ENVIRONMENTAL MOVEMENTS AND POLITICS

OF THE ASIAN ANTHROPOCENE

ENVIRONMENTAL MOVEMENTS AND POLITICS

OF THE ASIAN ANTHROPOCENE

Edited by

Paul Jobin
Ming-sho Ho
Hsin-Huang Michael Hsiao

ISEAS YUSOF ISHAK INSTITUTE

First published in Singapore in 2021 by
ISEAS Publishing
30 Heng Mui Keng Terrace
Singapore 119614

E-mail: publish@iseas.edu.sg
Website: <http://bookshop.iseas.edu.sg>

The responsibility for facts and opinions in this publication rests exclusively with the authors and their interpretations do not necessarily reflect the views or the policy of the publisher or its supporters.

ISEAS Library Cataloguing-in-Publication Data

Name(s): Jobin, Paul, editor. | Ho, Ming-sho, editor. | Hsiao, Hsin-Huang Michael, editor.
Title: Environmental movements and politics of the Asian Anthropocene / edited by Paul Jobin, Ming-sho Ho and Hsin-Huang Michael Hsiao.
Description: Singapore : ISEAS–Yusof Ishak Institute, 2021. | Includes bibliographical references and index.
Identifiers: ISBN 978-981-4951-08-1 (soft cover) | ISBN 978-981-4951-40-1 (pdf)
Subjects: LCSH: Political ecology—Asia. | Environmentalism—Asia.
Classification: LCC JA75.8 E61

Cover design by Wen-Tsen Lo

Top photo: Mailiao Coast-Yunlin Sixth Naphtha Industrial Zone, south estuary bank of the Chuoshui river, January 2003 (*background*) and Kaohsiung Linyuan petrochemical zone, May 2012 (*foreground*). Courtesy of Chin-yuan Ke.

Bottom (*background*): Students, monks, and activists gather with locals in the waters around Lovers' Island to bless and protect its mangrove forests from sand-dredging, Koh Kong Province, Southwest Cambodia; (*foreground*): A Cambodian woman discovers with dismay the mountains of sand dredged up and seized from her island of Koh Sralau at a storage facility in Singapore. ©Mona Simon/Lost World.

Back cover map: NASA Earth Observatory website, Land Surface Temperature map.

Typeset by International Typesetters Pte Ltd
Printed in Singapore by Markono Print Media Pte Ltd

"This collection provides a powerful and sophisticated analysis of how environmental movements influence politics in Asia, and how politics influences movements. It effectively comes to grips with the diversity of cases and regimes, and should be essential reading for all those who care about how growing environmental stresses and challenges are confronted in Asia."

John S. Dryzek
Centenary Professor, University of Canberra

"Interest in the environment never recedes; it is just reworked for a new era. This important book reflects the challenges and questions currently foremost in scholars', activists' and policy-makers' minds—the Anthropocene, environmental justice, China's Belt and Road Initiative, and post-politics—all addressed through the lens of environmental movements in Asia."

Jonathan Rigg
Professor at the School of Geographical Sciences,
University of Bristol

"How have authoritarianism, democratization and political change affected environmentalism in East and Southeast Asia? How have environmental mobilization and demands for environmental justice at the grassroots influenced politics there? What are the implications for the region's rampant environmental degradation, incessant resource extraction and burgeoning contribution to global pollution? These are among the vital questions answered by this insightful and well-crafted volume. It will be a valuable resource for researchers, students, activists and policymakers."

Paul G. Harris
Chair Professor of Global and Environmental Studies,
Education University of Hong Kong

"The anthropocene is not only about how humans have become the dominant influence in shaping our planet. It is also about the extent to which the environment has captured the imagination of our species and served to rework our societies and politics. This book shows convincingly that the concept is as relevant in Asia as anywhere. The editors' overall introductory argument and the impressive collection of finely nuanced country case studies make an important contribution to our understanding of environmental movements in East and Southeast Asia, both in their own right and as embedded in the wider politics of the countries in question."

Philip Hirsch
Emeritus Professor of Human Geography,
University of Sydney

"Despite its claims to universality, the Anthropocene concept remains largely a Western phenomenon. Yet the importance of Asia for the Anthropocene can hardly be overstated. This book is crucial in correcting this view by putting environmental movements in Asia center stage. Taking into account the diversity of the political, economic and social situations of Asian countries, it offers a differentiated overview of the landscape of ecological problems in the region. Finding solutions to the global ecological crisis will hinge, in large part, on Asia."

Eva Horn
Professor of Literature and Cultural History,
University of Vienna

CONTENTS

LIST OF TABLES, MAPS AND FIGURES

TABLES

MAPS

All maps are made by Gordon Shih-hao Jheng, with QGIS software, a free and open source Geographic Information System (www.qgis. org/en/site), and complementary data from Natural Earth, a public domain map dataset (www.naturalearthdata.com).

FIGURES

ACKNOWLEDGEMENTS

This book follows on the publication twenty years ago of another collective book, *Asia's Environmental Movements: Comparative Perspectives*, edited by Yok-shiu Lee and Alvin Y. So, which included the contribution of Hsin-Huang Michael Hsiao. As the twentieth anniversary of that publication was approaching, Hsiao invited Paul Jobin and Ming-sho Ho to work on a project for a collective update that would focus on how environmental movements have changed in the region during the first two decades of the twenty-first century.

A conference launched in December 2017 at the Institute of Sociology (IOS), Academia Sinica (in Taipei), and sponsored by the Asian Social Transformation Thematic Research Team, opened the discussion with presenters from Taiwan and Hong Kong (Paul Jobin, Alvin Y. So, James K. Wong, and Stephan Ortmann), and Southeast Asia (Francisco A. Magno, Fadzilah Majid Cooke, Jakkrit Sangkhamanee, and Suharko Suharko). We were fortunate to have stimulating feedback from Kuei-Tien Chou, Wen-Ling Tu, Hong-Zen Wang, Hua-Mei Chiu, Pin-Hsien Wu, Li-Hsuan Cheng, Mei-Fang Fan, Thung-Hung Lin, Mau-Kuei Chang, and Fu-Chang Wang. Unfortunately, despite his enthusiasm for this conference, our colleague Chun-Jie Chi, who was among the first scholars to introduce the environmental justice paradigm in Taiwan, was ultimately unable to join us as he was fighting a cancer that took his life a few months later. His spirit has nevertheless remained a source of inspiration for this book.

Transforming this conference into a book has been another exciting endeavour. In addition to the participants, who all agreed to take part in this collective volume, we were pleased to receive the contribution of Harvey Neo, James W.Y. Wang, and Adnan A. Hezri for additional chapters.

From the manuscript's early versions to its final submission, help was provided by Rebecca Fite in the form of editing and proofreading; her mix of rigour and enthusiasm was a great boost.

At the Institute of Sociology of Academia Sinica, we are indebted to Director Gwo-Shyong Shieh for his constant support and encouragement, as well as to our colleagues of the thematic research team on Asian Social Transformation in Comparative Perspective (Mau-kuei Chang, Jieh-min Wu, Fei-Yu Hsie, Ting-Hong Wong, Fu-chang Wang, Hong-zen Wang, Yen-Fen Tseng, and Alan H. Yang). And we must not forget our assistants Amanda Koh, Sherry Peng, Chi Wei Ying, Gordon Shih-hao Jheng, and Lulu Chen, without whom important tasks would not have gotten done, both for the conference and the book.

At ISEAS – Yusof Ishak Institute, Ng Kok Kiong's kind patience and support was another motivation to believe in this project. Catherine Ang and Sheryl Sin shepherded the manuscript through to book form.

We are, moreover, very grateful to two anonymous reviewers whose critical remarks and suggestions greatly helped to improve the final manuscript.

Thanks are due also to Wen-Tsen Lo for her beautiful design of the book cover, as well as documentary filmmakers Chin-yuan Ke and Kalyanee Mam for their magnificent photos. The photos provided by Kalyanee Mam, which also appear in the chapters on Singapore and Cambodia, capture our efforts to bring grassroots movements to the heart of the challenges of the Anthropocene across different Asian countries.

ABOUT THE CONTRIBUTORS

Adnan A. HEZRI is a Fellow of the Academy of Sciences Malaysia and the Chief Executive Officer of the Langkawi Development Authority, Malaysia.

Ming-sho HO is a Professor in the Department of Sociology, National Taiwan University, and Director of the Research Institute for the Humanities and Social Sciences, Ministry of Science and Technology (Taiwan).

Hsin-Huang Michael HSIAO is Chairman of the Taiwan-Asia Exchange Foundation, Chairman of the executive committee of the Center for Southeast Asian Studies, National Cheng-Chi University, and Chair Professor of Hakka Studies, National Central University. He is also Adjunct Research Fellow at the Institute of Sociology, Academia Sinica and Professor of Sociology at the National Sun Yat-Sen University.

Paul JOBIN is Associate Research Fellow and convener of the Asian Social Transformation Thematic Research Team at the Institute of Sociology, Academia Sinica, Taiwan.

Francisco A. MAGNO is Associate Professor in the Department of Political Science, and Founding Director of the Jesse M. Robredo Institute of Governance, at De La Salle University, Manila.

Fadzilah MAJID COOKE is a Research Associate at the Institute of Tropical Biodiversity and Sustainable Development, Universiti Malaysia Terengganu, and a Member of the International Steering Committee for Sustainability Initiative in the Marginal Seas in South and East Asia.

Harvey NEO is Senior Fellow and Head of Programme, Lee Kuan Yew Centre for Innovative Cities, Singapore University of Technology and Design.

Stephan ORTMANN is Adjunct Assistant Professor at the Centre for China Studies, Chinese University of Hong Kong.

Jakkrit SANGKHAMANEE is Associate Professor in the Faculty of Political Science, Chulalongkorn University in Bangkok, Thailand.

Alvin Y. SO is Professor Emeritus, Division of Social Science, Hong Kong University of Science and Technology.

Suharko SUHARKO is Associate Professor in the Department of Sociology at Universitas Gadjah Mada, Indonesia.

James W.Y. WANG is Assistant Professor, Department of Southeast Asian Studies, National Chi Nan University, Taiwan.

James K. WONG is Assistant Professor of Social Science Education, Division of Social Science and Division of Public Policy, Hong Kong University of Science and Technology.

1

ENVIRONMENTAL MOVEMENTS AND POLITICS OF THE ASIAN ANTHROPOCENE: AN INTRODUCTION

Paul Jobin, Ming-sho Ho, and Hsin-Huang Michael Hsiao

Two decades ago, several authors of the present book contributed to a collective publication on Asia's environmental movements in comparative perspective (Lee and So 1999).[1] As the editors pointed out (p. 15), while Western environmental movements developed in the context of advanced industrial economies and decades-old liberal democracies, their Asian counterparts emerged in either economically backward or newly industrializing countries, new democracies or authoritarian states. Distinct cultural and religious backgrounds have further shaped the specificities of environmentalism in Asia. The book therefore aimed to outline and compare the characteristics of Asia's environmental movements, and to examine their impact on the state, economy, and society—as well, of course, on environmental outcomes.

Around the same time, two other edited volumes attested to the effervescence of the academic attention to this range of topics in the context of East and Southeast Asia (Kalland and Persoon 1998; Hirsch and Warren 1998). The flourishing of bottom-up environmental activism reflected the quick pace of industrialization and an ascending position in the world economy. While social movements against industrial pollution in Japan started commenced in the late nineteenth century (Walker 2010; Stolz 2014), in the rest of Asia, similar movements did not appear until some hundred years later, starting with the "Four Asian Tigers" (South Korea, Taiwan, Hong Kong, and Singapore) in the 1970s; Thailand, the Philippines, and Malaysia in the 1980s; in China since the end of the 1990s; and still more recently in other countries, like Indonesia and Vietnam.

Our present collective volume examines how these popular protests engage with the environmental challenges in nine country-specific chapters, starting with Taiwan and Hong Kong for East Asia, then moving to Singapore, the Philippines, Indonesia, and Malaysia in maritime Southeast Asia, followed by Thailand, Vietnam, and Cambodia for the mainland area. The principal goal of the book is to present a qualitative assessment of how environmental movements have influenced the socio-politics of these countries and their environmental policies, and vice versa: how politics has influenced environmental movements.

The period covered focuses on the last two decades. Compared with the situation observed by Lee and So some twenty years ago, the state of the environment in the region—and indeed around the world—has not improved. On the contrary, the impact of anthropic activity on ecology had reached such a worldwide scope by the turn of the century that the epoch-marking term "Anthropocene" was introduced to describe it (Crutzen and Stoermer 2000). This neologism at first applied chiefly to the anthropogenic effects of global warming (or "global heating"[2]) on the earth system, whereas the emphasis is currently shifting to the massive extinction of animal and plant species. To give just two examples, tropical forests are on the eve of complete erasure, and plastic in the ocean will soon outnumber the fish. What is East and Southeast Asia's responsibility in this worldwide ecological crisis, and to what extent have environmental movements tried to cope with it?

Ever since East and Southeast Asia emerged as a powerful economic machine of global capitalism, in addition to their significant share in the emission of greenhouse gases, the massive production of waste and the drastic depletion of natural resources have been particularly alarming (Harris 2005; Harris and Lang 2015). The causes are multiple, starting with the logging of primitive forests and their replacement by cash crops (rubber, soya, palm). In addition to industrial pollution, major contentious issues have been mining activities, agribusiness monocultures, and forcible evictions for big dam projects.

The countries studied in this volume present a diversity of responses to the Anthropocene, reflecting a range of socio-political contexts, from real or flawed democracies to authoritarian regimes. Each chapter thus provides an updated and concise description of environmental movements during the last two decades, incorporating the analysis in the larger context of the country's evolving relations between society and politics, and looking at how political changes—such as democratization, constitutional reform, or military coup—have affected environmentalism, as well as whether environmental mobilizations have influenced national politics. The environmental movements include a large variety of organizational characteristics (grassroots-based, professionally led, confrontational, technocratic, deliberative, or cooperative) and people: from rural populations (such as "the villagers" of central and northern Thailand), indigenous and aboriginal peoples (in Taiwan, Borneo, and Vietnam's Highlands) to wealthy urban middle-classes (not only in Taiwan, Hong Kong, and Singapore, but also increasingly in places like Peninsular Malaysia, Java, Bangkok, Hanoi, and Saigon).

Given the planetary character of the crisis, the literature on the Anthropocene usually emphasizes the urgent need for effective transnational solutions (e.g., Dryzek and Pickering 2019, pp. 73–77). Although we basically agree, we have a couple of caveats. As pointed out by McAdam and Boudet (2012, p. 69), a "mobilization may span a country, but it almost never takes place nationally". It is "always embedded in and shaped by a local community context". Similarly, so-called "global issues" always start with people from specific locations, before they are gradually scaled up. The "global actor" is a myth, and if the catchphrase "think globally, act locally" might remain inspiring for environmental activists, it does not help in the sociology of transnational mobilizations, for what we need is to closely analyse the linkage between different scales of collective action.

We therefore understand that each country's environmentalism has its own unique characteristics and trajectories, and that these are worthy of attention. Keeping in mind the research agenda set by Lee and So (1999), we aim to provide a country-focused overview of the development of environmental movements in the region over the last two decades by profiling the main participants and opponents, depicting the main terrains of contention, assessing both achievements and weaknesses, and outlining the challenges ahead. By bringing these countries into comparative perspective, this volume aims to provide new theoretical insights into the changing interactions between social movements and political regimes in general, especially in the face of new challenges like the intensification of global warming and the other emergencies of the Anthropocene.

In this introductory chapter, we will first define what the Anthropocene epoch implies for Asia in general, and for East and Southeast Asia in particular. Then we will consider how environmental movements have interacted with politics, at the national level and beyond, and the resulting impact for the challenges of the ecological crisis.

The Anthropocene as Temporal Milestone

At the turn of the twenty-first century, Nobel Prize-winning chemist and atmospheric specialist Paul Crutzen and marine biologist Eugene Stoermer posited in a short article that, around the time of the industrial revolution in the eighteenth century, the earth left the Holocene—the post-glacial geological epoch of the past twelve thousand years—to enter a new geological period marked by the serious effects of anthropic activity, which they proposed to name the Anthropocene (Crutzen and Stoermer 2000). Two years later Crutzen published another one-page article in *Nature*, and the neologism "Anthropocene" became instrumental in raising awareness of a large range of big issues, such as the decisive impact of man-made gases on global warming and the massive depletion of biodiversity caused by a combination of global warming, habitat loss, pesticides, antibiotics, plastics, etc. Mass extinction, that is, the dying off of more than 50 per cent of the species on Earth, has generally been thought as a prehistoric phenomenon with five major instances, the best known of which was the disappearance of the dinosaurs. But since the publication of Elizabeth Kolbert's Pulitzer Prize-winning book *The Sixth Extinction* (2014), it is widely acknowledged that mass extinction currently threatens all kinds of plant and animal species (Ceballos et al. 2015). More recently, a United Nations report has confirmed that a mass extinction of the Earth's fauna and flora is already underway due to anthropic impact.[3]

These apocalyptic issues are often discussed under the catchword of "the Anthropocene".[4] The international community of geologists has received the neologism with reserve, preferring thus far to stick to the previous era, the Holocene; however, this was no great surprise, since it had taken fifty years of discussions to finally validate that designation at a conference in 1885. The term has also stirred fierce resistance among social scientists, although a great number of researchers have endorsed its use, particularly in the subfields dealing with environmental issues such as environmental history. As Jason Moore (2016, p. 3) puts it, "like globalization in the 1990s, the Anthropocene has become a buzzword that can mean all things to all people".

Much of the discussion on the Anthropocene has centred around where and when it started. Did it happen in Western Europe during the first industrial revolution, prompted by the invention of the steam engine and the sudden use of large quantities of coal? Or did it start after the Second World War with the "great acceleration" in the consumption of natural resources, driven in particular by the "American way of life" (Bonneuil and Fressoz 2013, pp. 28–33; Horn and Bergthaller 2020, chapter 11)? In this book, we cast aside this debate to retain the moment when, at the turn of the millennium, Crutzen and Stoermer (2000) introduced the concept to the scientific community. Although the idea that human activity was effecting cataclysmic changes to the Earth's systems was not new, the introduction of the Anthropocene as a concept has served to focus the attention, not only of researchers and scientists, but also of the wider public, around a single, coherent narrative.

Consequently, the thinking on environmental issues in the twenty years since has, to a large degree, engaged this concept; it is exactly these twenty years that we address in this book. The word thus acts as a chronological shorthand for the period studied here. While this certainly entails a much narrower view of the Anthropocene, we believe it carries heuristic values for our focus on environmental movements and politics. Moreover, even though individual chapters of this book may not discuss it, the use of this theoretical framework reminds us that the environmental destruction they reveal has entered a scale that was unknown, indeed unimaginable, some twenty years ago; this is not just another crisis that will soon end. In the remainder of this section, we present some salient points of the debate on the Anthropocene, which matter for the purposes of this book.

A major criticism of the Anthropocene concept is that it ascribes responsibility for the environmental crisis to humans in general, whereas many feel that the blame rightly belongs to just a portion of mankind. To some, the problem is its inherent Western-centrism, which deflects the responsibility of Western Europe and North America for the ecological crisis. In other words, the *anthropos* of the Anthropocene discourse is another version of the capitalist white male who finds in this narrative a renewed way to impose his neo-colonial domination (e.g., Davis and Todd 2017; Hecht 2018; Baldwin and Erickson 2020; Simpson 2020; Simangan 2020). This view is of importance for the post-colonial countries studied in this volume.

An unexpected challenge to this postcolonial criticism has come from Dipesh Chakrabarty (2009), a prominent author of postcolonial and subaltern studies. Chakrabarty admits that all the anthropogenic factors contributing to global warming are part of the imperial domination imposed by the West on the rest of the world. Western countries bear a moral burden, and other countries like China—which has now surpassed the United States as the largest emitter of carbon dioxide—are "prospectively guilty". Chakrabarty concludes that, while post-colonial scholarship's "hermeneutics of suspicion is an effective critical tool in dealing with national and global formations of domination", it is of little help in addressing global warming. Chakrabarty's article has provoked heated debates. Andreas Malm and Alf Hornborg (2014), for instance, endorse the notion of the Anthropocene, but they tag Chakrabarty's approach as a "flawed argument" that overlooks the differentiated vulnerability inherent in the power game between the rich and the poor (see also Beau and Larrère 2018; Reszitnyk 2020).

Other scholars believe that, while the West was undeniably the primary source of anthropogenic activities, the true culprit is capitalism. Its conception and early development were Atlantic-centred, but its subjugation of nature to capital accumulation has been adopted by much of the world, exponentially accelerating its devastating effects on the environment. For this reason, it has been suggested that the term "Anthropocene" should be replaced or at least completed by the concept of the "Capitalocene" (Moore 2016). The bulk of the many suggested alternatives for the Anthropocene have had little or no theoretical impact; the Capitalocene is a notable exception. Historian Jason Moore argues that capitalism seized on a completely new attitude toward nature: one that ceaselessly expanded the use of free—or almost free—labour, food, energy, and raw materials, through their appropriation and exploitation in lands both near and far. This reliance on "cheap nature" (2015) became the fundamental capitalist law of value.

Another left-wing criticism of the Anthropocene discourse argues that it tends to depoliticize the debate. For instance, Erik Swyngedouw (2015) posits that the Anthropocene discourse tends to avoid criticism of global corporations and tax-free polluters, thereby reducing the political discussion to a consensual and managerial approach within the neoliberal framework of "good governance". In his contribution to the present book, Harvey Neo analyses why this notion fits in very well with Singapore's approach to the Anthropocene.

Nonetheless, the Anthropocene is not necessarily a depoliticizing concept. Bruno Latour, who has generally endorsed the term (e.g., 2014, 2015), has also addressed a sharp criticism of the consensual "good governance" and the mirage of a world government that would be able to impose the right decisions on everyone. The problem, as Latour argues, is rather to fully acknowledge the *geo* in geopolitics. For instance, the Covid-19 pandemic, which has been a tremendous disruption to the traditional world order, is a dramatic reminder of the geopolitical force of the Anthropocene (Latour 2020). Latour accordingly invites us to look "down to earth" as closely as possible to the ground level of politics, so as to gradually map the frontlines of conflicts at different levels—local, national, regional, and international—but step by step (Latour 2015, 2017). This book is an attempt to do so through an analysis of selected cases of Asian environmental movements.

The Anthropocene in Asia

Another question of equal importance for the purpose of this book is how does Asia fit in the Anthropocene? As a concept aimed to define a very long period of time on a universal scale, the Anthropocene is not supposed to be confined within a particular place. However, an overwhelming proportion of authors who discuss the Anthropocene, both advocates and opponents of the notion, are from Western Europe, North America, and Australia. Moreover, scholars from other regions have so far shown little enthusiasm for this debate. This discrepancy engenders empirical shortages and theoretical flaws, sometimes openly assumed (e.g., Corlett 2013). Departing from the domination of Western paradigms in the Anthropocene literature (Marquardt 2019), a few scholars have therefore deemed it necessary to redefine the concept from the perspective of Africa (Hecht 2018), and Asia (Hudson 2014; Chatterjee 2020; Simangan 2019, 2020; see also Horn and Bergthaller 2020, chapter 12). This regionalist approach includes elements of the postcolonial criticism already presented, but it also offers further perspectives.

Hudson (2014) paved the way by identifying three research axes: the role of Asia in Anthropocene histories, the social and ecological vulnerabilities this epoch poses for Asia today, and how Asia addresses these global challenges. Our book focuses on the latter two questions through the relatively narrow angle of social movements and politics. But as Dahlia Simangan, a young researcher from the Philippines (2019, p. 565), aptly notes: "In a discourse saturated by universalising agenda, a regional level of analysis is an attempt to bridge global action and local capacity." Moreover, in an echo of *Provincializing Europe*—Chakrabarty's seminal book for subaltern studies—the historian of India Elisabeth Chatterjee (2020) invites researchers to "provincialize" the notion, and depart from the Western focus on the history of coal and oil (e.g., Malm 2016) to study other drivers of the Anthropocene, such as hydroelectricity, which has been instrumental in the modernization of Asian countries.

However, the geography of contemporary Asia is intertwined with the logic of asymmetrical world exchanges. Consider, for instance, that the Organization for Economic Co-operation and Development (OECD), which includes Japan and South Korea, accounts for more than two-thirds of the world's gross domestic product, but less than 20 per cent of its population. What Alf Hornborg (2013) terms "time-space appropriation" and an "unequal ecological exchange" have meant a huge transfer of wealth and resources from the "rest of the world" to Europe and North America. As he further observes (2018), this transfer still operates to the advantage of economic alliances, such as the OECD, because while these countries import and consume merchandise from China, carbon emissions resulting from the production of these imports are attributed to China (see also Zhang et al. 2017; Sims Gallagher and Xuan 2018; cf. Harris 2011).

The philosopher and member of the Australian Greens, Clive Hamilton (2017), tackles the argument of unequal relations thus: as

China reorients its economy toward domestic consumption, its share of emissions arising from export manufacture is declining. China is now the world's biggest carbon-emitter, and it is becoming harder to place all of the responsibility on its exports. At the 2015 climate change conference in Paris, Chinese diplomats were compelled to give up this line of argument, which had sabotaged the negotiations at the 2009 Copenhagen conference. Following on Chakrabarty, Hamilton (2017, p. 31) therefore fully endorses the notion of the Anthropocene: "If the 'Anthropocene' was a Eurocentric idea when it was coined, it is now Sino-Americo-Eurocentric, and in a decade or two it will be Indo-Sino-Americo-Eurocentric." Or as Horn and Bergthaller (2020, p. 173) see it: "The old industrial nations of Europe and North America may have started the recent transformation of the Earth system, but they are no longer in the driver's seat. Today the Asian nations are as much a part of the problem—and they must be a part of the solution, if there is to be one."

Indeed, according to the Germanwatch Institute, from 1998 to 2017, five of the top ten countries most affected by climate change were in Asia: Myanmar, the Philippines, Bangladesh, Pakistan, and Vietnam (Burck et al. 2020; cf. Sovacool 2015). Inversely, the same research institute shows that Taiwan, Japan, and South Korea rank at the bottom of the countries that most need to reduce their carbon emissions (Eckstein et al. 2019). The Asia-Pacific region as a whole is the highest contributor of greenhouse gas emissions to the atmosphere, with 40 per cent of global emissions in 2015; this percentage is projected to increase until 2030, with 89 per cent of Asia-Pacific's contribution coming from China, India, and Indonesia (Simangan 2020).

Regarding the concrete consequences of what the Anthropocene means for Asia, a great deal of discussion has so far focused on climate change and its most immediate consequences, like rising sea levels or stronger typhoons. For instance, Jakarta has been proclaimed "the city of the Anthropocene" for its vulnerability to rising sea levels and the resilience of the *kampong*—its floating slums (Chandler 2017). The Indonesian government is thus planning to transfer the capital to East Kalimantan (on the island of Borneo), with possibly detrimental effects for local indigenous populations and lush rainforests that are home to orang-utans and countless other animal species. Singapore is another city threatened by rising sea levels, with 35 per cent of its territory lying less than five metres above sea level; but from Lee Kuan

Yew's vision of a "Garden City" to its iconic Supertrees, Singapore's techno-nature and green-washing policy reflect the firm intention of the city-state to become a champion of resilience in the Anthropocene (Schneider-Mayerson 2017).

Along with rising seas, biodiversity loss in Southeast Asia is a major issue—if not the main issue—of the Asian Anthropocene. In addition to the oceans' depletion of fish and corals (Bush and Marschke 2017), the rivers' flora and fauna have been drastically decreasing due to the astounding number of hydroelectric dams under construction (Middleton 2017). Terrestrial species are similarly under attack, due to continued deforestation. After the Amazon and the Congo, Southeast Asia is the world's third-largest zone of tropical forests and a concomitant repository of terrestrial biodiversity (Seymour and Kanowski 2017; Hughes 2017). Boomgard (2017) stresses that anthropic impact on the Southeast Asian environment dates back to long ago, the current scale of decimation really started after the 1960s (cf. Stibig et al. 2013). By 2004, a strong warning was issued that Southeast Asia could lose three-quarters of its forests and up to 40 per cent of its biodiversity before the end of the twenty-first century (Sodhi et al. 2004). Sixteen years later, as the pace of deforestation has continued apace, Southeast Asia's biodiversity is at the forefront of "mass destruction" (Seymour and Kanowski 2017; Hughes 2017; Zeng et al. 2018), and at so rapid a rate that current data quickly becomes obsolete.

Social mobilizations against deforestation in Southeast Asia have long been a core research topic of political ecology (e.g., Tadem 1990; Lohmann 1993; Peluso 1994; Hirsch and Warren 1998; Dauvergne 2001; Ross 2001; Greenough and Lowenhaupt Tsing 2003; McElwee 2016; Vandergeest and Roth 2017). A famous case occurred at the end of the 1990s, when an international boycott campaign against Malaysian timber raised awareness of the issue (Keck and Sikkink 1998). Since then, mobilizations of local people and transnational networks have continued unabated, as in the 2009 Greenpeace campaign to enforce control over the expansion of oil palms in Indonesia. Nevertheless, the last two decades have seen an acceleration of forest loss in the region, as if no human force nor any law could possibly stop the chain saws and bulldozers from encroaching further on "protected" forest areas, not until the very last tree is cut down.

Furthermore, the disastrous consequences of continued deforestation for the biodiversity of plant and animal species go hand in hand with brutal attacks on human and cultural diversity, or what Aiken and Leigh (2015) call development by displacement and resettlement, whether through forced eviction or land-grabbing by false promises (of brand new houses, and modern conveniences like electricity, tap water, tarmacked or paved roads, etc.). Local populations of farmers or indigenous peoples often pay the highest price in an economy based on bulldozers, tons of concrete, and pesticides. The construction of large hydroelectric dams, and the expansion of mining and monocultures are almost inevitably accompanied by the displacement of entire communities, massive pollution of land and rivers, and a homogenization (and oversimplification) of human and natural ecology.

This violence is nothing new; it started during colonial times, was further aggravated by post-colonial regimes, and has been described by an abundant literature (e.g., Tadem 1990; Lohmann 1993; Hirsch and Warren 1998). What is more specific to the Anthropocene paradigm is that departing from the naive belief that brutal infrastructure projects and the expansion of agribusiness are "sustainable development", there is now a large consensus among international organizations that further destruction of the "cultural and natural heritage" must be avoided. However, despite announcements or stricter enforcement of regulation encouraged by various international initiatives, like the UN's REDD (Reducing Emissions from Deforestation and Forest Degradation), and despite the apparent willingness of major industries and high finance to adopt ethical standards via Corporate Social Responsibility programmes and the Equator Principles—if only for marketing reasons, national governments are likely to push unsustainable business as usual (Welker 2009; Hughes 2017; De Koninck and Pham 2017; Seymour and Kanowski 2017).

Several chapters shed light on the pathology of ongoing resource extraction. In Indonesia, Malaysia, Thailand, Philippines and Cambodia, social movements against the major causes of deforestation (industrial logging, agribusiness, and hydroelectric dams) remain major causes of contention, often entangled with a disregard of land rights of rural communities, indigenous peoples in particular.

But these considerations on the Anthropocene of Asia intertwine also with geopolitical concerns. As a mark of its ascendancy, China has undertaken a comprehensive global investment programme, the Belt and Road Initiative (BRI), with the aim of fashioning a China-centred economic sphere, by developing and economically integrating the countries along the historic Silk Road. With an estimated value by 2049 of US$8 trillion spread over a total of seventy-two countries, the BRI could be the largest infrastructure project in human history (Morris-Jung et al. 2018; Diokno et al. 2019), with possibly devastating consequences for biodiversity (Hughes 2019) and a further increase in global warming emissions due to the export of coal-burning power plants (Maréchal 2018). In addition, the new Silk Road is likely to increase China's political influence in the countries receiving these large investments. This question will be addressed in particular through the case of Chinese hydroelectric investments in Cambodia (Chapter 10).

What is the current pace of mobilization to curb the massive forces of destruction presented above? To what extent can traditional social movements cope with such challenges? Will these mobilizations be able to act quickly and efficiently enough to prevent the last forests being completely erased, or the Mekong and other rivers becoming so dammed up that only a few dozen species out of thousands will survive? To answer these questions, as evoked above through Swyngedouw's post-politics and Latour's redefinition of geopolitics, we need to examine the interaction between environmental movements and politics.

Environmental Movements and Politics

The dialectics of environmental movements with politics can be analysed through different prisms, but to put it simply, one perspective focuses on the contribution of environmental movements to environmental issues themselves; another angle concerns their influence on socio-politics on a par with other social movements (such as labour or gender movements), as well as how the legal and institutional framework allows them to flourish or not. At the local and national stages, decisive factors are the role of elections (if any), liberty of association (to initiate collective action and raise awareness on a specific issue), freedom of speech and of the press, and the right to protest (to influence public opinion). Beyond the national level, local non-governmental organizations (NGOs) must spend efforts in networking with bigger organizations like Greenpeace to open the doors of international organizations like the UN climate change conferences. In this section, we present key features of this interaction between environmental movements and national or international politics from the country cases studied in this volume, as well as the main theoretical frameworks used by the authors.

In Search of Environmental Justice and Political Opportunities

The chapters in this volume borrow from different disciplines and fields of studies, such as environmental politics, political ecology, human geography, and environmental sociology. But they share common references, notably two streams of theoretical background; one is Environmental Justice (EJ) and the other is Political Opportunity Theory (POT). Both theoretical frameworks have become dominant in the political sociology of social movements in the literature in English (and with a large number of case studies located in the United States), and by extension, the rest of the academic world. This intellectual domination of North American literature tends to neglect other theoretical perspectives and minimize cultural specificities when, at a critical time for biodiversity, we should also pay attention to a broader diversity of theoretical approaches. But POT and EJ share a common concern for grassroots mobilization—a basic requirement for bringing environmental politics "down to earth" (Latour 2017), and this conjunction has so far proved sufficiently helpful in a variety of contexts (Guha and Martinez-Alier 1997a; Pellow 2017; Sicotte and Brulle 2017). In many countries, including in Asia, environmental activists have mobilized under a rallying call for EJ (or related slogans such as "climate justice"), which implies a moral criticism of state policy and corporate behaviour. Moreover, in their analysis of environmental movements, social scientists from various countries have borrowed the ethical prism of EJ, or preferred the more neutral lenses of POT, and sometimes they have combined both approaches. The following chapters will reflect this ideological and theoretical atmosphere.

This heterogeneous repertoire needs some further explanations. POT, which is also known as the Political Process Theory or Political Opportunity Structure, appeared in the 1970s, soon after Resource Mobilization Theory (RMT) was developed by authors like Charles Tilly, at his debut a prominent historian of the French Revolution. RMT looked at both societal support and constraint of social movements, paying attention to "the variety of *resources* that must be mobilized, the linkages of social movements to other groups, the *dependence* of movements upon external support for success, and the *tactics* used by authorities to control or incorporate movements" (to borrow from a seminal article by McCarthy and Zald 1977, italics added).

In contrast, POT emphasized the role of the political environment and, in particular, the windows of opportunity that might favour social change (like the emergence of elites sympathetic to the cause), but also considered various threats and constraints like state repression or deeper social change; hence the addition of *structure*, which should not however be interpreted as a tribute to structuralism (Tilly 1978; Tarrow 1994; McAdam et al. 1996, 2001; Goodwin and Jasper 2011). A major contribution of POT to the theory of collective action was to "debunk the myth of social movements as spontaneous and autonomous forces" (Cefaï 2007, p. 273; see also Jasper 2010, Ho 2019), bringing back the emphasis on their interactions with the larger social, political, and legal environment, as well as their degree of integration with political institutions.

Environmental Justice started in the 1980s in the United States as a catchword for the mobilization of black and other ethnic minorities against what they had come to perceive as an unfair distribution of risk between white middle-class neighbourhoods and communities of Black, Hispanic, Asian, or Native Americans on the "fence line" of industrial zones (Bullard 1983, 1990). The ontology of North American EJ scholarly work, as well as its Australian variation (e.g., David Schlosberg), is still marked by this outcry against structural racism. In the United States, the Environmental Protection Agency and other state institutions have gradually endorsed the notion of EJ in the consensual mode of neoliberal multiculturalism and its coded way of talking about racism (Pulido 2017, p. 16), hence the development of a new, radical stream of EJ (Pellow 2018); a similar institutionalization of EJ as well as a new radical movement can be observed in other countries like Taiwan (Chapter 2). In Asia, generally speaking, rather than problems of racism in its U.S. understanding of the term—i.e., with obvious references to skin colour—EJ is a frequent reference for addressing class struggles and land conflicts between the dominant group and ethnic minorities or indigenous peoples.

During the last fifty years, there has been an increasingly strong coordination and recognition of indigenous peoples around the world, with highlights including the awarding of the 1992 Nobel Peace Prize to Maya activist Rigoberta Menchú, and the United Nations' designation of 1993 as the International Year of the Indigenous Peoples (Niezen 2003). This trend has continued in the new century, leading to the growing acknowledgement of indigenous peoples—or "aboriginal peoples" or "first nations"—with striking insistence in countries like

New Zealand, Canada, Australia, and Taiwan. The level of recognition depends on the agenda of the dominant ethnic group (Whites in Australia, Han in Taiwan, Kinh in Vietnam, and more controversially, *Bumiputra* in Malaysia). Sometimes, the ruling ethnic group expresses sincere remorse for past oppression, such as land grabbing or a ban on indigenous languages. Yet, with the possible exception of New Zealand's Māori, for the great majority of indigenous groups, concrete results and better living conditions are slow to come, rather in the way that "protected areas" do not necessarily prevent deforestation. Moreover, symbolic recognition of indigenous cultures is often reduced to electoral opportunism or political correctness. But like the biodiversity depletion that accompanies the vanishing rainforests, threats of the partial or complete cultural genocide of many indigenous peoples have become a symbolic feature of the Anthropocene, generating guilty feelings among the elites and urban middle classes, or what Boltanski (2009) calls a "distant suffering".

In this book, the chapters on Taiwan, Malaysia, Thailand, Indonesia, and the Philippines address this problematic issue. For instance, in the states of Sabah and Sarawak (or East Malaysia, on the island of Borneo), where the native peoples represent two-thirds of the total population (about three million), the defence of customary land rights is a core issue in stopping deforestation by the state, mining companies, and agribusiness. Despite the early support of transnational advocacy networks against the deforestation of Sarawak (Keck and Sikkink 1998, pp. 150–63), and despite growing recognition by the Malaysian courts, indigenous organizations of East Malaysia have gained few results in the fight against big dam projects (Aiken and Leigh 2015, pp. 82–83). However, as Majid Cooke and Hezri show in this book (Chapter 7), in a number of cases, East Malaysian courts have provided some significant progressive judgments, transforming the postcolonial legacy of English Common Law into a powerful leverage tool for those less endowed with economic and symbolic capital. Taiwan, Indonesia, Malaysia, and the Philippines present other examples of the important role of the courts in delivering environmental justice to the victims of land-grabbing or industrial pollution. However, the results are uncertain, and long-delayed, especially with transnational issues like global warming policies (Chapter 5) or the class action launched in Taiwan by Vietnamese fishermen (Chapter 2).

Climate Justice

Although still a matter of debate for prominent climate change deniers, increasingly frequent and violent weather disasters such as typhoons have motivated EJ-inspired ecologists to frame climate change as an unfair distribution of environmental risk on a worldwide scale (Lyster 2015; Harris 2016). Seeking mitigation and adaptation for climate change-related disasters has become a rallying cry for the most vulnerable, such as the coastal populations of the Philippines, Thailand, and Indonesia (see Chapters 5 and 7). In 2000, the UN climate change conference held in The Hague (the 6th meeting of the Conference of the Parties) made it clear that environmental justice was a global problem urgently needing to be addressed through international networks (Roberts and Parks 2009).

Since then, the worldwide movement for climate justice has gained momentum, usually in conjunction with UN climate summits, which offer good windows of opportunity through exposure to the global media. Almeida (2019, pp. 5, 169–70) has counted more than one thousand protest events in 175 countries between 2014 and 2018 alone, making it the most extensive transnational movement in history, with a growing proportion of Global South actors like the World Social Forum. The 13th UN climate change conference held in Bali in 2007, is a good example. As Suharko shows (Chapter 6), a coalition of Indonesian NGOs seized the opportunity to push the Indonesian government and other participating countries to look beyond the neoliberal targets of carbon trading—which consider any kind of forests or agribusiness plantation as sufficient for capturing carbon emissions—and engage in more concrete action against the ravaging of primitive forests in "protected areas".

Like the Occupy movements, the mobilizations for climate justice denounce the negative impact of neoliberal policies, which tend to neglect state regulation and impose a heavier burden of taxes on the most vulnerable. For instance, in France, after months of protest in 2018–19, the *Gilets Jaunes* ("Yellow Vests") movement against a carbon tax has finally convinced the government that technical solutions from neoliberal economists will not be accepted if they increase social inequalities. In East and Southeast Asia, neoliberalism still operates within the institutional framework of the developmental state (Barney 2017). While this is most obvious in one-party regimes like Vietnam (see Ortmann, Chapter 9), Magno argues that in the Philippines, the state remains weak and environmental activists must confront strong rent-seeking and commercial interests evading social and environmental accountability (Chapter 5).

When things go well, the dynamics of environmental movements generate a collective expertise that influences national legislation and international agreements on environmental policy. Beyond the national level, as evidenced by the UN climate change conferences, the role of international organizations like Greenpeace or Friends of the Earth is decisive in echoing the voice of Southeast Asian organizations. Twenty years ago, Lee and So (1999, p. 14) noted that these Western NGOs were being vilified as vehicles of neo-colonialism by strong-arm regimes like that of Mahathir. In contrast, Greenpeace is now being criticized by Taiwanese NGOs for its lack of political concern regarding China's bullying of the island nation (Chapter 2), whereas in the Philippines and Indonesia, local NGOs seem to appreciate its initiatives for lobbying states and global firms on climate change (Chapters 5 and 6).

Extending Environmental Justice to Other Species

Alongside the movement for climate justice, certain threatened animal species, such as polar bears, Borneo's rhinoceros and orang-utans, marine turtles hurt by plastic waste, and bee populations decimated by insecticides, have captured the world's attention through campaigns by international organizations like Greenpeace and the World Wide Fund for Nature (WWF). But the vast majority of threatened plants and animal species do not attract support beyond specialized scientists and a few local NGOs. In addition, while social scientists are keen to study social movements and political change, in comparison, the cause of "non-humans" has sparked very little research.

Despite its focus on the activities of man, the Anthopocene narrative generally champions the rights of an enlarged diversity of living species (Tønnessen et al. 2016). Similarly, inspired by the outcry of indigenous peoples against the neo-colonial disrespect for both people and non-human natures, Pellow (2017) seeks to extend political opportunity structures to non-humans. As he argues, cutting ties with human-centred ideologies implies a departure from a utilitarian understanding that reduces land, plants, and animals to mere resources for the sake of man, and indeed, all too often, an economic development model that is set by mining companies or agribusiness.

Harvey Neo further shows (Chapter 4) that despite the increased number of NGOs dedicated to animal welfare—such as the Jane Goodall Institute—and the apparently benevolent attitude of Singaporean authorities, non-humans remain excluded from substantive political debate. For instance, Singapore has joined international conventions for the protection of endangered wild species, yet the state keeps granting permits for the import of wild dolphins by marine resorts and does very little to stop the encroachment of housing on the reserve habitat of wild macaques. So, in spite of an apparent government commitment to the protection of wild animals, NGOs dare not openly denounce the hypocrisy of the state, even for the advocacy of such iconic mammals as dolphins and monkeys. In the context of Singapore's post-politics, every stakeholder has an equal say in the debate—providing one does not challenge the happy narrative of the "Garden City" state.

More generally speaking, in wealthy countries like Singapore, the "environmentalism of the rich" (cf. Guha and Martinez-Alier 1997b; Martinez-Alier 2002) cares little about the import of natural resources, such as sand from Cambodia and Indonesia, which is devastating for those countries' coastal ecosystems. So, while the façade of Singapore's Garden City boasts the iconic Supertrees, its backyard is a big pack of contradictions and double standards. Singapore is not alone in such green-washing. It stands rather as a marketing model for other wealthy cities like Hong Kong, Shanghai, Taipei, Tokyo, Seoul, Kuala Lumpur, etc.

While signs of the apocalypse, exemplified by global heating and the mass extinction of species, call for an urgent response, even large mobilizations of people do not guarantee results and success. Yet, we fully agree with Laura Pulido (2017)'s statement that "power concedes nothing without struggle, and that for all their messiness and disappointments, social movements, including massive shifts in political consciousness, are the *only* way to create meaningful change".

Environmental Activism: A Dangerous Job?

Environmental double standards and dubious green policies can be challenged by a combination of local mobilizations and transnational advocacy networks. But those who face the most serious risks are the local groups. After all, the principle of seizing a favourable political opportunity does not mean waiting passively for the opportunity to come. But such action does not come without danger, and those facing the most serious risks are the local organizations. Given the small chance of quick and positive results, to what extent are risks worth taking for activists? The rational actor model would expect activists to calculate the risk before any commitment. But activists do not always have enough time to make calculated decisions. As Ho Ming-sho (2019) shows in the case of Taiwan and Hong Kong in 2014, social movements do not necessarily emerge because of favourable political opportunities; they may also occur because of an acute perceived threat, which can be induced, for example, by the police's aggressive use of tear gas or other anti-riot weapons against unarmed citizens. In the Sunflower Movement in Taiwan and the Umbrella Movement in Hong Kong, an important driver of contention was the fear of a possible erosion of civil rights under the pressure of Beijing's authoritarian rule.

The same mechanism applies to environmental mobilizations. Intimidation, imprisonment, torture, murder, rape, and other human rights violations are the common lot of environmental activists around the world (Pellow 2017; Woods 2017). For instance, in 2012, the murders of Cambodian environmental activist Chut Wutty and journalist Taing Try attracted international attention to illegal logging involving the Cambodian army (Wang, Chapter 10). But many other activists have been killed with almost no media coverage.

As Magno aptly puts it, "environmental protection is indeed a dangerous business" (Chapter 5). In the Philippines, twenty-eight environmental activists were killed in 2016 alone, behind only Columbia and Brazil—although this may seem minuscule in comparison to the 22,000 extra-judicial killings of President Duterte's "war on drugs". However, despite this deployment of police forces and vigilantes around the country, as Magno emphasizes, the Republic of the Philippines remains a weak state. Indeed, that crusade has further siphoned off government resources that might otherwise be used to enforce the rather considerable environmental protections afforded by the law; without them, the spoliation of nature goes largely unchecked. Despite resistance from civil society organizations, which share an interesting mix of Christian and Marxist ideologies, the rampant climate of gun violence, as well as alternating periods of democratic and dictatorial regimes, bring the Philippines closer to Latin America than to its immediate neighbours Taiwan and Vietnam.

Compared to the Philippines, both Taiwan and Vietnam present the characteristics of a strong developmental state, but in contrasting ways. As presented by Jobin in Chapter 2, there is a plethora of environmental injustices in Taiwan. But since the transition to democracy in 1987, civil rights have been well respected and, apart from a policeman who died accidentally during a 1991 clash with anti-nuclear protesters, environmental mobilizations do not end in bloodshed. The situation is quite different in Vietnam. For instance, after a major incident of marine pollution in Central Vietnam attributed to the Taiwanese firm Formosa Steel, street protests were brutally repressed by the police and several activists were arrested and condemned to long prison sentences (Ortmann's analysis of the case in Chapter 9; see also Chapter 2). Such reactions, typical of an authoritarian regime, are certainly not the best expression of a "strong state", but at least they are distinct from the bloody killings occurring in the Philippines and Cambodia.

Setting aside the extreme cases of extrajudicial killing or capital punishment after a show trial, a good indicator of the state and corporate response to environmental mobilizations lies in their tendency to respond either by brutal repression or by dialogue and negotiation. The red line is the guarantee given to civil rights, or what Cefaï (2007, pp. 274–75) calls the demarcation line of a polity. But as Benedict Kerkvliet (2010) has highlighted from the case of Vietnam, the red line often moves so randomly that people might be unaware they have already crossed it.

To what extent do groups that challenge authoritarian regimes have their say in the polity without fearing harassment or arrest? Do the political and economic elites renounce state violence or the repression of civil liberties? While Marxist and Foucauldian scholars tend to look at the judiciary as another tool of oppression for bourgeois regimes to maintain their power and privileges, drawing on EJ and POT, several authors of this book attribute a more positive role to the courts. If existing laws reflect the domination of political and economic elites, as the US civil rights movement—a seminal reference for EJ and POT—has proved, laws can be changed. Another option that POT literature emphasizes is the co-option of mobilization leaders by their integration into the existing political system (e.g., Heijden 1997). In any case, the red line remains the use of state violence and repression

MAP 1.1

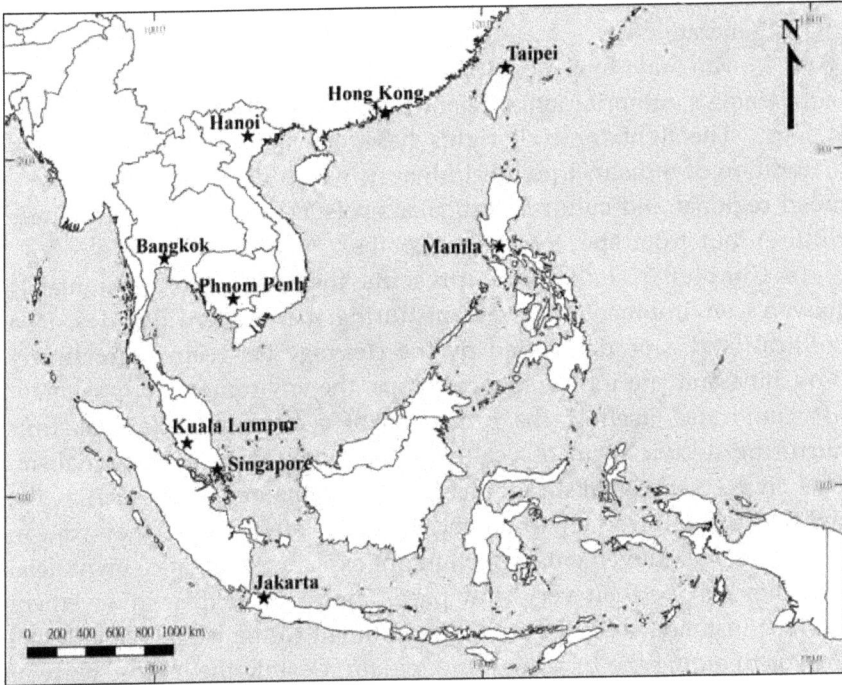

Taiwan, Hong Kong, and the capital cities of the Southeast Asian countries studied in this book

Source: QGIS and Natural Earth.

of basic civil rights. This problem brings us to the difficult issue of the interactions between environmental movements, democracy, and authoritarian regimes. This will be the topic of the concluding chapter focusing on the particular context of East and Southeast Asia.

Outlook of the Following Chapters

In the remainder of this book, the authors look at how environmental mobilizations forge their own path between authoritarian and democratic regimes to provide an answer to our initial question—how political changes have affected environmentalism in the region, and conversely, how environmental mobilizations have influenced national politics, and what sorts of environmental outcomes these interactions might generate.

In Taiwan and Hong Kong, as already mentioned, the confrontation with Beijing's authoritarianism stands at the core of social mobilizations at large. The fight for civil rights has gone hand in hand with the maturation of a distinct political identity, which does not result from a broad regional and cultural particularism (such as a Southern Chinese culture), but from specific political paths.[5]

In Chapter 2, Paul Jobin presents the main achievements of Taiwan's environmental movement during the last two decades. In a political landscape dominated by the cleavage between the relatively pro-China and pro-independence camps, the environmental movement has committed itself to the protection of a democratic Taiwan, thus nurturing a civic form of ecological nationalism or eco-nationalism. This civic eco-nationalism emphasizes problems of justice, such as the right to a toxin-free environment. Lawyers often play a key role in environmental movements, which might explain the reliance on judicial remedies despite their very slow pace. The scope of their involvement has, for instance, widened from commitment to the island's aboriginal groups to aiding the fishermen of Vietnam. Despite the impossibility of Taiwan's state agencies to join a large range of international meetings, and in particular all those set by United Nations organizations like the UN climate change conferences, these civic groups play a crucial role in collecting information and pushing for policy change.

The recent mobilizations for democracy in Hong Kong have attracted the attention of the world's media. In Chapter 3, James K. Wong and Alvin Y. So show that the fight for universal suffrage and more guarantees regarding civil rights has intimate links with the battles for land justice and the protection of cultural patrimony, which cannot simply be reduced to nostalgia for British colonialism. These early street protests have set the tone of a struggle for the recognition of a distinct polity. Despite its promise of respecting the principle of "one country, two systems", Beijing has increased pressure on the semi-autonomous territory to speed up its subjugation and its integration with the rest of China. This strategy has included the development of mega infrastructure projects. However, to the surprise of Beijing, and in contrast with the business-oriented environmentalism that prevailed before, a new generation of activists has reacted more and more strongly against this policy, launching protests against the demolition of heritage sites, the construction of a high-speed railway, the third airport runway, and other projects. Many of these protests have been organized by grassroots environmental groups, which have promoted new political personalities who are deeply involved in the movement for democracy and more radicalized than ever before.

Singapore has friendlier relations with Beijing. But if Singapore is not yet a fully free electoral democracy, neither is it the authoritarian champion of green governance as some portray it. First, the city-state owes a huge ecological debt to other nations, starting with its neighbours in the region. Second, during the last two decades, civic rights have kept expanding, especially during the post-Lee Kuan Yew era (since 2015). As Harvey Neo suggests in Chapter 4, environmental mobilizations are good exemplars of this evolution. An atmosphere of post-politics implies the persistence of rigid institutional constraints and the obstacles to addressing problems in a frank and open political debate. More windows of opportunity could nevertheless appear, if ecological activists decide to pressure the authorities of the Garden City toward more coherence between its national brand marketing and its effective practices.

Since the mid-1980s, political life in the Philippines has been characterized by a vibrant civil society as well as rampant gun violence. While both have remained basic features of the twenty-first century, the intensity of climate-related typhoons has become a new central issue. If some countries suffer more than others in the Anthropocene, the Philippines are surely among them. As Francisco Magno highlights in Chapter 5, the legal battle launched against the Carbon Majors is probably the most distinctive contribution of Philippine environmentalism to the international movement for climate justice. Another important struggle of the Philippine environmental movement deals with the extractive industry. While the Catholic Church has played an important role in this battle, the influence of this environmental activism on the political life in the Philippines remains elusive.

Compared to the three decades of Suharto's autocracy, "post-New Order" Indonesia (since 1998) has seen significant democratization of the country, with regular and fair elections being held since 2004. Although elections still rely more on the charisma of populist leaders like Yudhoyono and Jokowi (Kenny 2018, pp. 53–54), the number of civil society organizations has grown steadily, partly compensating for the structural weakness of the political parties. In Chapter 6, Suharko posits that environmental NGOs have become an important component of Indonesian civil society. With a median age of 28.3 years, in the fourth most populous country in the world, these environmental NGOs' members are young and creative. As the struggle against deforestation is a priority, they have been working hard to amend an odious law that transferred the majority of forests into the hands of state patrons and their cronies in the palm oil and logging companies, ignoring the customary rights of local populations. The young activists also pressure the international banks that finance forest-razing projects. With the cooperation of Oxfam and Greenpeace, they lobby climate change conferences so that carbon trading does not provide a blank cheque for more deforestation. In addition, they bring support to the numerous fisher folk of the Indonesian archipelago, who are vulnerable to the consequences of global warming and who must also resist against coastal reclamation for real estate developments, as in Bali, a global tourist mecca. Through these mobilizations, Indonesian environmental NGOs not only reshape the Indonesian polity, they are on the forefront of the Anthropocene's main challenges.

In Chapter 7 on Malaysia, Fadzilah Majid Cooke and Adnan A. Hezri show that, despite the long stranglehold on the country by the coalition Barisan Nasional, environmental activists have obtained several successes that led to major political change. The authors devote particular attention to the battles of indigenous peoples for their customary land rights against rapacious corporations. As in Indonesia, these environmental organizations have also relied on the judicial system; despite many defeats, the Malaysian courts, whose common law jurisdiction is a legacy of British colonial rule, have tended to recognize the rights of indigenous peoples to their ancestral lands. Since 2008, another major environmental cause has been the opposition to a rare earth refinery by a subsidiary of Lynas, an Australian company. This local mobilization gradually morphed into a nationwide campaign that combined slogans for clean environment and clean politics. In the general elections of 2013, one leader of the campaign against Lynas nearly defeated the Barisan Nasional candidate. The political turnover eventually occurred in the general elections of May 2018: after sixty-one years in power, the Barisan Nasional was defeated by a landslide victory. Beyond the spectacular comeback of Mahathir in the 2018 elections, the authors analyse the contribution of several environmental activists that underpins this long-term process of political liberalization through the maturation of civil society.

In contrast with the countries presented so far, the last three chapters present rather gloomier perspectives both for democracy and for the environment. In Chapter 8 on Thailand, Jakkrit Sangkhamanee focuses on the gradual co-option of environmental NGOs from a commitment to the rural poor to collaboration with autocratic forces. In the 1990s, environmentalism flourished thanks to popular movements like the Assembly of the Poor, which contributed to launching a new Constitution in 1997. In contrast, during the last two decades, as Sangkhamanee argues, environmental NGOs and other civil society organizations have gradually renounced their commitment to their idealized community of "villagers" and eventually gave up their consistent criticism of the state's ecologically destructive policies. Thaksin Shinawatra's authoritarian populism and the two coups d'état that punctuated his rule (in 2006 against Thaksin, and again in 2014 against Thaksin's sister Yingluck) contributed to this process. Thaksin had forged strong links with the rural population, while centralizing decision-making to boost exports through the increased exploitation of natural resources. The NGOs felt so betrayed by the villagers that in the end they endorsed the reactionary mindset of oligarchic groups and the military. The military regimes that overthrew Thaksin and Yingluck have increased the pressure on freedom of speech, and despite the NGOs' support, they do not perform any better for the environment. But the worst may be the double-standard bias that has divided urban elites from the rural populace.

In Vietnam, the Communist Party maintains strong control over society. In Chapter 9, Stephan Ortmann posits that, despite a coherent set of environmental laws and a certain tolerance for media reporting about environmental problems, a robust environmental movement is unlikely to emerge. An important reason for this lies in the reluctance of Communist Party officials, even the reform-minded, to allow more autonomy to NGOs. As in China, NGOs are very much controlled by state authorities, such as the Vietnam Union of Science and Technology Associations (VUSTA). The very notion of NGOs and civil society remains problematic. Ortmann argues that environmental protests and their reporting are tolerated provided they are circumscribed in time and space. If they become nationwide, they are seen as a threat to the regime and repression sets in, as indeed happened in the two rare nationwide cases of environmental protest: the campaigns against bauxite mining and the marine pollution by Formosa Ha Tinh Steel. In both cases, the considerable amount of foreign investment, as well as the politically sensitive roles of China and the Catholic Church, triggered repression from above.

The last country analysis is devoted to Cambodia. Since 1985, Hun Sen has been prime minister of the country with a joint record of longevity and corruption and electoral fraud. James W.Y. Wang makes clear how, through control of the Cambodian People's Party (CPP), Hun Sen and associates have built a patronage network that has captured the state apparatus and practices an intense expropriation of natural resources. Efforts by the West to promote democracy in Cambodia through financial aid have ended in complete failure; and China, which has no concern for democracy, has become the primary donor and largest investor. China's strategy is twofold: first, to gain geostrategic access to the Gulf of Thailand; and second, to exploit Cambodia's natural resources, starting with hydropower capacities, through state-owned companies like Sinohydro Corporation, which holds 50 per cent of the world market. Eight hydroelectric dams are already under construction and several others are planned, threatening to destroy the country's last forests and rivers. Despite all kinds of threats and harassment, an assemblage of local monks and villagers, plus an environmental NGO founded by a Cambodia-based foreign activist, has successfully mobilized against one of these dam projects. Such hard-won battles remain nevertheless as fragile as Cambodian electoral system.

In the 1980s, there was a dominant wishful thinking in the West that China's two-digit economic growth would bring about its democratization. The outbreak of the Covid-19 pandemic has made it clear that China is not ready for a democratizing path, to say the least. The long-wished-for prospect of democratization through economic development has now given way to a certain admiration for China's "strong" responses to climate change, pandemics, and other symptoms of the Anthropocene. In the concluding chapter,

Jobin draws on the findings of the previous chapters to examine the temptation of environmental authoritarianism, with China and Singapore the dominant models, and the significance of Taiwan and Hong Kong as democratic challengers to this model. The chapter presents a theoretical framework for further studies into the interactions between environmental mobilizations and different political regimes, with a focus on East and Southeast Asia.

NOTES

1. These are Alvin Y. So, Hsin-Huang Michael Hsiao, Ming-sho Ho and Francisco Magno.
2. In this book, although we might also use the expression of climate change, we have a preference for "global warming". As Latour (2015, p. 25) reminds, "climate change" was astutely introduced in 2003 by the American oil industry and its Republican supporters to mitigate the threatening impact of "global warming". Inversely, some researchers have recently proposed to level up "global warming" to "global heating" (Watts 2018). On climate change "denial countermovement", see Dunlap and McCright (2015)'s exhaustive research.
3. For a summary, see IBPES (2018) and IBPES (2019) for Asia. The 1,800-page report, which consisted of more than 15,000 scientific publications, stresses that three-quarters of the Earth's environment today has been altered by human activity, and if there is no quick solution, another one million animal and plant species will be threatened with extinction. The five main culprits of biodiversity loss are land use (agriculture, deforestation), direct exploitation of resources (fishing, hunting), climate change, pollution and invasive species. For example, plastic pollution has increased tenfold since the 1980s, and between 300 and 400 million tonnes of heavy metals, solvents, toxic sludge, and other wastes from industrial sites are dumped annually into the oceans. Fertilizers entering coastal ecosystems have produced more than 400 "dead zones" in the oceans, totalling 245,000 square kilometres, or the size of the United Kingdom.
4. In addition to a burgeoning number of articles using the Anthropocene in their title or as keyword (for literature reviews in humanities and social science, see Marquardt 2019, Simangan 2020), there are already three academic journals entirely devoted to it. The quarterly *Anthropocene*, which started in 2013 with Crutzen on the editorial board, is hosted by the scientific publisher Elsevier; *Elementa: Science of the Anthropocene*, an

online open access journal was launched the same year by the University of California; and the *Anthropocene Review,* another quarterly which welcomes scholars in the humanities and social sciences, debuted in 2014 and is hosted by Sage.

5. If the Southern Chinese culture was the main component of the recent mobilizations in Taiwan and Hong Kong, similar resistance to Beijing would also occur in places like Macao, Guangzhou or Fujian province, but this is far from being the case.

REFERENCES

Aiken, S. Robert and Colin H. Leigh. 2015. "Dams and Indigenous Peoples in Malaysia: Development, Displacement and Resettlement". *Geografiska Annaler: Series B, Human Geography* 97: 69–93.

Almeida, Paul. 2019. *Social Movements: The Structure of Collective Mobilization.* Oakland: University of California Press.

Baldwin, Andrew and Bruce Erickson. 2020. "Introduction: Whiteness, Coloniality, and the Anthropocene". *Environment and Planning D: Society and Space* 38, no. 1: 3–11.

Barney, Keith. 2017. "Environmental Neoliberalism in Southeast Asia". In *Handbook of Environment in Southeast Asia,* edited by Philip Hirsch. London: Routledge, pp. 99–114.

Beau, Rémi and Catherine Larrère, eds. 2018. *Penser l'Anthropocène.* Paris: Sciences Po.

Boltanski, Luc. 2009. *Distant Suffering: Morality, Media and Politics.* Cambridge: Cambridge University Press.

Bonneuil, Christophe and Jean-Baptiste Fressoz. 2013. *L'évènement Anthropocène.* Paris: Seuil.

Boomgard, Peter. 2017. "Environmental Histories of Southeast Asia". In *Handbook of Environment in Southeast Asia,* edited by Philip Hirsch. London: Routledge, pp. 31–45.

Bullard, Robert D. 1983. "Solid Waste Sites and the Black Houston Community". *Sociological Inquiry* 53, no. 2/3: 274–88.

———. 1990. *Dumping in Dixie: Race, Class, and Environmental Quality.* Boulder, CO: Westview Press.

Burck, Jan, Ursula Hagen, Niklas Höhne, Leonardo Nascimento, and Christoph Bals. 2020. *Climate Change Performance Index.* Bonn: Germanwatch Institute.

Bush, Simon R. and Melissa Marschke. 2017. "Social and Political Ecology of Fisheries and Aquaculture in Southeast Asia". In *Handbook of Environment in Southeast Asia,* edited by Philip Hirsch. London: Routledge, pp. 224–38.

Ceballos, Gerardo, Paul R. Ehrlich, Anthony D. Barnosky, Andres Garcia, Robert M. Pringle, and Todd Palmer. 2015. "Accelerated Modern Human-Induced Species Losses: Entering the Sixth Mass Extinction". *Science Advances* 1: e1400253. https://doi.org/10.1126/sciadv.1400253.

Cefaï, Daniel. 2007. *Pourquoi se mobilise-t-on? Les theories de l'action collective.* Paris: La découverte.

Chakrabarty, Dipesh. 2009. "The Climate of History: Four Theses". *Critical Enquiry* 35: 197–222.

Chandler, David. 2017. "Securing the Anthropocene? International Policy Experiments in Digital Hacktivism: A Case Study of Jakarta". *Security Dialogue* 48, no. 2: 113–30.

Chatterjee, Elisabeth. 2020. "The Asian Anthropocene: Electricity and Fossil Developmentalism". *The Journal of Asian Studies* 79, no. 1: 3–24.

Coleman, J.L., J.S. Ascher, D. Bickford, D. Buchori, A. Cabanban, R.A. Chisholm, K.Y. Chong, P. Christie, G.R. Clements, T.E.E. dela Cruz, W. Dressler, D.P. Edwards, C.M. Francis, D.A. Friess, X. Giam, L. Gibson, D. Huang, A.C. Hughes, Z. Jaafar, A. Jain, L.P. Koh, E.P. Kudavidanage, B.P.Y.-H. Lee, J. Lee, T.M. Lee, M. Leggett, B. Leimona, M. Linkie, M. Luskin, A. Lynam, E. Meijaard, V. Nijma, A. Olsson, S. Page, P. Paroli, K.S.-H. Peh, M.R. Posa, G.W. Prescott, S.A. Rahman, S.J. Ramchunder, M. Rao, J. Reed, D.R. Richards, E.M. Slade, R. Steinmetz, P.Y. Ta, D. Taylor, P.A. Todd, S.T. Vo, E.L. Webb, A.D. Ziegler, and L.R. Carrasco. 2019. "Top 100 Research Questions for Biodiversity Conservation in Southeast Asia". *Biological Conservation* 234: 211–20.

Corlett, Richard T. 2013. "Becoming Europe: Southeast Asia in the Anthropocene". *Elementa: Science of the Anthropocene* 1: 000016. http://doi.org/10.12952/journal.elementa.000016.

Cramb, Rob. 2017. "Shifting Cultivation and Human Interaction with Forests". In *Handbook of Environment in Southeast Asia*, edited by Philip Hirsch. London: Routledge, pp. 180–203.

Crutzen, Paul J. 2002. "Geology of Mankind". *Nature* 415, no. 6867: 23.

Crutzen, Paul J. and Eugene F. Stoermer. 2000. "The Anthropocene". *Global Change Newsletter IGBP* 41: 17–18.

Dauvergne, Peter. 2001. *Loggers and Degradation in the Asia-Pacific: Corporations and Environmental Management.* Cambridge, UK: Cambridge University Press.

Davis, Heather and Zoe Todd. 2017. "On the Importance of a Data, or, Decolonizing the Anthropocene". *ACME: An International Journal for Critical Geographies* 16, no. 4: 761–80.

De Koninck, Rodolphe and Pham Than Hai. 2017. "Population Growth and Environmental Degradation in Southeast Asia". In *Handbook of Environment in Southeast Asia*, edited by Philip Hirsch. London: Routledge, pp. 46–47.

Diokno, Maria Serena I., Hsin-Huang Michael Hsiao, and Alan H. Yang. 2019. *China's Footprints in Southeast Asia.* Singapore: National University of Singapore Press.

Dryzek, John S. and Jonathan Pickering. 2019. *The Politics of the Anthropocene.* Oxford: Oxford University Press.

Dunlap, Riley E. and Aaron M. McCright. 2015. "Challenging Climate Change: The Denial Countermovement". In *Climate Change and Society: Sociological Perspectives,* edited by Riley E. Dunlap and Robert J. Brulle. New York: Oxford University Press, pp. 300–32.

Eckstein, David, Marie-Lena Hutfils, and Maik Winges. 2019. *Global Climate Risk Index.* Bonn: Germanwatch Institute.

Goodwin, Jeff and James M. Jasper, eds. 2011. *Contention in Context: Political Opportunities and the Emergence of Protest.* Stanford, CA: Stanford University Press.

Greenough, Paul and Anna Lowenhaupt Tsing, eds. 2003. *Nature in the Global South: Environmental Projects in South and Southeast Asia.* Durham: Duke University Press.

Guha, Ramachandra and J. Martinez-Alier. 1997a. *Varieties of Environmentalism: Essays North and South.* London: Earthscan Publications Ltd.

———. 1997b. "The Environmentalism of the Poor". In *Varieties of Environmentalism: Essays North and South.* London: Earthscan Publications Ltd., pp. 3–21.

Hamilton, Clive. 2017. *Defiant Earth: The Fate of Humans in the Anthropocene.* Sydney: Allen & Unwin.

Harris, Paul G., ed. 2005. *Confronting Environmental Change in East and Southeast Asia: Eco-politics, Foreign Policy and Sustainable Development.* Tokyo: United Nations University Press; and London: Earthscan.

———, ed. 2011. *China's Responsibility for Climate Change.* Bristol: The Policy Press.

———. 2016. *Global Ethics and Climate Change,* 2nd ed. Edinburgh: Edinburgh University Press.

Harris, Paul G. and Graeme Lang, ed. 2015. *Routledge Handbook of Environment and Society in Asia.* London: Routledge.

Hecht, Gabrielle. 2018. "The African Anthropocene". *Aeon* (online), 6 February 2018.

Heijden, Hein-Anton van der. 1997. "Political Opportunity Structure and the Institutionalisation of the Environmental Movement". *Environmental Politics* 6, no. 4: 25–50.

Hirsch, Philip, ed. 2018. *Handbook of Environment in Southeast Asia.* London: Routledge.

Hirsch, Philip and Carol Warren, eds. 1998. *The Politics of Environment in Southeast Asia: Resources and Resistance.* London: Routledge.

Ho, Ming-sho. 2019. *Challenging Beijing's Mandate of Heaven: The Sunflower Movement in Taiwan and the Umbrella Movement in Hong Kong.* Philadelphia: Temple University Press.

Horn, Eva and Hannes Bergthaller. 2020. *The Anthropocene: Key Issues for the Humanities.* London: Routledge.

Hornborg, Alf. 2013. *Global Ecology and Unequal Exchange: Fetishism in a Zero-Sum World.* London: Routledge.

———. 2018. "La magie mondialisée du Technocène. Capital, échanges inégaux et moralité". In *Penser l'Anthropocène*, edited by Rémi Beau and Catherine Larrère. Paris: Sciences Po, pp. 97–112.

Hudson, Mark. 2014. "Placing Asia in the Anthropocene: Histories, Vulnerabilities, Responses". *The Journal of Asian Studies* 73, no. 4: 941–62.

Hughes, Alice C. 2017. "Understanding the Drivers of Southeast Asian Biodiversity Loss". *Ecosphere* 8, no. 1. https://doi.org/10.1002/ecs2.1624.

IPBES (United Nations' Intergovernmental Science-Policy Platform on Biodiversity and Ecosystem Services). 2018. *The Regional Assessment Report on Biodiversity and Ecosystem Services for Asia and the Pacific.* www.ipbes.net.

———. 2019. *Global Assessment Report on Biodiversity and Ecosystem Services (Summary for Policymakers).* www.ipbes.net.

Jasper, James. 2010. "Social Movement Theory Today: Toward a Theory of Action". *Sociology Compass* 4, no. 11: 965–76.

Kalland, Arne and Gerard Persoon, eds. 1998. *Environmental Movements in Asia.* Richmond, UK: Curzon Press and the Nordic Institute of Asian Studies.

Keck, Margaret and Kathryn Sikkink. 1998. *Activists Beyond Borders: Advocacy Networks in International Politics.* Ithaca, NY: Cornell University Press.

Kenny, Paul D. 2018. *Populism in Southeast Asia.* New York: Cambridge University Press.

Kerkvliet, Benedict. 2010. "Governance, Development, and the Responsive–Repressive State in Vietnam". *Forum for Development Studies* 37: 33–59.

Kolbert, Elizabeth. 2014. *The Sixth Extinction: An Unnatural History.* New York: Henry Holt and Company.

Latour, Bruno. 2014. "Agency at the Time of the Anthropocene". *New Literary History* 45: 1–18.

———. 2015. *Facing Gaia: Eight Lectures on the New Climatic Regime.* Cambridge, UK: Polity.

———. 2017. *Politics in the New Climatic Regime.* Cambridge, UK: Polity.

———. 2020. "Is This a Dress Rehearsal?" *Critical Inquiry*, 26 March 2020.

Lee, Yok-shiu F. and Alvin Y. So, eds. 1999. *Asia's Environmental Movements: Comparative Perspectives.* New York: M.E. Sharpe.

Lidskog, Rolf and Claire Waterton. 2016. "Anthropocene: A Cautious Welcome from Environmental Sociology?" *Environmental Sociology* 2, no. 4: 395–406.

Lohmann, Larry. 1993. "The Political Ecology of Southeast Asian Forests: Transdisciplinary Discourses". *Global Ecology and Biogeography Letters* 3, no. 4: 180–91.

Lyster, Rosemary. 2015. *Climate Justice and Disaster Law*. Cambridge: Cambridge University Press.

Malm, Andreas. 2016. *Fossil Capital: The Rise of Steam Power and the Roots of Global Warming*. London: Verso.

Malm, Andreas and Alf Hornborg. 2014. "The Geology of Mankind? A Critique of the Anthropocene Narrative". *The Anthropocene Review* 1, no. 1: 62–69.

Marquardt, Jens. 2019. "Worlds Apart? The Global South and the Anthropocene". In *The Anthropocene Debate and Political Science*, edited by Thomas Hickmann, Lena Partzsch, Philipp Pattberg, and Sabine Weiland. London and New York: Routledge.

Martinez-Alier, Joan. 2002. *The Environmentalism of the Poor: A Study of Ecological Conflicts and Valuation*. Cheltenham, UK: Edward Elgar.

McAdam, Doug and Schaffer Hilary Boudet. 2012. *Putting Social Movements in their Place: Explaining Opposition to Energy Projects in the United States, 2000–2005*. Cambridge: Cambridge University Press.

McAdam, Doug, John D. McCarthy, and Mayer N. Zald, eds. 1996. *Comparative Perspectives on Social Movements: Political Opportunities, Mobilizing Structures and Cultural Framings*. New York: Cambridge University Press.

McAdam, Doug, Sidney Tarrow, and Charles Tilly. 2001. *The Dynamics of Contention*. Cambridge: Cambridge University Press.

McCarthy, John D. and Mayer N. Zald. 1977. "Resource Mobilization and Social Movements: A Partial Theory". *American Journal of Sociology* 82, no. 6: 1212–41.

McElwee, Pamela. 2016. *Forests are Gold: Trees, People, and Environmental Rule in Vietnam*. Seattle: University of Washington Press.

Middleton, Carl. 2017. "Water, Rivers and Dams". In *Handbook of Environment in Southeast Asia*, edited by Philip Hirsch. London: Routledge, pp. 204–23.

Moore, Jason W. 2015. *Capitalism in the Web of Life: Ecology and the Accumulation of Capital*. London/New York: Verso.

———, ed. 2016. *Anthropocene or Capitalocene? Nature, History, and the Crisis of Capitalism*. Oakland, CA: PM Press and Kairos Books.

Morris-Jung, Jason, ed. 2018. *In China's Backyard: Policies and Politics of Chinese Resource Investments in Southeast Asia*. Singapore: ISEAS – Yusof Ishak Institute.

Niezen, Ronald. 2003. *The Origins of Indigenism: Human Rights and the Politics of Identity*. Berkeley: University of California Press.

Pellow, David N. 2017. "Environmental Justice Movements and Political Opportunity Structures". In *Handbook of Environmental Justice*, edited by Ryan Holifield, Jayajit Chakraborty, and Gordon Walker. London: Routledge, pp. 37–49.

———. 2018. *What is Critical Environmental Justice?* Cambridge: Polity.

Peluso, Nancy. 1994. *Rich Forests, Poor People: Resource Control and Resistance in Central Java*. Berkeley: University of California Press.

Pulido, Laura. 2017. "Historicizing the Personal and the Political: Evolving Racial Formations and the Environmental Justice Movement". In *Handbook of Environmental Justice*, edited by Ryan Holifield, Jayajit Chakraborty, and Gordon Walker. London: Routledge, pp. 15–24.

Reszitnyk, Andrew. 2020. "The Descent into Disanthropy: Critical Theory and the Anthropocene". *Telos* 190: 9–27.

Roberts, Patrick, Nicole Boivin, and Jed O. Kaplan. 2018. "Finding the Anthropocene in Tropical Forests". *Anthropocene* 23: 5–16.

Roberts, Timmons J. and Bradley C. Parks. 2009. "Ecologically Unequal Exchange, Ecological Debt, and Climate Justice: The History and Implications of Three Related Ideas for a New Social Movement". *International Journal of Comparative Sociology* 50, no. 3–4: 385–409.

Rootes, Christopher and Eugene Nulman. 2015. "The Impacts of Environmental Movements". In *The Oxford Handbook of Social Movements*, edited by Donatella Della Porta and Mario Diani. Oxford, UK: Oxford University Press.

Ross, Michael Lewin. 2001. *Timber Booms and Institutional Breakdown in Southeast Asia*. Cambridge, UK: Cambridge University Press.

Schneider-Mayerson, Matthew. 2017. "Some Islands Will Rise: Singapore in the Anthropocene". *Resilience* 4, no. 2–3: 166–84.

Seymour, Frances and Peter Kanowski. 2017. "Forests and Biodiversity". In *Handbook of Environment in Southeast Asia*, edited by Philip Hirsch. London: Routledge, pp. 159–79.

Sicotte, Diane M. and Robert J. Brulle. 2017. "Social Movements for Environmental Justice Through the Lens of Social Movement Theory". In *Handbook of Environmental Justice*, edited by Ryan Holifield, Jayajit Chakraborty, and Gordon Walker. London: Routledge, pp. 25–36.

Simangan, Dahlia. 2019. "Situating the Asia Pacific in the Age of the Anthropocene". *Australian Journal of International Affairs* 73, no. 6: 564–84.

———. 2020. "Where is the Asia Pacific in Mainstream International Relations Scholarship on the Anthropocene?" *The Pacific Review*. https://doi.org/10.1080/09512748.2020.1732452.

Simpson, Michael. 2020. "The Anthropocene as Colonial Discourse". *Environment and Planning D: Society and Space* 38, no. 1: 53–71.

Sims Gallagher, Kelly and Xiaowei Xuan. 2018. *Titans of the Climate: Explaining Policy Process in the United States and China*. Cambridge, MA: MIT Press.

Sodhi, Navjot S., Lian Pin Koh, Barry W. Brook, and Peter K.L. Ng. 2004. "Southeast Asian Biodiversity: An Impending Disaster". *Trends in Ecology and Evolution* 19, no. 12: 654–60.

Sovacool, Benjamin K. 2015. "Vulnerabilities to Climate Change: Adaptation in the Asia-Pacific Region". In *Routledge Handbook of Environment and Society in Asia*, edited by Paul G. Harris and Graeme Lang. London: Routledge, pp. 353–66.

Stibig, H.-J., F. Achard, S. Carboni, R. Rašil, and J. Miettinen. 2013. "Change in Tropical Forest Cover of Southeast Asia from 1990 to 2010". *Biogeosciences Discussions* 10: 12625–53. https://doi.org/10.5194/bgd-10-12625-2013.

Stolz, Robert. 2014. *Bad Water: Nature, Pollution, and Politics in Japan, 1870–1950*. Durham, NC: Duke University Press.

Swyngedouw, Erik. 2015. "Depoliticized Environments and the Promises of the Anthropocene". In *The International Handbook of Political Ecology*, edited by Raymond Bryant. Cheltenham: Elgar, pp. 131–45.

Tadem, Eduardo. 1990. "Conflict over Land-based Natural Resources in the ASEAN Countries". In *Conflict over Natural Resources in South-East Asia and the Pacific*, edited by Lim Teck Ghee and Mark J. Valencia. Singapore: Oxford University Press, United Nations University Press.

Tarrow, Sidney. 1994. *Power in Movement: Social Movements and Contentious Politics*. Cambridge: Cambridge University Press.

Tilly, Charles. 1978. *From Mobilization to Revolution*. New York: McGraw-Hill.

Tilly, Charles and Sidney Tarrow. 2015. *Contentious Politics*, 2nd ed. New York: Paradigm.

Tønnessen, Morten, Kristin Armstrong Oma, and Silver Rattasepp, eds. 2016. *Thinking about Animals in the Age of the Anthropocene*. Lanham, MD: Lexington Books.

Vandergeest, Peter and Robin Roth. 2017. "A Southeast Asian Political Ecology". In *Handbook of Environment in Southeast Asia*, edited by Philip Hirsch. London: Routledge, pp. 82–98.

Walker, Brett L. 2010. *Toxic Archipelago: A History of Industrial Disease in Japan*. Seattle: University of Washington Press.

Watts, Jonathan. 2018. "Global Warming should be called Global Heating, says Key Scientist". *The Guardian*, 13 December 2018.

Welker, Marina A. 2009. "'Corporate Security Begins in the Community': Mining, the Corporate Social Responsibility Industry, and Environmental Advocacy in Indonesia". *Cultural Anthropology* 24, no. 1: 142–79.

Woods, Kerri. 2017. "Environmental Human Rights". In *Handbook of Environmental Justice*, edited by Ryan Holifield, Jayajit Chakraborty, and Gordon Walker. London: Routledge, pp. 149–59.

Zeng, Zhenzhong, Lyndon Estes, Alan D. Ziegler, Anping Chen, Timothy Searchinger, Fangyuan Hua, Kaiyu Guan, Attachai Jintrawet, and Eric F. Wood. 2018. "Highland Cropland Expansion and Forest Loss in Southeast Asia in the Twenty-first Century". *Nature Geoscience* 11: 556–62.

Zhang, Qiang, Xujia Jiang, Dan Tong, Steven J. Davis, Hongyan Zhao, Guannan Geng, Tong Feng, Bo Zheng, Zifeng Lu, David G. Streets, Ruijing Ni, Michael Brauer, Aaron van Donkelaar, Randall V. Martin, Hong Huo, Zhu Liu, Da Pan, Haidong Kan, Yingying Yan, Jintai Lin, Kebin He, and Dabo Guan. 2017. "Transboundary Health Impacts of Transported Global Air Pollution and International Trade". *Nature* 453: 705–17.

2

ENVIRONMENTAL MOVEMENTS IN TAIWAN'S ANTHROPOCENE: A CIVIC ECO-NATIONALISM

*Paul Jobin**

Over the last two decades, despite threats and pressure from China, Taiwan has consolidated its democracy and its identity in the international community. So, too, have its environmental movements. Hsin-Huang Michael Hsiao (1999) has described how the emergence of an environmental movement in the mid-1980s played a significant role in the popular mobilization that put an end to forty years of authoritarianism, paving the way for the country's democratization. Hsiao further defined the three pillars—or what he prefers to call *streams*, a more dynamic and natural metaphor—of that environmental mobilization as follows: (1) a grassroots, victim-conscious, anti-pollution movement against heavy industry; (2) an urban middle-class movement for the conservation of natural habitats and animal species; and (3) an anti-nuclear movement, which the author detached from anti-pollution protests to emphasize a greater level of public concern and connection with national politics.

Nearly twenty years later, in addition to these three streams of mobilization, Hsiao (2017) notes the emergence of two additional movements: 4) a movement against high-tech industrial hazards that arose around the turn of the century and bears characteristics distinct from the initial anti-pollution protests (see also Tu 2007, 2017a; Tu and Lee 2009; Chiu 2011, 2014); and 5) a movement for energy transition toward a low-carbon society (see also Hsu et al. 2016). Kuei-tien Chou (2015, 2017) further argues that Taiwan's anti-pollution movements are now reshaping their episteme to cope with the new challenges of climate change; the fight against industrial hazards now goes hand in hand with a struggle to reduce the intensive consumption of energy and natural resources like water. Indeed, among the three hundred associations registered by the Environmental Protection Administration (EPA), around thirty claimed that global warming is their main matter of concern.[1]

This trend suggests that Taiwan's environmental movements have reached a critical turn, which reflects the dynamism of Taiwanese civil society and its solid connections with the international community. The notion of the Anthropocene has also prompted academic discussions, though thus far they remain limited to a small circle (e.g., Lin 2018; Chuang 2020; Lee 2020; Chuang and Gong 2020). But as Hsiao (1999) also noted, the impossibility for Taiwan to sign various international agreements—and consequent lack of obligations thereunder—has lessened the pressure of global environmentalism on the island. Taiwan's fragile diplomatic standing in the world is reflected in the fact that it has no listing in the Global Footprint Network and is referred to as "Chinese Taipei" in the Climate Change Performance Index.

We do at least have some indicators of Taiwan's "ecological balance sheet" as compared to other countries. Yale University's Environmental Performance Index not only refers to Taiwan as "Taiwan", it gives the island a good ranking: although its overall score has decreased from 79.1 (out of 100) in 2002 to 72.84 in 2018, Taiwan remains in the top thirty globally, right after New Zealand, Japan, and Australia in the Asia-Pacific area. However, according to the Germanwatch Institute, "Chinese Taipei" is both a victim *and* a perpetuator of global heating: in certain years, the island is one of the countries most exposed to the consequences of the climate crisis;[2] but it also ranks among the bottom ten (of fifty-seven) nations for its poor results in reducing carbon emissions and other greenhouses gases.[3]

Situated at the convergence of four tectonic plates, Taiwan experiences intense seismic activity. For geologists, the island is located on a "destructive plate boundary". In addition, because of its tropical and subtropical weather, Taiwan is subject to typhoons, which are becoming ever more ferocious with global heating. The violent winds and heavy rains provoke floods, rapid erosion, and landslides. This combination of geological and meteorological factors makes the island a hotspot for the study of "critical zones", a recent subfield of earth science (Latour 2014; Jobin 2018a, 2020), and puts Taiwan at the forefront of the Anthropocene.

Taiwan also finds itself a geopolitical hotspot; in that sense, as well, Taiwan is a "critical zone". Far from abating, the pressure from the Chinese regime has continued to grow, and uncertainties remain about strategic support from the United States. And while it remains unclear whether Taiwan's efforts will be sufficient to cope with the challenges of the Anthropocene (such as the threat to its populated urban shoreline from rising sea levels), what is certain is that the island cannot ignore the pressure from China. This unique situation has been a basic component of social movements in Taiwan for the last forty years. Despite the tremendous geopolitical pressure—or perhaps owing to it—Taiwanese civil society has consolidated the country's democracy over the last two decades, resulting in the excellent scores on various democracy indexes.[4] I argue in this chapter that environmental movements have played a significant role in this process, through what I call *civic eco-nationalism*, or a civic form of ecological nationalism. After introducing this argument, its theoretical framework, and the conditions that gave rise to it, this chapter reviews the main characteristics of Taiwan's environmental movements during the last two decades, through the existing literature—which is abundant both in Chinese and English—and my own observation since 2008. A good deal of fieldwork was conducted as a participating observer, which enables an ethnographic immersion over the long run.[5]

The environmental movements are organized into three sections. The first two involve public campaigns aimed at influencing government policy and public opinion: in nationwide concerns, such as nuclear energy and air pollution, and then with regard to local matters, as in cases involving indigenous peoples. The third looks at mobilizations against private companies, using the courts as a means to effect change.

A Civic Eco-nationalism

Environmental issues and national identity are usually distinct fields of research. When the two issues are discussed together, they are most often devised within the critical prism of prevention against "eco-fascism", especially in the context of Western Europe (cf. Stephens 2001; Biehl et al. 2011). Although this remark is less pertinent in the Asian context, studies of how ecology and nationalism interact nevertheless remain scarce overall.

The work of Jane Dawson (1995, 1996) is thus all the more precious, as her thorough study of the post-Chernobyl USSR presented the intersection between ecology and nationalism as a research topic worthy of a nuanced approach. After the Chernobyl nuclear disaster, anti-nuclear movements emerged all over the Soviet Union. Curiously, as Dawson showed, after the mutation of the USSR into the Federation of Russia and fifteen independent republics, anti-nuclear movements vanished completely. And yet, the mobilizations against nuclear plants had played an instrumental role in this drastic geopolitical transformation. Dawson called this mix of environmentalism and nationalism ecological nationalism, or *eco-nationalism*. She further showed that in small republics like Armenia, Lithuania, and Crimea, the anti-nuclear movement clearly served as a surrogate cause for criticism of Moscow's colonialism. But the anti-nuclear movement's usefulness as a safe proxy for national independence struggles disappeared with the fall of the USSR, and opposition to nuclear power plants plummeted. Thereafter, despite the dramatic and long-term consequences of the Chernobyl disaster, most of these countries resumed their development of nuclear power plants.

Taiwan's anti-nuclear movement—and the environmental movement at large—can also be understood as an expression of ecological nationalism. But contrary to what Dawson observed in the case of the post-Chernobyl USSR, Taiwan's environmental movements have not been hiding a nationalist purpose behind their ecological discourse, and environmental groups not only remain numerous and very active, they have become an essential part of Taiwan's civil society. I therefore argue that, in Taiwan, environmentalism is not a surrogate cause or a substitute for nationalism but a congruent factor. Ecological mobilizations do not only resist against techno-authoritarianism, they share a common goal of defending Taiwan's democracy. This includes protecting its *de facto* independence against the threat from China.

At the end of the 1970s, ecological worries developed in parallel with the rise of a Taiwanese "native identity" (*bentu yishi*), or the "indigenization movement" (*benduhua yundong*), against the China-centred ideology of the Kuomintang (Nationalist Party of China, or KMT), the one-party émigré regime in Taiwan. In that context, claims for environmental protection (*huanbao*) became a way to show concern for Taiwan (Jobin 2010, p. 47). The early discourse of environmental leaders such as Edgar Lin attributed the KMT's lack of care for Taiwan's environment to the fact that its ultimate goal was the recovery of China (*fangong dalu tongyi Zhongguo*). Or, as aptly put by Linda Arrigo:

> Taiwan's environmental morass was not merely the result of a tardy awakening to the ills of rapid industrialization, but the outcome of a particular political and economic order, which [can be summarized] as: a refugee government that at first thought of Taiwan mainly as a launching pad for retaking mainland China (Arrigo 1994, p. 23; see also Arrigo and Puleston 2006).

Departing from such a China-centred identity, Hsiao's (1987) early description of Taiwan's environmental movement was untitled "We have only one Taiwan" (*Women zhi you yige Taiwan*), to make it clear that there was no way back to the "ancestor's land" (*zuguo*), and that Taiwan was now generally identified as the true homeland.

As Lepesant observes more recently (2018, p. 108), environmental issues nowadays "constitute an important space for the politicization of young Taiwanese citizens", creating "a sense of crisis and urgency [...] that the economic model that brought prosperity to Taiwan is now on the verge of collapse". He concludes that "environmental issues contribute to reinforcing identification with Taiwan as a nation-state", and rally "the young generation to a political commitment on the margins of the partisan sphere" (p. 118, my translation). I fully endorse the first part of this statement and argue that this interaction between a growing concern for ecology and an attachment to Taiwan as a democratic nation extends beyond the young to a large segment of the population, starting with environmental activists. Moreover, while broadly non-partisan, these activists will enter into temporary political alliances in the furtherance of specific issues, as they also will during presidential and legislative elections, when concern for Taiwan's precarious status takes on a higher priority.

Still, the explicit raison d'être of environmental activists is not partisan politics but ecology; it is their main daily concern, their "core business". Consequently, the actors might not explicitly formulate their attachment to Taiwan's *de facto* independence or, if they do, it is with many nuances from one individual to another. We therefore need to read between the lines of environmental discourses, beyond explicit narratives, and consider the general orientation of environmentalism, its frequent social practices, and its interactions with local and national politics, as well as with foreign actors.

Borrowing John DeWitt's (1994) notion of *civic environmentalism*, Ching-ping Tang (2003) observed in mid-1990s Taiwan the emergence of this phenomenon: in addition to the grassroots mobilizations of the 1980s focusing on the "narrow" and "self-interested" problem of compensation for industrial pollution, "newly created civic groups engaged in issues of a broader public interest" (Tang 2003, pp. 1036–37). Although I would not label the early grassroots mobilizations as "narrowly defined self-interest groups" (cf. McAdam and Schaffer Boudet 2012; Hager and Haddad 2015), I think the idea of a civic form of environmentalism can still apply today to denote a broad public interest and a scaling up of environmental justice topics.

I further posit that civic environmentalism is compatible with nationalism. The issue of nationalism and its interaction with democracy is a complex and hotly debated problem. Contrary to a common view casting nationalism as the main cause of ethnic hatred and as incompatible with the spirit of liberal democracy, the evolution of Taiwan over the last two decades offers a perfect example that the rise of a specific national identity can reinforce the development of a democratic society (Chuang 2013; Muyard 2018).

As explained by Craig Calhoun in his fundamental book *Nations Matter* (2007; in particular, chapter 6), ethnic and civic nationalism are not necessarily antithetical, but I believe it is important to explicitly retain the adjective *civic* to emphasize the non-xenophobic character of this ecological nationalism and its substantial contribution to Taiwanese civil society.[6] For a majority of ecological activists have gradually come to care for the future of Taiwan as a free democracy, through a civic form of engagement that is perhaps naive but is at least faithful to both the causes of ecology and democracy. Despite many loopholes, such as recurrent irregularities in Environmental Impact Assessment procedures and the lack of severe punishment against persistent polluters, most activists would probably adhere to the view that environmental protection has achieved significant progress in Taiwan thanks to the democratization of the country.

Claims made about the supposed efficiency of China's environmental authoritarianism (Beeson 2010, 2016) have so far had little influence in Taiwan, where the rejection of authoritarianism is at least as strong as the motivations for ecological engagement. An anecdote illustrates this resistance. In July 2017, a group of environmental activists in Taiwan noticed that Greenpeace was mapping Taiwan as a part of China. This sparked a controversy on the Taiwanese web, with netizens turning against Greenpeace for profiting from the donations of Taiwanese citizens, while it showed no concern for Taiwan as a democracy threatened by China's authoritarian regime (Ho 2017).

Taiwan's nationalism should not, however, be misunderstood simply as anti-China sentiment. If the resistance against Beijing's irredentism has played a crucial role, the development of Taiwanese nationalism is mostly the outcome of an explicit move towards a distinct identity, resulting from a specific historical path, and correlated with a national project resolutely engaged with democracy, especially among the younger generations. Over the years, this civic nationalism has forged strong links with the environmental movement. Based on my observation in the case of Taiwan, I define civic eco-nationalism as a mix of nationalism, ecology, and the spirit of democracy.

Following on previous discussions of civic nationalism (Calhoun 2007; Hsiau and Wang 2016; and Muyard 2012, 2018) and civic environmentalism (DeWitt 1994 and Tang 2003), I posit that civic environmentalism crisscrosses between ecology and democracy when it stresses the importance of freedoms of speech and assembly, as well as elections and an independent judiciary. In addition, civic nationalism includes the protection of national sovereignty and the promotion of a national polity that delivers equal civil rights to the different components of the nation (ethnic groups, sub-nations of indigenous peoples, religious and sexual minorities), which implies efforts to contain ethnic hatred and homophobic movements. Figure 2.1 sums up the three spheres composing civic eco-nationalism: nationalism, concern for ecology, and the spirit of democracy. Eco-nationalism stands at the intersection of ecology and nationalism.

Civic eco-nationalism may not be the biggest sphere of a national polity, but it matters for the equilibrium of the whole, and as I will try to show, in Taiwan, it gives a decisive impulse to environmental movements. In other words, I do not mean to claim that Taiwan's environmentalism is always about nationalism. For instance, in the class actions presented in the last section, the civic sphere is clearly the more decisive element. Yet the national sphere is never entirely absent from these mobilizations.

FIGURE 2.1

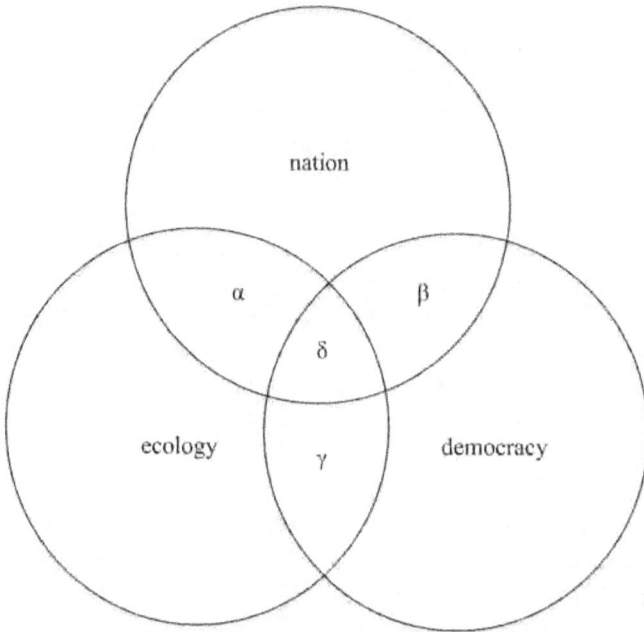

The three composing spheres of civic eco-nationalism: nationalism, ecology, and democratic spirit

Notes: α: Eco-nationalism; β: Civic nationalism; γ: Civic environmentalism, or ecological democratic spirit; δ: Civic eco-nationalism

Protecting "Our Island"

Chang and Slovic (2016) have described Taiwan as an epicentre of "eco-criticism". This notion refers to the cultural production—e.g., literary writing, theatre, film-making, and other visual arts—dealing with our critical epoch of ecological crisis.

A good manifestation of Taiwan's eco-criticism, and what I describe here as a civic eco-nationalism, is the weekly public television broadcast *Women de dao* (Our Island), which was launched at the founding of the Public Television Service in 1998. The lead producer is the award-winning documentary filmmaker Ke Chin-yuan. As he and his colleagues Yu Li-ping and Chang Dabbie Daiping explain, the initial idea of the title and its insular focus was to explore the country's seashore and ocean life; under martial law, the seashore had been off limits to civilians—quite a paradox for islanders—so this was a novel approach.[7] The programme is characterized by a mix of sharp criticism of the structural causes of industrial pollution—starting with corporate negligence and state indolence—and a candid tone in presenting numerous initiatives to protect biodiversity, develop alternative energies, etc. The programme thus offers other journalists, scholars, and environmental activists a reliable and easy-access databank, available on YouTube.

Another small-scale example of Taiwan's civic eco-nationalism can be seen in the numerous initiatives of "touring around the island" (*huandao*) for the sake of environmental protection, usually abbreviated as *huanbao* (for *huanjing baohu*), a catchword for various purposes, from collecting cigarette butts, plastic, and other waste, to more systematic citizen science with regular observation of the evolution of seashore pollution. The practice of *huandao* has become particularly popular among youth, either just for fun, as a self-imposed rite of passage, or to have physical contact with their natural surroundings. Many ride bicycles or motorbikes, or walk or hitchhike, while others take the train. But making a civic commitment such as cleaning up trash adds deeper meaning to the trip. The mode of participation varies from individuals on their own, or on collective tours arranged by local environmental activists or schoolteachers (e.g., Huang 2019), to religious groups staying in temples (C-W. Lin 2019), a frequent practice of Chinese folk religions in Taiwan.

An early sign of *huandao*, but with a stronger political meaning, dates back to 1994, when pro-democracy movement leader Lin Yi-hsiung launched the "Bitter March of One Thousand Kilometres" (*qianli kuxing*), an island-wide pilgrimage to protest the construction of Nuclear Power Plant Number Four (NPP4) (Ho 2018, p. 452). He undertook a similar march in 2009 with Cheng Li-chun (who thereafter served as Minister of Culture), under the slogan "The People as Master" (*renmin zuozhu*); in addition to a referendum on NPP4, they called for a second referendum to circumvent a commercial treaty with China. This last example suggests rather well how environmental issues may become entangled with nationalism. Before we look more in depth at other cases, the next section presents basic features of Taiwanese politics, with a focus on their linkage to environmental issues.

Green and Blue Camps

For forty years after the end of World War Two, Taiwan was under the authoritarian rule of the KMT, controlled by Generalissimo Chiang Kai-shek, followed by his son Chiang Ching-kuo. In September 1986, the opposition was able to launch the Democratic Progressive Party (DPP), and one year later, martial law was lifted. In order to maintain its position, the KMT was compelled to adapt to the democratization of the island's institutions. Meanwhile, the DPP continued to develop, but it was not until 2000 that its candidate, Chen Shui-bian, was able to win the presidential election. Chen won another four-year mandate in 2004, but in 2008, the KMT and its candidate Ma Ying-jeou returned to power for two consecutive mandates. Their rule ended in 2016, when the DPP made a triumphal comeback with the election of Tsai Ing-wen. The entire period since the end of martial law has been a difficult and complex transition, marked by several critical episodes, like the missile crisis of 1996 when China threatened to attack, and the attempted assassination of President Chen Shui-bian and Vice-President Annette Lu during their 2004 campaign for re-election.

In the 1970–80s, the physical pain and frustration from exposure to chronic industrial pollution encouraged people to express discontent (Lii and Lin 2000); these protests contributed to the chain of events that put an end to martial law. In the 1990s, protests against petrochemical plants and other big polluters grew in importance. These protests were concrete signs of democratization, and they contributed to challenging the KMT's control of the country (Hsiao 1999). Consequently, it was easier for the environmental movement to find political relays within the DPP than in the KMT, hence the tendency for partisan polarization thereafter. The Taiwan Environmental Protection Union (TEPU, *Taiwan huanbao lianmeng*), for example, was inclined to become dependent on the DPP (Ho 2003). The Green Party Taiwan (GPT) founded in 1996 was an attempt to break with such dependency, but it never managed to obtain parliamentary seats despite a gradual increase in popularity after 2008 (Fell and Peng 2017).

In contrast to the left-right—or liberal-conservative—divide that structures the political landscape of many contemporary democracies, the fault line of Taiwanese politics lies in a split between the so-called blue and green camps, or roughly speaking, between pro-China and pro-independence partisans, with the former led by the KMT and the latter by the DPP. The "green" designation derives from the DPP's flag, which presents a green map of Taiwan set in the middle of a white cross on a green background.[8] As we will see below, the map of Taiwan is often used as a symbol during environmental protests. Nonetheless, the green camp should not be misunderstood as an ecological alliance with the DPP's flagship.

Indeed, when the DPP is in power, it tends to adopt a low profile with big polluters, provoking recurrent friction with environmental activists who react more and more critically to the gap between electoral promises and post-election policies. Ho (2016) observes that both the DPP and the KMT have often contradicted their respective ideologies to better fulfil their electoral agendas. For those who wish to challenge the incumbents, it is therefore crucial to minimize the gap between the initiatives taken and the party's traditional line.

So far, the KMT and DPP have dominated the political landscape and other parties have never really challenged this domination or the blue-green split of Taiwanese politics; this includes those with legislative seats, such as the blue camp's People First Party, or the green's Taiwan Solidarity Union and New Power Party. However, the past decade has seen the Taiwanese polity undergo a substantial evolution.

One shift has been the increased influence of a radical left wing, especially in the green camp. In the 1990s, radical leftists had very little influence. But the effects of globalization and the transfer of industrial jobs to China have nurtured a "collapsing generation" (*bengshidai*) of those born between 1970 and 1990 (Lin et al. 2011). Compared to the generation of their parents, who had greater economic opportunities despite their lower level of education, it has become much harder for these young people to find stable and well-paid jobs, a situation somewhat similar to that observed in Japan and Western Europe beginning in the 1990s. Added to the growing threat that China has become for Taiwanese democracy, this social transformation has contributed to generating a stronger left wing within the green camp, that is, a leftist sub-branch of Taiwan's independence partisans (*zuodu*). This sociopolitical evolution partly explains the Sunflower Movement of March–April 2014 against the incumbent KMT's secret commercial agreement with China (Ho 2019).

A more recent development is the emergence of populist leaders, which has disrupted the rules of the game. This phenomenon started in 2014, after the Sunflower Movement, with the election of non-party-affiliated Ko Wen-je as Mayor of Taipei. Ko has since blurred the traditional divide between the blue and green camps with an ambivalent stand on cross-Strait politics (Hsiao 2019). Further upheaval came in 2018–19, when Han Kuo-yu and Terry Gou began to deeply disturb the KMT's long system of patronage with their unconventional styles. This latter phenomenon is comparable to Koizumi Junichirō's takeover of the Liberal Democratic Party in Japan, or to the case of Narendra Modi and India's Congress Party; these leaders develop direct contact with the people to bypass the complexities of institutional mediation (Kenny 2017). The difference in Taiwan is that several indices suggest that an external power—China—has been backing these populist candidates. As we will see later, Han Kuo-yu has benefitted as well from the conflict over air pollution.

The Anti-Nuclear Movement: From Renaissance to Radicalism

In the history of environmental movements in Taiwan, the anti-nuclear movement holds a special significance, by its length, its scope of action, and its intimate link with partisan politics. By the time the DPP was founded in the mid-1980s, Taiwan already had three nuclear plants operating, producing half of its electricity, and the construction of a fourth plant was planned. But an accidental fire in one of the three operating plants, followed soon after by the Chernobyl accident, aroused considerable concern among scientists, leading to the birth of a large opposition movement with a particular focus on the construction of NPP4, located not far from Taipei (Hsiao 1999, pp. 37–38). In 2000, Chen Shui-bian was elected with a promise to cancel the NPP4 project. But the KMT, which still controlled the parliament, blocked this effort and went so far as to drive an impeachment recall against President Chen, provoking a severe state crisis. Chen was finally forced to resume the construction, which many anti-nuclear activists interpreted as a betrayal. But the ultimate fate of NPP4 has yet to be resolved, as its controversial nature keeps it at the centre of an ongoing political tug of war.

The Chen Shui-bian years (2000–8) and the first half of Ma Ying-jeou's presidency (2008–12) were a sort of dark tunnel for the anti-nuclear movement and many other environmental mobilizations. Nonetheless, during this period there emerged a new generation of activists, like the Green Citizens' Action Alliance (GCAA), who were more grassroots-based and autonomous from the DDP compared to the scientist-led TEPU (Jobin 2010; Ho 2014a, 2018; Grano 2015).

The nuclear disaster of March 2011 in Fukushima reinvigorated Taiwan's anti-nuclear movement—indeed, more than any other in Asia except Japan's—sparking large demonstrations and the formation of new anti-nuclear groups, such as the Stop Nukes Now coalition (Ho 2014a, 2018; Grano 2015, 2017; cf. D-S. Chen 2011). The Ma government maintained its plan to bring NPP4 to completion, but politicians could no longer ignore or minimize the risk attached to the country's nuclear plants.

A second important episode occurred right after the Sunflower Movement of March–April 2014. This considerable mobilization against a secret trade deal with China provoked a major turnover in the political scene. The GCAA and activists from the Stop Nukes Now coalition played an active role in the successful twenty-three-day occupation of the parliament. As Grano (2017, pp. 166–67) emphasizes, anti-nuclear activists and other young protesters shared a common rejection of opaque and authoritarian decision-making. In addition to anti-nuclear groups, several other grassroots environmental organizations, such as Citizens of the Earth, Taiwan, played an instrumental role in the Sunflower Movement.[9] Ho (2019, pp. 74–79) further observes that the movement can be traced back to early initiatives around 2008–9 by groups of students, such as the Wild Strawberry Movement and the Taiwan Rural Front for land justice (*tudi zhengyi*).

Anti-nuclear activists were nevertheless worried by the declining interest in the nuclear issue. At the end of April 2014, seventy-three-year-old prominent politician Lin Yi-hsiung held a hunger strike against NPP4. As a senior pro-democracy leader and former DPP chairman, well-respected across partisan lines, his dramatic act kindled a wave of sympathy across the country, causing embarrassment for the government.[10] It also spurred young anti-nuclear activists and leaders of the Sunflower Movement, such as Chen Wei-ting, to conduct a series of disruptive street protests that ended in clashes with the police. These radical actions broke with the past moderation of anti-nuclear rallies and, combined with Lin's hunger strike, eventually compelled the incumbent pro-nuclear KMT to suspend NPP4's start of operations. For Ho (2018), the decisive factor was the emergence of a militant citizen movement led by a new generation of more radical activists.

MAP 2.1

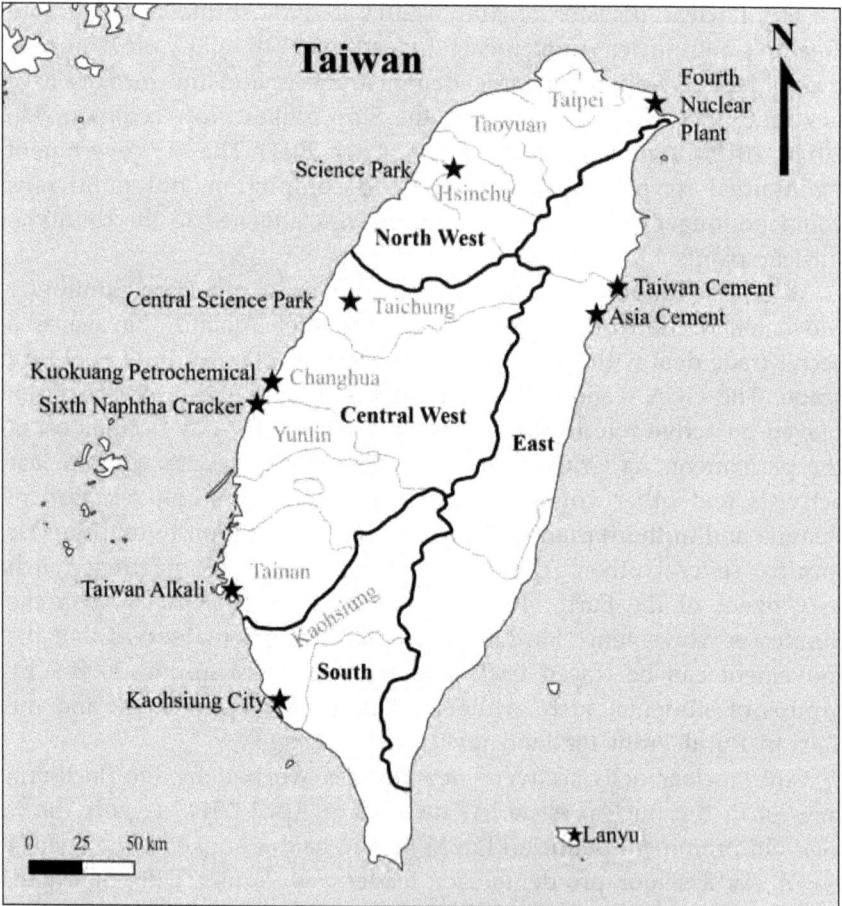

Selected sites of environmental disputes in Taiwan

Source: QGIS and Natural Earth.

After a period of hesitation at the beginning of her mandate in May–July 2016, the government of Tsai Ing-wen has remained firm in its decision to definitively halt the construction of NPP4 and announce the enforcement of a "nuclear free homeland" by 2025. But as we will see below, this decision has once again been challenged by the KMT.

"One Sky, but Two Taiwans"

The movement against air pollution (*fan[kong]wu yundong*) is another example of an aggregation of local mobilizations that has gradually scaled up to force awareness of this major public health concern and turn it into an important electoral issue.

Although the urban areas of northern Taiwan (Taipei, Taoyuan, Hsinchu) have been exposed to significant levels of vehicle emissions, as well as long-range transports from China in winter, the problem of air pollution has been resented with more bitterness in the South around Kaohsiung City, and in the Central West area around Taichung City and Yunlin County, where heavy industries like steel mills, petrochemical plants, oil refineries, and thermal plants are concentrated. These sites have been more often exposed to red alerts and "purple explosions" (*zibao*) of air pollutants than other areas of the island.[11]

The movement against air pollution has carried on the legacy of early battles against the hazards of heavy industry, in places like Houchin and Linyuan districts in Kaohsiung, which have been organized into self-help associations (*ziqiuhui*) around local temples (Hsiao 1988; Ho 2005b, 2014b; Lu 2016). Another hotspot has been the fence-line communities around the petrochemical zone of the Sixth Naphtha Cracker (controlled by Formosa Plastics) in Yunlin and Changhua counties. The dramatic increase of cancer incidence, less than ten years after the cracker's start of operations in 1998, has attracted the attention of public health researchers, lawyers, and activists.[12] Consequently, in 2010–11, a project to extend the zone by Kuokuang Petrochemical triggered a nationwide opposition movement (Ho 2014b, 2016; Grano 2015).

A new wave of actors in the movement is the urban middle-class, worried about the frequent smog and the consequences for their children's health of regular exposure to carcinogenic pollutants like PM2.5 (Chen and Ho 2017). This concern has been particularly strong in Kaohsiung and Taichung and has attracted the solidarity of Taipei-based scholars and environmental organizations. For instance, on 19 February 2017, Nobel Prize chemistry laureate Lee Yuan-Tseh and other celebrities joined thousands of people for a demonstration in Taichung City under the banner of "One Sky, but Two Taiwans" (*yige tiankong, liangge Taiwan*), a slogan that decries the geographical inequalities and implicitly longs for an idealized national unity (see Figures 2.2–2.4). The protesters stressed the responsibility of heavy industry and the central government's lack of commitment to solving the pollution problem in South and Central Taiwan.

FIGURE 2.2

Demonstration against air pollution in the shape of Taiwan with the banner "One Sky, but Two Taiwans", in Taichung, 19 February 2017

Source: Apple Daily.

FIGURES 2.3–2.4

Demonstration against air pollution in Taichung, 19 February 2017.
Top photo: a school teacher with his students wearing paper hats in the
shape of smokestacks. Bottom photo: personalities on stage, including Nobel
Prize winner Lee Yuan-Tseh.

Source: Paul Jobin.

The causes of chronic episodes of "purple explosions", as well as orange and red alerts, have been the topic of heated disputes among specialists. Researchers working with the EPA tend to emphasize the diversity of sources (i.e., not only industries, but also vehicles, merchant ships, etc.), as well as seasonal and geographic factors. These factors explain why even towns in non-industrialized areas in central Taiwan, like Chiayi and Nantou counties, have had bouts of record pollution, inspiring grassroots initiatives to reduce emissions from motorcycles or those resulting from burning plant waste and, in a common religious practice, incense and paper money (Liu 2019). However, for other experts and environmental organizations, the main culprits remain the heavy industries that frequently disregard emissions standards and use all kinds of camouflage to present positive data. Firms like Formosa Plastics and Taipower have shown a special gift for this exercise.

Another tactic for these big polluters is to shift the blame onto vehicle emissions, and long-range transports from China, which account for up to 40 per cent of total annual air pollution in Taiwan on average according to certain specialists, but no more than 30 according to others (Jobin 2018b). In December 2017, Tsai's government briefly attempted to point to air pollutants from China as the main source of air pollution, but this argument was not convincing. According to a survey conducted in 2017, in answer to the question "Who should be held accountable for air pollution in Taiwan?", 37 per cent of respondents put industry first, followed by the central government (26 per cent); China came in third with a relatively low 14 per cent.[13] While the Taiwanese may fear a military attack by China, when it comes to air pollution, they do not feel overwhelmed by a "Chinese invasion" of toxic air. Eco-nationalism does not mean blindness to scientific evidence.

Data, of course, is not monolithic; where it originates and how it is used influences its impact. According to Taiwan EPA, the level of PM2.5 has been gradually decreasing over the last ten years throughout the country, although the south (the region of Kaohsiung) and the central west (Taichung) continue to bear the brunt of it (see Figure 2.5). However, independent data-sharing platforms of citizen science have increased awareness of the risk.[14] From time to time, discrepancies between these data sets spark debate on social media, with concerned citizens or environmental groups accusing the EPA of falsifying its computations (Jheng 2019).

Both scientists and grassroots mobilizations of citizen scientists have played a role in this movement (Tu 2019). In contrast with the nuclear issue, characterized by a rather pro-nuclear blue camp and a generally anti-nuclear green camp (excluding a period of ambiguous positions during the presidency of Chen Shui-bian, and brief opportunistic moves from the KMT), no such clear-cut distinction can be made in the debate on air pollution. What can be seen instead is a clash between activists on the one hand, and the EPA, the Ministry of Economic Affairs, and heavy industry on the other hand, each side backed by arguments from different groups of scientists.

A structural element of the debate is the division between the North and South of the island. This opposition has been a constant factor in Taiwanese politics (with a broadly pan-green South and pan-blue North), and is marked by differing sociological characteristics (with the South experiencing higher rates of unemployment, lower levels of education, and steady out-migration towards the North). In the next section, we will see how air pollution and the nuclear issue facilitated the first success of the KMT in environmental politics in southern and central western Taiwan.

FIGURE 2.5

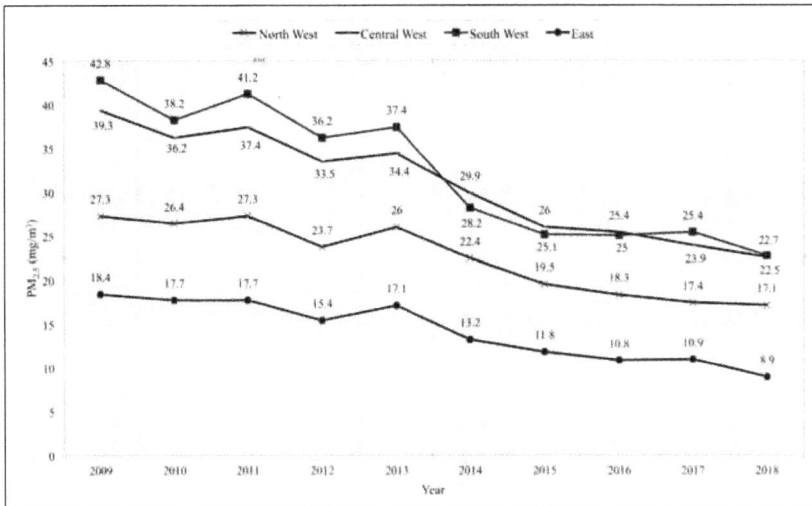

PM2.5 in Taiwan, 2009–18

Source: Data from Taiwan EPA (graph by Gordon Shih-hao Jheng).

Political Uses of Environmental Issues

In August 2017, a power blackout affected millions of homes, offices, and factories, prompting an apology from President Tsai and the resignation of the Minister of Economic Affairs. The outage was caused by human error concerning gas supply from a power station, which had little to do with the energy mix. But the KMT jumped at the chance to simultaneously denounce the DPP administration and promote nuclear energy. As previously observed by Hsiao (1999, p. 49), KMT-backed pro-nuclear advocates manipulated public ignorance to instil a fear of energy shortages as well as the necessity of keeping nuclear power plants online.

The problem of air pollution, however, provided the KMT a much greater opportunity to renew its pro-nuclear stance. In March 2018, Huang Shih-hsiu, who was the founder of a pro-nuclear group and served as an adviser to former KMT chairwoman Hung Hsiu-chu, came up with a proposal to forestall the withdrawal of nuclear energy, using the "green for nuclear" (yihe yanglü) rationale—that is, promoting nuclear energy as a means of reducing air pollution from coal-burning thermal plants. Huang spearheaded efforts to stop the DPP's plans to phase out nuclear energy by putting the matter to a public vote in a referendum.

In the past, referenda on environmental matters were initiated by local communities opposed to incinerator or waste storage, and by the anti-nuclear movement with the support of the DPP (Hsiao 1999, p. 49; Ho 2006, pp. 327–36). It was, however, difficult to stir up enough attention or sufficient voter support at the national level, except in the wake of Lin Yi-hsiung's hunger strikes against NPP4 (supra, and Ho 2018). And at the local level, powerful groups with financial interests could divert a referendum away from its initial goal of implementing grassroots democracy (Ho 2006, pp. 340–43).

A December 2017 reform of the Referendum Act rendered it far easier to introduce questions for public approval. During the course of 2018, numerous referendum questions were proposed for inclusion on the ballot for the November municipal elections. The end result was a mishmash of ten questions about energy, food safety, national identity, and LGBT rights. Huang's bid to ensure the maintenance of nuclear energy made the list, as did two KMT initiatives to cut coal-based energy production. The KMT also backed a proposal to stop the scrapping of the import ban on food from five prefectures affected by the Fukushima nuclear disaster, a diplomatic move planned by the Tsai government to reinforce links with Japan.[15] Anti-nuclear groups like the GCAA were not opposed to the reform provided the food products would be carefully checked by customs. But the KMT distorted the problem as a lack of concern by the government for food safety and the public health. Some gangsters with suspected KMT links even disrupted a public hearing on the case.[16]

The very limited time between the approval of the referendum questions and election day made it almost impossible to fight back with rational arguments, in particular on technical issues like energy and air pollution.[17] The presence of such hot-button topics as same-sex marriage further marginalized these matters. The multi-question referendum ultimately served as a wholesale denunciation of the DPP and the Tsai government and contributed to the election of KMT candidates. Among them were Han Kuo-yu in Kaohsiung (long a DPP stronghold) and Lu Shiow-yen in Taichung, both of whom made reducing air pollution a central campaign pledge. Yet obvious contradictions persisted; Han claimed, for instance, that he would clear the city of air pollution, while nevertheless maintaining heavy industries, including thermal plants.

Although this section has focused on the KMT, the DPP and other parties have also been guilty of manipulating environmental issues for partisan gains. However, such instrumentalization is not limited to national movements, like those against nuclear energy and air pollution. The next section will examine these phenomena in the cases of two local movements and how the environmental justice movement in aboriginal lands has contributed to developing a civic form of eco-nationalism.

Environmental Justice and Indigenous Nationalism

Aborigines make up a very small proportion of Taiwan's population, but their ancestral lands cover a large part of the east and central mountain areas. Due to social barriers to higher education and consequent difficulties in contending with the dominant Han, indigenous people have been the most vulnerable to the rapacity of the state and big corporations. They have seen their lands transformed into national parks or into mining areas by cement companies, whereas they themselves are denied land use for building houses, hunting, and cutting down trees (Chi 2001, 2015a, 2015b; C-T. Huang 2012; Lin 2003; Simon 2017). Of the 217 mining areas in Taiwan, 80 per cent are located in aboriginal territories.[18] Thus, in addition to suffering from culturally destructive assimilationist policies, Taiwan's indigenous people have also paid a heavy price for the rapid growth of post-war industrialization.

This disadvantaged state prompted the adoption in the mid-1990s of the notion of environmental justice (Chi and Wang 1995; Chi 1997, 2001). Environmental justice was developed in the United States in the 1980s, in response to the racist and classist distribution of toxic hazards and the heavy burden imposed on communities of black people. It advocates the equal distribution of environmental risks and benefits across all parts of society; in Taiwan, with regard to its indigenous population, this clearly did not exist.

After her study on post-Chernobyl anti-nuclear movements, Jane Dawson (2000) looked at other examples of eco-nationalism around the world, including cases of subnationalism. She observed that indigenous groups can gain more appeal, both domestically and globally, if they frame their demands for social justice and the recognition of their specific identity in terms of environmental justice. However, she pessimistically concluded that the environmental component tended to be limited to instrumental and tactical considerations, rather than a lasting union with the cause of a national or subnational identity. This observation works as a reminder to avoid the naive and romantic views that weaken many studies on environmental justice and indigenous rights. Yet, under certain conditions, the association between environmental justice and indigenous (sub)nationalism might well bring positive results.

A survey conducted in 1999 showed that a majority of Taiwanese endorsed the principles of environmental justice and expressed sympathy for aboriginal people (Chi and Hsiao 2003). For instance, around two-thirds agreed that aborigines should be allowed to hunt or build their homes in national parks and acknowledged that consolation payments are not enough to compensate them for the storage of nuclear waste.

This last issue, one of the most shocking cases of environmental injustice and state racism, concerns the placement of a storage facility for nuclear waste on Orchid Island (or Lanyu), the home of the Tao (Yami) people. Kept purposely isolated during Japanese rule and much of the martial law period, the Tao have preserved their own language and cultural practices. The government was therefore able to exploit the language barrier to hide the purpose of the facility (it was widely believed to be a canning factory). When martial law was lifted, the site's true nature was revealed and protests emerged (Hsiao 1999). The Tao have continued their campaign against the facility ever since, transforming their traditional beliefs and rituals into striking forms of street protest (Chi 2001; Fan 2006; Jobin 2010; and my observation at a protest in Taipei in March 2013).

Still, after thirty years and numerous projects for relocation, the waste storage facility remains on Lanyu; the alternative site is another tribal people's township. Fan (2009) shows that, despite residents' and workers' legitimate concern for their health, both the Taipower Company and the government regard them as ignorant and "technophobic". Notwithstanding, President Tsai's 2016 formal apology to the Tao for the waste site—as well as the injustices borne by Taiwan's indigenous people in general—and the extensive use of environmental justice discourse by the EPA itself, the basic rules of distributive and procedural justice have continued to be ignored (C-L. G. Huang 2012; Huang et al. 2013; Tu 2017b).

But the problems of environmental injustice cannot be detached from a more fundamental issue, which has been the central claim of Taiwan's aboriginal communities since the late 1980s: the struggle for the retrocession of their lands (*huan wo tudi*). While their battles have gained appeal among the Han, their claim for acknowledgment of their specific subnational identities has been manipulated by both the KMT and DPP for partisan purposes (Friedman 2018). For although indigenous groups account for only 2.2 per cent of Taiwan's population, they hold 5.3 per cent of the seats in the legislature (Simon 2017, p. 249). However, there are important nuances between the parties. The KMT has pursued its pork-barrel tactics to maintain domination, paying little respect to the cultural values of indigenous people, or at best as folklore for tourists. In contrast, the DPP and green-camp oriented organizations—such as the Presbyterian Church, which enjoys a large indigenous membership—have tended to show more respect for Austronesian characteristics, as a way to reinforce Taiwanese identity and break with the "Great China" imaginary (Sia 2014, 2016, 2018). For the green camp, indigenous peoples therefore represent a symbol of great value. Consequently, the Han environmental activists who have developed the strongest relationships with aboriginal activists tend to be pan-green or at least very critical of the KMT domination over local politics. As a Truku activist fighting against an Asia Cement mining operation sums up: "We have been used by both the KMT and DPP, but at least when the government is ruled by the DPP, we have more opportunities to discuss and express our views. We feel more respected."[19]

Simon (2017) found that despite indigenous communities' keenness to mobilize over livelihood issues—as in protests against nuclear waste storage, destructive mass tourism, and post-disaster reconstruction (like after Typhoon Morakot in 2009, the deadliest so far; see also Sia 2014)—they nevertheless "are often distrustful of other social movements, especially the environmental movements, which they perceive as dominated by Taiwanese Buddhists and thus intrinsically opposed to hunting" (p. 252). It used to be that a large majority of indigenous activists were Presbyterians, which tended to alienate members of other churches, such as Roman Catholic and the True Jesus Church, which were also well implanted among aborigines. But Simon (2017, pp. 245–47) has further observed a rise in non-church actors during the last decade, such as the Indigenous Youth Front (*yuanzhu minzu qingnian zhenxian*) and the Taiwan Indigenous People Society (*Taiwan yuanshe*).

In the movement against Asia Cement (see Figure 2.6), these groups of young aborigines are quite open to environmental activists, even if they are Han, provided they build mutual trust in the long run.[20] Like the protest against nuclear waste storage on Lanyu, the mobilization had scaled up from a local issue to a national symbol of environmental injustice, with indigenous people at the forefront (Simon 2002; Lin 2010; Jobin 2018a, 2020).

As posited by Simon (2017, p. 253), "the indigenous movement is not at all about the emergence of a Taiwanese Volk", a national identity distinct from China. Rather, mobilizations of indigenous people represent a sort of subnationalism and their environmental efforts may likewise be considered eco-(sub)nationalism. Although the indigenous rights movement may have its own logic and momentum, cooperation between aborigines and Han environmental activists has become an essential component of Taiwan's civic eco-nationalism.

This eco-(sub)nationalism is an emblematic expression of sometimes desperate attempts to cope with the anxiety of the Anthropocene.

Anthropologist Yi-Tze Lee observes that Taiwanese aborigines have recently multiplied rituals of "returning to ancestral land" (*fanhui zujudi*), which can be seen as a renewed form of the 1980s movement for the retrocession of ancestral lands (*huan wo tudi*):

> These actions reunite the bodily memories of the indigenous people themselves, and connect the scales of traditional knowledge with its relationship to the future. Indigenous peoples' efforts to reflect and narrate their relationships with landscapes retrace the steps of their renewal kinships; a new bonfire within the lives of indigenous people is enkindled in the Anthropocene (Lee 2020, p. 143).

FIGURE 2.6

Demonstration against Asia Cement in the shape of Taiwan, Taipei, 25 June 2017

Source: Courtesy of Citizens of the Earth, Taiwan.

Mobilizing Around Legal Action

In this final section, we take a look at collective lawsuits as another important form of mobilization for environmental justice, one that targets private companies that cause pollution, rather than lobbying the government. During the last two decades, a growing number of environmental conflicts have gone to the Taiwanese courts. One reason lies in the failure of Taiwan's Public Nuisance Disputes Mediation Act (*gonghai jiufen chulifa*, voted in 1992) to offer satisfying solutions to the victims of industrial pollution (Ho and Su 2008; Shih and Tu 2017). Another is that the compensation schemes or various "good neighbour policies" (*dunqin mulin*), offered by big companies to buy the consent of fence-line communities, do not always meet their goals (Wang and Hsiao 2004; Jobin 2021). Going to court has thus been one of the few options left to convey dissent and seek more righteous policies.

However, the average time for getting a judicial ruling is very long. For farmers and residents of rural areas with few resources or social capital, such litigation would be impossible without strong support. Instrumental in this have been the Legal Aid Foundation (LAF), launched in 2004 after a vote by the parliament, and non-governmnetal organizations (NGOs) like the Environmental Jurists Association (founded in 2010). Below are some examples.

In Tainan, the residents living near a petrochemical plant were exposed to one of the worst concentrations of dioxins in the world. The Taiwan Alkali plant, which produced a pesticide, was a colonial legacy of the Japanese imperial army. The Tainan branch of LAF offered to help the residents and some former workers sue the parent company, the China Petroleum Development Company, and the state for compensation (Jobin 2013). It took more than ten years for the plaintiffs to obtain a fairly positive decision from the District Court (2015), which was later confirmed by both the High Court (2017) and the Supreme Court (2018). The company and the state were ordered to pay 160 million Taiwan dollars (around US$5.6 million) to 229 plaintiffs, a relatively small sum, however, when compared to similar cases in the United States.

In August 2018, after twenty years of mobilization, the Taiwan Supreme Court handed down a landmark ruling in the case of Taiwan RCA, an American company, which had produced television sets in Taiwan from 1970 to 1992. After the plants were closed and production moved to China, the land and the ground water around the main plant in Taoyuan were found to be highly polluted by organic solvents. Former workers, most of whom were women, found themselves stricken with all sorts of cancers and other health problems. In 2007, with the help of the LAF, around five hundred workers sued their former employer and its parent companies, U.S. conglomerate General Electric and Thomson Consumer Electronics of France (today Technicolor SA). The "corporate veil", which protects a corporation from being liable for its subsidiaries' obligations, was a major obstacle for the plaintiffs' lawyers (Jobin and Tseng 2014).

The main task was to prove causation between the toxicants the workers had been exposed to, either at work or because they had drunk the area's contaminated ground water (H-H. Chen 2011). Thanks to the striking testimony of the plaintiffs and their experts, in 2015, the District Court judges recognized that the workers had been poisoned and ruled against RCA and Technicolor (Y-P. Lin 2018). Two years later, the High Court ruling confirmed these conclusions, and tacked on the liability of General Electric, ruling that the defendants were all fully responsible for negligently exposing the workers to a wide range of thirty-one toxicants. This was a breakthrough given the one-chemical-one-disease view of causation that usually dominates toxic torts (Jobin et al. 2018). The Supreme Court confirmed the decision for half of the plaintiffs, and sent the case back to the High Court for the other half; another group of 1,100 plaintiffs is also pending in the High Court. In this case, the fact that the defendants are foreign firms has fuelled left-wing criticism, thereby framing Taiwan as a victim of global capitalism, another aspect of Taiwan's civic eco-nationalism.

Before the cases of Taiwan Alkali and RCA reached the Supreme Court, their success in the lower courts served as encouragement for fence-line residents of the Sixth Naphtha Cracker in central Taiwan (*supra*) to sue the Formosa Plastics Corporation. The plaintiffs suffer from cancers attributed to toxic air emissions from this huge petrochemical zone. The case was initiated (in 2015, at the District Court of Yunlin County) by Thomas Chan, an environmental lawyer who served as EPA vice minister in the first Tsai cabinet (*supra*). As the company accounts for around 10 per cent of Taiwan's GDP, the plaintiffs and their lawyers face an enormous disparity in resources and influence. Four years after the lawsuit was launched, the trial is still going around in circles. They nevertheless receive support from a solid network of scholars and environmental activists, coordinated by the Environmental Rights Foundation (ERF). The foundation was itself established thanks to a lawsuit launched in 2010 by a humble group of six farmers against the extension of the Central Taiwan Science Park, one of the island's three high tech parks.[21] More recently, the support group is closely cooperating with environmental activists in Texas and Louisiana who successfully sued Formosa Plastics USA for chronic water pollution and persistently breaking the law.

Lastly, Taiwan's civic environmentalism is also about pressuring Taiwanese companies to fulfil their environmental duties abroad. The ERF, the Environmental Jurists Association, and a Vietnamese priest in Taiwan have coordinated an international network (composed mainly of overseas Vietnamese and the Catholic Church in Vietnam) for a mammoth collective lawsuit. In June 2019, a group of 7,875 Vietnamese plaintiffs filed a civil action in Taipei District Court against Formosa Plastics, China Steel, Japanese steel maker JFE, and their joint subsidiary company in Vietnam, Formosa Ha Tinh Steel, as well as five chief executives and eighteen other related companies including offshore concerns (C-N. Lin 2019; Jobin and Ying 2020). See Figure 2.7.

The plaintiffs seek justice for the marine pollution that occurred in Central Vietnam in April 2016, causing tremendous environmental damage and threatening the livelihoods of the region's inhabitants (see Ortmann, chapter 9). The case is being heard in Taiwan because the plaintiffs do not trust in the independence of Vietnamese courts and fear state repression. In addition, the one-party rule in Vietnam presents serious constraints for more traditional forms of protest and lobbying. Taiwan, however, boasts the encouraging precedents set by RCA and other class actions. It will probably be a legal and technical nightmare for the judges and lawyers, but this movement is another sign of the dynamism of Taiwan's civil society.

In addition to professors, journalists, and grassroots activists, lawyers have become essential actors in environmental movements in many countries. The modern Taiwanese legal system was developed out of the legislative framework established by the 1947 Republic of China Constitution. In addition, it has been heavily influenced by German and Japanese jurisprudence, as well as the American judicial system. This legal framework explains why Taiwan's collective lawsuits (*tuanti susong*) often refer to Japanese anti-pollution litigation, which began at the end of the 1960s (Jobin 2013). In Japan, these lawsuits are

FIGURE 2.7

Press conference in front of Formosa Plastics' annual shareholders' meeting in Taipei, on the day the lawsuit was launched at the Taipei District Court, 11 June 2019

Source: Courtesy of Environmental Jurists Association, Taiwan.

an essential part of the environmental movement, or what Japanese lawyers call a "lawsuit movement" (*soshō undō*). In addition, despite differences between continental and common law, the country's strong links with the United States have made the American model of class actions another important influence. Reference is seldom made, on the other hand, to Chinese cases, despite the development of environmental litigation in China and their shared use of Mandarin Chinese (Stern 2013). An obvious reason for this is the perception that Chinese courts lack independence and make arbitrary use of the law for political repression. In contrast, notwithstanding the lengthy process of Taiwanese courts, environmental groups engaged in these lawsuits show a good deal of trust in the independence of the courts and in Taiwan's rule of law. Although this legal confidence may be not an explicit marker of national identity, it is an essential component of Taiwan's civic environmentalism.

Conclusion

In this chapter, I aimed to highlight the main achievements of Taiwan's environmental movements in the last two decades, focusing on how ecological issues are entangled with national politics. As the fault line of Taiwanese politics lies not so much on a traditional left-right divide, but on differing positions toward China, it is not surprising that, for countrywide issues like nuclear energy and air pollution, China is a major factor (as, for instance, during the 2009 march for referenda against NPP4 and trade with China), or that environmental activists take an active role in mobilizations for the sake of Taiwan as a nation, like during the Sunflower Movement of 2014. I identify this phenomenon as an expression of eco-nationalism. Other examples include the controversy against Greenpeace, demonstrations in the shape of Taiwan, or on a more modest scale, environmental protection tours around the island.

Although environmental groups have gained more partisan independence compared to the 1990s, links between ecologists have remained stronger with the green camp than the blue (this is most obvious when activists look for support among lawmakers). However, during the multi-question referendum and local elections of November 2018—thanks to the support of pro-nuclear greens and conservative groups opposed to homosexual marriage—the KMT gained votes by capitalizing on nationwide concern about air pollution and local opposition to coal-burning thermal plants. A few months after the elections, it was already clear that air pollution was no longer a matter of concern for the newly elected KMT mayors. I therefore call for a distinction between the crude opportunism of politicians of any party who are only motivated by temporary electoral targets, and environmental groups in search of windows of opportunity for significant policy change; I define the latter as a *civic* eco-nationalism.

But the description of this civic eco-nationalism would be incomplete without two other components, substantially more important. Both deal with environmental justice. First are the movements of indigenous peoples for the recognition of their land rights and their distinct subnational identities. Second are the class actions for the victims of industrial hazards, such as the fence-line communities of farmers in southern and central Taiwan, former RCA electronics workers, and Vietnamese fishermen hurt by Formosa Steel. Environmental activists involved in these battles share a common sense of justice, a quest for equality, and respect for those segments of the population with less economic and symbolic capital.

Environmental protection (*huanbao*) has therefore nurtured a spirit of protecting the homeland, for the sake of Taiwan as a certain type of nation: democratic and multicultural. As seen recently in Western Europe, eco-nationalism may turn into a reinforcement of xenophobic or egoistical attitudes, but so far, I have seen no such example in Taiwan. Most of its eco-nationalism is composed of a left-wing liberal criticism, open to the world. A good example of this eco-criticism (Chang and Slovic 2016) can be found in the TV broadcast "Our Island". This programme was, for instance, the first in Taiwan to deliver a solid and detailed report on the marine disaster in Vietnam.

What general assessment can we then make of Taiwan's civic eco-nationalism? If we look only at Taiwan's carbon footprint, the result is quite disappointing. In addition to continuous massive emissions from its petrochemical "heavy smokers", it remains to be seen what contribution Taiwan can provide on dramatic and urgent issues like plastic waste in the oceans, the depletion of biodiversity, overfishing and coral destruction in the South China Sea, or the massive deforestation in Southeast Asia. One might therefore think that authoritarian China could do a better job of fixing these problems, as Beeson (2010) argues. But at best, as Shahar (2015) aptly notes, eco-authoritarianism is only capable of matching the performance of market liberalism, and at the clear cost of renouncing individual and political rights. Dryzek and Pickering (2019, p. 149) further argue that democracy must be redeemed in the Anthropocene, because only it allows the ecological reflexivity needed to cope with its challenges, whereas environmental authoritarianism prescribes the solutions through top-down directives with uncertain results. Today's environmental problems are exceedingly daunting, and response to them too long delayed, but civic eco-nationalism at least reconciles the global concern for the climate with a no less legitimate concern: the protection of democracies and national sovereignties against authoritarianism and neo-imperialism.

With its unique position as geological, meteorological, and geopolitical hotspot—not to mention its political history and industrial activity—Taiwan is particularly well placed to judge which system can best meet the demands of the age. Moreover, though it has a long way to go to turn the tide, the dynamism of its environmental movement, in embracing the democratic spirit, has an opportunity to prove it.

NOTES

* Thanks are due to Hsin-Huang Michael Hsiao, Ming-sho Ho, Wenling Tu, and two anonymous reviewers for judicious remarks to improve drafts of this chapter, as well as my research assistants Chee-Wei Ying, Fei-hsin Chang, Shih-hao Jheng, and Yi-ying Tsai for their help in collecting elements of analysis, transcription of interviews, etc.

1. As of January 2019, Taiwan EPA has listed a total of 323 environmental organizations. One of the most active groups on climate change policy is the Taiwan Youth Climate Coalition (*Taiwan qingnian qihou bianqian lianmeng*), with 15,000 followers as of July 2019.

2. According to the Germanwatch Institute's Climate Risk Index, in 2017, Taiwan ranked 7th.

3. According to the Germanwatch Institute's Climate Change Performance Index, in 2018, Taiwan ranked 54th, down from 32nd in 2009. See also Pan (2017) and Chapter 11 of this book.

4. Examples include the Freedom House (Washington), The Economist Intelligence Unit (London) and the V-Dem Institute (University of Gothenburg, Sweden), all available online. See also Chapter 11 of this book.

5. My first encounter with environmental issues in Taiwan dates back to 1998, when a PhD classmate invited me to visit some former workers of the RCA electronics factories, who were stricken with cancer. From 2008 until today, I have regularly participated in the class action of these workers and, since 2016, in another class action launched by fence line residents against Formosa Plastics in Yunlin, as well as by the victims of Formosa Steel in Vietnam. Other fieldwork observations include the anti-nuclear movement (in particular from 2011 to 2014), following on from interviews conducted in 2002 with nuclear plant workers; a class action on a case of dioxin pollution in Tainan (from 2008 to 2013); another class action on asbestos pollution; and, since 2016, the movement against air pollution, in particular through the specific role of an expert. More recently, I have started a research project on the case of Asia Cement.

6. For a discussion of civic and ethnic nationalism in the context of Taiwan, see Muyard (2012), pp. 341–48. See also Hsiau and Wang (2016).

7. As Ke explains, under martial law, except for a few beaches allowed for bathing, ordinary people could not access the seaside in an effort to prevent Taiwanese from leaving for China. Our interviews of Ke Chin-yuan, Yu Li-ping, and Chang Dabbie Dai-ping, 29 December 2017 and 15 January 2018, at the Public Television Service's office in Taipei. See the magnificent five hundred-page photo album that Ke published to commemorate his thirty years of filmmaking (Ke 2018).

8. The flag was designed around 1985, by which time the anti-nuclear movement and anti-pollution protests were on the rise, but it is unclear if these inspired the green colour chosen by the flag's designer, Ou Hsiu-hsiung, a Christian architect (Ch'iu 2016).

9. Informal discussions with GCAA members in July 2014, and additional testimony from movement insiders on the important role played by GCAA and Citizens of the Earth Taiwan, congruent with Grano (2015), Chuang (2018) and Ho (2018, 2019).

10. An example of the heavy price that Lin has paid for his political commitment: on 28 February 1980, while he was in prison, his mother and his young daughters were stabbed to death, probably as an act of intimidation against him and other pro-democracy activists.

11. The maps released by Taiwan EPA's website use different colours to symbolize the changing levels of air pollution, from green when safe to yellow, orange, red, violet and purple for levels with risk for public health. A "purple explosion" (*zibao*) has become a common way to raise the alarm on social media. Since 2012, Taiwan EPA's Pollutant Standard Index (PSI) has released measurements of PM10, ozone 3, sulphur and nitrogen dioxide, and carbon monoxide. In 2016, PM2.5 were added to the measurement and the PSI was renamed Air Quality Index, as in the United States (Jheng 2019, p. 59).

12. Field research in Yunlin from March 2016 onward.

13. Courtesy of the survey's principal investigator, Yang Wen-shan (Research Fellow, Institute of Sociology, Academia Sinica). The survey, which was conducted by the Center for Survey Research, Academia Sinica, as part of the Taiwan Social Change Survey, has not yet been made public.

14. Cheng Ling-Jyh, a researcher from Academia Sinica has developed a light measuring device—called Airbox—which he managed to produce at a low price with the help of Taiwanese electronics makers, for a current network of around 7,000 users (Jheng 2019). On Facebook, another network named *PM2.5 Ziqiuhui: zixun ying gongkai, jujue zang kongqi* [PM2.5 Self-help Association: information should be made public, rejecting dirty air] has gathered 24,000 followers as of July 2019. See also Air Clean Taiwan (www.airclean.tw).

15. Interview with a high-ranking officer from Taiwan's Ministry of Foreign Affairs, Taipei, June 2018.

16. Testimony from two attendants at the public hearing on November 2017. See also Ho (2018), pp. 461–62.
17. Interview with one environmental activist (in her thirties, with seven years' experience in the movement), Taipei, 18 December 2018.
18. These data were presented by New Power Party's lawmaker Kawlo Lyun, during a press conference on 4 April 2018 (source: Citizens of the Earth, Taiwan).
19. Interview in Sincheng Township (Hualien County), 14 January 2019.
20. For instance, in the case of Taiwan Citizens of the Earth, Taiwan, Hualien-based Huang Jing-ting (alias Hsiao-nan) has been fully integrated into a group of young Truku, while Taipei-based Tsai Chong-yue is a member of a national association called *Taiwan yuanzhumin zhengce xiehui*.
21. See Tu (2007), Chiu (2014), and the foundation's website: www.erf.org.tw.

REFERENCES

Arrigo, Linda Gail. 1994. "The Environmental Nightmare of the Economic Miracle: Land Abuse and Land Struggles in Taiwan". *Bulletin of Concerned Asian Scholars* 26, no. 1–2: 2–44.

Arrigo, Linda Gail and Gaia Puleston. 2006. "The Environmental Movement in Taiwan after 2000: Advances and Dilemmas". In *What Has Changed? Taiwan Before and After the Change in Ruling Parties*, edited by Dafydd Fell, Henning Kloter, and Chang Bi-Yu. Wiesbaden: Harrassowitz Verlag, pp. 165–84.

Beeson, Mark. 2010. "The Coming of Environmental Authoritarianism". *Environmental Politics* 19, no. 2: 276–94.

———. 2016. "Environmental Authoritarianism in China". In *The Oxford Handbook of Environmental Political Theory*, edited by Teena Gabrielson, Cheryl Hall, John M. Meyer, and David Schlosberg. Oxford: Oxford University Press, pp. 520–32.

Biehl, Janet and Peter Staudenmaier. 1995. *Ecofascism Revisited: Lessons from the German Experience*. Porsgrunn, Norway: New Compass.

Biehl, Janet, et al. 2011. *Ecofascism Revisited: Lessons from the German Experience*. Porsgrunn, Norway: New Compass Press.

Calhoun, Craig. 2007. *Nations Matter: Culture, History and the Cosmopolitan Dream*. London: Routledge.

Chang, Chia-ju and Scott Slovic, eds. 2016. *Ecocriticism in Taiwan: Identity, Environment, and the Arts*. Washington, D.C.: Lexington Books.

Chen, Dung-sheng. 2011. "Taiwan's Antinuclear Movement in the Wake of the Fukushima Disaster, Viewed from an STS Perspective". *East Asian Science, Technology and Society: An International Journal* 5: 567–72.

Chen, Hsin-hsin. 2011. "Field Report: Professionals, Students, and Activists in Taiwan Mobilize for an Unprecedented Collective-Action Lawsuit against a

Former Top American Electronics Company". *East Asian Science, Technology and Society: An International Journal* 5: 555–65.

Chen, Yi-an and Ho Ming-sho. 2017. "Taiwan fan kongwu yundong 2.0" 臺灣反空污運動 2.0 [The movement against air pollution 2.0]. In *Neng zenme zhuan: qidong Taiwan nengyuan zhuanxing yaoshi* 能怎麼轉：啟動臺灣能源轉型鑰匙 [How to turn? Keys for starting energy transition in Taiwan], edited by Chou Kuei-tien and Kuo-hui Chang. Taipei: RSPRC/Liwen.

Chi, Chun-chieh and Hsin-Huang Michael Hsiao. 2003. "Dangqian Taiwan huanjing zhengyi de shehui jichu" 當前台灣環境正義的社會基礎 [The social foundation of environmental justice in Taiwan]. *National Policy Quarterly* 國家政策季刊 2, no. 3: 169–80.

Chi, Chun-jie. 1997. "Huanjing zhengyi: huanjing shehuixue de guifanxing guanhuai" 環境正義：環境社會學的規範性關懷 [Environmental justice: A normative concern in environmental sociology]. In *Huanjing jiazhiguan yu huanjing jiaoyu xueshu yantaohui lunwenji* 環境價值觀與環境教育學術研討會論文集 [Proceedings of the conference on environmental values and education]. Tainan: National Cheng Kung University Centre for Taiwan Culture Studies.

———. 2001. "Capitalist Expansion and Indigenous Land Rights". *The Asia Pacific Journal of Anthropology* 2, no. 2: 135–53.

———. 2004. "From Environmental Injustice to Ethnic Reconciliation Taroko People and Taroko National Park in Taiwan". *Tamkang Review* 34, no. 3/4: 53–68.

———. 2015a. "Yilan xian: Taiwan de lüse dianfan" 宜蘭縣：台灣的綠色典範 [Yilan county: a green model for Taiwan]. In *Taiwan difang huanjing de jiaoxun: wudou sixian de dadaizhi* 臺灣地方環境的教訓：五都四縣的大代誌 [Lessons from Taiwan local environment: big issues in five municipalities and four counties], edited by Hsin-Huang Michael Hsiao. New Taipei City: Juliu 巨流, pp. 293–332.

———. 2015b. "Hualien xian: cong ziyuan xiequ yu gongye dameng dao guangguang fazhan" 花蓮縣：從資源擷取與工業大夢到觀光發展 [Hualien county: from the capture of resources and industrial big dream to the development of tourism]. In *Taiwan difang huanjing de jiaoxun: wudou sixian de dadaizhi* 臺灣地方環境的教訓：五都四縣的大代誌 [Lessons from Taiwan local environment: big issues in five municipalities and four counties], edited by Hsin-Huang Michael Hsiao. New Taipei City: Juliu 巨流, pp. 333–60.

Chi, Chun-jie and Shun-shiu Wang. 1995. "Huanjing zhengyi: yuanzhumin yu guojia gongyuan chongtu de fenxi" 環境正義：原住民與國家公園衝突的分析 [Environmental justice: analysis of the conflicts between indigenous people and national parks]. In *Taiwan de shehuixue yanjiu: huigu yu zhanwang lunwenji* 台灣的社會學研究：回顧與展望論文集 [Sociology research in Taiwan:

proceedings of retrospect and prospect], edited by Song-ling Lin and Jenn-Hwan Wang. Taichung: Tunghai University.

Chiu, Hua-mei. 2011. "The Dark Side of Silicon Island: High-Tech Pollution and the Environmental Movement in Taiwan". *Capitalism, Nature and Socialism* 22, no. 1: 40–57.

———. 2014. "The Movement against Science Park Expansion and Electronics Hazards in Taiwan: A Review from an Environmental Justice Perspective". *China Perspectives* 3: 15–22.

Ch'iu, Wan-hsing. 2016. "Minjindang dangqi de shejizhe Ou Hsiu-Hsiung" 民進黨黨旗的設計者歐秀雄 [Ou Hsiu-Hsiung, the man who designed the DPP's flag]. *Taiwan People News*, 9 September 2016.

Chou, Kuei-tien. 2015. "From Anti-Pollution to Climate Change Risk Movement: Reshaping Civic Epistemology". *Sustainability* 7, no. 11: 14574–96.

———. 2017. *Qihou bianqian shehuixue: gaotan shehui ji qi zhuanxing tiaozhan* 氣候變遷社會學：高碳社會及其轉型挑戰 [Sociology of climate change: high carbon society and its transformation challenge]. Taipei: National Taiwan University Press.

Chou, Kuei-tien et al. 2019. *Richang shenghuo de nengyuan geming* 日常生活的能源革命 [Energy revolution in daily life: eight pioneers of energy transition in Taiwan]. Taipei: Springhill & RSPRC.

Chuang, Chun-mei. 2020. "Renleishi zhong de nuxing zhuyi: lizudian, difang yu shijian" 人類世中的女性主義：立足點、地方與實踐 [Feminism in the anthropocene: standpoints, places and practices]. *Chung-Wai Literary* 中外文學 49, no. 1: 13–60.

Chuang, Chun-mei and Jow-jiun Gong, eds. 2020. "Yishu celiang, renleishi meixue pipan" 藝術測量・人類時美學批判 [Artistic measuring, aesthetic critique in anthropocene epoch]. *ACT: Art Critique of Taiwan* 藝術觀點 80: 4–128.

Chuang, Ya-chung. 2013. *Democracy on Trial: Social Movements and Cultural Politics in Postauthoritarian Taiwan*. Hong Kong: The Chinese University Press.

———. 2018. "Democracy under Siege: *Xiangming* Politics in Sunflower Taiwan". *Boundary 2* 45, no. 3: 61–77.

Dawson, Jane. 1995. "Anti-Nuclear Activism in the USSR and its Successor States: A Surrogate for Nationalism?" *Environmental Politics* 4, no. 3: 441–66.

———. 1996. *Eco-Nationalism: Anti-Nuclear Activism and National Identity in Russia, Lithuania, and Ukraine*. Durham, N.C.: Duke University Press.

———. 2000. "The Two Faces of Environmental Justice: Lessons from the Eco-Nationalist Phenomenon". *Environmental Politics* 9, no. 2: 22–60.

DeWitt, John. 1994. *Civic Environmentalism: Alternatives to Regulation in States and Communities*. Washington, D.C.: CQ Press.

Dryzek, John S. and Jonathan Pickering. 2019. *The Politics of the Anthropocene*. Oxford: Oxford University Press.

Fan, Mei-fang. 2006. "Environmental Justice and Nuclear Waste Conflicts in Taiwan". *Environmental Politics* 15, no. 3: 417–34.

———. 2009. "Public Perceptions and the Nuclear Waste Repository on Orchid Island, Taiwan". *Public Understanding of Science* 18: 167–76.

Fan, Mei-fang and Kuei-tien Chou. 2017. "Environmental Justice in a Transitional and Transboundary Context in East Asia". In *Handbook of Environmental Justice*, edited by Ryan Holifield, Jayajit Chakraborty, and Gordon Walker. Abingdon: Routledge.

Fan, Yun. 2019. *Social Movements in Taiwan's Democratic Transition: Linking Activists to the Changing Political Environment*. London: Routledge.

Fell, Dafydd and Peng Yen-wen. 2017. "The Revival of Taiwan's Green Party after 2008". In *Taiwan's Social Movements under Ma Ying-jeou: From the Wild Strawberries to the Sunflowers*, edited by Dafydd Fell. London: Routledge.

Friedman, Kerim P. 2018. "The Hegemony of the Local: Taiwanese Multiculturalism and Indigenous Politics". *Boundary 2* 45, no. 3: 79–105.

Grano, Simona. 2015. *Environmental Governance in Taiwan: A New Generation of Activists and Stakeholders*. London: Routledge.

———. 2017. "The Evolution of the Anti-Nuclear Movement in Taiwan since 2008". In *Taiwan's Social Movements under Ma Ying-jeou: From the Wild Strawberries to the Sunflowers*, edited by Dafydd Fell. London: Routledge.

Hager, Carol and Mary Alice Haddad, eds. 2015. *Nimby is Beautiful: Cases of Local Activism and Environmental Innovation around the World*. Oxford: Berghahn.

Ho, Hsin-jie. 2017. "Lüse heping zhengyi zhihou: sanzhong ditu liangan hongxian yu women de yige diqiu" 綠色和平爭議之後：三種地圖、兩岸紅線與我們的一個地球 [After the greenpeace dispute: three kinds of map, a red line between two straits and one planet]. *Theinitium.com*, 13 July 2017.

Ho, Ming-sho. 2003. "The Politics of Anti-Nuclear Protest in Taiwan: A Case of Party-Dependent Movement (1980–2000)". *Modern Asian Studies* 37, no. 3: 683–708.

———. 2005a. "Weakened State and Social Movement: The Paradox of Taiwanese Environmental Politics after the Power Transfer". *Journal of Contemporary China* 14: 339–52.

———. 2005b. "Protest as Community Revival: Folk Religion in a Taiwanese Anti-Pollution Movement". *African and Asian Studies* 4, no. 3: 237–69.

———. 2006. *Lüse minzhu: Taiwan huanjing yundong de yanjiu* 綠色民主：台灣環境運動的研究 [Green democracy: a study on Taiwan's environmental movement]. Taipei: Socio Publishing.

———. 2010. "Co-Opting Social Ties: How the Taiwanese Petrochemical Industry Neutralized Environmental Opposition". *Mobilization: An International Journal* 15, no. 4: 447–63.

———. 2014a. "The Fukushima Effect: Explaining the Recent Resurgence of the Anti-Nuclear Movement in Taiwan". *Environmental Politics* 23, no. 6: 965–83.

————. 2014b. "Resisting Naphtha Crackers: A Historical Survey of Environmental Politics in Taiwan". *China Perspectives* 3, no. 3: 5–14.

————. 2016. "Making an Opportunity: Strategic Bipartisanship in Taiwan's Environmental Movement". *Sociological Perspectives* 59, no. 3: 543–60.

————. 2018. "The Historical Breakthroughs of Taiwan's Anti-Nuclear Movement: The Making of a Militant Citizen Movement". *Journal of Contemporary Asia* 48, no. 3: 445–64.

————. 2019. *Challenging Beijing's Mandate of Heaven: The Sunflower Movement in Taiwan and the Umbrella Movement in Hong Kong.* Pennsylvania: Temple University Press.

Ho, Ming-sho and Su Feng-san. 2008. "Control by Containment: Politics of Institutionalizing Pollution Disputes in Taiwan". *Environment and Planning (A)* 40, no. 10: 2402–18.

Hsiao, Hsin-Huang Michael. 1987. *Women zhi you yige Taiwan: fanwuran, shengtai baoyu yu huanjing yundong* 我們只有一個台灣：反污染、生態保育與環境運動 [We have only one Taiwan: anti-pollution, ecological protection, and environmental movements]. Taipei: Booklife 圓神.

————. 1988. *Qishi niandai fanwuran zili jiuji de jiegou yu guocheng fenxi yu guocheng fenxi* 七○年代反污染自力救濟的結構與過程分析 [Structure and process analysis of anti-pollution self-help associations in the 1980s]. Taipei: EPA.

————. 1999. "Environmental Movements in Taiwan". In *Asia's Environmental Movements: Comparative Perspectives*, edited by Yok-shiu F. Lee and Alvin Y. So. Armonk, New York: M.E. Sharpe, pp. 31–54.

————, ed. 2003. *Sustainable Development for Island Societies: Taiwan and the World.* Taiwan: Center for Asia-Pacific Area Studies, Academia Sinica and National Central University.

————. 2017. "Forty Years of Environmental Movements in Taiwan: Main Streams and New Trends to Enhance". Paper presented at the Conference on Taiwan Environmental Protection Movement: Review and Prospect, National Taiwan University, 21 October 2017.

————. 2019. "Observations on Rising Populism in Taiwan Politics". *Global Taiwan Brief* 4, no. 15 (31 July 2019). http://globaltaiwan.org.

Hsiao, Hsin-Huang Michael and Hua-pi Tseng. 1999. "The Formation of Environmental Consciousness in Taiwan: Intellectuals, Media, and the Public Mind". *Asian Geographer* 18, no. 1–2: 99–109.

Hsiao, Hsin-Huang Michael and Hwa-jen Liu. 2002. "Local Practice of Violence in Environmental Protests in Taiwan since the 1980s". *Ritsumeikan Journal of Asia Pacific Studies* 9: 45–57.

Hsiao, Hsin-Huang Michael, Russell Stone, and Chun-chieh Chi. 2002. "Taiwan Environmental Consciousness: Indicators of Collective Mind toward Sustainable Development". *Sustainable Development* 4, no. 2: 1–33.

Hsiau, A-chin and Horng-luen Wang, eds. 2016. *Zhuqun, minzhu yu xiandai guojia – jingyan yu lilun de fansi* 族群，民族與現代國家－經驗與理論的反思 [Ethnicity, nation, and the modern state: rethinking theory and experience in Taiwan and China]. Taipei: Institute of Sociology, Academia Sinica.

Hsu, Keng-ming, Chun-chieh Chi, and Hsin-Huang Michael Hsiao. 2016. "Qihou bianqian shidai zhengyi yu yongxuxing: gainian zhibiao yu zhengce" 氣候變遷、世代正義與永續性：概念、指標與政策 [Climate change, intergenerational justice and sustainability: concept, indicators and policy]. *Taiwan Economics Forecast and Policy* 臺灣經濟預測與政策 46, no. 2: 259–85.

Hsu, Shih-jung and Hsin-Huang Michael Hsiao. 2006. "Wurang changzhi zailiyong zhengce zhi yanjiu: Meiguo yu Taiwan zhi bijiao" 污染場址再利用政策之研究：美國與台灣之比較 [Comparative study on the reutilization policy for contaminated sites: US and Taiwan cases]. *City and Planning* 都市與規劃 33, no. 2: 143–67.

Huang, Chao-yung. 2019. "Congbu huandao 57 tian...Lese haitan tang heishui" 從步環島 57 天...垃圾海灘淌黑水 [Walking around the island in 57 days... beach of waste and black water, looking at your and my selfishness]. *United Daily News*, 22 April 2019.

Huang, Chi-lun Gillan. 2012. "Environmental Justice and Public Participation: A Case of Nuclear Waste Management and Policy in Taiwan". PhD dissertation, University of Newcastle.

Huang, Chi-lun Gillan, Tim Gray, and Derek Bell. 2013. "Environmental Justice of Nuclear Waste Policy in Taiwan: Taipower, Government, and Local Community". *Environ Dev Sustain* 15: 1555–71.

Huang, Chih-tung. 2012. "One Park, Two EJs: When Two Environmental Justices Collide Head-on in Taiwanese National Parks". *Environmental Justice* 5, no. 6: 298–305.

Huang, Chih-tung and Ruey-chyi Hwang. 2009. "'Environmental Justices': What We Have Learned from the Taiwanese Environmental Justice Controversy". *Environmental Justice* 2, no. 3: 101–7.

Jheng, Gordon Shihao. 2019. "Huiji gongming liliang de kongwu zhandouqi: kongqi hezi" 匯集公民力量的空污戰鬥器：空氣盒子 [Air pollution fighting machines that bring citizens together: airboxes]. In *Richang shenghuo de nengyuan geming* 日常生活的能源革命 [Energy revolution in daily life], edited by Chou Kuei-tien et al. Taipei: Springhill & RSPRC, pp. 76–93.

Jobin, Paul. 2010. "Hazards and Protest in the 'Green Silicon Island': The Struggle for Visibility of Industrial Hazards in Contemporary Taiwan". *China Perspectives* 83, no. 3: 46–62.

———. 2013. "Beyond Uncertainty: Industrial Hazards and Class Actions in Taiwan & Japan". In *Environmental History in East Asia: Interdisciplinary Perspectives*, edited by Ts'ui-jung Liu. London & New York: Routledge, pp. 339–82.

―――. 2018a. "Entre typhons et menace chinoise, Taiwan zone critique de la géo-politique". *Monde Chinois Nouvelle Asie* 56, no. 4: 120–35.

―――. 2018b. "Air Pollution in Taiwan: Self-determination or China Factor?" Paper presented at the 15th Annual Conference of the European Association of Taiwan Studies (EATS), University of Zurich, 4–6 April 2018b.

―――. 2020. "Extractivism in the Critical Zone". In *Critical Zones: The Science and Politics of Landing on Earth*, edited by Bruno Latour and Peter Weibel. Cambridge, MA: MIT Press, pp. 80–83.

―――. 2021. "Our 'Good Neighbor' Formosa Plastics: Petrochemical Damage(s) and the Meanings of Money". *Environmental Sociology* 7, no. 1: 40–53.

Jobin, Paul and Chee Wei Ying. 2020. "Taisu qu yuenan datie: gonghai shuchu de 'nanxiang'?" 台塑去越南打鐵：公害輸出的「南向」? [Formosa Plastics goes to Vietnam to make steel: a 'southbound turn' for pollution export?]. In *Nanfang shehuixue jiaokeshu* 南方社會學教科書 [A manuel for southern sociology], edited by Chao En-jie. Taipei: Rive gauche 左岸.

Jobin, Paul, Chee Wei Ying, and Gordon Shih-hao Jheng. 2017. "Formosa and the Geopolitics of Industrial Hazards". Paper presented at 6th International Symposium on Environmental Sociology in East Asia, Taipei, 20–21 October 2017.

Jobin, Paul, Hsin-hsing Chen, and Yi-ping Lin. 2018. "Translating Toxic Exposure: Taiwan RCA". *Toxic News*, 1 February 2018. https://toxicnews.org.

Jobin, Paul and Yu-hwei Tseng. 2014. "Guinea Pigs Go to Court: Epidemiology and Class Actions in Taiwan". In *Powerless Science? Science and Politics in a Toxic World*, edited by Soraya Boudia and Nathalie Jas. Oxford, New York: Berghahn, pp. 170–91.

Ke, Chin-yuan. 2018. *Women de dao: Taiwan sanshinian huanjing bianqian quanjilu* 我們的島：臺灣三十年環境變遷全記錄 [Our island: complete records of thirty years of environmental change in Taiwan]. New Taipei City: Acropolis.

Kenny, Paul. 2017. *Populism and Patronage: Why Populists Win Elections in India, Asia, and Beyond*. Oxford: Oxford University Press.

Latour, Bruno. 2014. "Some Advantages of the Notion of 'Critical Zone' for Geopolitics". *Procedia Earth and Planetary Science* 10: 3–6.

Lee, Yi-tze. 2020. "Renlei shixia de yuanzhumin: dijing xushi yu jichu jianshe renshilun" 人類世下的原住民：地景敘事與基礎建設認識論 [Indigenous people in the anthropocene: landscape narratives and epistemology of infrastructure]. *Chung-Wai Literary* 中外文學 49, no. 1: 133–43.

Lepesant, Tanguy. 2018. "Les questions environnementales, espace de (re) politisation de la jeunesse taïwanaise". *Monde Chinois Nouvelle Asie* 56, no. 4: 108–18.

Lii, Ding-tzann and Wen-yuan Lin. 2000. "Shehuili de wenhua genyuan: Lun huanjingquan ganshou zai Taiwan de lishi xingcheng, 1970–86" 社會力的文化根源：論環境權感受在台灣的歷史形成 [The cultural origins of social forces: the historical formation of environmental rights in Taiwan, 1970–86]. *Taiwan shehui yanjiu qikan* 38: 133–206.

Lin, Chia-nan. 2019. "Thousands of Vietnamese Sue Investors of FPG Unit". *Taipei Times*, 12 June 2019.

Lin, Ch'ien-wei. 2019. "Huanbao Mazu ganjing Taiwan: Huandao jingtan" 環保媽祖乾淨台灣—環島淨灘 [Environmental protector [Goddess] Mazu cleans Taiwan: touring the island to purify the seashore]. *Taiwan News Review*, 1 June 2019.

Lin, Ching-hsiu. 2010. "Women and Land: Privatisation, Gender Relations and Social Change in Truku Society, Taiwan". PhD thesis, Department of Social Anthropology, University of Edinburgh.

Lin, Chun-yin. 2018. "Liugei ziran bange diqiu: shenmei de tiyan" 留給「自然」半個地球—審美的體驗 [Preserve half the surface of the earth to nature: the aesthetic experience]. *Applied Ethics Review* 應用倫理評論 64: 217–37.

Lin, Thung-hong et al. 2011. *Bengshidai: Caituanhua pinqionghua yu shaoziniühua de weiji* 崩世代：財團化、貧窮化與少子女化的危機 [The collapsing generation: the crises of corporate domination, pauperization and low fertility rate]. Taipei: Taiwan Labor Front.

Lin, Yih-ren. 2003. "Yuanzhumin shoulie wenhua yu dongwu jiefang yundong keneng jiemeng ma? Yige tudi lunli xue de guandian" 原住民狩獵文化與動物解放運動可能結盟嗎？一個土地倫理學的觀點 [Can indigenous hunting culture and animal liberation movement be allied? a viewpoint from land ethic]. *Chung Wai Literary* 中外文學 32, no. 2: 73–102.

Lin, Yiping. 2018. "Reconstructing Genba: RCA Groundwater Pollution, Research and Lawsuit in Taiwan, 1970–2014". *Positions: Asia Critique* 26, no. 2: 305–41.

Liu, Hwa-jen. 2015. *Leverage of the Weak: Labor and Environmental Movements in Taiwan and South Korea*. Minneapolis, MN: University of Minnesota Press.

Liu, Yiting. 2019. "Ziji de kongqi ziji jiu: Jiayishi yu Pulizheng fankongwu gushi" 自己的空氣自己救：嘉義市與埔里鎮反空污故事 [Solving our air problem by ourselves: the anti-air pollution stories of Chiayi City and Puli Township]. In *Richang shenghuo de nengyuan geming* 日常生活的能源革命 [Energy revolution in daily life], edited by Chou Kuei-tien et al. Taipei: Springhill & RSPRC, pp. 53–75.

Lu, Hsin-yi. 2016. "Tudi, shequn, xinyang: jiexi sumin huanjing lunshu" 土地、社群、信仰：解析俗民環境論述 [Land, community, and faith: an analytical model of folk environmental discourse]. *Taiwanese Journal for Studies of Science, Technology and Medicine* 科技、醫療與社會 22: 6–108.

McAdam, Doug and Hilary Schaffer Boudet. 2012. *Putting Social Movements in Their Right Place: Explaining Opposition to Energy Projects in the United States, 2000–2005*. Cambridge: Cambridge University Press.

McAdam, Doug, John D. McCarthy, and Mayer N. Zald, eds. 1996. *Comparative Perspectives on Social Movements: Political Opportunities, Mobilizing Structures and Cultural Framings*. New York: Cambridge University Press.

Muyard, Frank. 2012. "The Formation of Taiwan's New National Identity Since the End of the 1980s". In *Taiwan Since Martial Law*, edited by David Blundell. Taipei: National Taiwan University Press, pp. 297–366.

———. 2018. "The Role of Democracy in the Rise of the Taiwanese National Identity". In *A New Era in Democratic Taiwan*, edited by Jonathan Sullivan and Chun-Yi Lee. London: Routledge, pp. 35–62.

Pan, Jason. 2017. "Government Urged to Act on Environment". *Taipei Times*, 23 November 2017.

Shahar, Dan Coby. 2015. "Rejecting Eco-Authoritarianism, Again". *Environmental Values* 24, no. 3: 345–66.

Shih, Chia-liang and Wenling Tu. 2017. "Huanjing guanzhi xinzheng de kexue jishu kuangjia yu juece jiangju: liu qing gong an shijian huanping guocheng xi lun" 環境管制行政的科學技術框架與決策僵局：六輕工安事件環評過程析論 [The scientific framework and decision deadlock in the environmental administrative procedures: examining the EIA of the fire accident in the no. 6 naphtha cracking]. *Journal of Public Administration* 公共行政學報 52: 81–111.

Sia, Ek-hong Ljavakaw. 2014. "When Weak Communities Meet Strong NGOs: Collaborative Governances in the Post-Disaster Reconstruction". Paper presented at the 11th Annual Conference of the European Association of Taiwan Studies (EATS), University of Portsmouth, UK, 30 April–2 May 2014.

———. 2016. "Crafting the Taiwanese Nation: Exclusivist and Inclusivist Theses of the Postwar Taiwanese Nationalism". *Berliner China-Hefte – Chinese History and Society* 47: 56–84.

———. 2018. "Crafting Aboriginal Nations in Taiwan: The Presbyterian Church and the Imagination of the Aboriginal National Subject". *Asian Studies Review* 42, no. 2: 356–75.

Simon, Scott. 2002. "The Underside of a Miracle: Industrialization, Land, and Taiwan's Indigenous Peoples". *Cultural Survival Quarterly Magazine*, June 2002 (online).

———. 2005. "Scarred Landscapes and Tattooed Faces: Poverty, Identity and Land Conflict in a Taiwanese Indigenous Community". In *Indigenous Peoples and Poverty: An International Perspective*, edited by Robyn Eversole, John-Andrew McNeish, and Alberto D. Cimadamor. London: Zed Books, pp. 53–68.

———. 2017. "All Our Relations: Indigenous Rights Movements in Contemporary Taiwan". In *Taiwan's Social Movements under Ma Ying-jeou: From the Wild Strawberries to the Sunflowers*, edited by Dafydd Fell. London: Routledge, pp. 236–59.

Stephens, Piers H.G. 2001. "Blood, Not Soil: Anna Bramwell and the Myth of 'Hitler's Green Party'". *Organization & Environment* 14, no. 2: 173–87.

Stern, Rachel. 2013. *Environmental Litigation in China: A Study of Political Ambivalence*. Cambridge, UK: Cambridge University Press.

Tang, Ching-ping. 2003. "Democratizing Urban Politics and Civic Environmentalism in Taiwan". *The China Quarterly* 176: 1029–51.

Tang, Ching-ping, Shui-yang Tang, and Chung-yuan Chiu. 2011. "Inclusion, Identity, and Environmental Justice in New Democracies: The Politics of Pollution Remediation in Taiwan". *Comparative Politics* 43, no. 3: 333–50.

Tilly, Charles and Sidney Tarrow. 2015. *Contentious Politics*, 2nd ed. New York: Paradigm.

Tu, Wenling. 2007. "IT Industrial Development in Taiwan and the Constraints on Environmental Mobilization". *Development and Change* 38, no. 3: 505–27.

———. 2015. *Huanjing fengxiang yu gonggong zhili: tansuo Taiwan huanjing minzhu shijian zhi dao* 環境風險與公共治理：探索台灣環境民主實踐之道 [Environmental risks and public governance: exploring practical way of Taiwan environmental democracy]. Taipei: Wunan Books.

———. 2017a. "An Uphill Battle to Hold High-Tech Corporations Accountable: Lessons Learned from the Siaoli River Disputes in Taiwan". *Toxic News*, 7 August 2017a. https://toxicnews.org.

———. 2017b. "Social Dialogue for Environmental Justice: Civil Forums on Nuclear Waste in Taiwan". Paper presented at the Environmental Justice Conference: Looking Back, Looking Forward, Sydney University.

———. 2019. "Combating Air Pollution through Data Generation and Reinterpretation: Community Air Monitoring in Taiwan". *East Asian Science, Technology and Society: An International Journal* 13: 235–55.

Tu, Wenling and Yujung Lee. 2009. "Ineffective Environmental Laws in Regulating Electronic Manufacturing Pollution: Examining Water Pollution Disputes in Taiwan". In *2009 IEEE International Symposium on Sustainable Systems and Technology*, pp. 1–6.

Wang, Ting-jieh. 2012. "Communicating Environmental Protests: The National Rescue Chilan Cypress Forests Campaign in Taiwan". *Environmental Politics* 21, no. 1: 70–87.

Wang, Yiwen and Hsin-Huang Michael Hsiao. 2004. "Huanjing zhengyixing gonggong sheshi de huikui zhidu: dui heyichang, heerchang ji Taizhong huoli fadianchang de fenxi" 環境爭議性公共設施的回饋制度：對核一廠、核二廠及台中火力發電廠的分析 [The compensating institution of public facilities for nimby syndrome: the case studies of nuclear and thermal power plants in Taiwan]. *City and Planning* 都市與規劃 31, no. 1: 65–90.

Williams, Jack F. and David Ch'ang-yi Chang. 2008. *Taiwan's Environmental Struggle: Toward a Green Silicon Island*. New York: Routledge.

3

ENVIRONMENTAL MOVEMENTS IN POST-HANDOVER HONG KONG: BETWEEN MANAGERIALISM AND RADICALISM

James K. Wong and Alvin Y. So

In the latter half of the twentieth century, Hong Kong was considered one of Asia's little dragons. Rapid industrialization in the post-World War II era has led to the worsening of the environment in the city. Subsequently, nascent environmental movements rose up to address the issues of air, water, and soil pollution. However, the opening up of China in 1978 led to the de-industrialization of Hong Kong. Over the course of a decade, almost all the polluting factories moved across the border to the Pearl River Delta. In the 1990s, Hong Kong was further transformed from an industrial city to a global centre of finance, trade, and business services. With the growth of its service industry, the issues addressed by Hong Kong's environmental movements also changed to reflect the post-materialistic concerns of the new middle class, such as lifestyle and cultural preservation.

The political context changed dramatically towards the end of the twentieth century. After Hong Kong became a Special Administrative Region (SAR) of China in 1997, the city experienced two phases of national integration with the Mainland. In the first phase (1997–2002), Beijing did not intervene in Hong Kong's affairs, and thus the city's economy, society, politics, and environmental movements remained largely the same as before. During this phase, environmental issues did not arouse great debate or controversy in civil society. The major environmental organizations were, as in the past, absorbed into the formal political structure to advocate piecemeal policy change through consensual environmental campaigns and an institutionalization similar to the process described by Heijden (1997). Before 2003, Hong Kong's environmental movements may be considered as more or less *managerial*.

However, in the second phase (2003–present), Beijing intervened in Hong Kong to speed up the national integration process. In response to the re-scaling exercises and the mega infrastructure projects, environmental protests began to take place over a number of preservation, conservation, and anti-development issues. The demolition of heritage sites in 2006–7 sparked opposition from a new generation of activists who mobilized protests against a variety of developmental projects. Many of these protests were organized by local environmental groups. These emerging environmental forces have become more politically significant in recent years, and Hong Kong's environmental movements more radicalized than ever before.

This chapter seeks to investigate the continuity and change of Hong Kong's environmental movements since the sovereignty transfer in 1997. It focuses on depicting how the city's environmental politics have been depoliticized by the institutionalized environmental movements, as well as how a new set of social forces have emerged to resist such depoliticization of the environment. The argument is that, owing to the changing political contexts over the past two decades, the environmental movements in post-handover Hong Kong have been oscillating between "managerial" and "radical" forces. In the face of increasing political pressure from Beijing, the repoliticization of the environment can be interpreted as a democratic struggle against China's (environmental) authoritarianism.

The discussion is structured as follows. The first section summarizes the traditions of environmental movements in Hong Kong under British rule. The second section outlines the environmental movements in the first phase of post-colonial Hong Kong (1997–2002), a period dominated by what this chapter labels as "managerial environmentalism"—a piecemeal, non-confrontational, and institutionalized approach to environmental problem-solving (Dryzek 2013; Perkins 2010). In the third section, the focus turns to the second phase of Hong Kong's development (2003–present) and examines how, despite the persistence of managerial environmentalism, alternative types of environmental forces have emerged to capture the political space. Such forces, which this chapter labels as "radical environmentalism", are more progressive, confrontational, and non-institutionalized compared to managerial environmentalism. Finally, the conclusion reviews some lessons learned.

For the purpose of discussion, "environmental movements" are defined broadly as networks of individuals and groups of actors who engage in collective action and share similar concerns regarding not

MAP 3.1

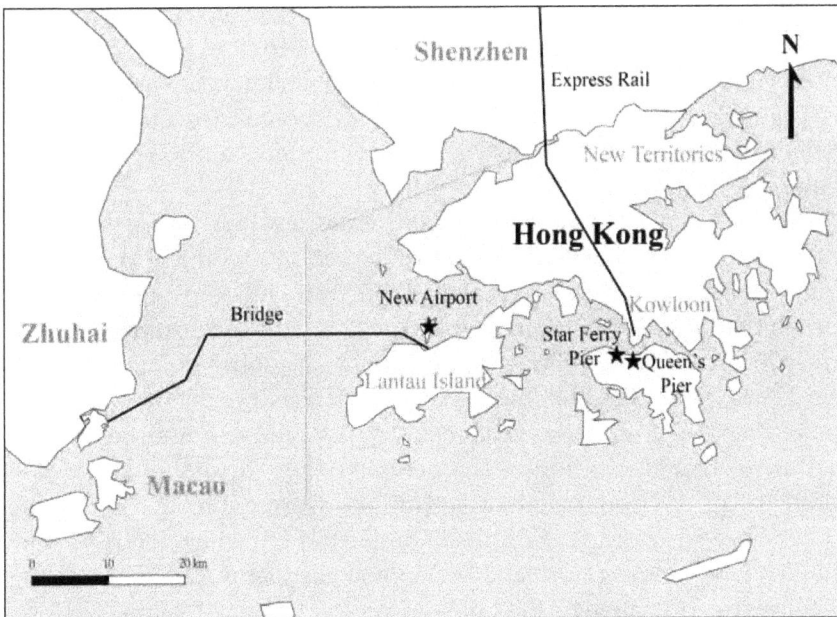

Selected sites of environmental disputes in Hong Kong

Source: QGIS and Natural Earth.

only the physical environment, but also the built environment and cultural environment (Rootes 1999). In other words, environmental movements refer to movements against the pollution of air, water, and soil as well as those against the demolition of old neighbourhoods, the destruction of local and cultural environments, and the disappearance of agriculture and rural communities.

Environmental Movements in Hong Kong under British Rule

The origins of Hong Kong's environmental movements can be traced back to 1968 when the Conservancy Association was founded to exert pressure on the government over policies related to the environment. This was followed by the establishment of local branches of the World Wide Fund for Nature in 1981, Friends of the Earth in 1983, and Green Power in 1988. Another key organization was Greenpeace, which established a local office in 1997. These four major environmental organizations left significant footprints on the early development of Hong Kong's environmental movements. In particular, the Conservancy Association, Friends of the Earth, and Green Power at one time even engaged in confrontational anti-establishment struggles, such as protesting against industrial pollution, the construction of an oil refinery plant, and the construction of the nuclear power plant in Daya Bay (Chiu et al. 1999).

All the main environmental organizations, however, were gradually pacified by the authorities: they were invited to join the government's advisory committees, conduct research projects, and promote consensual campaigns, such as environmental education, green consumerism, and green lifestyles. After Hong Kong became a global financial city in the 1990s, confrontational environmental actions became less common and, when they did occur, tended to take the form of judicial reviews within formal institutions (Chiu et al. 1999).[1] In other words, the mainstream environmental organizations were "absorbed" into the governance structure of the British administration, which followed "the defined rules of the game" and "seldom formed strong alliances among themselves to challenge the colonial regime" (Lai 2000, pp. 284–85). They received financial support from the government for environmental education and research and, in the process, developed professionalism by specializing in different areas of interest and supplying inputs to environmental impact assessments (Lai 2000).[2]

Environmental movements in Hong Kong under British rule produced some limited impact on institutional structures and public attitudes. The first environmental agency—the Environmental Protection Unit—was set up in 1977, then later renamed the Environmental Protection Agency in 1981 and the Environmental Protection Department in 1986. This nomenclature reflects the increasing importance of environmental issues in government administration, following the rise and growth of several major environmental organizations (Chiu et al. 1999).

Despite the time and resources these organizations spent on advocating green lifestyles, people remained generally unmotivated to take concrete actions to protect the environment. The emphasis on promoting green lifestyles also ignored the structural constraints on environmental protection (Chiu et al. 1999). Members of the mainstream environmental organizations were predominantly educated people of high socio-economic status from the expatriate community. In this sense, only a confined range of social groups were mobilized for environmental action. The shift to consensual campaigns by these organizations also resulted in a smaller number of environmental protests and confrontations, and hence they attracted less attention from both the mass media and the local community (Lai 2000).

Trajectory from the British Colonial Era

Chiu et al. (1999) suggest three observations about the environmental movements towards the end of the British colonial era (i.e., from the mid-1980s to the mid-1990s). First, the environmental social forces were either absorbed into the institutional structures or marginalized by democratic forces. On the one hand, the voices of environmental organizations were incorporated into the consultative machinery, and thus their incentives for oppositional and confrontational actions were reduced. On the other hand, in the run-up to the sovereignty transfer in 1997, the societal agenda was dominated by issues of democratic reform. This marginalized other political issues and social movements not directly related to democratization or liberalization, including environmental movements. It also intensified the competition for resources, especially the participatory resources of activists, between environmental and other political groups.

Second, the mobilization structures for most environmental organizations in Hong Kong were largely weak. Their membership bases were small, and most campaigns relied on the intermittent participation of uncommitted volunteers. In turn, the shortage of funding as a result of small membership incentivized organizations to accept financial support from the government and even private corporations. Both conditions favoured the consensual approach to environmental movements. In addition, territory-wide environmental organizations were not inclined to build networks and coalitions with local environmental groups. Bottom-up mobilization, therefore, had difficulty emerging and was easily pacified by rural elites who benefitted from local economic development at the cost of environmental deterioration (Chiu and Hung 1997).

Third, Hong Kong's environmental organizations tended to frame environmental problems as technical problems. Instead of demanding structural transformations, they sought "optimal decisions" based on expert and professional knowledge (Man 1996). This provided a favourable context for a consensual, rather than confrontational, approach to environmentalism. However, the advocacy of green lifestyles—such as green or ethical consumerism—failed to draw much resonance from a grassroots population whose livelihood or survival was at stake. There existed no cultural framework that successfully bonded grassroots' livelihood problems and broader environmental concerns together (Chiu et al. 1999).

Projecting the future of environmental movements in post-handover Hong Kong, Chiu et al. (1999) suggest that confrontational politics would be unlikely to flourish in Hong Kong under China's sovereignty. The Chinese government has, since then, prioritized economic development in its national agenda. Thus, any confrontational or grassroots struggles against developmental projects would result in significant repression. As a result, the city's environmental movements would "be channelled toward an emphasis on individual life-styles, conservation, and education" (p. 86).[3]

To sum up, the traditions of environmental movements in Hong Kong under British rule consisted mainly of prominent environmental organizations absorbed into the formal institutional structure, advocating a consensual or lifestyle-oriented approach to environmentalism.

Their membership bases were small, and they emphasized expert and professional knowledge for environmental problem-solving. They produced some limited structural and sensitizing impacts. It was projected that the consensual, non-confrontational and institutionalized environmental movements would persist after 1997. To what extent did these projections turn out to be true?

Environmental Movements in the First Phase of Post-handover Hong Kong (1997–2002): Depoliticization of the Environment

The Context

In 1997, the sovereignty of Hong Kong was transferred from Britain to China. During the first phase of the Hong Kong SAR's history (1997 to 2003), the Beijing government adopted a hands-off policy of not intervening in Hong Kong's affairs, based on the principle of "One Country, Two Systems". With little influence from Beijing, Hong Kong's environmental movements from 1997 to 2002 were mostly shaped by its own developmental policy.

The first aspect of Hong Kong's urban development was urban renewal. This policy aimed to attract global corporations and their expatriate workforce to set up offices in the city. For this purpose, old neighbourhoods were torn down and modernized into high-rise office buildings, high-class residential apartments, luxury hotels, and sizable shopping malls. For example, a historic landmark in Wanchai (close to the Central Business District) was demolished and turned into a 46-storey residential building.

The second aspect concerned real estate development more generally. Since Hong Kong's de-industrialization in the 1980s, the real estate sector has been the most essential pillar of the city's economy. Its significance lay in the fact that land development would bring business to other economic sectors, especially construction and banking. For a long time, not only has property-related lending accounted for a high percentage of the city's GDP, the government has also benefitted from the booming real estate sector.[4]

Given the existence of the growth coalition, the government failed to effectively regulate the real estate sector, resulting in the rise of a real estate hegemony (Cheng 2015). The real estate development of Hong Kong has been dominated by a handful of tycoons, namely Cheung Kong Holdings, Sun Hung Kai Properties, Henderson Land Development, and New World Development Company. These tycoons were known to have formed close relationships with the government ("government-business collusions") in new town development and urban renewal projects.[5] The limited supply of public and subsidized housing by the government of Hong Kong after the handover to China has also created a heavy reliance on the private housing market, which further intensified the real estate hegemony. This dominance has contributed to the disputes over land use in development and regeneration projects.

Urban renewal projects have, therefore, led to a drastic transformation of the city's built environment in many local communities. In response, both urban renewal projects and the real estate hegemony itself were highly contested by nascent urban environmental movements. They battled against the indiscriminate demolition of the built environment for the preservation of historical districts, cultural landscapes, inclusive open markets, and diverse street life (Chen and Szeto 2015). New groups were formed, comprising activists and participants residing in crisis neighbourhoods, as well as cultural workers, artists, architects, urban planners, academics, and college students. They demanded the preservation of the local cultural environment, like local social institutions, small business networks, and the lifestyles experienced by the city's grassroots population. They also demanded to "reclaim the public space" from the government and property developers in order to restore the autonomy and participation of the grassroots community (Chen and Szeto 2015).

These urban environmental movements criticized the real estate capitalists and articulated social justice for the poor, marginalized communities, and the grassroots population. They also contested the lack of democracy and community participation in urban renewal and planning. Nevertheless, these movements were very small in scale and their calls for preserving neighbourhood spots such as Wanchai's Lee Tung Street did not receive broad support across Hong Kong society. The environmental protests also had little impact on the government's urban renewal policy, as the neighbourhood in Lee Tung Street was eventually demolished.[6] Notwithstanding the limitations, such urban environmental forces planted the seeds for radical environmentalism in the second phase of post-handover Hong Kong.

Managerial Environmentalism: Depoliticization of the Environment

Despite the emergence of small-scale environmental protests, the mainstream environmental movements in the first phase of post-handover Hong Kong stayed broadly similar to those in the British era. The emphasis was still on individual lifestyle, education, and research. The major environmental organizations remained inside the formal institutions, advocating a piecemeal and consensual approach to environmentalism. Such an approach was managerial, as it sought rational solutions for environmental problem-solving rather than striving for structural or institutional change.

The managerial approach to environmentalism was made possible by the neoliberal strategy of development. One crucial role of a neoliberal state is to uphold institutional arrangements that guarantee individual freedoms. However, when it comes to environmental problems, such a state faces a dilemma. On the one hand, it has an interest in pursuing environmentalism, since the existence of environmental problems reduces individual freedoms. On the other hand, fixing environmental problems may require behavioural changes, but a neoliberal state prefers not to coerce individuals or restrict their freedoms. It is hence in the state's interest to frame environmentalism as the pursuit of individuals' environmental consciousness and to substantiate environmental solutions with robust evidence and research. Both actions are consistent with neoliberalism, which emphasizes individual voluntarism as well as expert knowledge and governance (Harvey 2005).

Under the neoliberal framework of governance, environmental politics is understood as essentially post-political. According to post-politics, despite the presence of environmental problems, the environment per se is not a subject for political conflict or antagonism. In this view, environmental problems are technical issues that can be resolved by techno-managerial solutions alone. This is a widely shared consensus within the neoliberal paradigm (Mouffe 2006; Swyngedouw 2011; Žižek 1999; see also Anshelm and Haikola 2018). Erik Swyngedouw (2015) suggests that, in the context of neoliberalism, the Anthropocene discourse is often used as a consensual narrative to displace disagreements and confrontations, as well as to limit the debate to environmental problem-solving or governance (see also Chapter 1).

Such post-political discourse has been dominant in Hong Kong since as early as the British era, resulting in the depoliticization of the city's environmental politics. There are three types of depoliticization according to Hay (2007). The first is the process of demotion from the governmental sphere to the public sphere, in which contestation and conflict over a political issue are pacified by some objective, standard procedures of problem-solving. The second type is the demotion from the public sphere to the private sphere, in which the political issue is reduced to a private matter that possesses little value for public deliberation. Third comes the relegation process of demotion from the private sphere to the realm of necessity, where the political issue is framed as a settled consensus or "fate" that cannot be altered.

While the depoliticization of Hong Kong's environmental politics dates back to the British period, this process continued to evolve into the post-handover era, during which the government spearheaded the mainstream environmental movements. Under this arrangement, the mainstream environmental organizations took up the role of promoting environmental education and research, while the government served as a facilitator and sponsor of various environmental initiatives. Such corporatist relationships were desirable for maintaining the consensual approach to environmentalism and assimilating any radical pockets within environmental movements. The focus of environmental education and research was also important, since they constituted an effective means of depoliticization—research for the first type and education for the second and third.

The Environmental Campaign Committee was a remarkable initiative. Established in the early 1990s, the Committee was charged with a mission to promote public awareness of environmental issues and encourage people to protect the environment. Its first slogan— "environmental protection starts with me"—spoke of the emphasis placed on individual choice and responsibility. To achieve its mission, the Committee organized campaigns, publicity and educational programmes, and collaborated and communicated with stakeholders in the community. Members of the Committee were appointed by the Chief Executive (the head of government), including representatives from the Environmental Protection Department and other relevant government departments.[7]

Most major environmental organizations acted in line with the framework of managerial environmentalism set out by the government. They placed strong emphasis on environmental education, community participation, and collaborative environmental problem-solving. For example, Green Power expressed in its mission statements that "education is the ultimate means of transforming our thinking and behaviour".[8] The Conservancy Association aimed not only to organize "various kinds of environmental activities to promote environmental protection", but also to support and facilitate "community groups or organisations in planning and organising activities to promote environmental protection".[9] Similarly, Friends of the Earth envisioned engaging "government, business and community to act responsibly" and offered "equitable solutions to help create environmentally sustainable public policies, business practices and community lifestyles".[10] And the World Wide Fund for Nature even specified that it would "seek dialogue and avoid unnecessary confrontation", "create conservation solutions through a combination of field based projects, policy initiatives, capacity building and education work" and "build partnerships with other organizations, governments, businesses and local communities".[11]

Some organizations also conducted research projects to find solutions to environmental problems. For example, Friends of the Earth carried out studies on wind power on outlying islands and on the social return on investment of the proposed third runway at the Hong Kong International Airport. The World Wide Fund for Nature carried out research projects on biodiversity in Hong Kong's wetlands. In 2000, an independent think tank, Civic Exchange, was established to conduct public policy research related to the natural environment, urban planning, and overall well-being. For the past two decades, Civic Exchange has completed a list of environmental projects on air quality, biodiversity, waste, water security, and climate change. Like other prominent environmental organizations, Civic Exchange aims to make use of research findings to engage policy stakeholders, such as the government, academics, non-governmental organizations, and the general public, in the hope of eventually driving policy and behavioural changes.[12]

Through incorporation, the government was able to maintain collaborative and non-confrontational relationships with the major environmental organizations.[13] It is true that these organizations sometimes exerted pressure on the government to address environmental problems, but that came mostly in the form of lobbying that complied with institutional practices, such as urging the government to impose green taxes on electronic waste and plastic shopping bags. Overall, the government managed to steer the environmental movements to remain largely consensual, with an emphasis on individuals and research.

That being said, there were occasional moments of confrontational action. The first few years of post-handover Hong Kong witnessed a few examples of public complaints, judicial reviews, and non-violent direct actions by the main environmental organizations. For example, in 2003, Friends of the Earth filed a complaint with the Audit Commission against the maladministration of the government in misusing public money to construct Hong Kong Disneyland.[14] In the same year, the Society for Protection of the Harbour successfully applied for judicial review against the government's reclamation plan for violating the Protection of the Harbour Ordinance.[15] But while there were occasional instances of contention, most confrontational actions took place within the formal institutional structure, which was consistent with the neoliberal practice of mediating conflict and opposition.

In sum, the environmental movements in the first phase of post-handover Hong Kong more or less continued to follow the managerial approach from the British era. Most major environmental organizations regarded environmental issues as problems that could be resolved through environmental education (for promoting individual responsibility) and research (for seeking rational solutions). Such an emphasis demoted environmental issues from the governmental sphere to the realm of necessity, and thereby depoliticized the city's environmental politics. This echoes the "post-politics" or "post-democracy" of the neoliberal framework, which marginalizes dissent and tends to permeate the Anthropocene discourse. The continued domination of such institutionalized environmental movements aligns with the projections of Chiu et al. (1999) and Lai (2000) twenty years ago.

As Hsiao and Wan (2006) have argued, the administrative absorption and professionalization of the mainstream environmental organizations has increasingly alienated local forces in Hong Kong's civil society (King 1975). As a result, environmental movement forces failed to strengthen and complement other social forces in Hong Kong's democracy movements. However, things started to change in the mid-

2000s, when a new set of local forces arose to capture the political space in an attempt to repoliticize the city's environmental politics.

Radical Environmentalism in the Second Phase of Post-handover Hong Kong (2003–present): Repoliticization of the Environment

The Context

The year 2003 constituted the turning point for the development of post-handover Hong Kong. The city's economy hit rock bottom following the Asian financial crisis and the Severe Acute Respiratory Syndrome (SARS) epidemic. In the same year, the proposed legislation of the national security law (Article 23) sparked fierce opposition from the public. On 1 July, half a million people protested against Article 23, making it one of the largest protests in post-handover Hong Kong (So 2008, 2011).

The massive protest in 2003 marked a significant new phase in the city's development. After the protest, Beijing intensified the national integration process and incorporated Hong Kong into the orbit of Mainland China. Hong Kong's urban development turned to focus on re-scaling, so that it would become synchronized with the development of the mainland. The re-scaling exercise involved joint infrastructure projects and new urban development plans in rural areas.

The mega infrastructure projects included: (1) the Hong Kong-Macao-Zhuhai Bridge, linking Hong Kong to Macao and to the West Pearl River Delta by road; (2) the Guangzhou-Shenzhen-Hong Kong Express Rail Link and a number of new freeways, connecting Hong Kong to cities in the Pearl River Delta and throughout the mainland; and (3) the Hong Kong-Shenzhen Western Corridor and the Lok Ma Chau Spur Line, which aimed to enhance the flow of cross-boundary passengers and vehicles between Hong Kong and the mainland, especially in the Pearl River Delta (or the Greater Bay Area).[16]

In addition, facing keen competition from other cities in the Delta region, the Hong Kong government recognized the need to cooperate and establish closer relations with its neighbour cities, especially Shenzhen, Macao, and Zhuhai. In a remote area in the New Territories, the government proposed to build a new town with multiple functions, known as the Northeast New Territories New Development Areas

Planning, that included private and public residential areas, tertiary education, tourism, commercial and business zones, as well as logistical support.[17] This remote area, consisting mostly of agricultural land, was chosen for development due to its proximity to Shenzhen. Through the infrastructure projects and new urban development plans, Hong Kong was envisioned to become the most advanced city in the Delta region and a Chinese metropolis.

At the same time, the New Development Areas Planning served to expand environmental concerns from urban Hong Kong to the rural New Territories. The re-scaling exercise turned valuable agricultural lands, wetlands, and fishponds into parking lots, storage areas, shopping malls, and residential estates, with transport links for cross-border trucks and logistic industries. This development resulted in the pollution of farmland and streams, the destruction of natural habitats, and the dissolution of village communities in the New Territories. In April 2012, protests sprang up outside a rural subway station against the construction of a ventilation building as part of the high-speed railway system (Hui 2017).[18]

In this respect, the mega infrastructure projects and new developments in the New Territories since 2003 have not only expanded the environmental movements from the urban to the rural areas, they have also strengthened the budding radical environmental movements from the first phase of post-handover Hong Kong.

Radical Environmentalism: Repoliticization of the Environment

In social movements, "radicalism" is taken as the values, beliefs, and actions of radical movement actors. These actors, on the one hand, favour a strategy of high-risk, extreme activities, which often include violence and other unconventional actions (Cross and Snow 2011). On the other hand, they advocate structural changes as movement goals, such as changes in the institutional or alliance structures (McCormack 1957). For collective actors, radicalism can emerge internally, whereby the group structures are less hierarchical and external, and grassroots participation exerts a greater role in mobilization than professional resources (Diani and Donati 1999).

In the post-2003 era, Hong Kong's radical environmental movements consisted of activists and groups at the local level. Compared to the large, mainstream environmental organizations, these local forces were less institutionalized and professionalized, with limited hierarchies, resources, and membership bases. They were also more radical in the following ways. First, they focused on contentious or disruptive actions, or what Hui (2017) labels as "transgressive tactics", rather than conventional negotiations. Second, they were critical of, and sought fundamental changes to, the existing structures and institutions. Some groups were ad hoc in nature, formed in response to specific issues, such as the demolition of local communities and cultures.

The radical environment forces built upon their earlier struggles against the urban renewal project in Wanchai during the first phase of post-handover Hong Kong (see above). They quickly expanded the scope, size, and frequency of their protests during the second phase. For example, in 2006 and 2007, as part of the reclamation project of Victoria Harbour, the government decided to demolish the Star Ferry Pier and Queen's Pier in the central business district, two monuments that symbolized the British era. In November 2006, soon after the departure of the last ferry, several protestors gathered at the Star Ferry Pier and occupied the site. They accused the government of prioritizing economic development at the cost of sacrificing historical and cultural heritage and people's collective memories. Their occupation was supported by other citizens in a candlelight vigil, in which protestors demanded conversations with government officials.[19]

Following the removal of the Star Ferry Pier, a local group—Local Action—was formed by several environmentalists, including Chow Sze Chung, Eddie Chu Hoi Dick, Ho Loy, and Bobo Yip Po Lam, to advocate democratic participation in city and town planning. The group size of Local Action was small, consisting of a few dozen members mostly from the 1970s and 1980s generations (Ip 2011).

In 2007, members of Local Action protested against the government's demolition of Queen's Pier and demanded its preservation in the same location.[20] They negotiated with government officials, occupied the site, collected signatures for petitions, and organized talks, forums and mini-concerts. Other social groups and activists, such as the Conservancy Association, the Society for the Protection of the Harbour, the Hong Kong Institute of Architects, and the Hong Kong Federation of Students, also joined the protests. Even though the Pier was eventually assessed by the Antiquities Advisory Board as a Grade I historic building—

meaning that it was of outstanding merit and should be preserved whenever possible—the government perceived the Board's assessment as merely advisory and eventually secured funding from the Legislative Council for demolition. In July 2007, three activists from Local Action decided to go on hunger strikes until the government withdrew the demolition plan. In August, the government imposed a lockdown of the area around the Pier and removed all protestors.[21]

Although the protests were ultimately unsuccessful, the establishment of Local Action demonstrated the possibility of a radical approach to environmentalism, which involved contentious actions against undemocratic decision-making in city and town planning. Notwithstanding its small scale, Local Action was able to unite the dissident forces in the critical public sphere and organize confrontational actions against the government, which signified the shift of Hong Kong's environmental movements from predominantly managerial to a more radical direction. This also marked the beginning of the repoliticization of the city's environment.

Repoliticization is a response to depoliticization. As illustrated in the previous section, the depoliticization of the environment is prominent in the Anthropocene discourse that tends to minimize the political space of disagreement and antagonism over environmental issues. Such displacement is realized in the framework of neoliberal governance, in which environmental issues are demoted from the governmental to the public sphere (Type 1), then to the private sphere (Type 2), or even to the realm of necessity (Type 3) (Hay 2007). Repoliticizing the environment means reversing the above demotions, so that environmental issues are moved from the realm of necessity back to the private sphere, the public sphere, or eventually the governmental sphere.

In Hong Kong, the resistance by local environmental groups and activists can be seen as efforts to repoliticize the city's environment. For example, through protest actions, Local Action challenged the settled consensus of economic development at the cost of historical and cultural heritage and collective memories. They also emphasized the public nature of city and town planning, and that there should be a democratic process of decision-making and governance. More importantly, they did not regard the demolition of the heritage sites as an issue that could be resolved through technical solutions, nor did they seek to achieve consensus with actors within the formal institutions. Instead, they demonstrated the value of contention and conflict in debating environmental issues, which were, after all, essentially political. In this manner, Hong Kong's environmental politics no longer consisted of just problem-solving and consensus-seeking but also confrontations and antagonism.

Following the protests at the ferry piers, in 2009, some members from Local Action, together with a number of ad hoc concern groups consisting mostly of the post-1980s generation, mobilized for protests against the construction of the Guangzhou-Shenzhen-Hong Kong Express Railway Link. They accused the project of being cost-ineffective as well as creating noise and air pollution. In January 2010, some twenty activists organized "ascetic" protests [*fu hang* 苦行] across five legislative constituencies, which involved intermittent kneeling, rising, and walking over a few days, in a campaign against the proposed project and for the conservation of the rural land affected.[22] Other protestors started to gather outside the Legislative Council building and scrutinized the deliberation of the project funding application. Similar to the protests in 2006–7, there were carnivals, mini-concerts, talks, and forums to publicize their contentions. Several activists also went on hunger strikes.[23] In mid-January 2010, protestors beset the Legislative Council after the funding application was passed with the support of the pro-establishment camp and the commercial sector.[24]

At the same time, some activists, including Eddie Chu and Bobo Lam, launched protest actions to stop the government from demolishing Choi Yuen Village, a rural village in the New Territories, whose location was designated for the sidings and emergency rescue station of the proposed express railway. A series of conflicts broke out during the land resumption in January 2011. Chu and dozens of villagers failed to achieve any consensus after negotiations with the railway company, and some activists were injured when the site was eventually cleared by the police.[25] Although the defence against the demolition was unsuccessful, it facilitated the rise of another environmental organization, the Land Justice League, which has in recent years become increasingly influential in Hong Kong's environmental movements.

The Land Justice League was founded in 2011 by twelve concerned groups, including the People's Action Plan, the New Territories Northeast Development Study Group, and the Central and Western District Concerned Group (Hui 2017). Through its robust protest activities against environmental injustice, several of its activists became renowned in Hong Kong's civil society, notably Eddie Chu, Bobo Lam, Chen Yun Chung, and Szeto May. Its platform consisted of six major demands: (1) the co-existence of rural and urban areas and the restoration of local agriculture; (2) justice in land use and ecology; (3) the right to residency and participation in the community; (4) the dissolution of the real estate hegemony; (5) an end to government-business collusions; and (6) democratic participation in urban and city planning.

Unlike the big conventional environmental organizations, the Land Justice League did not regard environmental issues as technical problems, but as something attributable to the formal structures and institutions. For example, it aimed to tackle environmental injustices—ranging from unsustainable rural development and disappearing green spaces to the commodification of land and accommodation—by reforming the social, political and economic institutions. In addition, they also sought to mobilize for social transformation through public participation in decision-making and democratic planning in the government, making Hong Kong a just city free of privilege, hegemony, and monopoly ownership.[26]

Since its establishment, the Land Justice League has been protesting against a number of environment-related issues, such as the gentrification of the New Territories, government disregard for agriculture, and the development of the Northeast New Territories area. Notably, in June 2014, it organized rallies and sit-ins with a list of ad hoc groups and activists to oppose the funding application for the Northeast New Territories development plan.[27] In one of their joint statements, they made accusations against the police (for its violence in arresting the protesters) and against the legislative process (for being dominated by the pro-establishment camp) as well as the undemocratic political system at large. In another statement, they attributed their contestation to structural and institutional factors, including the elite-driven and elite-dominated developmentalism and planning, collusion between the government and real estate developers, and the institutional violence of the authorities. The Land Justice League remained active in mobilizing protest actions against the government over land resumptions in the New Territories, the development plan on Lantau Island and in the country park peripheries, and also fly-tipping in a number of rural sites.[28]

In this respect, the rise of the Land Justice League has blurred the boundary between environmental and democratic movements, as it called for both the resolution of environmental issues and the transformation of the political system so as to usher in democracy in urban and city planning (Hui 2017). "Democracy" here refers not merely to democratic participation in policymaking but also to democratic resistance against an undemocratic political system, characterized by state repression, elite domination, and interest collusion. Arguably, Hong Kong's environmental movements have been further repoliticized since the emergence of the Land Justice League.

FIGURE 3.1

Members of the Land Justice League and the League of Social Democrats protesting against the construction of the Guangzhou-Shenzhen-Hong Kong Express Railway Link, 19 March 2016

Source: The Land Justice League.

Radical Environmentalism: Environmental or Democratic Movements?

Towards the second half of the 2010s, the radical environmental forces became further involved in the democratic struggles against authoritarianism. In the Legislative Council election of 2016, the Land Justice League formed coalitions with other groups and individuals, including Democracy Groundwork, Demosistō, and Edward Yiu, to advocate universal suffrage and self-governance through democratic self-determination.[29] Eddie Chu won a seat in the New Territories West constituency as an independent candidate, garnering the highest number of votes among the geographical constituencies.[30] However, some of his allies—including Lau Siu-lai (founder of Democracy Groundwork), Nathan Law (founding president of Demosistō), and Edward Yiu—were subsequently disqualified by the court from taking office in the Legislative Council, for their failure to swear allegiance to the Hong Kong SAR during the swearing-in ceremony.[31] The disqualifications were later attributed to their self-determination and pro-independence stances which, as proclaimed by the authorities, violated the principle of the constitutional framework—i.e., "one country, two systems"—as stipulated in the Basic Law.[32]

In 2018, Chu initiated the Village Charter 2018 to advocate the democratization of village representation in the New Territories. At the same time, he ran in the election for Village Representative in a rural constituency. His nomination was subsequently disqualified by the authorities on the grounds that he consented to the independence of Hong Kong as a viable option for self-determination, which, similarly, contradicted the "one country, two systems" principle of the Basic Law. It was believed that the disqualification of Chu was linked to his rebellious stance on the political future of Hong Kong vis-à-vis Mainland China.[33]

In 2019, Chu, together with the Land Justice League, participated in one of the largest movements in Hong Kong's history—the anti-extradition protests. The Land Justice League associated the threats of environmental injustice in Hong Kong with the authoritarian regime in the mainland. They expressed doubts over the Chinese judicial system which, in the face of elite domination such as forced evictions and land resumptions, could not uphold justice and human rights for ordinary people. They worried that, once the extradition bill was passed, people would censor their own contentions even in Hong Kong, owing to the fear of extradition to a less transparent jurisdiction on the mainland.[34] At the same time, Chu was one of the advocates for the five demands by the anti-extradition protestors, which included the enactment of universal suffrage for both the Chief Executive and Legislative Council elections.[35] In late 2019, Chu ran in the District Council elections as a pan-democracy candidate in a New Territories constituency, though he eventually lost.[36]

The above examples demonstrate that, since the mid-2010s, the radical environmental movements in Hong Kong have expanded their engagements in other domains of political contestation, in the form of the democratic resistance against authoritarian institutions and practices in Hong Kong as well as those associated with the mainland. The boundary between environmental and other social movements— particularly democratic movements—thus became further obscured. In a sense, these radical forces have attempted to repoliticize not only the city's environment but also its democratic development. While democracy has been dominating the political agenda in recent years, the radical environmental movements have collaborated with the democracy movements to resist authoritarianism. Chiu et al. (1999) were correct in predicting that local environmental forces would be repressed by the authorities after the sovereignty transfer in 1997. Yet, what went beyond their predictions was that such repression was not entirely attributable to the battles against developmental projects but also the resistance against authoritarian institutions and practices. Instead of treating the democracy movements as competitors, the radical environmental movements were able to construct coalitions with these forces to enlarge the political space for contestation. As a result, the city's environmental forces were no longer marginalized by their democratic counterparts as in the late period of the British regime.

Conclusion

This chapter has reviewed the evolution of environmental movements in post-handover Hong Kong, with both continuity and change noticed in the past twenty years. The traditions of consensual, piecemeal, and lifestyle-oriented environmental movements—i.e., managerial environmentalism—inherited from the British colonial era have largely persisted since the sovereignty transfer in 1997. Even nowadays, most major environmental organizations regard environmentalism as a collection of technical problems that can be resolved by promoting behavioural change and individual responsibility (through education) and seeking rational solutions (through research). The neoliberal context of development facilitated managerial environmentalism to remain feasible and dominant in post-handover Hong Kong. This continuity was very much consistent with the projections that Chiu et al. (1999) and Lai (2000) made twenty years ago. Until the mid-2000s, Hong Kong's environmental politics was largely depoliticized as in the Anthropocene discourse.

However, managerial environmentalism, despite being the mainstream, was far from the only form of environmental movement in post-handover Hong Kong. Since the mid-2000s, new local groups and activists have emerged to address environmental issues through a distinct approach challenging the fundamental principle of developmentalism. They have highlighted the sociopolitical costs of various infrastructure and development projects that sacrificed local cultures, collective memories, and environmental justice. They have even engaged in democratic struggles against authoritarian institutions and practices. The unconventional actions—confrontational, transgressive, and critical of formal structures and institutions—used in the protests against the demolition of heritage sites have become increasingly common in many subsequent protests over environmental as well as other political issues, notably democratic development. This new form of environmental movement—radical environmentalism—was a change not quite anticipated by Chiu et al. (1999) and Lai (2000). These radical environmental forces have been responsible for the repoliticization of Hong Kong's environmental politics since the mid-2000s.

In summary, the continuity and change of environmental movements in post-handover Hong Kong have produced two streams of environmentalism (see Table 3.1): managerial environmentalism within the formal institutional framework, and radical environmentalism advocating structural and institutional change through contestation. Owing to the changing political contexts over the past two decades under the new rules set by Beijing, the environmental movements in Hong Kong have oscillated between these managerial and radical forces.

The radical environmental forces might have been marginalized before the mid-2000s, but they have gradually evolved to become more significant actors in Hong Kong's environmental politics than ever before. The Umbrella Movement in 2014, for example, included environmental activists who advocated the need for environmental preservation and alternative lifestyles against crony capitalism (Veg 2016). Realistically, with such environmental radicalism on the rise, it is becoming less feasible for the government, the media, conservatives, and the public to ignore it. It remains to be seen whether these forces will further radicalize Hong Kong's environmental movements—as well as other social and political movements—or whether they will eventually be co-opted into the mainstream managerial environmentalism.

TABLE 3.1
Two Streams of Environmentalism in Hong Kong

	Managerial environmentalism	Radical environmentalism
Active period	The early 1990s to the present	The mid-2000s to the present
Organizational form	Professionalized and institutionalized movement organizations	Local activists and groups; Ad hoc, issue-specific groups
Membership and resource bases	Small membership; Expert and professional knowledge; Green funding	Small membership; Participatory resources
Scope	Environmental "problems"	Social, political and/ or economic structures and institutions behind environmental issues
Tactics	Research; Education; Lobbying; Limited contention (e.g., public complaints and judicial reviews)	Confrontational, disruptive, contentious actions
Prevailing strategies by authorities	Incorporation; Assimilation	Repression; Exclusion
Values/ ideology	Neoliberal developmentalism; Rationality; Individual responsibility	Scepticism of developmentalism, authoritarianism, and existing structures/ institutions

NOTES

1. An example was the judicial review filed by Friends of the Earth and other environmental groups in 1992 to block the proposal for turning the country parkland, Sha Lo Tung, into a private property development.
2. Apart from the major organizations, there were small-scale environmental groups founded in the local communities. For example, the Tsing Yi Concern Group was formed in 1983 to advocate against the potential environmental hazards from the petrochemical plants and chemical engineering industries; it adopted mainly confrontational means, such as protests and demonstrations. Many other local environmental groups emphasized, instead, the promotion of green lifestyles, which could be found in local community centres, schools, and universities (Chiu, Hung and Lai 1999).
3. Similarly, Lai (2000) points out that environmental organizations would be unlikely to secure partnership from any independent counterparts on the mainland, hence further reducing the likelihood of the development of distinct environmental movements.
4. For example, at the end of 2013, the outstanding values of mortgage loans were HK$900 billion, accounting for 40 per cent of the city's GDP.
5. According to *The Economist*'s crony-capitalism index, Hong Kong was ranked first among twenty-three countries in 2014.
6. *Hong Kong Economic Times*, 28 December 2007, p. 20.
7. Environmental Campaign Committee, www.ecc.org.hk (accessed 18 May 2018).
8. Green Power, www.greenpower.org.hk (accessed 18 May 2018).
9. The Conservancy Association, www.cahk.org.hk (accessed 18 May 2018).
10. Friends of the Earth, www.foe.org.hk (accessed 18 May 2018).
11. WWF (Hong Kong), www.wwf.org.hk (accessed 18 May 2018).
12. Civic Exchange, http://civic-exchange.org/ (accessed 18 May 2018).
13. It is worth mentioning that in 2003, Mei Ng, the then director of Friends of the Earth, received the Bronze Bauhinia Star from the government in recognition of her contribution to environmental protection. In 2012, Christine Loh, the founder of Civic Exchange, was appointed Undersecretary for the Environment.
14. *Ming Pao Daily News*, 24 June 2003, p. 19.
15. The Society for the Protection of the Harbour Ltd., Hong Kong, www.harbourprotection.org (accessed 18 May 2018). Throughout the years, Greenpeace has also carried out various scales of direct action, including hanging banners, occupying sites, projecting slogans, and other creative actions. For example, in 2009, Greenpeace hung a banner outside the government headquarters blaming and shaming Donald Tsang, then Chief Executive, for ignoring the issue of climate change in his administration. In

2015, the organization occupied the lobby of a government office building in protest of the customs department's failure to combat the smuggling of endangered species.

16. The express railway project was particularly controversial because it was over-budget (with the cost increasing from US$66 billion to an estimated US$85 billion) and dismantled Choi Yuen Village (see the latter discussion).

17. North East New Territories New Development Areas Planning and Engineering Study, https://www.nentnda.gov.hk/ (accessed 5 May 2020).

18. *Apple Daily*, 20 April 2012, p. 22.

19. *Ming Pao Daily News*, 25 December 2006, p. 4.

20. *Ming Pao Daily News*, 19 July 2007, p. 4.

21. For a detailed discussion of the protests, see Ip (2010).

22. *Hong Kong Daily News*, 6 January 2010, p. 1.

23. *Apple Daily*, 13 January 2010, p. 4.

24. For a detailed discussion of the protests, see Cheung (2014).

25. *Sing Pao*, 22 January 2011, p. 8.

26. Land Justice League, Hong Kong, https://landjusticehk.org/ (accessed 18 May 2018).

27. *Sing Tao Daily*, 7 June 2014, p. 6. The list of groups included Kwu Tung North Development Concern Group, League of Fanling North Villages and Residents, Ta Kwu Ling/Ping Che Alliance for "Saving Our Home", Age of Resistance, and so on.

28. Ibid.

29. *Sing Tao Daily*, 6 September 2016, p. 4.

30. Apart from the Legislative Council Election in 2016, Eddie Chu (and four other members of Land Justice League) ran in the District Council Election in 2011 in the Central and Western District, Pat Heung, San Tin, and Lamma Island, although none of the five candidates managed to secure a seat.

31. *Sing Tao Daily*, 15 July 2017, p. 2. See also Haas (2017).

32. *Sing Tao Daily*, 13 October 2018, p. 1.

33. *Ming Pao Daily News*, 3 December 2018, p. 2.

34. Land Justice League, Hong Kong, https://landjusticehk.org/ (accessed 1 March 2020).

35. *Apple Daily*, 18 October 2019, p. 6. The five demands consisted of: (1) complete withdrawal of the extradition bill; (2) retraction of the "riot" proclamation for the protests on 9 June 2019 and 12 June 2019; (3) withdrawal of criminal charges against all protestors; (4) investigation into the police's abuse of power; and (5) implementation of universal suffrage for the Chief Executive and the Legislative Council elections.

36. *Apple Daily*, 25 November 2019, p. 4.

REFERENCES

Anshelm, Jonas and Simon Haikola. 2018. "Depoliticization, Repoliticization, and Environmental Concerns – Swedish Mining Politics as an Instance of Environmental Politicization". *ACME: An International Journal for Critical Geographies* 17, no. 2: 561–96.

Chen, Yun-chung and Mirana M. Szeto. 2015. "The Forgotten Road of Progressive Localism: New Preservation Movement in Hong Kong". *Inter-Asia Cultural Studies* 16, no. 3: 436–53.

Cheng, Joseph. 2015. "Business-Government Nexus: The Special Case of Hong Kong". *Asian Education and Development* 5, no. 4: 454–67.

Cheung, Chor-yung. 2014. "Hong Kong's Systemic Crisis of Governance and the Revolt of the 'Post-80s' Youths: The Anti-Express Rail Campaign". In *New Trends of Political Participation in Hong Kong*, edited by Joseph Y.S. Cheng. Hong Kong: City University Press.

Chiu, Stephen Wing-kai and Ho-fung Hung. 1997. "The Paradox of Stability Revisited: Colonial Development and State Building in Rural Hong Kong". *China Information* 12: 66–96.

Chiu, Stephen Wing-kai, Ho-fung Hung, and On-kwok Lai. 1999. "Environmental Movements in Hong Kong". In *Asia's Environmental Movements: Comparative Perspectives*, edited by Yok-shiu F. Lee and Alvin Y. So. New York/London: M.E. Sharpe.

Cross, Remy and David Snow. 2011. "Radicalism within the Context of Social Movements: Processes and Types". *Journal of Strategic Security* 4, no. 4: 115–29.

Diani, Mario and Paolo Donati. 1999. "Organizational Change in Western European Environmental Groups: A Framework for Analysis". *Environmental Politics* 8, no. 1: 13–34.

Dryzek, John S. 2013. *The Politics of the Earth: Environmental Discourses*. 3rd ed. Oxford: Oxford University Press.

Haas, Benjamin. 2017. "Hong Kong Pro-democracy Legislators Disqualified from Parliament". *The Guardian*, 14 July 2017.

Harvey, David. 2005. *A Brief History of Neoliberalism*. Oxford: Oxford University Press.

Hay, Colin. 2007. *Why We Hate Politics*. Cambridge: Polity Press.

Heijden, Hein-Anton van der. 1997. "Political Opportunity Structure and the Institutionalisation of the Environmental Movement". *Environmental Politics* 6, no. 4: 25–50.

The Heritage Foundation. 2018. *Index of Economic Freedom*. Washington. www.heritage.org/index/.

Hsiao, Hsin-Huang Michael and Po-shan Wan. 2006. "Environmental Protests in Taiwan and Hong Kong: 1987–2002". In *Trends and Challenges of Social*

Development: Experiences from Hong Kong and Taiwan, edited by Lau Siu-kai et al. Hong Kong: Hong Kong Institute of Asia-Pacific Studies, The Chinese University of Hong Kong (in Chinese).

Hui, Dennis Lai Hang. 2017. "Environmental Governance and the Rise of Environmental Movement in Hong Kong". In *Interest Groups and the New Democracy Movement in Hong Kong*, edited by Sonny Shiu-hing Lo. Abingdon, Oxon: Routledge.

Ip, Iam Chong. 2011. *Nostalgia for the Present: The Past and Present of Cultural Preservation*. Hong Kong: Hong Kong Institute of Asia-Pacific Studies, The Chinese University of Hong Kong (in Chinese).

King, Ambrose Yeo-chi. 1975. "Administrative Absorption of Politics in Hong Kong: Emphasis on the Grass Roots Level". *Asian Survey* 15, no. 5: 422–39.

Lai, On Kwok. 2000. "Greening of Hong Kong? – Forms of Manifestation of Environmental Movements". In *The Dynamics of Social Movement in Hong Kong*, edited by Stephen Wing Kai Chiu and Tai Lok Lui. Hong Kong: Hong Kong University Press.

Legislative Council Secretariat. 1999. *Relocation of the Manufacturing Sector Outside Hong Kong in the 1990s* (Original title in Chinese: 製造業於80年代 及90年代初期遷離香港). Hong Kong: Legislative Council Secretariat (立法 會秘書處). www.legco.gov.hk.

Man, Si-wai. 1996. "De-constructing the Management Approach to the Environment". *The Centre for Environmental Studies Newsletter* (The Chinese University of Hong Kong) 5, no. 2: 1–7.

McCormack, Thelma H. 1957. "The Motivation of Radicals". In *Collective Behaviour*, edited by Ralph Turner and Lewis Killian. Englewood Cliffs, NJ: Prentice Hall.

Mouffe, Chantal. 2006. *On the Political*. London: Routledge.

Perkins, Richard. 2010. "The Internationalisation of Managerial Environmentalism: Globalisation, Diffusion and Territorialisation". *Geography Compass* 4, no. 8: 1069–83.

Rootes, Christopher. 1999. "Environmental Movements: From the Local to the Global". *Environmental Politics* 8, no. 1: 1–12.

So, Alvin Y. 2008. "Social Conflict in Hong Kong After 1997: The Emergence of a Post-modernist Mode of Social Movements?" In *Hong Kong SAR's First Decade: Retrospect and Prospects*, edited by Ming K. Chan. Hong Kong: City University of Hong Kong Press.

———. 2011. "One Country, Two Systems and Hong Kong-China National Reunification: A Crisis-transformation Perspective". *Journal of Contemporary Asia* 41, no. 1: 99–116.

Swyngedouw, Erik. 2011. "Interrogating Post-democratization: Reclaiming Egalitarian Political Spaces". *Political Geography* 30: 370–80.

————. 2015. "Depoliticized Environments and the Promises of the Anthropocene". In *The International Handbook of Political Ecology*, edited by Raymond Bryant. Cheltenham: Edward Elgar.

Veg, Sebastian. 2016. "Creating a Textual Public Space: Slogans and Texts from Hong Kong's Umbrella Movement". *The Journal of Asian Studies* 75, no. 3: 673–702.

Žižek, Slavoj. 1999. "Carl Schmitt in the Age of Post-politics". In *The Challenge of Carl Schmitt*, edited by Chantal Mouffe. London: Verso.

4

THE POST-POLITICS OF ENVIRONMENTAL ENGAGEMENT IN SINGAPORE

Harvey Neo

Twenty years ago, sociologist Daniel Goh commented that Singapore is a strange place for environmentalism (Goh 2000). The reasons for this are two-fold. First, ruled by a single, dominant political party since its independence in 1965, the room for civil society in general has been circumscribed in the best of times, and suppressed in the worst of times. Second, as a small island-state, which reached near complete urbanization as early as the 1980s, Singapore is seen as a place where environmentalism is dissonant with reality. This dissonance becomes more acute as far as nature conservation—an enduring environmental issue—is concerned. Put another way, nature conservation is seen as increasingly irrelevant given the hyper-development of the city-state because there is little space left to conserve in urbanized Singapore. Suffice to say, the perennially weakened state of the environmental movement explains in part why, when it comes to the tug-of-war between conservation and development, the conservationists have more often than not ceded ground to the state. In addition, as this chapter will illustrate, the developmentalist posturing of the Singapore state makes it ideologically challenging for the environmental movement to defend nature conservation. Yet, the latter is but one of the many concerns of the environmental movement.

Indeed, mirroring global trends, the local environmental movement, especially in recent years, has incorporated a plethora of interests beyond nature conservation. How have issues such as animal rights and sustainable living (broadly defined), relatively new forms of environmental concerns here, play out within the environmental politics of Singapore, as compared to the concerns of more "traditional" environmental groups? Further to that, how have the general ebb and flow of the Singaporean political climate affected the development of the environmental movement? These questions, the focus of this chapter, are related in a symbiotic manner. To put it simply, commentators have argued that the introduction of newer, non-traditional environmental concerns spearheaded by younger environmental organizations nudge open the political space in Singapore (Kong 1991), and the latter once opened—even if gingerly—can encourage the further emergence and consolidation of environmental groups.

To be sure, it is undeniable that political space for environmental concerns has opened up in Singapore during the last decades. However, through a series of vignettes, I argue that such politicization is marked by a subtle self-selection and sanctioning process whereby the issues that are allowed political space and debate (as well as the ways such issues are framed) are those that do not disrupt the developmental ethos and legitimacy of the Singaporean state. Drawing on the concept of post-politics, I hence argue that there are limits to which environmental engagement as seen in Singapore can bring forth an emancipatory society-nature relationship in the age of the Anthropocene.

This chapter is divided into five sections. Following this introduction, I will briefly lay out the political realities of Singapore as a one-party state, particularly how this has affected the growth of civil society in general, and environmental movements in particular. This will be done through a quick recap of significant contestations between the state and environmental groups in the 1980s and 1990s. I will then highlight how, since the new millennium, the state has for various reasons ostensibly attempted to involve non-state actors to manage a range of social issues.

In the third section, I argue that such engagements are subtly linked to a post-political society. In explaining what post-politics entails, I show how such political engagements are well-suited to, and indeed favoured by, a paternalistic state such as Singapore. In brief, post-politics presents an aura of political openness without necessarily ceding political ground and political legitimacy to non-state elements, both in the way political issues are identified and defined, and in how they might be resolved. In the fourth section, I detail how animal-society politics have burgeoned and show that, while commendable, it falls squarely within the logic of post-politics. This, in effect, curtails what animal issues are engaged publicly and how.

In the final section, I critically reassess the relationship between post-politics, environmental engagement, and the Anthropocene. In so doing, I argue that while there have been clear signs of political opening up as far as environmental issues (broadly defined) are concerned, this openness is circumscribed by a climate of post-politics. I conclude that, as far as meeting the most critical challenges of the Anthropocene is concerned, post-political Singapore, with its alignment to a "cooperative" political engagement, falls short.

Evolving Politics and Environmentalism Under the Weight of Development

Since independence, the People's Action Party (PAP) has ruled Singapore with little threat to its parliamentary supermajority. Even today, with its weakest hold on parliament, the PAP still commands a total of 81 out of 87 elected seats. Such political dominance extends to all spheres of life in Singapore. For example, labour unions have long been subsumed entirely within the political orbit of PAP, with the post of Secretary General of the National Trades Union Congress traditionally being held by a senior PAP politician. Even community organizations such as national sports associations are helmed by PAP Members of Parliament. Elsewhere, I have also shown how something as innocuous as community gardening has been considerably politicized (Tan and Neo 2009; Neo and Chua 2017). As Singam (2017, p. 3) describes vividly: "the PAP established a structure of overwhelming control. An apt analogy is that of an octopus, the PAP leadership is the brain and body of accumulated power, while the bureaucracy and institutions of the party machine provide the tentacles, which extend to various institutions and agencies of control". Such political entrenchment, where the dominant party is wary of any challenges to its total rule, directly shapes the development of civil society in Singapore.

This is not to suggest that challenges have not been mounted, nor that dissent is unheard of in Singapore. Indeed, the environmental movement, even at the height of PAP's hegemony in the early 1990s, has launched various bids to contest decisions by the state. In what follows, I will illustrate two pivotal case studies where the Nature Society of Singapore (NSS) was involved with contestations over the conservation of nature sites in Singapore. The ensuing discussion draws in part from some of my earlier works (Neo 2007, 2013).

MAP 4.1

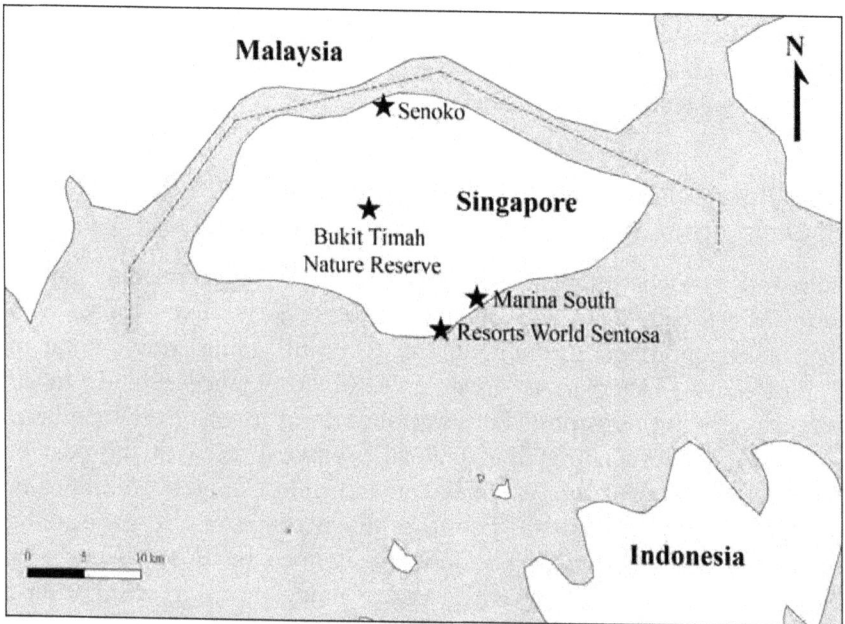

Selected sites of environmental disputes in Singapore

Source: QGIS and Natural Earth.

The Marina South Duck Ponds

During the 1980s, there was massive reclamation at the southern tip of Singapore, close to the Central Business District. The resultant land, called Marina South, was an eleven-hectare piece of "idle" land, poised for the future expansion of the city and was left undeveloped for close to a decade after its initial reclamation. During this time, ponds were filled from subsidence of the ground and a spontaneous ecosystem was formed. Marina South then developed naturally to become a roosting ground for rare migratory ducks, including the lesser tree duck, common moorhen, and the wandering tree-duck. According to a survey conducted by the Nature Society in 1991, several of the species spotted there had never been seen in Singapore before (NSS 1991, p. i). However, barely a year after NSS's glowing assessment of Marina South, the Ministry of Environment (it has since been renamed the Ministry of Environment and Water Resources (MEWR) and the rest of the chapter adopts this new name) drained the ponds and covered up the hollows. The manner in which the Marina duck ponds were lost offers an insight into the particular way in which the environmental movement engaged with the state in the heady days of development.

The case of the Marina duck ponds was set in a period of rapid development in Singapore. Concomitantly, it was also paradoxically situated in the late 1980s to early 1990s, a period when the "environment" figured constantly in the public arena. Certainly, the inaugural Earth Summit in Rio de Janeiro (where Singapore's Ambassador-at-large, Mr Tommy Koh, was co-chairperson) subsequently propelled the flurry of environmental initiatives in Singapore (e.g., *The Singapore Green Plan*). The afterglow of the government's decision to designate Sungei Buloh Wetlands, an area Northwest of Singapore, as a bird sanctuary had yet to dissipate. Coupled with the then newly elected Goh Chok Tong-led PAP government's promise of building a "kinder, gentler society", the early 1990s represented an unprecedented open window of political opportunities for environmental non-governmental organizations (NGOs) to pursue their respective agendas.

Thus, the NSS swung into action when, to its surprise, the MEWR declared that the ponds were going to be filled in to "rectify the surface drainage system at Marina South" (*Straits Times*, 20 April 1992). As the organizational capability of the NSS was limited, the usual recourse to influence the government's decisions was through direct talks with the relevant agencies and, more frequently, stating their stance through the media. For this episode, the NSS first questioned the exact nature of the alleged "drainage problems" through the press (*Straits Times*, 20 April 1992). This query was never answered by the MEWR. Contrary to the MEWR's claim that they would "be arranging to meet representatives from the NSS to see how best [they] can balance the need to ensure [the] public health problem of mosquito breeding and the desire to preserve the natural habitats of the wild ducks can be met" (*Straits Times*, 24 April 1992), the NSS stated that the MEWR "did not meet the society although NSS did try to contact the ministry about the ponds" (*Straits Times*, 12 May 1992).

Drawing on developmentalist discourse, the MEWR justified the reclamation and framed the dispute as one of conservation versus development, with little room for any sort of creative planning compromise. The Ministry of National Development (MND) also chimed in to state, somewhat rhetorically, that the site was meant for "future urban development" (*Straits Times*, 12 May 1992). Second, it revealed that "there were several complaints in the papers on the mosquito nuisance at Marina South" and thus "to resolve the problem and to prevent future mosquito breeding, the ministry decided to fill up these ponds" (*Straits Times*, 24 April 1992). This justification drew from both a communitarian ideology (i.e., getting rid of the mosquito nuisance will benefit the public), as well as the developmentalist ethos that getting rid of the mosquitoes must be done "rationally" and "efficiently". This is despite the fact that there appeared to be little chance of a public health menace even if there were mosquitoes breeding there, simply because the area was so secluded. Furthermore, the NSS argued that the fish in the pond would have fed on mosquito larvae; this was an ecological response to the alleged problem as opposed to the state's technocratic and so-called rational solution.

The MEWR further insisted that "no wildlife was observed in the area" (*Straits Times*, 24 April 1992), a direct contradiction to the environmental report put forth by the Nature Society just two years prior. Doubling down, the MEWR maintained that the site was "not natural" to start with—the ponds being dug out by humans—implying that to consider it for "nature conservation" was absurd. The opportunity costs of alternative uses of the site were claimed to be too high, as it was "too commercially valuable to be set aside as a bird sanctuary". Finally, in an attempt to downplay the ecological value of the site, it was claimed that the migratory ducks "were not rare and common to the region".

In its official newsletter, the NSS stated that they were "not against the eventual development of the area" (*Nature News* 1992, p. 18), but asked for more time to resettle the birds safely and completely. Nonetheless, the MEWR stood firm and went ahead to fill in all the ponds in the site. The only concession was the relocation of the ducks to Sungei Buloh or, if unable to adapt there, to the Jurong Bird Park in Singapore's West Region.

In critically reflecting on this episode, Goh (2000, p. 138) writes that several inconsistencies in the MEWR's arguments (e.g., the MEWR had initially said that it expected the birds to fly to other swamp areas in the region when the ponds were filled but later claimed that it would work with other relevant government agencies and the Jurong Bird Park to resettle the birds) suggest that they were just "post-hoc justifications for an already-made decision to fill up the ponds". However, I wish to argue that while the decision may be *a priori*, the justifications were not as post-hoc as they appeared. Rather, the MEWR drew on established developmentalist discourse to justify its reclamation. It downgraded the suitability of the ponds as a bona fide nature area through codified criteria as well. Against these two strategic manoeuvres, the NSS had no replies and the ponds were irrecoverably lost. It is perhaps ironic that more than twenty years later, the completely artificial Gardens by the Bay stands in part where the Marina duck ponds once rested.

This case illustrates that contestations between environmental groups and the authorities are very much circumscribed by the extent to which developmental impetus is a key concern. In other words, where the development imperative is high, the space for political negotiation is limited. Not least, such an imperative is deemed to resonate with the citizenry at large. As will be elaborated later, this resonance is critical in the formation of a post-political condition that requires a broad, albeit often vague, consensus within society as to what is acceptable and desirable. For now, we turn to the next example, which will see the developmental imperative echo even more strongly.

Senoko

By far the most contested site between the environmental movement and the state was Senoko. Located in the western part of Singapore, Senoko was a 120-hectare piece of land that was given the highest conservation rating (five star) by the most comprehensive nature survey ever completed by the Nature Society (NSS 1990). The land was remarkable for being the nesting grounds of over 180 species of birds including two internationally and nineteen locally endangered species. Following NSS's assessment, the Urban Redevelopment Authority indicated that Senoko would be integrated with any future urban development as a nature park (URA 1991, p. 31). Further reassurance also came from the MND, as late as October 1992, that Senoko would be conserved in some ways (*Nature News* 1993, p. 9). Despite such positive pronouncements, it was suddenly announced in September 1993 that Senoko had been earmarked for "housing needs" (*Straits Times*, 20 September 1993, p. 142) and would be completely cleared.

The Senoko case shows how the state's stance on matters such as conservation can swiftly change dramatically. At some level, this is surprising, given Singapore's reputation as a city governed by a polity obsessed with planning. On the other hand, such rapid backtracking of major developmental and environmental decisions had precedence. For example, Neo (2015) has written how, in a matter of a few months in the early 1980s, the Singaporean government vacillated between modernizing the local pig production industry through capital injections and the complete phasing-out of the polluting industry. The case of Senoko had distinct parallels with the Marina incident, which occurred barely a year before. For instance, even more obvious than before, the authorities in standing their ground drew persuasive strength from the critical need for development. More significantly, there was a palpable hardening of the authorities' attitude towards environmental groups like the NSS (specifically, the way the latter challenged its legitimacy).

While the NSS sees Senoko as "the richest bird site in Singapore in terms of species and numbers" (*Straits Times*, 20 September 1993), then Acting National Development Minister, Mr Lim Hng Kiang, in an argument reminiscent of one that was used in the Marina tussle, stated that Senoko was "not a natural area for a hundred years" (*Straits Times*, 19 March 1994). Believing in his position of power and his own sense of how development was the key concern of Singaporeans, Mr Lim threw a challenge, perhaps somewhat rhetorically, to the NSS: "so if the NSS can give me a petition to take 17,000 applications of upgraders from my waiting list, then we will keep the Senoko land and keep it for the birds".

It probably came as a surprise to everyone, not least the Minister himself, that civil society (led by NSS) took up his challenge and, with the implicit encouragement of the Minister, set about to embark on a political lobbying strategy hitherto unheard of locally. What followed was an act of civil activism in post-independence Singapore where the society started an appeal letter in order to save Senoko. Claiming themselves to be the "Friends of Senoko", some twenty-five thousand people put their names on the appeal letter (bear in mind this was long before the emergence of online petitions!). Significantly, many prominent civil society and political elites put their names to the petition: Professor Tommy Koh, Kuo Pao Kun (a renowned playwright who has since passed away), Tay Kheng Soon (a renowned architect), Kawaljit Soin and Hedwig Anuar (both past presidents of another prominent NGO, AWARE—the Association of Women's Action and Research).

While such mass petitions are common in other developed countries as an activism strategy, it was new in Singapore. In any case, it was ineffectual against the state's discourse of development. The priority use of Senoko was the construction of public housing, as stated plainly by Mr Lim: "with the pressing needs of Singaporeans, I think Singaporeans' needs come before birds" (*Straits Times*, 19 March 1994). There was a strict dichotomy here with limited room for compromise (such as to conserve part of Senoko). I suggest that the state had taken on such an uncompromising position for several reasons.

The legitimacy of the Singapore state is derived largely from continued economic progress and development. Thus, any attempts to conserve land slated for development directly contravenes their modes of legitimacy and governance. Public housing is one of the most important tools in the state's striving for legitimacy (Chua 1997). Second, the state might have been disturbed by the speed with which the Friends of Senoko could get twenty-five thousand signatures to lobby for Senoko's preservation. Finally, a few years prior to the Senoko incident, the NSS had successfully lobbied to prevent the government from building a golf course within the Central Catchment area, so the government was now unwilling to cede ground again. A former Chair of the NSS, concurred that the political climate for the environmentalists changed for the worse in the Senoko affair as well:

My interpretation is that the whole thing goes way back... It has much to do even with the [Lower Peirce] golf course... Maybe the golf course was their pet project but they were denied that. So they were not happy with that so they had a hard feeling against greenies. So when proposals were put to Senoko, they are not too keen to conserve it. I mean things like that happen, things can happen in an irrational way (Ho, cited in Neo 2007).

While the conservation of the Senoko bird sanctuary was a lost cause, the impact of each environmental political engagement goes beyond mere material objectives. I suggest that at a broader level, such politicization is heuristic in drawing the state's attention to the potential of civic activism; an increased awareness of alternative conceptions of living as well as the inevitability of a rising desire for activism among the citizenry. Clearly, this awareness would bear material and ideational impacts on the institutional forms and social-political norms of the regulatory state. In short, as suggested earlier, environmental engagement and political space has an iterative relationship.

Senoko was finally bulldozed to make way for 17,000 flat units. Dr Ho Hua Chew, then Chair of NSS, addressed the issue of housing in a letter to the Forum page of the *Straits Times* six years after the Senoko incident. He argues for an overhaul of the housing policies aimed at preventing home owners from profiteering from the sale of their subsidized flats (*Straits Times*, 27 August 1998) and reflects on the paradox that Singapore continues to develop public housing when more than 85 per cent of the population are already residing in public housing. "Housing for development" represents a powerful discursive and material justification for the developmental state to clear nature areas. What Dr Ho tried to do in retrospect, and in vain, was to critique and unsettle this hegemonic ideology.

Dr Ho was ahead of his time. In early 2002, two related developments combined to dent this hegemonic ideology. Quite unexpectedly, a Minister without portfolio in the Prime Minister's Office, Mr Lim Boon Heng, asked rhetorically: "We have one of the highest savings rates in the world, yet many do not have enough cash for retirement. Why? Is there too much invested in property?" (*Straits Times*, 4 April 2002). Predictably, the *Straits Times* followed his comments with a flurry of articles asking, for instance, "Are Singaporeans sinking too much into property?" (*Straits Times*, 13 April 2002) and reminding that "a home may cost more than you think" (*Straits Times*, 12 May 2002). Interspersed between these articles was a report that the Housing Development Board (HDB) had started "pulling out the stops to woo buyers". Apparently, buyers in the queue to purchase the flats were not doing so because the unsold flats were located in undesirable areas and, perhaps more likely, the weak economic climate was holding back buyers' commitment. The report notes that after a prolonged promotional blitz, the HDB only managed to sell 3,200 units of its backlog. In what can only be described as a cruel twist of fate, the number of units of flats in the backlog was revealed to be 17,000 (*Straits Times*, 12 April 2002). More recently, public housing emerged in the public spotlight again when there was debate over what exactly happens when the ninety-nine-year lease of public housing ends.

The above case studies offer two perspectives of environmental engagement in Singapore. First, the discourse of development triumphs over ethical concerns relating to the conservation of land. Second, that the Nature Society has the voice and space to mount such diametrically opposing world views against the dominant political party is itself commendable, regardless of their eventual outcome. Such high-profile confrontations between the environmental movement and the state have not been repeated since 2000, although there have been sporadic tensions (such as the proposed cross-island train system that will run through parts of the Central Catchment area by 2030). In part, this is due to the fact that, by the turn of the millennium, there were hardly any significant tracts of land in Singapore that still could be developed. This geographical reality, however, does not mean that environmental engagement ceases in Singapore. Rather, it merely shifts to other environmental issues, especially those that are not fundamentally opposed to the developmental imperative. Concomitantly, the overall political environment of Singapore has also shifted appreciably to involve non-governmental organizations. These two insights coalesced into a particular post-politics of environmentalism in Singapore. The ensuing sections will elaborate more on this point.

The Post-Politics of Environmentalism

What is post-politics? How and why does it emerge in any given society? To be sure, a post-political condition is ostensibly a sign of political openness, and hence always preferable to a repressive state. However, it is a particularistic kind of political opening. Key to the post-politics perspective is the rejection of ideological divisions and the explicit universalization of particular political demands. Among other things, "the post-political condition is one in which a consensus has been built around the inevitability of neoliberal capitalism as an economic system and parliamentary democracy as the political ideal" (Swyngedouw 2007, p. 24). In other words, post-politics eschews ideological divisions in favour of a common ideal. It sidesteps any demands of specific groups that may run counter to hegemonic (neoliberal) social structures and, more importantly, it endeavours to prevent these demands from resonating in the wider society. Rather, it packages or rearticulates such demands to be complementary to and complicit with existing political economy structures of neoliberalism or, in the case of Singapore, developmentalism. To be sure, Perry et al. (1997) define Singapore's developmentalism as implying a political legitimacy based upon continual economic progress. In that sense, particular aspects of the environmental agenda are not at odds with this ethos. For example, improvements to the urban built environment (paving roads, modernizing sanitation, and provision of clean water supply) are often conduits towards economic expansion.

In viewing Singapore as both developmental and post-political, I argue that possible socio-political outcomes in political contestations (e.g., nature conservation as discussed earlier) cannot be contrary to the discursive imaginaries of development and communitarianism. Both of these aligned discursive realities ultimately sustain the neoliberal, hegemonic state. And both of these realities spring from the siege mentality present amongst the citizenry and cultivated by the hegemonic state. In other words, in a post-political society, politics is not suppressed and, indeed, for the most part, is often actively materialized. However, some forms of political engagement and political demands are "disallowed" if they are deemed "non-consensual" (chiefly because they contravene hegemonic political economic realities). Hence, if it is believed that the issues being contested have compromised (or will compromise) development and the "overall well-being of society" (however it is defined), the government will be uncompromising to a fault.

Transposed to the focus of our chapter, a post-politics of environmentalism holds a few features. First, environmental issues that seep into the public's consciousness are those aligned with developmentalism. Put differently, the emergence and resolution of environmental issues (or more accurately, particular kinds of environmental issues, such as recycling or the "Greening of Singapore") are means to an end. Amongst other things, this end strengthens pre-existing political-economic structures in Singapore that are geared towards ever-increasing growth. The most obvious example of such "sanctioned environmental-ism" is the "Garden City" vision that essentially defines Singaporean environmental history. As Schneider-Mayerson (2017, pp. 170–71) notes, the voices of advocates who agitate for the conservation of wilderness are overwhelmed by the top-down manufacture of the Garden City, where nature "exists as the final product in a deliberate (but rarely deliberative) process" and greenery becomes a "signifier of stability, prosperity and control".

Second, the *manner* in which these issues are resolved veers towards non-confrontational means and behind-the-scenes negotiations with the relevant agencies. Indeed, this is one of the distinctive features of a post-politics of the environment, in that the opposition is rarely eliminated through brute suppression. Rather, they are co-opted, discredited (often by asserting that dissenting views do not understand the exceptionalism of Singapore), or simply ignored. Third, the narratives surrounding these environmental issues revolve around key motifs of the broader society, and it is through these motifs that Singapore exceptionalism is composed. To elaborate on the third feature, Perry et al. (1997, p. 6) have argued that "the political style of Singapore's leadership is to cultivate a continual sense of crisis and urgency amongst the population". Such cultivation thrives on various motifs, including the creation of a "siege mentality" that capitalizes on Singapore's "vulnerability" and "limited space" (i.e., its "small size", "lack of human and natural resources", etc.). These motifs provide the moral suasion for the ruling PAP government to institute extensive curbs, controls, and policies over many aspects of citizen life. Such curbs include the lack of press freedom (Seow 1998), coercive family planning policies (Cheng 1989), and the state's control of education, particularly in the area of language acquisition (PuruShotam 1998 and Tremewan 1994). As mentioned earlier, the extent of control extends to almost all facets of social life. More importantly, these motifs buttress the understanding of environmental issues and provide the basis for solving environmental problems. For example, as Neo (2010) writes, recycling as an environmental problem is continuously given the greatest attention, in part because of the widely promulgated worldview that Singapore's small size limits space for landfills. Hence, apocalyptic imaginaries of the island state being buried in ever-increasing trash are often conjured to encourage recycling.

The emergence of a post-political condition is also partly due to the state being cognisant of the fact that heavy-handed political manoeuvring is increasingly untenable as the electorate matures. Yet, for the first three decades since Singapore's independence from British colonial rule in 1965, through various policies and regulations, the state has long taken a totalizing role in transforming the urban facets of Singapore. Unsurprisingly, the physical development of Singapore is historically a depoliticized process where protests against state-initiated land use policies are rare. The powerful Land Acquisition Act is one of the practical and extensive means ensuring that the PAP government's planning is unhindered. The Land Acquisition Act ensures that the state has the final say in all land use matters, even on non-state land. This powerful Act allows the state to acquire *any* particular piece of land, should it be needed:

> for any *public* purpose; by any person, corporation or statutory board, for any work or an undertaking which, in the opinion of the Minister [for National Development], is of *public benefit* or of *public utility* or in the *public interest*; or for any residential, commercial or industrial purposes (Section 5(1), Land Acquisition Act, Chapter 152).

Consequently, the state has become the largest land-owner in Singapore. Acquisitions are compensated by the state at an amount that in its "opinion should be allowed for the land" (Land Acquisition Act, Chapter 152, Section 10 (1)). Underpinning the Land Acquisition Act is a broad communitarian ideal that emphasizes the interest of the "public" over potential and conflicting private interests. It further signals the exceptionalism of Singapore's physical size in necessitating such a law. The Act further grants immense power to the state (with the National Development Minister as its proxy) where it is the sole arbitrator for deciding what constitutes "public benefit". More importantly, the Land Acquisition Act exemplifies two state-society relationships in Singapore. First, the Act rests upon the proven managerial and planning track record of the PAP government, so that many Singaporeans would eventually accept it. Second, should such faith in the managerial capabilities of the government diminish, the Act does not preclude the possibility of the government turning rogue and authoritarian.

This brief example of land acquisition attests to the observation of Campbell and Marshall (2002, p. 163): "the legitimisation of planning has rested on the proposition that the state's intervention in land and property development is necessary to safeguard public interest". This is why, as they note, what constitutes public interest is highly contentious. Furthermore, Chua has similarly argued that "what is politically articulated as the 'collective' interest at a specific point in time is a device for excluding unacceptable voices and opinions rather than the accommodation of a plurality of views and interests" (2000, p. 75), a view that is consistent with the policymaking in a post-political hegemonic state. In the context of Singapore, "public" or "collective" interest compels the minority to yield to the will of the majority in land use matters. And the will of the majority is frequently driven by profit, "efficiency", and the interests of the hegemony.

Indeed, as Chua (1995, p. 197) writes, "Singaporean-style communitarianism" is "constrained within the ideological/conceptual space of national interests [such that] no individual or group can assert its own right as a basic condition of existence lest the assertion be read as unacceptable self-interest, potentially detrimental to the whole". Simply put, the central idea of communitarianism is that "collective interests should have primacy over individual ones" (Perry et al. 1997, p. 66) and significantly, more often than not, it is the state that explicitly (or implicitly) defines collective interests. Such an understanding of communitarianism aligns well with post-politics.

Clearly, as far as land use planning is concerned, there is a kind of post-politics at work where the minority voice opposing the manner in which land is acquired and used is deemed irrelevant and out of the realm of what is set as "rational". That realm is defined largely in economic-developmentalist terms which themselves are pivoted on particular notions of what it means to be communitarian and communal, as well as what counts as a legitimate collective interest. In this case, extra-economic objections (e.g., for the sake of nostalgia and natural heritage) to land use change are often considered irrelevant and unwarranted. Moreover, state agencies like the Ministry of National Development and the Urban Redevelopment Authority, emboldened by powerful legislation like the Land Acquisition Act, remain unchallenged in terms of land use policies in Singapore. Such a state of affairs is mirrored in NGO politics where the Societies Act (part of Singapore's Constitution) bestows absolute power on the Minister for Home Affairs to refuse the registration of any NGO (thereby rendering its existence illegal) or order the dissolution of existing organizations if their activities are considered to be "contrary to national interest" (Singapore Statutes 1966 [2014]: 4(2) (d)). Given such far-reaching political control wielded by the political structures over its citizenry, the emergence of a post-political state in Singapore is almost inevitable. In the next few sections, I will show how communitarianism, the hegemonic state, and development intersect to produce a post-politics of environmentalism in Singapore.

The Post-Politics of Animal-Society Relations in Singapore

From the mid-2000s onwards, the value and place of animals in society has gained increasing public attention. The interest in animals is a departure from earlier instances of the nature-society dichotomy for two main reasons. First, in both policy and public spheres, animals have been very much neglected in deference to the "purely green" (e.g., trees, parks, forests, green spaces) agenda. Nonetheless, there has been a slow but sure inclusion of animals into the popular imagination of what counts as the natural environment. Such inclusion, if nothing else, suggests that Singapore will see nature-society issues being debated more frequently. Second, while some contentious issues, like the feeding of stray cats in housing estates and the encroachment of macaques into residential areas, are local in nature, other issues are simultaneously tied to global ethical-political concerns. This includes wildlife trafficking, captive dolphins in marine parks, and the anti-shark-fin campaign. Concomitant to the proliferation of such varied animal-society contestations is the increased number of NGOs (both formal and informal) that are dedicated to animal welfare, such as ACRES (Animal Concerns Research and Education Society) and the Cat Welfare Society. Global organizations like the Jane Goodall Institute have also set up offices in Singapore. In any case, as detailed above, whether NGOs are endogenous to Singapore or local affiliates of global organizations, they are similarly subject to the post-political reality of Singapore, as are the causes which they agitate for. This also explains why environmental issues that have global resonance, such as damming, deforestation, and the degradation of the coastlines of neighbouring countries, such as Malaysia and Indonesia, are relatively muted in Singapore. It is not so much due to the fact that Singapore is complicit in these environmental problems because of its insatiable demand for resources to develop. Rather, the muting of these issues is to pre-empt any disruption of Singapore's developmental trajectory.

Suffice to say, animal-society issues are for the most part "safe". Moreover, the changing physical landscape of Singapore has seen increasingly built-up areas, which result in animals becoming more present in public spaces. This has given rise to particular human-animal conflicts that are difficult to resolve. Yeo and Neo (2010) argue that the encroachment of condominiums and landed housing (such as terraced houses, bungalows, etc.) into the fringes of the Bukit Timah Nature Reserve has resulted in the heightened presence of macaques in residents' home spaces. However, the behavioural change of these animals is not solely due to the shrinking space of their living environments. Ironically, the increased number of visitors to the Nature Reserve to "enjoy nature" has also seen more people feeding the monkeys. Indiscriminate feeding has emboldened these primates, making them more aggressive. In that sense, animal lovers have insisted that it is human action that altered the macaques' behaviour.

FIGURE 4.1

A long-tailed macaque with her baby at the fringe of Bukit Timah Nature Reserve, Singapore

Source: Harvey Neo.

FIGURE 4.2

Macaques feeding by the roadside in the western part of Singapore, 2012
Source: Ria Tan.

The macaque example is notable in that, while it received attention from the relevant authorities, the root and resolution of the problem were framed somewhat differently by NGOs and animal lovers, compared to the authorities. As Yeo and Neo (2010) note, while all parties agree that one of the important factors contributing to the conflicts between macaques and humans is the persistence of indiscriminate feeding; animal lovers and animal rights group go further to criticize the complicity of the planning authorities in allowing housing to be built so close to the nature reserves. As noted earlier, housing has always been framed positively in a developmentalist perspective and, furthermore, the might and right of the planning agencies is seldom questioned. In this example then, we see how the contours of the debate are circumscribed in such a way that the framing and possible resolution of environmental conflicts do not problematize key socio-economic tenets of the country. To be sure, this does not mean that animal rights groups *cannot* voice such views. Rather, it suggests that the authorities have chosen to not engage substantively in animal rights protection, restricting themselves solely to framing the root of the conflict as a "behavioural problem" of the people.

The second example concerns the use of captive dolphins by Resorts World Sentosa. For the owners of this theme park, dolphin performances offer genuine enjoyment to visitors and their captivity for this purpose is hence justified. The argument for the release of the dolphins, on the other hand, stresses the cruelty of placing such sentient and intelligent beings in captivity and that such animals have intrinsic value and fundamental rights to roam free in the oceans. As I previously reflected with Ngiam, "thinking through this debate might be a conceptual, ethical, and practical struggle but if we do not take up such a task, we abandon them to those who use Nature to justify… the domination of nature by humans" (Neo and Ngiam 2014, p. 254).

We have further elaborated that the controversy over the captive dolphins has seen the authorities taking a decidedly neutral stance, where they are content to let the owners of the theme park fend off the protests of animal rights groups (led by ACRES) in Singapore. This is despite the complicity of the authorities in, amongst other things, granting permits for the import of wild dolphins, whereas a case could be made for the illegality of such an act (due to the Convention on International Trade in Endangered Species of Wild Fauna and Flora regulations). Compared to the case of the macaques, the authorities were even more removed from this debate. With their palpable absence, the framing of this conflict is reduced to one that does not concern "majority interest" but rather only the narrow interests of animal rights groups. More speculatively, it can be said that the dolphins are understood to be instrumental to the overall attractiveness of the resort, hence opposition to it would not have gotten any traction with the authorities (Neo and Ngiam 2014). In other words, as mentioned earlier, a post-politics of environmentalism will see the emergence and resolution of conflicts compliant to the growth ethos of Singapore. Anbarasi Boopal (2017, p. 41), Deputy Chief Executive of ACRES, reflects that this failure to free the captive dolphins counts as one of the organization's "greatest disappointments".

In both examples above, there were clear, appreciable NGO-led politics that magnified the conflicts in the public sphere and saw varying degrees of engagement with the government. However, the success of their politicization is arguably dependent on the extent to which these issues compromise the socio-economic and developmental ethos. In other words, where the point of contention is deemed to have contravened the "public interest" (as defined by the government), the state will prove to be unyielding and minimally engaging. This point is illustrated more starkly in the next example: the culling of cats in the early 2000s.

The problem of stray cats (and dogs) in Singapore had its genesis in the urbanization process, beginning in the late 1950s (Chan 2016). Cats, which roamed free in the rural areas, began to appear in newly urbanized housing estates. Teo (2011), in her study of stray cats roaming in housing estates, details the tensions between cat lovers and residents who see the cats as a nuisance. This view is aligned with the government's longstanding perception that strays are a "problem" that needs to be solved (Chan 2016, p. 310). On the grounds of public health and to create pleasant living environments, the government for the most part sees urban spaces as spaces of exclusion for such animals. Teo argues against such a stance and calls for a (re)integration of animals into our urban landscapes. The ultimate goal then is geared towards "ameliorating the anthropocentric city and moving towards a place where humans can live morally in concert with a diversity of non-human animals—a 'zoopolis'" (Teo 2011, p. 71). Put another way, it is to assert the fundamental right of stray cats to share our urban space and to recognize the intrinsic value of their very presence. Such a perspective is an admirable, albeit modest reaction against the Anthropocene, insofar as any gesture to mediate the extensive change wrought by humans to the environment should be welcomed. In that sense, populating urban spaces with nature (in this case, cats) is a worthwhile goal. In highlighting this case study, however, one must not forget the myriad ways in which Singapore's environmental impacts extend much further afield (e.g., the importation of sand for reclamation from countries such as Cambodia and Indonesia), often with devastating consequences.

Formed in 1999, the Cat Welfare Society (CWS) is the most prominent animal welfare group in Singapore dedicated to promoting better human-cat relationships in the built environment. While acknowledging the problems that overpopulation of stray cats can bring, the CWS is resolutely against the culling of cats. Instead, since its inception, it has advocated for the neutering and release of strays into the

FIGURE 4.3

Students, monks, and environmental activists gather hand in hand with the local community, in chest-high water to bless and protect the mangrove forests at Lovers' Island (Kaoh Bang កោះ បង and Kaoh Aun កោះ អូន) from sand-dredging in Koh Kong Province, Southwest Cambodia

Source: Mona Simon/Lost World.

FIGURE 4.4

Phalla Vy stands before mountains of sand piled at a storage facility in Singapore, discovering for the first time what happened to the sand that was dredged up and seized from her homeland of Koh Sralau, Koh Kong Province, Southwestern Cambodia

Source: Mona Simon/Lost World.

community as a sustainable solution. By 2003, just three years after it was founded, CWS with the cooperation of AVA (the Agri-food and Veterinary Authority), had neutered ten thousand cats under its "Stray Cat Rehabilitation Scheme" (SCRS). To be sure, culling by AVA still proceeded, albeit at a lower rate, even as they partnered with CWS for this scheme. Nonetheless, given the government's obsession with cleanliness, order, and control, that the SCRS was even launched is testament to the tenacity of NGOs like CWS.

As mentioned earlier, one of the features of a post-politics of environmentalism is that the emergence and resolution of environmental issues strengthens (or at the very least does not weaken) pre-existing political-economic structures in Singapore. Second, the manner in which these issues are resolved veers towards non-confrontational means, such as behind-the-scenes negotiations with the relevant agencies. Third, the narratives surrounding these environmental issues revolve around key motifs of the broader society. The flipside of these features is that any gains in the environmental movement, particularly in championing their specific causes and enrolling the government in their efforts, can be easily unravelled when any of the key motifs of society is contravened.

This was indeed what happened to CWS when, in 2003, the SCRS was terminated without notice. The catalyst behind this was the outbreak of Severe Acute Respiratory Syndrome (SARS) in Singapore, where public health authorities had suspected cats could be a vector for the virus. While this conjecture proved subsequently to be unfounded, overnight "cats started disappearing from the streets" (Lau 2017, p. 29). Meanwhile, with no success in seeking clarifications from AVA as to what was actually happening, a group of animal welfare organizations (led by CWS) called a press conference to publicize their suspicion that a nationwide stealth culling was underway.

This 2003 incident was a textbook example of what an NGO should *not* have done in a post-political Singaporean society. Notwithstanding the refusal by the relevant authorities to confirm if a nationwide culling was indeed underway, in their eyes, to have unilaterally called the government's bluff in a highly publicized press conference was not the "right", consensual way to practise activism. Not least, the advocates went further than just giving a simple press conference, but also conducted a memorial service for all the cats that had been culled. As with previous examples of engagement where the communal interest of the majority was thought to have been threatened, the authorities took a hard, uncompromising stance. This is evinced by the anecdote told by a past Vice President of the CWS about the society's meeting with a cabinet minister after their press conference:

> Finally, a cabinet minister agreed to meet CWS's Director of Operations Dawn Kua and other cat advocates. They discovered that it was not a dialogue but a dressing down. The activists were told they were impeding the clean-up process and threatening the safety of the nation (Lau 2017, p. 30).

After this clash, CWS underwent a decade of stuttering growth before managing to re-launch the sterilization programme in 2011. In the following year, the CWS successfully lobbied the government to begin a pilot project of allowing public housing residents in selected towns to keep cats as pets (this had previously been forbidden). Finally, in a major breakthrough in 2018, AVA appointed CWS as "community mediators" for human-cat conflicts and more importantly, the CWS will be given funds by AVA to perform this responsibility.

Conclusion

One needs to be careful when generalizing about the development of the environmental movement in the last few decades. By some indicators—such as the number of registered environmental groups in Singapore, which grew from less than fifteen in the 1990s to more than forty in 2015 (Green Future Solution 2015)—activism has indeed become more vibrant. In part, this is due to the rallying call of the Anthropocene, where the actions of humans are said to have caused irreversible, negative change to the global environment. These impacts run the gamut from climate change to mass extinctions to the depletion of natural resources. Yet, as the editors of this volume have argued in the introduction, "Anthropocene" as a concept to encapsulate human-environment interaction is still highly contentious. Debate rages over how we should determine the implications of the Anthropocene, as well as what kinds of responses to make at the local and global scale.

For the Singapore government, one might venture that "climate change" is seen as the most obvious product of the Anthropocene.

The National Climate Change Secretariat (NCCS) was established on 1 July 2010 "to develop and implement Singapore's domestic and international policies and strategies to tackle climate change" (NCCS 2020). That the NCCS is under the direct supervision of the Prime Minister's Office shows the importance the government placed on this issue. From a post-political lens, it is also simultaneously a concerted effort for the government to develop the narrative of climate change and its mitigation, thereby circumscribing the contours of climate change politics in Singapore. This narrative does not stray from the core motifs described and elaborated earlier, in that it emphasizes mitigation, adaptation, and most importantly, exploring "green growth" opportunities (in other words, making the proverbial lemons of negative climate change impacts into entrepreneurial lemonade). There is also the fear that if the government does not take any action to set the tone and agenda, "citizens will take their cause to the streets", as our Minister for the Environment and Water Resources warned (cited in *Straits Times*, 21 October 2019). If nothing else, the Anthropocene as a concept is sufficiently galvanizing in rousing citizen activism and also remarkably encompassing in the range of environmental issues that can be folded into it.

Given this reality, the first generalization one can make about the environmental movement in Singapore is that its growth mirrors global trends in both the quantity of groups being formed and the diversity of their interests. In Singapore, for example, more than a third of registered environmental groups are animal-interest organizations. The remaining two-thirds focus on a wide array of special interests, with a slight leaning towards anti-consumerism and nature conservation. For the most part, these groups are focused on local issues.

The second salient characteristic of the recent development of environmentalism in Singapore is the proliferation of social media and how it has enabled different ways of amplifying the causes of environmental groups. This is a clear improvement from the 1990s when the only way the public could hear of environmental activism was through a print media that has a symbiotic relationship with the government.

Third, as discussed earlier, stemming from its perennial goal of making Singapore a "city in a garden", the government is happy to engage with NGOs that focus on "brown issues" such as food wastage, resource conservation, and of late, community-driven urban food farming. Unsurprisingly, these are issues that do not compromise the government's key ethos of growth, development, and communitarianism.

Beyond NGOs, there is also sustained interest from academia in the scientific research of flora and fauna in Singapore. Most representative of this is the Raffles Museum of Biodiversity Research (RMBR), which was renamed the Lee Kong Chian Natural History Museum in 2014. The RMBR itself has an interesting backstory that speaks to the post-colonial anxiety of a young nation. The RMBR was established in 1998 and its collection inherited from the Zoological Reference Collection, which had opened in 1988. The latter had in turn been hived off from the National Museum when it was decided that the National Museum should focus on historical and cultural—not natural—exhibits. The predecessor of the National Museum was the Raffles Museum, established by the British colonizers in the 1870s; its first name change occurred in 1965, as a symbolic assertion of breaking with colonial ties. It is therefore curious that the RMBR was regressively named as such in 1998, harking back to its colonial past. In any case, the most recent name change, to Lee Kong Chian Natural History Museum, pays homage to one of the most famous local philanthropists and finally assumes a complete break from any residual colonial memory.

Finally, following on from the point above, while not diminishing the growth of the environmental movement, one needs to be more circumspect about the prospects of the movement achieving further breakthroughs in the near future. As this chapter has tried to show, the post-political Singapore places subtle restrictions and nudges the environmental movement in specific ways, both in terms of its focus as well as its modes of engagement with the authorities. In that sense, the concept of post-politics critically moderates the hope that "eco-authoritarian" states like China and Singapore can make positive environmental changes where other state formations falter (see also Schneider-Mayerson 2017). Essentially, post-politics tells us that eco-authoritarian states will only pursue environmentalism of their own volition; it further informs us that even when citizens rebel against explicit authoritarian rule, post-political rule can subtly manage such dissent. Hence, while the post-political state (unlike, say, bona fide authoritarian states) does not place overt curbs on the issues NGOs can champion, given the concentration of political power in Singapore, if the societal consensus groomed by the state using long-standing national motifs is breeched, then the repercussions would be palpable, as the CWS experienced. This last point implies that post-politics and authoritarianism (of varying shades) are not mutually exclusive, although one must assume that there is no reason for an extreme authoritarian state to partake in post-politics. That being said, some degrees of authoritarianism do ease the emergence of a post-political society.

Yet when all is said and done, one can still be cautiously optimistic about the future of the environmental movement in Singapore (see also Grundy-Warr and Savage 2017). Working within the confines of a state-mandated and sustained national consensus requires deft activism but it is not insurmountable. In part, this is because the contours for debate and activism are more or less understood by all. Hence, the more astute NGOs would continuously frame and amplify their cause in nuanced ways that do not necessarily shatter the consensus but stretch it with care. Such stretching is an important iterative process between the state and NGOs. One can hope that, eventually, environmental engagement can sidestep the darkest side of post-politics, which demands a constantly submissive demeanour from the NGOs, and progress to a more liberating politics, unfearful of imagining a different Singapore, in a different world.

REFERENCES

Boopal, Anbarasi. 2017. "The Importance of Generating Conversations". In *The Art of Advocacy in Singapore*, edited by Constance Singam and Margaret Thomas. Singapore: Ethos Books.

Campbell, Heather and Robert Marshall. 2002. "Utilitarianism's Bad Breath? A Re-evaluation of the Public Interest Justification for Planning". *Planning Theory* 1, no. 2: 163–87.

Chan, Ying-Kit. 2016. "No Room to Swing a Cat? Animal Treatment and Urban Space in Singapore". *Southeast Asian Studies* 5, no. 2: 305–29.

Cheng, Lim Keak. 1989. "Post-independence Population Planning and Social Development in Singapore". *Geojournal* 18: 163–74.

Chua, Beng Huat. 1995. *Communitarian Ideology and Democracy in Singapore*. London: Routledge.

———. 1997. *Political Legitimacy and Housing: Stakeholding in Singapore*. New York: Routledge.

————. 2000. "The Relative Autonomies of State and Civil Society in Singapore". In *State-Society Relations in Singapore*, edited by Gillian Koh and Ooi Giok Ling. Singapore: Institute of Policy Studies and Oxford University Press.

Goh, Daniel P.S. 2000. "Defending Nature in the 'Garden City': Nature and Social Power in Singapore". PhD dissertation, Department of Sociology, National University of Singapore.

Green Future Solution. 2015. "Singapore Green Landscape 2015". www.greenfuture.sg.

Grundy-Warr, Carl and Victor R. Savage. 2017. "Singapore: Sustaining a Global City-state and the Challenges of Environmental Governance in the Twenty-first Century". In *Routledge Handbook of the Environment in Southeast Asia*, edited by Philip Hirsch. New York: Routledge.

Kong, Lily. 1991. "'Environment' as a Social Concern: Democratizing Public Arenas in Singapore?" *Sojourn: Journal of Social Issues in Southeast Asia* 9, no. 2: 277–87.

Lau, Veron. 2017. "Speaking up for Singapore's Felines". In *The Art of Advocacy in Singapore*, edited by Constance Singam and Margaret Thomas. Singapore: Ethos Books.

National Climate Change Secretariat (NCCS). 2020. "About NCCS". www.nccs.gov.sg (accessed 6 March 2020).

Nature News. 1992. *Nature Society Singapore Newsletter*. Singapore: NSS.

————. 1993. *Nature Society Singapore Newsletter*. Singapore: NSS.

Nature Society Singapore (NSS). 1990. *Master Plan for the Conservation of Nature in Singapore*. Singapore: NSS.

————. 1991. *Conservation Proposal for Marina South*. Singapore: NSS.

Neo, Harvey. 2007. "Challenging the Developmental State: Nature Conservation in Singapore". *Asia Pacific Viewpoint* 48, no. 2: 186–99.

————. 2010. "The Potential of Large Scale Urban Waste Recycling: A Case Study of the National Recycling Programme in Singapore". *Society and Natural Resources* 23, no. 9: 872–87.

————. 2013. "Nature and the Environment as an Evolving Concern in Urban Singapore". In *Changing Landscapes of Singapore*, edited by Elaine Lynn-Ee Ho, Wong Chih Yuan, and Kamalini Ramdas. Singapore: National University of Singapore Press.

————. 2015. "Placing Pig Farming in Post-independence Singapore: Community, Development and Landscapes of Rurality". In *Food, Foodways and Foodscapes: Culture, Community and Consumption in Post-Colonial Singapore*, edited by Lily Kong and Vineeta Sinha. Singapore: World Scientific.

Neo, Harvey and Cheng Ying Chua. 2017. "Beyond Inclusion and Exclusion: Community Gardens as Spaces of Responsibility". *Annals of the Association of American Geographers* 107, no. 3: 666–81.

Neo, Harvey and Jing Zhi Ngiam. 2014. "Contesting Captive Cetaceans: (I) legal Spaces and the Nature of Dolphins in Urban Singapore". *Social and Cultural Geography* 15, no. 3: 235–54.

Perry, Matthew, Lily Kong, and Brenda Yeoh. 1997. *Singapore: A Developmental City State*. New York: Wiley.

PuruShotam, Nirmala. 1998. *Negotiating Language, Constructing Race: Disciplining Difference in Singapore*. New York: Mouton de Gruyter.

Schneider-Mayerson, Matthew. 2017. "Some Islands Will Rise: Singapore in the Anthropocene". *Resilience* 4, no. 2–3: 166–84.

Seow, Francis T. 1998. *The Media Enthralled: Singapore Revisited*. Boulder, Colorado: Lynne Rienner Publishers.

Singam, Constance. 2017. "When Ordinary People Do Extraordinary Things". In *The Art of Advocacy in Singapore*, edited by Constance Singam and Margaret Thomas. Singapore: Ethos Books.

Singapore Statutes. 1966 [2014]. *Societies Act: Chapter 311*. Original Enactment: Act 56 of 1966 (Revised Edition 2014). sso.agc.gov.sg/Act/SA1966.

Straits Times. 1992. "Rare ducks' pond being filled at Marina South". *Straits Times*, 20 April 1992.

———. 1992. "Work to fill ponds in Marina South stopped". *Straits Times*, 24 April 1992.

———. 1992. "ENV fills in ducks' pond despite appeals". *Straits Times*, 12 May 1992.

———. 1993. "Khatib Bongsu added to list of conservation sites". *Straits Times*, 20 September 1993.

———. 1994. "Not just for the birds – Senoko land will be developed". *Straits Times*, 19 March 1994.

———. 1998. "Tighten HDB rules to help conserve land". *Straits Times*, 27 August 1998.

———. 2002. "NTUC Chief suggests less CPF for housing". *Straits Times*, 4 April 2002.

———. 2002. "Sengkang four room flats snapped up". *Straits Times*, 12 April 2002.

———. 2002. "Are Singaporeans sinking too much into property?" *Straits Times*, 13 April 2002.

———. 2002. "A home may cost more than you think". *Straits Times*, 12 May 2002.

Swyngedouw, Erik. 2007. "Impossible 'Sustainability' and the Postpolitical Condition". In *The Sustainable Development Paradox*, edited by Rob J. Krueger and David Gibbs. New York: The Guilford Press.

Tan, Leon and Harvey Neo. 2009. "'Community in Bloom': Local Participation of Community Gardens in Urban Singapore". *Local Environment* 14, no. 6: 529–39.

Teo, Pamela. 2011. "Advocating a Place for Cats in Singapore". Honours
    dissertation, Department of Geography, National University of Singapore.
Tremewan, Chris. 1994. *The Political Economy of Social Control in Singapore*. New
    York: St. Martin's Press.
Urban Redevelopment Authority (URA). 1991. *Living the Next Lap*. Singapore:
    URA.
Yeo, Jun Han and Harvey Neo. 2010. "Monkey Business: Human-Animal Conflicts
    in Urban Singapore". *Social and Cultural Geography* 11, no. 7: 681–700.

5

ENVIRONMENTAL MOVEMENTS IN THE PHILIPPINES: CONTESTATION FOR JUSTICE IN THE ANTHROPOCENE

Francisco A. Magno

From the 1970s to the mid-1980s, environmental advocacy in the Philippines was subsumed within the broader demands of the democratic struggle. Elsewhere in Asia, opposition to authoritarianism triggered a strong partnership between environmental movements and democracy movements (Lee et al. 1999). The democratic transition in the late-1980s opened up political opportunities for the environmental movements to voice their agenda for change in the 1990s (Magno 1999). While democratization broke new ground for collaboration between civil society and government reformers, the politics of contention continued to simmer in resource conflict zones in the twenty-first century.

　　This chapter examines how political arrangements have influenced environmentalism, and conversely, how environmental movements have affected national politics in the Philippines in the past two decades. These processes are analysed through the framework of environmental justice and in the context of the historical period identified as the Anthropocene. According to Crutzen's seminal article (2002), the Anthropocene refers to the "human-dominated geological epoch" that started in the latter part of the eighteenth century. The notion has thus become a marker for the "profound, global and irreversible alterations of the Earth's ecosystems by collective human activity" (Cho 2014, p. 3). But the epochal shift characterized by human-driven environmental changes, including pollution, natural resource degradation, water scarcity, and climate change, are also accompanied by growing social inequalities (Stengers 2015). In this regard, the use of an environmental justice lens highlights "how the results of environmental and climatic change became differently distributed over the human populations of the world and which communities have carried the burden of the 'ecological footprints' of commodity consumption" (Lane 2015, p. 11).

In the Philippines, centuries of Spanish domination imposed a radically uneven access to land and natural resources, which has never been challenged by a comprehensive land reform programme (as happened, for instance, in Taiwan and Japan after World War Two). The landed nobility (*latifundistas*) has survived until today, metamorphosed into a political elite and a ruling class of capitalists. In reaction, social activists, progressive Church leaders, and trade union organizers have encouraged vulnerable communities to develop an "environmentalism of the poor".[1] In the face of the expanding state and commercial pressures of a neoliberal political economy, the poor struggle to protect the commons. These are often battles waged to retain control over natural resources tied up with basic local income sources. In other words, in a country like the Philippines where about a quarter of the population remains under the poverty line, environmental movements are triggered by threats to people's survival.

Moreover, environmental risks generally cause more distress to vulnerable or marginalized groups for they can less easily protect themselves or move away from the source of the risks (Pellow 2018). The uneven distribution of environmental benefits and burdens across social groups and geographical regions also fosters conflict throughout the production and consumption chains (Avila-Calero 2017, p. 994). These factors explain why environmental justice movements have usually originated in localized, place-based movements (Sicotte and Brulle 2018, p. 32). Support for these movements must avoid two kinds of traps: one is a tendency to pity and commiserate with marginalized groups; the other is a temptation to romanticize them or overestimate their agency. Nevertheless, their capacity for contestation and collective action provides the means to reassert cultural values, and to protect the land both from contamination and private appropriation (Anguelovski and Martínez-Alier 2014, p. 168).

An archipelagic nation with more than 7,000 islands, the Philippines used to enjoy a fabulous diversity of flora and fauna, as well as abundant mineral deposits. However, since the mid-1960s, growing exploitation of these resources has pushed the country into an "ecological deficit".[2] In 2008, the Philippines already required more than twice the capacity of its natural resources. Such "overspending" has persisted despite clear evidence of serious damage, from deforestation and depleted fisheries to ever greater climate instability (Global Footprint Network 2012, p. 20). Moreover, due to rapid population growth, the per capita biocapacity has decreased by 44 per cent (Global Footprint Network 2015).

In recent decades, forest degradation, mining pollution and, more recently, the effects of global warming have counted among the most salient issues addressed by the environmental justice movement in the Philippines. These three cases can also be seen as particularly representative of the Anthropocene. The Philippines has become especially vulnerable to strong typhoons, which a growing scientific consensus maintains are a direct consequence of global warming. Not only has the drastic depletion of natural resources continued unabated, increasingly violent typhoons have killed thousands of Filipinos and devastated their fragile habitats, affecting in particular impoverished people living in coastal areas. The mobilization for climate justice in the Philippines points to the liability of large global emitters of greenhouse gases (GHG), such as the United States, China, Europe, etc. But Filipino activists do not exempt the ruling elites of their country who, despite the rise in alarming event, have maintained their business as usual, namely grabbing and extracting land resources, and polluting the atmosphere with more coal burning.

This chapter therefore puts the emphasis on environmental movements that have been engaged against the powerful socio-economic forces driving these types of environmental damage. I consider the Anthropocene under the particular national context of blatant environmental injustices, set by a long legacy of uneven access to and control of natural resources. The following sections analyse local place-based efforts to defend the community and ecosystem from contamination and private appropriation. I start with citizen action in forest and fishery zones; second, comes the anti-coal movement; and the final section describes the movement for climate justice characterized by innovative advocacy anchored on web-based platforms, legal reforms, and human rights mechanisms. The strategic value of these engagements increases with their vertical links to national and international campaigns for environmental justice.

From Dictatorship to Democracy in a Weak State

A persistent problem in the Philippines has been the weakness of the state. The structural fragility of public institutions has fostered an uneven access to natural resources in which particularistic elite interests are favoured at the expense of local communities. The rapid expansion of the country's ecological deficit coincided with a political economy characterized by the allocation of natural resource permits for patronage purposes. Preferential access to these resources was awarded to political elites, as well as to friends and relatives of the regime in power. In the forestry sector, the state's issuance of Timber License Agreements (TLAs) was a highly politicized affair. Preferential access to TLAs has traditionally gone to private entities closely linked with power brokers like legislators, governors, mayors, and military officials. During the martial law period, timber licences were issued to close political allies of the Marcos regime (Magno 1992, p. 82).

As the dictatorship held sway from 1972 to 1986, the environmental movements were kept busy with the fight to restore democracy. With the return of formal democracy, collective action was recalibrated towards pushing the environmental agenda through the new governance mechanisms. The 1987 Constitution established in the post-authoritarian period stipulates that the state "shall protect and advance the right of the people to a balanced and healthful ecology in accord with the rhythm and harmony of nature" (Article 1). The Constitution further encourages non-governmental, community-based, or sectoral organizations promoting welfare. Guided by this fundamental law, legislation on governance and ecology has emphasized the participation of civil society in decision-making at both national and subnational levels.

Democracy may have been restored, but it is perched on the back of a weak state. The country would appear to have a strong legal design for public participation but in practice suffers from low participatory governance over environmental matters (Gerra 2016, p. 205). A significant list of environmental laws was enacted after the adoption of the 1987 Constitution. However, there is an enforcement gap, especially with respect to programme coordination. Many enforcement and regulatory bodies function in silos, insulated structures that are incapable of interoperability (Gonzalez 2017, p. 87). So, while the national economic planning agency acknowledges that there are sufficient rules and regulations mandating the sustainable use of resources, the weak and fragmented institutional infrastructure hinders effective policy implementation (NEDA 2017, p. 320).

The weak state has to contend with the threat of elite capture. There are localized sources of land use and environmental degradation linked to power relations in society that should not be taken for granted (Holden 2018, p. 23). Land policies are not created or carried out in a vacuum; as part of prevailing power arrangements, they tend to favour landed elites as well as powerful state officials and bureaucrats (Borras and Franco 2012, p. 50). Even if community and ancestral domain tenure rights are recognized by the national government, contending resource claims are common in the uplands, mountainous areas with slopes of 18 per cent and above (as defined under the Revised Forestry Reform Code). This results from the overlapping of formal and informal tenure arrangements there; while the former are prone to elite capture, the latter persist owing in part to the inability of the state to monitor these areas (Verbrugge et al. 2015, p. 52). Forest frontiers, such as the northern Sierra Madre (in the northeast of Luzon, see Map 5.1), suffer from environmental stress due to land use transitions, poverty, rapid social change, and chaotic and unaccountable governance (Van der Ploeg et al. 2016, p. 156).

The state's environmental authority in forest areas is highly precarious. There are only two thousand forest rangers to stop illegal loggers. In 2011, President Benigno Aquino III signed an executive order that prohibited timber cutting in natural and residual forests nationwide to address deforestation. The illegal timber trade persisted, however, backed up by coercive force. In the three-year span following the declaration, twenty forest rangers were killed trying to enforce the ban (Agence France Press 2012).

The election of Rodrigo Duterte in the 2016 elections led to political change with the installation of a populist presidency, but did little to improve the effectiveness of the country's formal environmental protections. President Duterte declared during his first State of the Nation address on 25 July 2016 that the government would protect the rural and indigenous communities and safeguard the environment. But while strong in rhetoric, populism proved to be wanting in performance. Aside from its failure to provide full support for the confirmation of its appointee to the highest post in the environment agency, the Duterte administration has thus far been unable to protect local communities and ecological systems from influential resource users who have exacerbated Anthropocenic climate change. Furthermore, the oversubscription of police forces in waging a drug war that has led to extrajudicial killings in urban areas has contributed to government neglect in regard to other important concerns, such as curbing the destructive environmental practices in the countryside or protecting those who protest against them.

Environmental protection is indeed a dangerous business. Globally, at least two hundred community activists, NGO workers, and other civilians on the frontlines of environmental defense were reported murdered in 2016. During that year, twenty-eight environmental killings were registered in the Philippines, with only Brazil and Colombia tallying more such murders. Similar to other countries on the hotspot list, the deaths in the Philippines are escalating as communities resist efforts by powerful economic interests to control increasingly scarce natural resources (Global Witness 2016).

As in many other countries, the fight for environmental justice in the Philippines is largely carried out through "contentious politics" (Tilly and Tarrow 2015) to open up opportunity structures and influence policy action. Political spaces are widened when social movements gain allies among the elite (Pellow 2018), or activists may take government positions and tackle issues that overlap with social movements (Pettinicchio 2012, p. 502). To create political opportunities, environmental movements must therefore expand their network of alliances, obtain public posts, or at least find potential allies in the state. But the menace of forced disappearance and extrajudicial killings render political contacts uncertain. Local politicians who serve as brokers can, if they wish, circumvent regulations to favour particularistic business interests and frustrate demands for environmental justice. Moreover, where the state is weak, it takes a long time for public decisions to be enforced on the ground, and in the meantime, people can be killed. In places like Mindanao, which is exposed to the guerilla warfare waged by communist and Islamic groups—and where Duterte first practised his political culture of violence—extrajudicial killings have become almost part of the "local culture".

The Philippine case illustrates how the continuity of a weak state serves as a key feature in a political ecosystem that encourages environmental killings. The international watchdog organization Global Witness reports that, since it started releasing data on environment-related murders in 2012, the Philippines has consistently posted the greatest number of deaths in Asia of people who resist illegal logging, destructive mining, or corrupt agribusiness. Indeed, Global Witness pointed out that, in 2018, "this trend of spiraling violence reached a disturbing new landmark: the Philippines became the country with the highest total number of such killings in the world" (Global Witness 2019, p. 3). A particularly dangerous field for environmental activists is the battle against logging companies, as we will see in the next section.

MAP 5.1

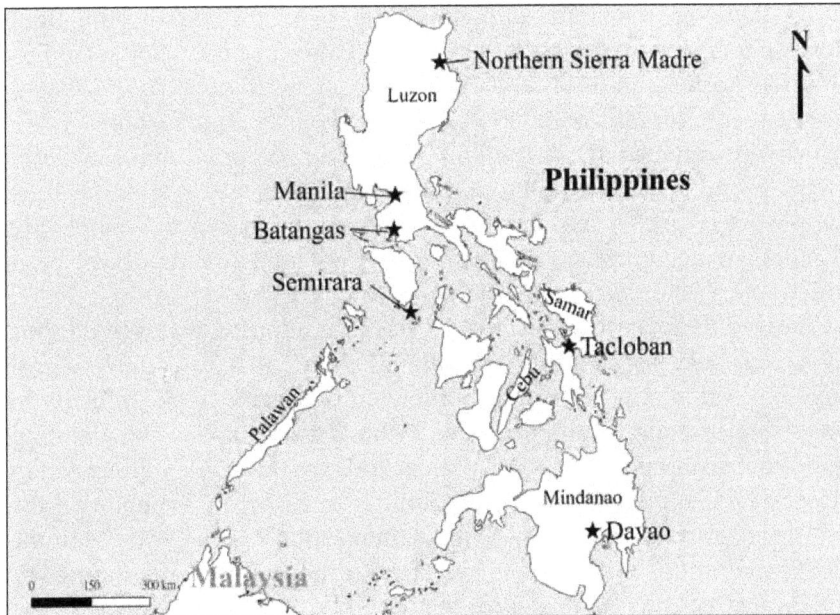

Selected sites of environmental disputes in the Philippines

Source: QGIS and Natural Earth.

Environmental Justice Against Forest Degradation

Over the last twenty years, the environmental movements that emerged in the Philippines have been focused on efforts to promote environmental justice in addressing the harm caused by forest degradation, mining pollution, and the increasingly violent typhoons caused by global warming. Given the weak autonomy and limited capacity of state actors to enforce regulations in distressed ecosystems, the fight for environmental justice requires the formation of social activism. A recurring theme in the environmental movement is the insistence of local communities to take direct action to protect their livelihoods and ecosystem. Local practices can also be used to critique the Western anthropocentrism that excludes indigenous ecocentric ontologies (Simangan 2019, p. 576). Nevertheless, as noted above, environmental activism can be a perilous exercise. In cases documented by Global Witness, environmental killings have attended efforts by local civil society and indigenous communities to protect upland and agro-forestry systems in the provinces of Palawan and Bukidnon (the latter on Mindanao island, see Map 5.1).

In Palawan province, known for its rich biodiversity, the fight against forest degradation is led by the Palawan NGO Network, Inc. (PNNI). Formed in 1991, the PNNI is composed of thirty-four non-governmental organizations (NGOs) and people's organizations (POs). It actively campaigns for the enforcement of the environmental laws in the province, including those that pertain to illegal logging. But the simple act of asking that laws be respected has proved to be a deadly business: a dozen members of the environmental coalition have been killed since 2001 (*Straits Times* 2017).

Instead of cowering in fear, the PNNI has adopted disruptive forms of action, such as arresting the citizens. Its goal is to counter illegal logging and derail operations that would otherwise be difficult to prosecute in court. Another PNNI tactic is to confiscate woodcutting and other equipment from violators of forestry laws. Such direct action relies on the support of local communities to gather information on the modus operandi of the illegal loggers. Interestingly, some of those in the PNNI operations team once worked with the logging and smuggling syndicates before crossing over to the other side (Anda 2010).

In addition, the PNNI has built a network of trained paralegal volunteers from the affected communities who have cooperated with it and served as intelligence assets. Over the past two decades, the paralegal enforcers of PNNI have confiscated more than seven hundred chainsaws, and even a fishing vessel that was used to smuggle logs and mangrove tanbark to Malaysia (AFP 2017). Provincial authorities who are supposed to enforce environmental regulations have themselves been accused of illegal logging. Proof of that corruption was found in the chainsaws used in clearing mangrove areas: after being confiscated by the PNNI, they were traced to business interests linked to the provincial governor (Global Witness 2019, p. 22). For these logging companies, long-term care of the forests is not an issue; only immediate profits count, and a weak state means greater opportunities to corrupt the local political elite.

In Bukidnon province, indigenous communities have tried to reclaim their rights to their ancestral forestlands from agribusiness companies supported by the government. The case of the Manobo Pulanguihon indigenous land claims represented by the Tribal Indigenous Oppressed Group Association (TINDOGA) presents a good illustration. In 2011, TINDOGA sought to regain control of their ancestral domain by building houses on land occupied by the Montalvan Ranch and the Kiantig Development Corporation, in which a municipal mayor had huge proprietary interests (Global Witness 2019, p. 12). Kiantig argued that the company had obtained a long-term Forest and Land Grazing Lease Agreement from the Department of Environment and Natural Resources (DENR). In addition, Kiantig had signed a contract with Dole Philippines, Inc., while the Montalvan Ranch had one with Del Monte Philippines. It was therefore obvious that their goal was to grow pineapples, not to protect the forest. Having been turned back in 2011 by armed men as they attempted to set up houses on indigenous soil, TINDOGA persevered by setting up protest camps, organizing rallies, and petitioning government officials (Global Witness 2019, p. 12).

A 2012 resolution signed by the National Commission on Indigenous People (NCIP)—the primary government agency that recognizes the ancestral domains of indigenous peoples—indicates "that the land Kiantig operates on, along with the land used by the Montalvan Ranch, was one of the four parcels of land stolen from the indigenous people by Don Manolo Fortich in 1921". The NCIP ruled in 2014 to return the land to the Manobo Pulanguihon. In the context of a weak state, however, public decisions are vaguely interpreted and not forcefully implemented on the ground. The local companies thus maintained de facto resource control, using coercion to prevent the indigenous people from reclaiming their land. A spate of violence exploded as the company's guards opened fire on the protesting TINDOGA community in 2015. In 2017, the secretary general of TINDOGA was killed. Despite the loss of their leader, the TINDOGA activists persisted with their courageous actions and ultimately convinced the NCIP to obtain police and military assistance to evict Kiantig and Montalvan and help the 480 families from the Manobo Pulanguihon to reclaim their ancestral land (Global Witness 2019, p. 13).

Anti-Coal Mining Movement

After languishing in the cellar as the "sick man of Asia" during the long years of authoritarianism, the Philippines rebounded with an economy that has grown consistently over the past decade. But this evolution has led to greater demand for energy, including that from coal-fired power plants, which produces soil, water, and air pollution. The fight against such pollution has thus become an important issue for the environmental justice movement.

The expansionary path taken by the country has driven new investments in the energy sector. Since the adoption of the Philippine Energy Plan 2008–2030, there has been a significant increase in coal-mining permits. In 2015 alone, environmental compliance certificates for the construction of twenty-one new coal-fired plants were issued. As of 2017, the Department of Energy (DOE) data indicated an installed generating capacity of 22,728 megawatts nationwide, with the bulk (8,049 megawatts) coming from coal-fired power plants (Flores 2018).

The rise in coal-mining projects and their negative environmental spillovers has provided the impetus for an explosion of anti-pollution protests in many parts of the country. In fact, almost all the proposed coal plants have been met by protests from local communities and stakeholders. Protest involves the collective use of unconventional modes of political participation to convince authorities to support a group's agenda; this is a key element that distinguishes social movements from routine political actors (Taylor and Van Dyke 2004, p. 263). In the anti-coal movement, the unconventional act of the prayer rally is a common feature in the protest repertoire. This reflects the active participation of the Catholic Church in the instances of contestation.

The Southern Luzon province of Batangas became a hotbed of protest against coal-mining activities. The *Alyansa Tigil Muna* (Alliance to Stop Mining), an environmental NGO, called for the cancellation of mining permits in the municipality of Lobo in Batangas province during a prayer rally on September 2015. In a position paper submitted to the DENR, the group referred to the municipality as part of the Verde Island Passage, which was designated in 1978 as a marine reserve by presidential proclamation and thereafter declared a tourist area by the Department of Tourism. The Archdiocesan Ministry on the Environment, which is a special unit of the Catholic Church, urged the DENR to uphold the ecological integrity of the town.

In another part of the province, the Church also backed a local movement of fishermen and other concerned citizens to stop a proposed 600-megawatt coal plant in Batangas City. In February 2015, the priests organized a prayer walk attended by three thousand people. Two months later, some three hundred Catholic priests, led by Lipa City Archbishop Ramon Arguelles, held a prayer rally before proceeding to a committee hearing called by the Batangas City Council to decide whether to issue a location permit for the project (Algo 2016).

Around ten thousand people marched in Batangas City to express their opposition to the coal plant in May 2016. The protest highlighted a national campaign called "Break Free Batangas! Break Free the Philippines!" (*Piglas Batangas! Piglas Pilipinas!*). The local anti-coal groups were joined by affected communities in other provinces, as well as civil society organizations from Metro Manila and other provinces in Southern Luzon (Algo 2016). In August 2017, the DENR held a public hearing on the coal plant in Batangas City, where various organizations—including the Philippine Movement for Climate Justice, Greenpeace, Health Care without Harm, and Archdiocesan Ministry on the Environment—expressed their opposition to the project. As of November 2018, the environmental movement appeared to have effectively derailed this coal project.

In the province of South Cotabato in Southern Mindanao, the members of the clergy from the Marbel Diocese issued a statement in November 2017 opposing the plan to allow coal mining in the town of Lake Sebu. The church leaders said coal mining should not be permitted because of a standing open-pit mining ban under the 2010 Provincial Environment Code of South Cotabato. In addition, the Bishop of Marbel released a statement with a strong claim that coal mining would lead to environmental plunder as well as the displacement of up to thirteen hundred tribal people (Catholic News Service 2017).

The active participation of the Church in supporting the local movement has led to positive outcomes on the island of Samar, where all three provinces adopted policies that banned mining. In 2003, Western Samar imposed a fifty-year moratorium on large-scale mining, while Eastern Samar declared an indefinite halt to the development of any new large-scale mines. Northern Samar followed suit in 2007 by disallowing all forms of large-scale mining for fifty years (Holden 2012, p. 851).

Coal mining and combustion processes bear grave toxic effects for the health of both people and the environment. Environmental justice movements have taken on a broader vision of health in their relationship to the social, ecological, cultural, and spiritual production of life. In this regard, health, democracy, and well-being concerns are connected and must have priority over private property and excessively economic-oriented social policies (Porto et al. 2016, p. 121). The anti-coal mining movement emphasizes the need to phase out coal plants and mines and to shift instead towards renewable energy. Unsurprisingly, the mining industry and environmental movements are often at loggerheads at the national level, as well as at local sites. The strife has been worsened by the continuing failure of Congress to pass a National Land Use Act because mining areas often neglect property rights (De La Cruz 2012). The ongoing dependence on coal energy is inconsistent with the country's commitments under the 2015 Paris Agreement (Algo 2016). While the state should step in, especially when policy lines are blurred, it rarely does.

One window of political opportunity to change that situation opened when the election of Duterte as president in 2016 led to the appointment of Regina Lopez as Secretary of DENR. Lopez was known for her anti-mining position, with the assertion that low-income farming and fishing communities were negatively affected by mining operations. She likewise disapproved of coal-powered plants and insisted that they do not provide cheap sources of energy but rather end up compromising the health and income of host communities (Yee 2016). In February 2017, as the new environment chief, she ordered the closure of twenty-three mining operations as well as the suspension of five other firms related to mining activities (Passion 2017).

This controversial decision did not sit well with the mining industry and key government officials, who accused the DENR of not following due process in its audit of mining activities (Santos 2017). In addition, the Department of Finance estimated a total revenue loss of 821 million pesos from sixteen local government units once the closure and suspension orders took effect. With strong lobbying by the mining industry and only weak endorsement from fellow cabinet officials, Lopez had to face three hearings from the Commission on Appointments, which is composed of twelve senators and twelve congressmen (Alvarez 2017). The legislators questioned her technical competence to lead the environment agency, and she was eventually dismissed from her post as DENR Secretary. Anti-coal mining activists thus lost an important ally in the government and with her a prime window of political opportunity. However, the localized mobilizations against coal mining gained ground through links with institutional activists in the state, and also with foreign NGOs. This effort to mediatize the conflicts beyond national borders has become an imperative to resist the projects of certain economic groups that act globally (Da Rocha et al. 2018, p. 717). But this is slow and patient work, which starts by developing national alliances.

Scaling-up the Movement for Climate Action

The first reason that local groups look for support from larger networks is to influence public policies that are decided in urban centres or within the premises of centralized government agencies (Bautista 2001, p. 211). Local campaigns have a better chance of elevating their demands to the status of national issues when they frame those concerns as translocal issues by networking with others with similar grievances. They are most likely to do this with the support of non-local actors like national NGO networks. Such assistance is given when the issue concerns a problematic government policy, and is sustained so long as that issue remains nationally salient for those organizations (Rootes 2013, p. 96).

As aptly put by Passy and Monsch (2014, p. 42), "being bridged to the contentious opportunity by networks leads activists to a higher degree of participation. *Networks are thus a crucial factor in bringing people to higher level of commitment*; that is, to engage in a more costly form of activism" (emphasis in the original). Broad coalitions are formed when organizations with shared concerns about the environment come together and are expected to engage in collective action and to be collaboratively networked (Saunders 2007, p. 240). And according to Di Gregorio (2012, p. 19), "network density in coalition work is predominantly driven by underlying communication processes among social movement organizations that share similar values and a common discourse".

The campaign against a coal plant in Batangas City in 2016, for example, has received support from the Philippine Movement for Climate Justice (PMCJ), a national network of 103 organizations representing fishing, farming, and forest communities, as well as indigenous people and environmental groups (Amilhamja and Regis 2017). The PMCJ has further invited the Green Thumb Coalition, *Alyansa Tigil Mina* (Alliance to Stop Mining), the Centre for Energy, Ecology and Development, and Alternative Law Groups, to join in staging a protest rally at the DENR central office in Quezon City on July 2017. The environmental groups urged the government to implement the policies on mining regulation and ecological protection programmes. The groups also criticized the decision of the Commission on Appointments to deny the confirmation of anti-mining advocate Lopez as DENR Secretary (Amilhamja and Regis 2017).

The call for environmental justice has also provided a unifying theme for building networks of civil society at the local, national, and international levels. In the Philippines, social movements, religious associations, and other civil society groups united to call for a strong and fair global climate agreement at the 2015 Paris Talks. Likewise, a protest caravan traversed across local coal hotspots from Semirara Island in Antique province to Batangas province, culminating in a 20,000-person-strong march in Manila. The Philippine Movement for Climate Justice played a leading role in forging connections between different organizations across the country into a national alliance. It has, moreover, developed links with the Thai Climate Justice Network and the Indonesian Civil Society Forum on Climate Justice (Chatterton et al. 2012).

A key feature of recent social movements has been the cross-national diffusion of protest ideas and actions through the adaption of similar forms of protest practices (Vicari 2014, p. 93). Or as Temper et al. (2015, p. 256) put it, "local political ecologies are becoming increasingly transnational and interlinked across space". Environmental actors at the grassroots level are linking local activities to similar efforts in other countries; the result is a network that is transnational in character. In order to exchange knowledge over national boundaries, these NGOs "are building co-activist strategies that address the concerns of both partners in a more effective way" (Pangsapa 2014, p. 48).

In recent years, the Philippine environmental movement has been more and more permeable to this transnational flow of ideas and practices of collective action. During the Rise for Climate Global Action in September 2018, some thousand events were organized in more than ninety countries to coincide with the three-day Global Climate Action Summit in San Francisco. The protest actions were meant to deliver two key messages. The first is to shift to a world powered by renewable energy rather than the earth-warming gas, oil, and coal. The second is to protect the people who are most vulnerable to the risks posed by rising seas and extreme weather patterns (Gascon 2018).

In Manila, hundreds of people took part in this climate action by marching through the streets to oppose the country's deep reliance on dirty energy sources like coal. The Oriang Women's Group joined the march to point out that the rising cost of rice and the importation of fish are symptoms of the neglect of natural resources, and how these affect the small farmers and fishermen who rely on them for their livelihood. At the same time, in Bangkok, dozens of workers

FIGURE 5.1

Catholic nuns participating in the march for climate justice in Manila, November 2015

Source: March for Climate Justice Pilipinas (www.climatejusticemarch.org).

and fishermen from the Gulf of Thailand, whose economic security is threatened by rising sea levels and coastal erosion caused by climate change, also joined the protest. Along with Manila and Jakarta, the Thai capital is projected to be among the world's urban areas most affected by climate change (AFP 2018).

The first two decades of the twenty-first century have seen the conceptual birth of the Anthropocene, that is, the moment when humans admitted that they had a geological impact on the planet. This awareness has been driven by global trends, primarily climate change, but also by economic liberalization and migration. This latter trend has a special resonance in the Philippines, where many people rely on money sent from migrant workers situated around the world. As global integration deepens, the synchronicity and connectedness of civil society responses come into play (Almeida and Chase-Dunn 2018, p. 191). Indeed, the demand for environmental justice provides a good platform for the formation of new coalitions, increasing solidarity between NGOs and state actors from developing countries (Allan and Hadden 2017, p. 601). It challenges the injustice that produces environmental spillovers, to the point that only the most privileged can remain immune to the disastrous effects of fossil fuel extraction and transport, the heat waves, droughts, storms, and flooding (Sicotte and Brulle 2018, p. 33).

Climate Justice and Web Activism

Collective action has inspired people to fight for climate justice by rallying in the streets, and in the online world to sign a petition or donate money (Dalton 2015). In 2013, the PMCJ launched the *Cut n' be Just* Web campaign to pressure industrialized countries to effectuate bold reductions in their greenhouse gas emissions. Referring to the Germanwatch Climate Risk Index, the call for signatures stressed that the Philippines ranked as "the fourth most vulnerable country to the damaging effects of climate change".[3] This appeal came after several years of devastating tropical cyclones and storms as a consequence of the climate crisis, which the PMCJ blamed squarely on the rich, industrialized countries and their failure to meet their obligations under the various climate accords. The online petition thus aimed to bring the demands of affected Filipinos directly to those countries' officials, urging them to undertake huge cuts in their greenhouse gas emissions to avoid the crisis reaching catastrophic proportions. The campaign mobilized university students and other writers to post Internet articles and blogs on climate change and to demand climate justice; it furthermore sought reparations for both past and future damage suffered by developing countries. Though modest, this online movement added to similar initiatives from other countries. After the failure of the Copenhagen summit in 2009, initiatives of this sort contributed to give a new impetus to the movement for climate justice before the negotiations leading up to the Paris Agreement in 2015.

Web activism played also a big role in the success of the 2016 campaign against the construction of a coal-fired power plant in the village (*barangay*) of Sawang Calero in Cebu City. Mindful of the negative health effects of the project, concerned citizens initiated a Change.org petition against the corporation that proposed the plant. The online campaign helped to disseminate information on the planned energy investment. NGOs from Cebu and Manila boosted the cause online by publishing material about the impact of coal on the environment and people's health. In response, the Cebu City Council finally decided in April 2016 to reject the coal plant proposal (*Mindanao Examiner* 2013).

To reflect on the lessons gained from web activism, a Climate Action PH workshop was organized by the online news website Rappler and the Climate Reality Project Philippines in November 2016. It was attended by various NGOs, including the Philippine Movement for Climate Justice, Oscar M. Lopez Center, Seed4Com, Sanlakas, and Greenpeace Southeast Asia. The victorious anti-coal resistance in Cebu was presented as a strategic case for adaptation to other battles, particularly in its use of social media to promote environmental justice. Another case of web activism that was discussed during the workshop was the National Youth Commission's climate change advocacy programme. As part of this effort, the agency launched an online campaign in cooperation with MovePH, its social media partner, which garnered over three million pledges from young Filipinos to help reduce carbon emissions (Matabuena 2016). As it navigates within a highly global context, the movement for climate justice in the Philippines—even more than other social movements—needs to widen its utilization of the Internet and social media in pursuit of communication and organizational aspirations, as well as for mobilizing resources and supporters (Ackland and O'Neil 2011). In the last sections, we look at another form of mobilization: litigation.

The Court as Terrain of Environmental Struggle

The environmental movement has been a driving force towards the inclusion of rights-based approaches in the use of natural resources and the environment in legal reforms. In the Philippines, environmental justice is a guaranteed state policy (UNDP 2014, p. 12).

In 2008, the Supreme Court designated 117 trial courts as environmental courts, vested with the jurisdiction to handle cases dealing with environmental conflict. The following year, the court organized a national forum on environmental justice and, in 2010, it certified new Rules of Procedure for Environmental Cases, which were seen as a world first and a vital reform in promoting access to justice for the poor in environmental matters (UNDP 2014, p. 15). These legal improvements were heartily welcomed by environmental NGOs. The new Rules came with a citizen's suit as a legal option that local communities can use to ask for the suspension of development activities that endanger the environment. Under the procedure called the Writ of Kalikasan (Writ of Nature), the Supreme Court or the Court of Appeals can issue a temporary or permanent order to protect the environmental rights of communities.[4]

In June 2017, several environmental groups and individuals tested the waters by filing a Writ of Kalikasan petition with the Supreme Court against two key government agencies, namely the DOE and the DENR, for failing to protect the environment.[5] The petitioners reminded the court that the DOE is mandated under the Renewable Energy Act to decrease national reliance on fossil fuels. The DENR, for its part, is required by the Clean Air Act to closely regulate coal-fired power plants due to the environmental and health risks they present. However, the DOE failed to set up a clear agenda to promote renewable energies, while the DENR neglected to update emission standards and sanction negligent coal plants. Furthermore, coal-fired power plants have been permitted to proliferate. Environmental groups therefore claimed that these agencies' dereliction of their duties made the country even more dependent on dirty energy, despite the existence of cleaner alternatives. Moreover, it seems to show a wanton disregard for the Philippines' pledge under the 2015 Paris accords to have reduced its carbon emissions by 70 per cent in 2030. They then called on the Supreme Court to compel the agencies to perform their duties as mandated by these two laws. In the meantime, they have asked the Court to issue a temporary environmental protection order barring the DENR and DOE from granting environmental compliance certificates and operating permits to coal-fired power plants (Geronimo 2017). This collective action paralleled an ambitious litigation effort.

Battling the Carbon Majors

In September 2015, Greenpeace Southeast Asia was joined by thirteen other NGOs, as well as typhoon survivors, in filing a complaint with the Commission on Human Rights (CHR) of the Philippines against forty-seven investor-owned oil, natural gas, and coal producers, as well as cement manufacturers, many of which have subsidiaries in the Philippines.[6] The petition alleged that these companies contribute to global warming and should be held accountable for the destruction caused by stronger typhoons and other phenomena attached to climate change. Conducting the inquiry in the country was timely since the Philippines served as the Chair of the Climate Vulnerable Forum in 2015. The Climate Vulnerable Forum is a partnership of countries that are most vulnerable to global warming. It serves as a South-South mechanism for cooperating governments to implement collective action to address climate change. Furthermore, the country is especially at risk since there are more tropical cyclones that enter the Philippine Area of Responsibility than any other place in the world.

The CHR is an independent National Human Rights Institution (NHRI) created under the 1987 Philippine Constitution. It was "mandated to conduct investigations into human rights violations, against marginalized and vulnerable sectors of society, involving civil and political rights".[7] The petition asked the CHR to exercise its investigative powers to look into the role of the respondents in the human rights implications of climate change and ocean acidification. These companies are among those termed the "Carbon Majors" for significantly contributing to climate change. The petition based its claims on a study by climate expert Richard Heede (2014), who revealed that "nearly two-thirds of historic carbon dioxide and methane emissions can be attributed to [the] ninety entities considered Carbon Majors".[8]

The complaint submitted to the CHR represents the second generation of private climate litigation. The first took place in the United States and was hampered by the inability of plaintiffs to establish sufficient causal connections between climate harm and defendant conduct.

Nevertheless, the move towards private climate litigation has been gaining traction, with plaintiffs incorporating innovative strategies to take advantage of advances in climate science. Ganguly et al. (2018, p. 587) argue that "developments in attribution science are likely to bring private climate litigation into closer alignment with asbestos and tobacco litigation, particularly since the cohort of potential defendants in climate litigation has become easier to identify and narrow down to a key set of players, the Carbon Majors".[9]

Environmental advocates are convinced that climate change caused by the Carbon Majors is overturning the rights of the Filipino people to the basic goods necessary for survival whenever a typhoon strikes and destroys entire communities. In November 2013, Super Typhoon Haiyan known locally as Yolanda, was one of the most powerful tropical cyclones ever recorded; it devastated the poorest areas of the Philippines, killing approximately 6,300 people. Following the storm, a breakdown of law and order was observed in Tacloban City, the provincial capital of Leyte, as people struggled to find food, water, and shelter (Yamada and Galat 2014). In an unparalleled step, the CHR agreed in December 2017 to investigate the petition to hold the Carbon Majors accountable. However, the powers of the CHR are limited. The Commission does not wield enforcement powers and cannot award compensation. It can only provide recommendations to prosecute human rights transgressions. Nevertheless, its decision could affect the prospects of climate change litigation in the future.

When the CHR held its first hearing on the issue in March 2018, the Chairperson Jose Luis Martin Gascon, a lawyer, recognized the relevance of the petition, and declared:

> We can no longer ignore the impact of significant changes in global temperatures and the rising sea levels on people's lives. We have been witness ourselves in this country to a spate of natural disasters and super typhoons (Araja 2018).

The political opportunities for the environmental movement to engage with the CHR are favourable since its high officials were former NGO leaders. Chairperson Gascon was the Executive Director of the National Institute of Policy Studies (NIPS), while Commissioner Cadiz previously served as the Executive Director of Libertas. Both NIPS and Libertas are members of the civil society coalition called the Transparency and Accountability Network. It is interesting that the petition against the Carbon Majors treats accountability for environmental harm as a central issue.

A series of three public hearings were conducted in Manila between March and August 2018. While the Carbon Majors did not participate in the proceedings, the CHR heard from victims of typhoons and a series of expert witnesses on climate change and human rights. It also conducted hearings in New York City in September 2018 and in London two months later. The overseas sessions were arranged with the aim of bringing the inquiry closer to the Carbon Majors' headquarters as well as to widen the awareness of the larger international community regarding the issue. The CHR injected the international context into the inquiry by inviting stakeholders from around the globe to participate in the process. The Inquiry Panel collaborated with the New York Bar Association and the London School of Economics to collect the statements of witnesses and reflect on the insights of experts and scholars on the topic.[10]

Despite the efforts made to hold hearings in the US and UK, the Carbon Majors did not show up. The seventeen companies that initially responded to the investigation in writing mostly disputed the authority of the Commission to investigate them because they do not operate in the Philippines. Contending that climate change is not a human rights issue under domestic or international law, they also argued that the Philippine Constitution only allowed the CHR to investigate cases involving civil and political rights. The Commission responded that it was its duty to examine the matter brought before it, emphasizing that all human rights are interdependent and indivisible. Since the Commission did not have the power to impose sanctions against any of the parties, instead of issuing summons, it could only persuade them to participate in the inquiry (Philippine News Agency 2018).

The Philippines is one of the pioneers of a global rise in legal suits demanding redress for climate change impact. Legal action in various countries, such as Germany, Pakistan, and the Netherlands, has sought to compel an urgent response to climate change and exact compensation from energy companies (Dancel 2018). In 2005, the Inuit people first attempted to create a connection between climate change and human rights in a case before the Inter-American Commission on Human Rights, a mechanism under the Organization of American States. However, the Inter-American Commission declined to take up the case. The 2015 petition filed in the Philippines was thus the second attempt to frame climate change as a human rights issue. In this regard, the CHR set an important precedent for a national human rights institution in probing the human rights responsibilities of corporations that contribute to climate change (Philippine News Agency 2018).

In clarifying what the investigation seeks to accomplish, Commissioner Cadiz stressed the following:

> The inquiry will not impose any penalties should it agree with the allegations made by the petitioners... their records will be available to the public should anyone intend to file cases in regular courts to pursue civil or criminal charges (Mateo 2018).

The CHR, as a result of this undertaking, expects to design procedures for hearing petitions from victims, specify clear standards for corporate reporting on greenhouse gas emissions, and outline the fundamental rights and duties linked to climate change (Savaresi and Setzer 2018). A finding that fossil fuel companies are responsible for human rights infractions could push the state to legislate more stringent environmental regulations, or it could encourage citizens to claim damage payments from fossil fuel companies. It might thus create a precedent triggering similar inquiries in other countries (Wang 2018).

Conclusion

In the Philippines, the environmental movement that emerged in the last twenty years features a strong demand for environmental justice. In the context of a post-authoritarian, neoliberal political economy, the movement fights to prevent pollution and the private appropriation of the commons. It further strives to protect their local ecology and livelihood systems.

Over the past two decades, the Philippine government moved towards a high-growth economic strategy and was unable to regulate resource practices that intensified Anthropocene-related problems, including forest degradation, pollution from coal mining, and climate change. Social movements emerged to protest against these anthropogenic pressures. Through these three cases, this chapter has examined how "political arrangements"—i.e., corruption—affect environmentalism and, conversely, how environmental movements influence national politics. For the citizen organizations, corruption can have a dramatic human cost. While the extrajudicial killings of environmental activists were high under the Aquino presidency, the numbers further increased under the Duterte administration. Despite its strong populist rhetoric about diminishing oligarchic influence over key economic sectors, the Duterte government has been unable to strengthen the state to exercise sufficient autonomy and capacity towards effective environmental governance, including the promotion of environmental justice for the poor he pretended to help.

In a recent article discussing the specificities of the Anthropocene in the Asia-Pacific region, Dahlia Simangan (2019, p. 573) observes that "corruption is also linked to poor public services and weak government institutions, draining the necessary support to climate-related initiatives and assistance to climate-affected industries and communities". Given a weak state and the problems associated with corruption and elite capture, environmental activists in the Philippines have had to engage in contentious politics as they confront strong rent-seeking and commercial interests that evade social and environmental accountability.

Environmental movements have substantially influenced national politics and policy. Through their protest actions, several collective actions have succeeded in stopping resource destruction and led to the adoption of anti-mining legislation in certain provinces. Environmentalists also engaged in innovative tactics including the use of the citizen's suit to ask for the suspension of development activities that endanger the environment through the Writ of Kalikasan (Writ of Nature) under the court system. A key accomplishment of the Philippine environmental movement in the age of the Anthropocene was convincing the human rights commission of the country to hear the case against the giant fossil fuel corporations for contributing to climate change that harms both human rights and the environment.

Local communities have had to rely on their reservoir of internal social capital, as shown in successful campaigns against illegal resource extraction and coal pollution. As local organizational resources are insufficient to challenge well-financed networks in the extractive sectors, the environmental movement had to take advantage of political spaces and opportunities to gain elite allies and civil society supporters to advance its goals. The cultivation of horizontal and vertical connections with translocal, national, and international coalitions has provided a way to expand public awareness and knowledge of environmental issues through the diffusion of protest ideas and actions, as evidenced by the creation of multi-level environmental justice networks. It has also opened up avenues for scaling up the strategic value and policy impact of environmental advocacy efforts.

The environmental movement is contributing to new knowledge in the politics of contention for environmental justice. As the Philippines grapples with climate change and extreme weather events, whose disastrous effects are felt more in poor communities and vulnerable sections of society, civil society innovations are emerging through the use of new online platforms, legal reform tools, and human rights mechanisms in strengthening the fight for environmental justice. While this range of collective actions may not be enough to "fix" the climate emergency and other threats posed by the Anthropocene, they constitute significant moves that are worthy of encouragement and further study.

NOTES

1. For a general introduction to this notion and its link with the environmental justice movement, see Guha and Martinez-Alier (1997) and Martinez-Alier et al. (2016).
2. The ecological footprint calculates the biologically productive land and marine areas a country requires in order to produce sufficient renewable resources (such as food, fiber, or timber) to both sustain its population and absorb the carbon dioxide and other waste that is emitted. This demand is then measured against the productivity of the available resources, that is, the area's bio-capacity. See also the concluding chapter of this volume.
3. http://climatejustice.ph/component/civicrm/?task=civicrm/petition/sign&sid=1&reset=1.
4. Its intention is to be "a remedy available to any person, natural or juridical, whose constitutional right to a balanced and healthful ecology is violated or threatened to be violated by an unlawful act or omission by any person, including the government, involving environmental damage of such magnitude as to prejudice the life, health, or property of inhabitants of two or more cities or provinces" (Philippine Judicial Academy 2012, p. 62).
5. The coalition included PCMJ, Environmental Legal Assistance Center, Philippine Earth Justice Center, Philippine Rural Reconstruction Movement, 350.org East Asia, Philippine Alliance of Human Rights Advocates, Philippine Human Rights Information Center, EcoWaste Coalition, Sanlakas, Nagkakaisang Ugnayan ng mga Magsasaka at Manggagawa sa Niyugan, Sentro ng mga Nagkakaisa at Progresibong Manggagawa, Nuclear Free

Bataan Movement, Alliance of Youth Organizations and Students-Bicol, Asian People's Movement on Debt and Development, Dakila, and Greenpeace Philippines.

6. In addition to Greenpeace Southeast Asia, the petition was signed by many organizations from the Philippines. The Carbon Majors named in the petition are investor-owned companies engaged in the oil and gas, coal, and cement businesses, including Chevron, ExxonMobil, British Petroleum, and Royal Dutch Shell.

7. Commission on Human Rights (CHR), Republic of the Philippines, http://chr.gov.ph/about-chr.

8. Editors' note: Richard Heede has further identified the twenty oil corporations most responsible for global warming, and which have been lobbying for decades to postpone reforms (see Taylor and Watts 2019).

9. Editors' note: Recent revelations that the fossil fuel companies were similarly aware of the harmful effects of their products but covered them up (*supra* note 4), may spur both private and government climate litigation, so that, like the victims of asbestos and tobacco before them, the populations most vulnerable to climate change can seek redress for the damage suffered.

10. The overseas sessions were organized with the additional support of the Asia Pacific Forum of Human Rights Institutions, Global Alliance of National Human Rights Institutions, Office of the UN High Commissioner on Human Rights, European Union, Spanish Aid Agency, and International Bar Association.

REFERENCES

Ackland, Robert and Mathieu O'Neil. 2011. "Online Collective Identity: The Case of the Environmental Movement". *Social Networks* 33: 177–90.

Acselrad, Henri. 2010. "The 'Environmentalization' of Social Struggles – the Environmental Justice Movement in Brazil". *Estudos Avançados* 24, no. 68: 103–19.

Agence France Press (AFP). 2012. "Rangers Losing Battle in Philippine Forests". *Inquirer.net*, 2 October 2012.

———. 2017. "Environmental Crusaders Risk Their Lives to Save Philippine Paradise". *The Guardian*, 6 December 2017.

———. 2018. "Global Wave of Climate Protests as Key UN Climate Talks Stumble". *Straits Times*, 8 September 2018.

Algo, John Leo. 2016. "Anti-Coal Movement Grows in Philippines". *Asia Sentinel*, 11 May 2016.

Allan, Jen Iris and Jennifer Hadden. 2017. "Exploring the Framing Power of NGOs in Global Climate Politics". *Environmental Politics* 26, no. 4: 600–20.

Almeida, Paul and Chris Chase-Dunn. 2018. "Globalization and Social Movements". *Annual Review of Sociology* 44: 189–211.

Alvarez, Kathrina Charmaine. 2017. "CA Rejects Gina Lopez as DENR Secretary". *GMA News Online*, 3 May 2017.

Amilhamja, Celine and Renz Paolo Regis. 2017. "Green Groups Urge Duterte to Act on 'Neglected' Environmental Policies". *Inquirer.net*, 20 July 2017.

Anda, Redempto. 2010. "Philippines: Citizens' Raids Hauling in Smugglers, Illegal Fishers". *Inter Press Service Agency*, 26 September 2010.

Anguelovski, Isabelle and Joan Martínez Alier. 2014. "The 'Environmentalism of the Poor' Revisited: Territory and Place in Disconnected Glocal Struggles". *Ecological Economics* 102: 167–76.

Araja, Rio. 2018. "CHR Holds Hearing to Probe Carbon Effect on Climate". *Manila Standard*, 27 March 2018.

Asian Development Bank (ADB). 2009. *Country Environmental Analysis 2008*. Mandaluyong City: ADB.

Austin, Rebecca. 2003. "Environmental Movements and Fisherfolk Participation on a Coastal Frontier, Palawan Island, Philippines". PhD dissertation, University of Georgia, Athens.

Avila-Calero, Sofia. 2017. "Contesting Energy Transitions: Wind Power and Conflicts in the Isthmus of Tehuantepec". *Journal of Political Ecology* 24: 992–1012.

Bautista, Germelino. 2001. "Environmental Degradation and Activist Intervention: Reflections on the Philippine Experience". *Asian Cultural Studies*: 199–213.

Borras, Saturnino, Jr. and Jennifer Franco. 2012. "Global Land Grabbing and Trajectories of Agrarian Change: A Preliminary Analysis". *Journal of Agrarian Change* 12, no. 1: 34–59.

Brower, Ralph S. and Francisco A. Magno. 2011. "A Third Way in the Philippines: Voluntary Organizing for a New Disaster Management Paradigm". *International Review of Public Administration* 16, no. 1: 31–50.

Brulle, Robert. 2010. "From Environmental Campaigns to Advancing the Public Dialog: Environmental Communication for Civic Engagement". *Environmental Communication* 4, no. 1: 82–98.

Catholic News Service. 2017. "Residents of Philippine Mining Town Protest Reopening of Coal Mine". 28 November 2017. www.ncronline.org/.

Chatterton, Paul, David Featherstone, and Paul Routledge. 2012. "Articulating Climate Justice in Copenhagen: Antagonism, the Commons, and Solidarity". *Antipode*: 1–19.

Cho, Ji-Hyung. 2014. "The Little Ice Age and the Coming of the Anthropocene". *Asian Review of World Histories* 2, no. 1: 1–16.

Cordero, Ted. 2018. "Ombudsman Verdict Looms vs. 600 Local Execs over Solid Waste Slip". *GMA News*, 24 March 2018.

Dalton, Russell J. 2015. "Waxing or Waning? The Changing Patterns of Environmental Activism". *Environmental Politics* 24, no. 4: 530–52.

Dancel, Raul. 2018. "'Carbon Majors' Accused of Rights Violations in the Philippines for Role in Driving Climate Change". *Straits Times*, 28 March 2018.

Da Rocha, Diogo, Marcelo Firpo Porto, Tania Pacheco, and Jean Pierre Leroy. 2018. "The Map of Conflicts Related to Environmental Injustice and Health in Brazil". *Sustainability Science* 13, no. 3: 709–19.

De La Cruz, Erik. 2012. "Philippine Mining at Policy Crossroads as Investment Sputters". *Reuters*, 24 September 2012.

DENR Administrative Order No. 2017–15. "Guidelines on Public Participation under the Philippine Environmental Impact Statement (EIS System)". 2 May 2017.

Devlin, John and Denise Isabel Tubino. 2012. "Contention, Participation, and Mobilization in Environmental Assessment Follow-Up: The Itabira Experience". *Sustainability: Science, Practice and Policy* 8, no. 1: 106–15.

Di Gregorio, Monica. 2012. "Networking in Environmental Movement Organization Coalitions: Interest, Values or Discourse?" *Environmental Politics* 21, no. 1: 1–25.

Flores, Alena Mae. 2018. "Increasing Philippine Demand Straining Power Supply". *Manila Standard*, 14 August 2018.

Ganguly, Geetanjali, Joana Setzer, and Veerle Heyvaert. 2018. "If At First You Don't Succeed: Suing Corporations for Climate Change". *Oxford Journal of Legal Studies* 38, no. 4: 841–68.

Gascon, Melvin. 2018. "Marchers Demand Aggressive Action on Climate Change". *Philippine Daily Inquirer*, 10 September 2018.

Geronimo, Jee. 2017. "Environment Groups File Case vs. DENR, DOE over Coal Plants Proliferation". *Rappler*, 30 June 2017.

Gerra, Weena. 2016. "Examining the Resilience of Public Participation Structures for Sustainable Mining in the Philippines". In *Legal Aspects of Sustainable Development*, edited by Volker Mauerhofer. Switzerland: Springer International Publishing, pp. 203–31.

Global Footprint Network. 2012. *A Measure for Resilience: 2012 Report on the Ecological Footprint of the Philippines*. Oakland (California).

———. 2015. *Philippines Case Study 2015*. Oakland (California), 25 August 2015. www.footprintnetwork.org.

Global Witness. 2016. "Defenders of the Earth: Global Killings of Land and Environmental Defenders in 2016". London. www.globalwitness.org.

———. 2019. "Defending the Philippines". London.

Gonzalez, Eduardo. 2017. "Judicialized Governance in the Philippines: Toward New Environmental Judicial Principles that Translate into Effective 'Green' Policies and Citizen Empowerment". *Philippine Political Science Journal* 38, no. 2: 81–103.

Guha, Ramachandra and J. Martinez-Alier. 1997. "The Environmentalism of the Poor". In *Varieties of Environmentalism: Essays North and South*. London: Earthscan Publications Ltd., pp. 3–21.

Heede, Richard. 2014. "Tracing Anthropogenic Carbon Dioxide and Methane Emissions to Fossil Fuel and Cement Producers, 1854–2010". *Climatic Change* 122: 229–41.

Holden, William N. 2012. "Ecclesial Opposition to Large-Scale Mining on Samar: Neoliberalism Meets the Church of the Poor in a Wounded Land". *Religions* 3, no. 3: 833–61.

———. 2018. "Endogenous Exacerbation of an Exogenous Problem: Climate Change, Environmental Degradation, and Unsustainable Development Practices in the Philippines". *Asian Geographer* 36, no. 1: 1–27.

Jalandoni, Apples. 2015. "World's First Human Rights Complaint vs. Climate Culprits Filed". *ABS-CBN News*, 23 September 2015.

Lane, Paul. 2015. "Archaeology in the Age of the Anthropocene: A Critical Assessment of its Scope and Societal Contributions". *Journal of Field Archaeology* 40, no. 5: 485–98.

Lee, Su-Hoon, Hsin-Huang Michael Hsiao, Hwa-Jen Liu, On-Kwok Lai, Francisco A. Magno, and Alvin Y. So. 1999. "The Impact of Democratization on Environmental Movements". In *Asia's Environmental Movements: Comparative Perspectives*, edited by Yok-shiu F. Lee and Alvin Y. So. New York: M.E. Sharpe, pp. 230–51.

Magno, Francisco A. 1992. "Weak State, Ravaged Forests: Political Constraints to Sustainable Upland Management in the Philippines". *Philippine Political Science Journal* 17, no. 33–36: 79–96.

———. 1999. "Environmental Movements in the Philippines". In *Asia's Environmental Movements: Comparative Perspectives*, edited by Yok-shiu F. Lee and Alvin Y. So. Armonk, New York: M.E. Sharpe, pp. 143–75.

———. 2007. "Environmental Capacity and Decentralized Governance in the Philippines". *Journal of International Development and Cooperation* 13, no. 1: 39–60.

Martin, David. 2018. "Global Climate Change Protests Kick Off as UN Talks in Bangkok Stall". *DW Newsletter*, 9 September 2018. www.dw.com/en/.

Martinez-Alier, Joan, Leah Temper, Daniela Del Bene, and Arnim Scheidel. 2016. "Is There a Global Environmental Justice Movement?" *The Journal of Peasant Studies* 43, no. 3: 731–55.

Matabuena, Jules. 2016. "#ClimateActionPH: Fighting Coal with Information Drives, Social Media". *Rappler*, 10 December 2016.

Mateo, Janvic. 2018. "'Carbon Majors' Snub CHR Inquiry on Climate Change". *Philippine Star*, 29 March 2018.

Mindanao Examiner. 2013. "Filipino Environmentalists Launch Campaign in the Philippines". 4 July 2013.

National Economic and Development Authority (NEDA). 2017. *Philippine Development Plan 2017–2022*. Pasig City: NEDA.

Pangsapa, Piya. 2014. "Environmental Justice and Civil Society". In *Routledge Handbook of Environment and Society in Asia*, edited by Paul G. Harris and Graeme Lang. London: Routledge, pp. 36–52.

Passion, Patty. 2017. "CA Rejects Gina Lopez as Environment Secretary". *Rappler*, 3 May 2017.

Passy, Florence and Gian-Andrea Monsch. 2014. "Do Social Networks Really Matter in Contentious Politics?" *Social Movement Studies* 13, no. 1: 22–47.

Pellow, David. 2018. "Environmental Justice Movements and Political Opportunity Structures". In *The Routledge Handbook of Environmental Justice*, edited by Ryan Holifield, Jayajit Chakraborty, and Gordon Walker. New York: Routledge, pp. 37–49.

Pettinicchio, David. 2012. "Institutional Activism: Reconsidering the Insider Outsider Dichotomy". *Sociology Compass* 6, no. 6: 499–510.

Philippine Judicial Academy. 2012. *Citizen's Handbook on Environmental Justice*. Manila.

Philippine News Agency. 2018. "CHR Ends Inquiry on Effects of Climate Change on Human Rights". 13 December 2018.

Porto, Marcelo Firpo, Diogo Rocha Ferreira, and Renan Finamore. 2016. "Health as Dignity: Political Ecology, Epistemology and Challenges to Environmental Justice Movements". *Journal of Political Ecology* 24, no. 1: 110–24.

Rootes, Christopher. 2004. "Environmental Movements". In *The Blackwell Companion to Social Movements*, edited by David A. Snow, Sarah A. Soule, and Hanspeter Kriesi. London: Blackwell, pp. 608–40.

———. 2013. "From Local Conflict to National Issue: When and How Environmental Campaigns Succeed in Transcending the Local". *Environmental Politics* 22, no. 1: 95–114.

Santos, Eimor. 2017. "CA Rejects Gina Lopez Appointment as DENR Chief". *CNN Philippines*, 4 May 2017.

Saunders, Clare. 2007. "Using Social Network Analysis to Explore Social Movements: A Relational Approach". *Social Movement Studies* 6, no. 3: 227–43.

Savaresi, Annalisa and Joana Setzer. 2018. "The Carbon Majors Inquiry Comes to London". Commentary, Grantham Research Institute on Climate Change and the Environment, London School of Economics and Political Science, 30 October 2018. www.lse.ac.uk.

Sicotte, Diana and Robert Brulle. 2018. "Social Movements for Environmental Justice through the Lens of Social Movement Theory". In *The Routledge Handbook of Environmental Justice*, edited by Ryan Holifield, Jayajit Chakraborty, and Gordon Walker. London and New York: Routledge, pp. 25–36.

Simangan, Dahlia. 2019. "Situating the Asia Pacific in the Age of the Anthropocene". *Australian Journal of International Affairs* 73, no. 6: 564–84.

Snow, David A., Sarah A. Soule, and Hanspeter Kriesi. 2004. "Mapping the Terrain". In *The Blackwell Companion to Social Movements*, edited by David A. Snow, Sarah A. Soule, and Hanspeter Kriesi. London: Blackwell Publishing Ltd., pp. 3–16.

Stengers, Isabelle. 2015. *In Catastrophic Times: Resisting the Coming Barbarism*. Lüneburg: Meson Press and Open Humanities Press.

Straits Times. 2017. "One Environmental Activist Killed Every 12 Days in the Philippines in 2016 as Criminals Grab Natural Resources". 6 December 2017.

Taylor, Matthew and Jonathan Watts. 2019. "Revealed: The 20 Firms Behind a Third of All Carbon Emissions". *The Guardian*, 9 October 2019.

Taylor, Verta and Nella Van Dyke. 2004. "Get Up, Stand Up: Tactical Repertoires of Social Movements". In *The Blackwell Companion to Social Movements*, edited by David A. Snow, Sarah A. Soule, and Hanspeter Kriesi. London: Blackwell Publishing Ltd., pp. 262–93.

Temper, Leah, Daniela Del Bene, and Joan Martinez-Alier. 2015. "Mapping the Frontiers and Front Lines of Global Environmental Justice: The EJAtlas". *Journal of Political Ecology* 22, no. 1: 255–78.

Temper, Leah, Mariana Walter, Iokiñe Rodriguez, Ashish Kothari, and Ethemcan Turhan. 2018. "A Perspective on Radical Transformations to Sustainability: Resistances, Movements and Alternatives". *Sustainability Science* 13, no. 3: 747–64.

Tilly, Charles and Sidney Tarrow. 2015. *Contentious Politics*. 2nd ed. Oxford: Oxford University Press.

United Nations Development Programme (UNDP). 2014. *Environmental Justice: Comparative Experiences in Legal Empowerment*. New York: UNDP.

Van der Ploeg, Jan, Dante M. Aquino, Tessa Minter, and Merlijn van Weerd. 2016. "Recognising Land Rights for Conservation? Tenure Reforms in The Northern Sierra Madre, The Philippines". *Conservation and Society* 14, no. 2: 146–60.

Verbrugge, Boris. 2015. "Decentralization, Institutional Ambiguity, and Mineral Resource Conflict in Mindanao, Philippines". *World Development* 67: 449–60.

Verbrugge, Boris, Jeroen Cuvelier, and Steven Van Bockstael. 2015. "Min(d)ing the Land: The Relationship Between Artisanal and Small-Scale Mining and Surface Land Arrangements in the Southern Philippines, Eastern DRC and Liberia". *Journal of Rural Studies* 37: 50–60.

Vicari, Stefania. 2014. "Networks of Contention: The Shape of Online Transnationalism in Early Twenty-First Century Social Movement Coalitions". *Social Movement Studies* 13, no. 1: 92–109.

Villarin, Tomasito. 2005. "A Green Patch in Davao's Blue Waters". In *Social Watch Philippines 2005 Report – Race for Survival: Hurdles on the Road to Meeting the MDGs in 2015*. Quezon City: Social Watch Philippines, pp. 105–8.

Wang, Ucilia. 2018. "Climate Accountability Probe Brings Philippines Human Rights Hearing to NYC". *Climate Liability News*, 20 September 2018.

World Bank. 2018. *Philippines Economic Update: Investing in the Future*. Macroeconomics, Trade and Investment Global Practice, East Asia and Pacific Region, April 2018.

Yamada, Seiji and Absalon Galat. 2014. "Typhoon Yolanda/Haiyan and Climate Justice". *Disaster Medicine and Public Health Awareness* 8, no. 5: 432–35.

Yee, Jovic. 2016. "Gina Lopez accepts DENR post". *Philippine Daily Inquirer*, 21 June 2016.

6

ENVIRONMENTAL NGOS IN "POST-NEW ORDER" INDONESIA: SAVING THE FORESTS THROUGH DEMOCRACY

*Suharko Suharko**

Given the importance of tropical rainforests in the struggle to mitigate global warming and save terrestrial biodiversity from the "Sixth Extinction", Indonesia represents a key area of the Anthropocene (Simangan 2019, p. 572). It is thus no accident that, in addition to English and four other major languages, a referent website like Global Forest Watch also offers its online data in Bahasa Indonesia.[1] Yet, in the literature on the Anthropocene, apart from a few exceptions (e.g., Chandler 2017), Indonesia is almost inexistent. As emphasized by the editors of this volume (see Chapter 1), the Anthropocene framework remains Western-centred; it has not yet been assimilated by Asian scholars, or its "indigenization" has started only recently. A rare exception in the literature in Bahasa thus far is a special issue of *Balairung*, edited by a group of students from Gadjah Mada University (Raja et al. 2018). Although it is a modest start, these young scholars nevertheless highlight that the Anthropocene concept opens a brand new theoretical gateway for understanding the specific meaning of the global ecological crisis for a country like Indonesia (Sugandi and Najjah 2018; Haekal and Suci 2018).

In this chapter, I analyse how Indonesian environmental non-governmental organizations (ENGOs) have come to address two emblematic issues of the Anthropocene: deforestation and the climate emergency. A decisive moment in that process was the engagement of Indonesian ENGOs during the 13th United Nations Climate Conference, which was held in Bali in 2007. We will look also at two related issues: the responsibility of banks and other financial institutions in deforestation, or what I call "unsustainable finance", and the problem of coastal reclamation as a result of land grabbing and developmentalist urbanization. These issues are emblematic of the Anthropocene in the fundamentally anthropic nature of the damage done to the environment. But if they have played a central role in the advocacy campaign of Indonesian ENGOs during the last two decades, it is also due to their entanglement with local and national politics. We follow on the editors of this volume to consider the Anthropocene as a heuristic time reference for the last two decades.

Since the notion of Anthropocene remains almost unknown to the majority of Indonesians, for our study of ENGOs and environmental politics, we consider another temporal framework: Suharto's authoritarian regime, the so-called "New Order" (1966–98), and the period of liberalization that followed, usually referred to as the "post-New Order". Although ENGOs were not entirely absent under Suharto, the political liberalization that followed his rule has allowed them more autonomy and freedom of speech. Their action, however, remains impeded by serious hurdles: the political oligarchy still colludes with environmentally destructive businesses, and the rise of populism has prevented true political debate on the socio-economic roots of environmental injustices.

This chapter nevertheless argues that ENGOs have become an active force of Indonesian civil society, and as such, they have contributed to make public institutions more accountable (or at least relatively less corrupt than during the New Order era). I start with a general description of Indonesian ENGOs in the post-New Order democracy, the scope of their ambitions, and the major sociopolitical constraints they are subject to. The following sections will then analyse specific issues of crucial importance in Indonesia—deforestation, climate change, and coastal reclamation—and how environmental groups have sought to address them.

ENGOs and the "Post-New Order" Democracy

The environmental movement in Asia emerged in the 1980s in response to a combination of rapid industrial development, environmental degradation, and deteriorating life prospects (Lee and So 1999; Kalland and Persoon 1998; Hirsch and Warren 1998). In Indonesia, although their room for manoeuvre was restricted under Suharto's authoritarian "New Order", the first ENGOs appeared in the early 1970s and, from the 1980s onward, they took an increasingly active part in the democratization process (Uhlin 1997). Those oriented toward policy advocacy have proven to be an important force in influencing and controlling environmental policy implemented by the state (Eldridge 1995; Ganie-Rochman 2002; Hadiwinata 2003).

After the resignation of Suharto in 1998 and the transition to democracy, ENGOs experienced significant development in terms of quantity and quality. They were able to build links with local communities, especially those suffering environmental damage, and promote community participation in making environmental regulations at the local level, as in participatory forestry management (Nomura 2007). Since 2004, general elections have been held regularly for both executive and legislative positions at the central and regional levels, while government agencies have been redesigned to mitigate state corruption. Decentralization and regional autonomy policies continue to operate as a form of power dispersion. Political liberalization has created a more inclusive democratic space that can increase actors' engagement in political life (Lay 2012).

However, the post-New Order democracy has faced serious problems. Under the presidency of Susilo Bambang Yudhoyono (2004–14), and even more under that of Joko Widodo (2014 to present), the elected presidents have adopted a populist style, which, despite important differences, are comparable to Thailand under the government of Thaksin or the Philippines since Duterte came to power in 2016 (Kenny 2018). To obtain popular support, both Yudhoyono and Widodo have offered social welfare programmes and adopted economic nationalism-oriented policies (Kenny 2018; Mietzner 2015). But these welfare programmes have not changed the structure of the economy: big business has kept a firm grip on it and economic inequalities remain high.

Moreover, democratic practices, decision-making, and public policy have been confined to a small group of individuals both inside and outside the government. This political and economic elite uses the democratic system to control resources, support mobilization through clientelistic networks, and develop alliances with business groups and communal leaders (Samadhi and Warouw 2009). Democratic practices in post-New Order Indonesia continue to be oligarchic and based on patronage (Robison and Hadiz 2004; Aspinall and Sukmajati 2015; Mietzner 2015), and political parties remain weak; no one party has yet received a majority of votes, so every government must forge a coalition. Savirani and Tornquist (2015) even argue that democratization has stagnated. Indeed, most democratic institutions remain ineffective. Political equality and collective action are so weak that it is hard to find major improvements in political representation and public policy.

Duile and Bens (2017) argue that, despite the presence of democratic institutions, political discourse in Indonesia has in fact been depoliticized through decades of a top-down imposition of consensus. Drawing on Slavoj Žižek's theory of depoliticization strategies, they show that Sukarno's consensual approach to democracy and Suharto's conception of the nation as a family (with himself as the father) still prevail today, centred around the foundational values of "the nation/the people" (*bangsa*) and "Islam". These two "transcendental signifiers" (a reference to Lacan via Žižek) ultimately form the basis for all political discourse, marginalizing other factors, such as economic inequality or the claims of indigenous peoples, and favouring a unifying populism that stifles true political debate. Despite these problems, civil society associations and organizations have been working hard to defend democracy (Mietzner 2012; Hanif and Hiariej 2015).

This context naturally imposes serious constraints on environmental organizations. Heinrich (2005) defined civil society as "the arena, outside of the family, the state, and the market, where people associate to advance common interests". This view implies that civil society is an arena of free association and deliberation, which can advocate for the public interest without pressure from the state or other political forces. Ideally, civil society organizations (CSOs) can become a restraining force on the state (Diamond 1999). For Beetham (1999), the general goal of democracy is to achieve "popular control over public affairs on the basis of political equality". In practice, popular control is achieved through direct participation or via a mediator (Stokke 2014; Tornquist 2013). CSOs can apply either one or both of these approaches to shape public affairs. In post-New Order Indonesia, ENGOs have been an active part of CSOs (Scanlon and Alawiyah 2015; Suharko 2011). From the time of their emergence, Indonesian ENGOs were often the mediator for local populations in campaigning for environmental issues. But ENGOs are more and more the embodiment of citizens advancing their own environmental interests and values. Indeed, an attempt was made to form a Green Party in 2012, but the movement was ultimately unable to meet the criteria to register the party to compete in elections.[2]

ENGOs' success in influencing public affairs ultimately depends on political opportunities and constraints (Tarrow 1994). A political environment may provide "a window of opportunity" or, conversely, be a threat or a barrier to change. In post-New Order Indonesia, environmental activists have gained greater political scope thanks to the guarantee of civil and political rights such as freedom of opinion and the right to organize. However, opportunities to create and organize advocacy actions are often restricted. As in many Global South countries that have transitioned towards democracy, the new regimes exhibit a formal, elitist democracy rather than encouraging popular participation; or they oscillate between the former habits of dictatorial rule and the new requisites of a substantive democracy (Stokke 2014; Levitsky and Way 2010). Such an ambivalent political context inhibits CSOs striving to influence policy changes.

The effect of change generated by CSO movements hinges on their interaction with actors in the larger social, political, and legal environments, as well as their degree of integration with political institutions (Ho 2019). Likewise, ENGOs' relations with the state, donors, and international networks contribute to the effectiveness of a movement (Bank and Hulme 2012). A democratic state tends to allow non-state actors, particularly CSOs, to be involved in public decision-making processes. However, in most developing countries, governments do not prioritize the participation of NGOs in policymaking, nor do they encourage their development (Lassa and Li 2015, p. 21).

In the broader sociopolitical context, international networks and donors provide important contributions (Lassa and Li 2015), as they can increase a movement's political leverage and strengthen its legitimacy. Nevertheless, the relationship with donors can be problematic for ENGOs: on the one hand they are a financial resource; on the other hand, this gives them the power to dictate the direction an organization takes (Ahmed and Potter 2006). Change created by the ENGO movement, to some extent, depends on its ability to maintain a balance between these two conflicting factors.

The next section provides a brief background on Indonesia's conflicting interests of environmental conservation pursuits and economic growth after 1998, a period that also corresponds with the Anthropocene as defined by the editors of this volume.

Indonesia in the Anthropocene

Indonesia is the largest archipelago nation in the world with approximately 17,000 islands. A vast variety of flora and fauna can be found throughout the islands, and it is estimated to make up 40 per cent of the biodiversity in the Asia-Pacific region. At the same time, Indonesia is the fourth most populous country in the world (after China, India, and the United States) with considerable population growth over the last two decades. Indonesia's population has continued to increase in the last two decades. But it is not proportionately distributed among its islands and provinces. More than half of Indonesians live on the island of Java, which covers less than 7 per cent of the total land area, and urban populations are growing faster than those in rural areas (BPS 2013). Sustaining this populace has put enormous pressure on the country's biocapacity, as governments prioritize development to meet its housing, energy, and infrastructure needs.

Indonesia's macroeconomic policies tend to rely on the utilization of natural resources, which provide a significant contribution to Indonesia's gross domestic product (GDP) and government budget. The agriculture, forestry, and mining sectors account for about 25 per cent of Indonesia's GDP and about 30 per cent of all government revenue (World Bank 2014). The majority of exports are still raw materials or resources that have been processed into commodities, such as mineral fuels, palm oil, coal, wood pulp, aluminum, rubber, and copper. Coal and palm oil have become the country's core export commodities. The export of manufactured goods remains relatively minor.

Most of these commodities are sold to China (Neilson 2017, p. 385). This point is of importance given the geopolitical context as outlined by the editors in the introduction. Since 2014, in line with the Belt and Road Initiative (BRI) implemented by the Chinese government, the Indonesian government has welcomed investment from Chinese corporations for the construction of roads, railways, ports, and other infrastructure projects to support industry development and improve domestic and international connectivity (Damuri et al. 2019; Blanchard 2017). Chinese corporations have also invested in a large range of other economic sectors, including electricity, gas and water supply, mining activities, and the metals industry.

The magnitude of this investment has aroused suspicion towards China's BRI, as was evident in recent political campaigns for the presidential and legislative elections (Hicks 2019). This political reaction, however, reflects not only concern about Indonesia's sovereignty and the protection of environmental resources; it is entangled with a long legacy of anti-Chinese sentiment.[3] Political parties and interest groups have fuelled this xenophobia to oppose government economic policies that were felt to be promoting too much foreign investment from China (Bharat 2018). The growing pressure of Chinese investments could thus provoke further episodes of violence against the communities of Chinese Indonesians.

In line with the country's wide-ranging economic development and rapid population growth, the demand for electricity continues to rise. In 2017, electricity consumption reached 1,012 KWH (kilowatts per hour) per capita, up 5.9 per cent from the previous year, and this will continue to increase in the coming years. The government seeks to achieve complete electrification for the whole country by 2025 (*Katadata* 2018). Electricity demands are overwhelmingly met by power plants using non-renewable energy sources like coal. Renewable energy sources, such as solar, wind, microhydro, biogas, and other hybrid energies, have been developed but only in very limited quantities.

All of these developments have contributed to Indonesia's worst environmental problem since at least the 1960s: deforestation. The rate of deforestation is currently about 1.13 million hectares per year. In the period from 2009 to 2013 alone, the country lost 4.5 million hectares of natural forest cover. This high rate of forest loss is driven by mining activities and agribusiness, particularly palm oil. Logging and the clearing of peatlands and tropical forests for industrial activities lead to the irremediable loss of wildlife and natural habitats for numerous species, as well as conflicts between various "stakeholders" (Forest Watch Indonesia 2014). They also contribute three-fold to the carbon emissions crisis: from the industrial activities that replace the woodlands, the thick smoke produced by slash-and-burn clearing practices, and the loss of carbon-absorbing trees and peatland. Last but not least, deforestation leads to "natural" disasters like droughts and fires, which occur more readily in agribusiness plantations than in moisture-retaining tropical rainforests.

This ongoing disaster can be partly attributed to a distorted form of political decentralization. According to the blueprint for democratization, redistributing power to local governments should be a good way to break the concentration of power, reduce corruption, and promote better governance practices at the local level. Since the early 2000s, the Indonesian central government has thus implemented institutional reforms to allocate more autonomy to regional governments. Unfortunately, no system of checks and balances was included in the process.

Moreover, although environmental policy—from laws to ministerial regulations—is generally drafted at the national level, implementation and decision-making are largely left to the regional heads. Consequently, as these regional heads (governors and mayors) have gained more power, no authority has been really able to control their decisions over the utilization of natural resources. In addition, many provinces and districts have created their own interpretations of existing national regulations, and have even sought to establish entirely new regulatory procedures. Decentralization has therefore encouraged some regional heads to ignore environmental policy standards that were decided at the national level (World Bank 2014). Furthermore, Chinese-backed banks and companies often appeal directly to local politicians to advance their BRI projects (Bharat 2018). Thus, while one might expect local authorities to be more protective of their immediate environment, the acquisition of more revenue and authority by local politicians and bureaucrats seems to have led to continued and even increased resource depletion in many areas (Neilson 2017, p. 384).

If the state, big business, and industry are the main culprits of the massive deforestation and a mode of development generally destructive for the ecology, it is also true that the general population is not really supportive of sustainable practices. To some extent, environmental damage and pollution, as well as the threatened loss of biodiversity and the depletion of natural resources are precipitated by a general lack of environmental awareness (Ministry of Environment 2012).

Those who are aware and informed are usually engaged in efforts to address environmental problems, typically members of ENGOs or other associations who take collective action to influence government policy. Young people, who represent a growing proportion of the populace, form the core members of CSOs and ENGOs; however, while students aware of the environmental crisis support national and international ENGOs, they tend to become actively involved in small-scale efforts regarding threats to their immediate environment (Nilan 2017).

ENGOs have long been engaged in various forms of environmental advocacy, through litigation and other channels. One organization in particular, Walhi (*Wahana Lingkungan Hidup Indonesia*, i.e., The Indonesian Forum for Environment), has been involved in a number of prominent environmental cases (Eldridge 1995). A national network of activists and environmental organizations, Walhi began to engage in advocacy efforts in the late 1980s and, in 1989, it became a member of Friends of the Earth International (FoEI), as Friends of the Earth Indonesia.

One of its most prominent actions was a lawsuit in 1989 against a pulp and rayon company, Inti Indorayon Ltd., which was contaminating Lake Toba in the north of Sumatra province. Although Walhi eventually lost the court case, this gave momentum to the whole Indonesian environmental movement. For the first time, an ENGO had been able to launch a lawsuit against a polluting firm. ENGOs have thereafer often used the justice system to fight against those who damage the environment. In 1997, the enactment of the Law on Environmental Management—revised in 2009 to become the Law on Environmental Protection and Management—granted citizens or CSOs the right to file a lawsuit for damage or loss due to contamination or environmental degradation (Walhi 2008). This legal change provided environmental activists with a more robust status within the judiciary.

In addition to Walhi, the Secretariat for Forest Conservation in Indonesia, known as Skephi (for *Sekretariat Kerjasama Pelestarian Hutan Indonesia*), has since the late 1980s been an active network characterized by a more radical approach. Collaborating with student groups, indigenous peoples, and other grassroots groups, Skephi has conducted large mobilizations to oppose developmentalist projects. Skephi consists of 250 groups and individual activists from all over Indonesia. It collects information and campaigns through *Setiakawan* magazine, renowned for its harsh criticism of the government's environmental policy (Uhlin 1997, p. 113).

MAP 6.1

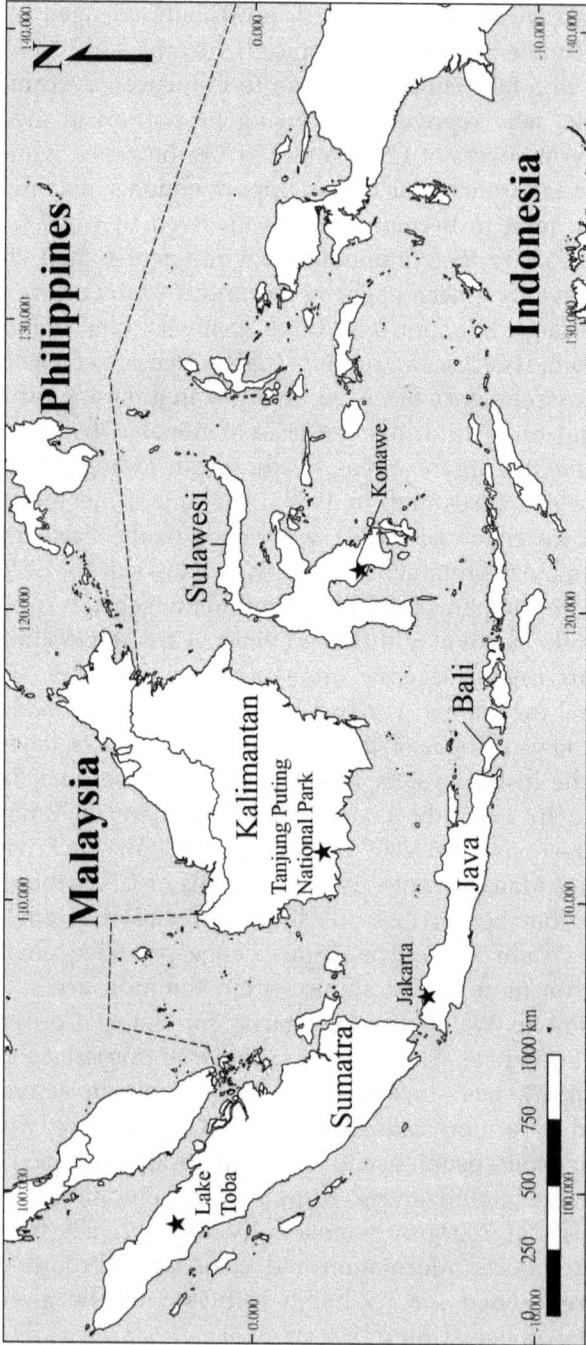

Selected sites of environmental disputes in Indonesia

Source: QGIS and Natural Earth.

Since the downfall of the New Order authoritarian government, numerous CSOs have flourished, engaging in various public activities, both cultural and political (Scanlon and Alawiyah 2015). The scope of organizations committed to environmental issues has increasingly widened. Some examples of grassroot organizations are the Mine Action Network (*Jaringan Aksi Tambang*/JATAM), Sawit Watch, Indigenous Peoples' Alliance of the Archipelago (*Aliansi Masyarakat Adat Nusantara*/ Aman), Forest Watch Indonesia (FWI), the International Center of Environmental Law (ICEL), and the Telapak Association (*Perkumpulan Telapak*). Moreover, the significance at the global level of issues such as the deforestation of Southeast Asian tropical rainforests encouraged Greenpeace to establish three offices in Southeast Asia, with Indonesia chosen in addition to Thailand and the Philippines. In Indonesia, the democratic climate has provided opportunities for these ENGOs to build alliances to actively oppose corporations, government agencies, and other actors considered to be harmful to the environment.

The following pages present environmental campaigns conducted during the last two decades on the major issues of forest degradation and the climate emergency, and two correlated matters: unsustainable finance and coastal reclamation. In Indonesia, these emblematic issues of the Anthropocene have led to the formation of a large advocacy movement led by ENGOs.

Shrinking Forests

Indonesia has vast areas of forest that contain a wealth of natural resources. The rapid rate of deforestation not only threatens a large range of animal and plant species but also worsens global warming. The deforestation is intrinsically linked to corporate businesses, such as the production of palm oil and the extractive industry mining for oil and coal. To cope with these big corporations, several ENGOs such as the Indigenous Peoples' Alliance of the Archipelago (Aman), Walhi, Telapak, and the Network for the Forests (*Jaringan untuk Hutan*/ JAUH) have been working together. One of their primary goals has been that indigenous peoples hold onto their rights to the customary forests of their ancestral lands. The government continues to regard customary forests as a part of the state forestland and, as such, has relinquished the management of these forests to corporations. In response, this ENGO coalition developed a community logging pilot project in Konawe, Southeast Sulawesi. The coalition facilitated the establishment of the Sustainable Forest Cooperative (*Koperasi Hutan Jaya Lestari*/KHJL) as an agency for forest management. Through the mass media, Walhi has presented this case of community logging as a model for other regions (Darsono 2011). But the replication on a broad scale of this successful case has proven difficult. Central and local governments still tend to favour corporate-based management systems, as is made obvious in a regulation that allows corporations to utilize protected forest zones.[4]

Another problem that ENGOs must fight against is the widespread and persistent practice of illegal logging. Led by Walhi, a coalition of NGOs—including Telapak, ICEL, and the Association for Community and Ecology Based Law Reform (*Perkumpulan untuk Pembaharuan Hukum Berbasis Masyarakat dan Ekologis*/HuMa)—has investigated a number of cases in several regions, such as Tanjung Puting National Park in Kalimantan. These campaigns against illegal logging are based on solid investigation and mapping, as well as legal and policy analysis. However, despite frequent reports in the mass media, very few of these illegal loggers have been brought to justice. The firmly embedded practice of corruption among economic and political actors in the forestry sector, together with the high demand for timber, makes it incredibly difficult to eradicate illegal logging in Indonesia (Darsono 2011).

One of the most important battles has been on the legal front. During the New Order era, customary forests (*hutan adat*) were unduly absorbed by state forests (*hutan negara*). This reflected a complete disregard for indigenous peoples' rights. Law No. 41 on Forestry, issued in 1999, acknowledged the existence of customary forests, but only as a subsection of state forests (Chapter II, Article 5, point 2). In practice, this meant that the government could grant the concession of any customary forest to private corporations for any use at all. This contempt for indigenous rights has often provoked the alienation of communities living around these forest areas. When conflicts have arisen between communities and corporations, the local government has generally supported the latter, camping on the legality of the concession. In response, HuMa formed the Coalition for Amending Forest Policy (*Koalisi untuk Perubahan Kebijakan Kehutanan*/KPKK).[5]

The Coalition started by documenting the grievances of local communities from a number of regions on the negative impacts of this law, before conducting a policy analysis with funding from the Rainforest Foundation Norway; the result was published in book form (KPKK 2007). In addition, the Coalition lobbied the central and local governments, the House of Regional Representatives, and the House of Representatives of Indonesia (DPR). For a while, the revision of the law was to be scheduled for the National Legislation Program's 2005–9 period. But in the end, the revision was not included in the agenda.

In March 2012, the indigenous organization Aman submitted a judicial review to the Constitutional Court to challenge the definition of customary forest in the Law on Forestry (No. 41). In May 2013, the Court granted a judicial revision so that customary forests would no longer be categorized as state forests. This decision meant that indigenous peoples were now entitled to manage forests on their ancestral lands. As a result, the government allocated 12.7 million hectares to community forestry (Astuti and McGregor 2017, pp. 450–51). The government has nonetheless continued to use the initial law to grant concessions to corporations in customary forest areas, and even accommodated the law to the interests of mining companies that claimed to be disadvantaged by the revision of 2013. Conflicts between indigenous peoples, corporations, and the government have thus remained unabated (Saturi 2013). ENGOs have tried to stop this hypocritical game being played by the government in concert with big businesses. Although no significant change has been obtained, the court decision of May 2013 became an entry point for ENGOs to address various problems, such as the economic marginalization of local communities deprived of access to state forests.

The Constitutional Court decision nevertheless encouraged indigenous communities to claim their land rights. It also offered an opportunity to the forest carbon initiative Reducing Emissions from Deforestation and Forest Degradation Plus (REDD+); Indonesia has become one of its pilot countries. Fairhead et al. (2012) contend that REDD+ and other carbon projects are a neoliberal "green grabbing" that brings benefits to the agencies and consulting firms involved in these programmes but marginalizes traditional communities of forest users. Departing from such criticism, Astuti and McGregor (2017) show that in Indonesia, REDD+ has enabled indigenous opportunities to pursue land claims and recover access to the forest. The problem, as the authors show, is rather that REDD+ propagates a romantic image of indigenous peoples that neglects gender, class, and ethnic diversity within indigenous communities, thus omitting inherent power relations, tensions, and conflicts. Haekal and Suci (2018) further point out the ambiguous role of countries like Norway in pushing for such carbon marketization of Indonesian forests through programmes like REDD+.

In May 2019, the Indonesian government published the first customary forest map to help indigenous communities establish their land rights and prevent land grabs by developers and corporations. However, it is rather likely that onerous bureaucratic requirements will hamper the process for legal recognition of customary forests. ENGOs have called for a presidential order to abolish such requirements and also to speed up deliberations over the law on the rights of indigenous peoples currently before the parliament, as a measure to bolster their land rights (Jong 2019).

Unsustainable Finance

Previously, environmental movements did not consider financial organizations such as banks or insurance funds to be important actors of deforestation. But the threats to tropical forests and the climate emergency have prompted ENGOs to find new forms of advocacy. Targeting financial institutions has now become an important form of engagement.

A pioneer for this form of action was TuK Indonesia (Transformasi untuk Keadilan Indonesia), founded in 2013 by environmental activists in Jakarta. TuK has advocated human rights and social justice for marginalized indigenous communities and other groups dependent on forests for their livelihood. The organization first targeted the owners of oil palm plantations that destroy the forest with bulldozers or by lighting fires, before extending its fight against the financial institutions backing this agribusiness (TuK Indonesia 2015). Activists further found that eight pulp and paper companies were also active in the destruction of Indonesian forests, with financial support from China (40 per cent), Japan (29 per cent), and Indonesia (15 per cent) (TuK Indonesia 2020).

TuK has formed the "Bank Response Coalition"[6] to influence the drafting of the Banking Bill (*Rancangan Undang-Undang tentang Perbankan*). An initiative of the House of Representatives, the Banking Bill was supposed to make banks liable for investments that might affect the environment, the management of natural resources, and the rights of local communities. Although the bill was actually an initiative of the House of Representatives, there was no indication that the lawmakers included or seriously considered the coalition's input (Nugraha 2015).

The coalition met with a more positive attitude from the Financial Services Authority (*Otoritas Jasa Keuangan*/OJK), a government agency, which in 2014 issued the Sustainable Finance Regulatory Plan (Saturi 2015). This roadmap was strategic for the coalition, as it could provide a legal foundation for preventing banks from financing companies whose operations impact negatively on communities and environmental sustainability. According to research conducted by TuK together with Rainforest Action Network (RAN) and Profundo (a Dutch consultant specialized in commodity chains), from 2010 to 2015 around US$38 billion in loans from banks in Southeast Asia potentially contributed to deforestation, as they pumped funds into palm oil production, pulp and paper mills, and rubber plantations (Arumingtyas 2016).

TuK has encouraged the OJK to monitor the funds being channelled to clients in the forestry sector with particular care, and to endorse tough sanctions when there is a blatant violation. The OJK has offered the coalition and other stakeholders the opportunity to provide input on the draft of the regulatory plan. The coalition gave a number of proposals targeting the decisive role of banks in environmental damage and the protection of human rights (Jalal and Winarni 2017).

The coalition was also involved in the Civil 20 summit, an international network of NGOs that was scheduled ahead of the G20 leaders' 2017 summit in Hamburg. This was an opportunity to seize, as the G20 meeting's agenda included "sustainable finance", and the president of Indonesia had declared his commitment to it (Winarni and Jalal 2017). Thanks to this collaboration with foreign partners, Indonesian NGOs increased their legitimacy vis-à-vis the OJK and the parliament. However, the Regulatory Plan has not yet been issued or ratified. Reluctant to place curbs on environmentally destructive businesses, banks have thus far prevented the state and politicians from going beyond promises and nice speeches on "sustainability".

Negotiating Climate Change

Indonesia's carbon dioxide emissions stemming from deforestation, forest degradation, and the impact of land-use change are among the greatest in the world (Hein 2013). The country did not show any political will to reduce its emissions until the early 2000s. Media campaigns and pressure from ENGOs and donor organizations, however, prompted the government to demonstrate its willingness to reduce emissions (Resosudarmo et al. 2013).

Instrumental in this was the 13th United Nations Climate Change Conference of the Parties (COP) held in Bali in December 2007. Ahead of the conference, a group of twenty-nine Indonesian CSOs established the Civil Society Forum for Climate Justice. Their goal was to act as a pressure group, as well as an information centre on regulatory negotiations about climate change at the national level (CSF 2009). The forum encouraged the Indonesian government to adopt its proposal as a reference in national policymaking and international negotiations. It consisted of four pillars: human security, ecological debt, land tenure, and the use of natural resources for economic purposes. Natural resource management needs to comply with human rights to ensure a guarantee of land tenure or ownership. Likewise, the ecological debt of developed countries should be paid, at the very least through emission cuts, so as to reduce the burden on developing countries. Production and consumption patterns create inequality, and the impacts of climate change are an impediment to the economic progress of developing countries.

However, as the forum noted critically, the COP focuses on carbon trading and market approaches that tend to disregard environmental sustainability and human safety. While discussions are monopolized by carbon trading, the targets for domestic emissions reduction in each country have been all but forgotten. For instance, beyond declarations of commitment to reduce carbon emissions, the Indonesian government has made few improvements to stop deforestation (CSF 2009).

With the support of Oxfam Great Britain, the forum later held a climate summit in November 2009 as a form of interactive dialogue between policymakers and those most hurt by climate change. The forum brought in nine fishing and farming representatives from several Indonesian regions to provide testimony on how their daily lives have become increasingly difficult due to more unpredictable rainfall affecting crops, and a higher frequency of storms that have made fishing at sea more difficult. The forum urged the government to devote more of its budget to help farmers and fishermen cope with these rapid changes (Burhani 2009). In an open letter, the forum also urged the National Council on Climate Change (*Dewan Nasional Perubahan Iklim*) to map the areas most vulnerable to disasters caused by climate change, based on data from the Meteorology, Climatology and Geophysics Agency and the National Disaster Management Agency (Rimayanti 2013).

Ahead of the climate change negotiations in Paris in December 2015, a coalition of twenty Indonesian NGOs formed the Civil Society Coalition to Save Indonesian Forests and the Global Climate (*Koalisi Masyarakat Sipil untuk Penyelamatan Hutan dan Iklim Global*).[7] This coalition again criticized the carbon trading approach in addressing climate change (TuK Indonesia 2015). Carbon trading has shifted the focus of solving climate change to a mere trading issue, and it has obviously failed to reduce global warming. In fact, no state or international policy can be effective without the involvement of local people. Unfortunately, negotiators from Indonesia and other nations of the COP treat the wisdom and knowledge of indigenous peoples with contempt (Firmansyah 2015).

For Walhi, the Paris agreement of December 2015, with its obvious focus on carbon trading, clearly ignored the interests of those most vulnerable to the effects of climate change. Aman emphasized, in particular, that the Paris agreement's operative text had weakened the rights of indigenous peoples (Saturi 2015). Greenpeace Indonesia further condemned the gap between the climate change policy and its implementation. The government declared its commitment to closing this gap, but, in reality, it has continued to build heavily polluting coal-fired power plants. Greenpeace Indonesia (2016) has therefore demanded that the government halt all plans for new coal-fired power projects and promptly transition from coal energy to renewable energy.

The ENGO coalitions have had good access to policy- and decision-makers at the national and international level regarding climate change adaptation and mitigation. It remains difficult, however, for these organizations to challenge the pro-market policies imposed by the developed countries on other countries, even those as big as Indonesia. Unsurprisingly, the government has continued to follow a market-based approach that has largely disregarded the interests of vulnerable groups affected by climate change.

Resistance Against Coastal Reclamation

As an archipelago nation, the effects of climate change are very tangible in Indonesia. Coastal communities and fishing groups are among the first victims. Furthermore, they have also been under pressure from coastal reclamation for the development of urban areas or industrial zones that threaten entire ecosystems. ENGOs must therefore also fight against the seizure of coastal lands and the resultant environmental impacts. This section presents two cases. In Jakarta Bay, ENGOs have worked with a local CSO to reject the reclamation development projects. In Bali's Benoa Bay, several ENGOs have become members of an alliance initiated by local CSOs.

Jakarta

Since the New Order era, many coastal environments have been transformed into residential and business areas. The growth of the capital city of Jakarta has taken place at an incredibly rapid rate to become "the city of the Anthropocene" (Chandler 2017), for the constant transformation of its slum dwellings (*kampongs*) can be seen as a model of adaptation to anthropic climate change. But the proliferation of slums is only one aspect of the city's growth, and given the limited land capacity, coastal reclamation for all sorts of landed property was deemed a viable solution to cope with urban expansion. In the bay of Jakarta, this process began in the early 1980s (Rosalina 2016), but it was officially established by presidential decree in 1995. The goal was to create a key area for urban and economic development.

After a series of legal disputes, in 2012, the Jakarta provincial government incorporated the development of the northern coastal area into Jakarta's Spatial and Regional Plan. Then, at the end of 2015, the governor issued reclamation permits for four of the seventeen artificial islands that are to be built. These artificial polders are designated simply by the letters from A to Q. For example, Island G is to welcome gas pipelines from Pertamina Hulu Energi Ltd., as well as cables belonging to the State Electricity Company and the Muara Karang Power Plant. These infrastructures would play a crucial role in the economy of the region. But Island G is on a waterway frequently used by traditional fishermen (Syalaby 2016).

The coalition Save Jakarta Bay (*Koalisi Selamatkan Teluk Jakarta*)[8] argues that the reclamation of Jakarta Bay must be stopped; otherwise it would have tremendous repercussions for the ecosystem and the livelihoods of local fishermen (Ambari 2016b). The coalition filed a lawsuit in the Jakarta State Administrative Court and won. In response, the Jakarta provincial government appealed the decision and it was overturned. The coalition turned to the Supreme Court, which rejected its appeal in August 2017. The central government and the Jakarta governor, Basuki Tjahaja Purnama, then issued a decree for the continued reclamation of the bay (Ambari 2017; Arumingtyas 2017).

The coalition was nevertheless determined to block the application of these decrees and the activists got their revenge through politics. Their opposition movement found a window of opportunity during the election for governor of Jakarta in mid-October 2017. The issue captured so much attention during the electoral debate that Anies Baswedan, the main challenger for the post, endorsed most of the activists' claims (Ambari 2017). After the election, Baswedan ordered a re-evaluation of the whole development project and formulated measures to stop coastal reclamation (Friana 2017). In September 2018, Baswedan declared the cancellation of the principle permits held by seven developers for the construction of thirteen of the seventeen planned islets in Jakarta Bay (*Jakarta Post* 2018). This was a victory for Indonesian ENGOs.

However, in August 2019, the government of Joko Widodo argued that since Jakarta is sinking at a pace of 20 centimetres a year, the capital should be displaced to the province of East Kalimantan, on the island of Borneo, starting in 2024. If this radical move helps to reduce gridlock and air pollution in Jakarta, the city will certainly remain an economic megacity for decades. Worse, this solution might only extend such problems in Borneo and cause further loss of habitat to wild species like orangutans, which are already threatened with extinction due to logging, palm oil production, and other agribusiness. For now, at least, Borneo has no need of coastal reclamation. This is not the case for Bali, as shown in the next section.

Bali

Bali has become a leading destination for global tourism and, as such, has attracted the attention of many investors. With the support of the Bali provincial government, one of these investors, Tirta Wahana Bali International Ltd., a national private company that belongs to the sino-indonesian businessman Tomy Winata (one of the richest Indonesians, according to Forbes), has reclaimed a huge part of the Benoa Bay area, in the south of Bali. Inspired by the Palm Beach of Dubai, this vast real estate and resort project called Nusa Benoa ("two islands") would cover a total surface of 838 hectares, or one third of the whole bay (2,800 hectares). Only one hundred hectares would be allocated to tourist accommodations as such. The rest would be devoted to the construction of public facilities, such as an art exhibition centre, a craft exhibition building, a sports arena, places of worship, schools, etc., plus the "development" of four hundred hectares of mangroves (to extend the existing mangrove). The project therefore claims to be "eco-friendly"; instead of "reclamation" (*reklamasi*), it was framed under the slogan of "revitalization" (*revitalasi*).

But the whole project would involve the creation of new islands covering seven hundred hectares and will require forty million cubic metres of sand. It is therefore hard to believe that the polderization would not affect the ecosystem of the bay. Several scientific assessments, like the study conducted by the local university Udayana, have pointed to the risks of coastal abrasion, the destruction of the coral reefs, threats to the mangrove ecosystems, and the risk of flooding. The project has thus sparked the resistance of a large and motley gathering of people under the leadership of the Balinese People Forum Reject Reclamation (*Forum Rakyat Bali Tolak Reklamasi* or ForBali). ForBali defines itself as a cross-sectoral alliance of Balinese civil society, gathering students, artists (like the local painter Made Bayak, and musicians like the rock bands Nosstress and "Superman is Dead"), academics, and other individuals, in addition to NGOs and other organizations that believe that this project implies the destruction or commodification of Bali's rich natural and cultural environment.

The mobilization has been initiated through demonstrations, attitude statements, and online petitions demanding the revocation of the governor's decree granting the reclamation of Benoa Bay. In addition to seminars in collaboration with universities, the presence of artists has delivered powerful messages through music concerts, protest songs, T-shirts, posters, banners, and billboards. In addition, a strong characteristic and exotic attraction of this movement is a series of actions driven by local customs of Hindu rituals (Suantika 2015). Meanwhile, Walhi, as a member of ForBali, filed a lawsuit against the governor of Bali to revoke the 2012 reclamation decree (Walhi 2014, 2015). Walhi won the case, and in August 2013 ForBali forced the governor to issue a new decree. However, this new decree was merely a revision of the old one, and the reclamation plan remained in place. In addition, in 2014, the central government issued a Presidential Regulation that altered the conservation status of Benoa Bay into a buffer zone or general use zone. This top-down decision from Java has since become the main driver of the local opposition, as expressed by the creative banners and artistic placards that can be found all around the bay.

In early 2016, fourteen Balinese customary village heads went to the presidential office to demand the revocation of the presidential regulation (Nugraha 2016). Customary village leaders also took part in a demonstration attended by about ten thousand people at Ngurah Rai Park near the Bali International Airport, to express their anger at the government's slow response (Suriyani 2016). ForBali has received the support of the National Human Rights Commission (*Komisi Nasional Hak Asasi Manusia*), which issued a letter of recommendation in February 2017 to the central government and the Bali provincial government to withdraw the reclamation plan. The letter stated that if the plan were executed, it would lead to serious social conflict (Muhajir and Doaly 2017). With the support of ENGOs like Walhi, local CSOs have to some extent succeeded in forcing authorities to delay, or at least act cautiously, in executing these reclamation projects. Indeed, in June 2019, Indonesia's Environment Minister affirmed that the government would decline to grant a crucial permit to develop the bay, as long as local opposition to the project remained so high (Gokkon 2019).

Conclusion

Indonesia's post-New Order democratic political system has allowed environmental NGOs more scope to advocate for the protection of forests and for policies to cope with the devastating effects of global heating. They have lobbied central and regional parliaments to encourage the revision of the Forestry Law. They have also demanded from the parliament and the government's Financial Services Authority (OJK) the ratification of sustainable finance laws. They filed a judicial review with the Constitutional Court against the Forestry Law in order to prevent the marginalization of indigenous communities. And despite long and complex procedures that require substantial resources and do not always end in positive results, legal actions remain a powerful weapon in curbing government policies and corporate practices. Finally, strong criticism has been directed at international policies that pretend to fix the climate emergency with carbon trading and carbon storage programmes like REDD+, which generally benefit developed countries without necessarily aiding indigenous and other marginalized people. During the United Nations 13th Conference of the Parties on climate change, held in Bali, ENGO coalitions therefore lobbied the Indonesian negotiating team to shift the focus to the protection of vulnerable groups.

ENGOs have developed collaborative networks with international NGOs and donors in the form of coalitions and networks. As members of international NGOs, Walhi, Greenpeace Indonesia, and Friends of the Earth Indonesia have been engaged in anti-deforestation movements and lobbying to reform international and national policies that exacerbate environmental damage and global warming. Indonesian ENGOs have established robust networks and obtained resource support from European NGOs, such as the Rainforest Foundation Norway (RAM), Oxfam in the United Kingdom, and Profundo in the Netherlands. A coalition established by TuK Indonesia is part of an international movement (launched during the Civil 20's summit) to advocate for sustainable finance. Nonetheless, it is still difficult for these mobilizations to manage the political constraints that derive from elitist and oligarchical democratic practices. ENGOs constantly face unyielding economic and political forces at both the local (Welker 2009) and national levels (Hadiz and Robison 2014) that are resistant to any change in public policy.

In opposing the reclamation of Jakarta Bay and Bali's Benoa Bay, the coalition formed by Jakarta-based ENGOs along with local CSOs has been able to influence decision-making processes by seizing political opportunities. The Save the Jakarta Bay coalition utilized the momentum from a 2017 change of governor for its advocacy purposes. Through mass mobilization, ForBali was able to consistently reject Benoa Bay's reclamation. ForBali and the Save the Jakarta Bay coalition used litigation channels to reject reclamation attempts. In the end, the national government did not grant the Benoa Bay reclamation permit, and the Jakarta governor stopped the reclamation of Jakarta Bay.

Although it is not easy to make a generalization regarding the changes and effects generated by ENGO movements, as they need to be considered on a case-by-case basis, I have tried to show that ENGOs have been able to profit from the democratization during the post-New Order period. By establishing alliances with local CSOs and international NGOs, Indonesian ENGOs have become a social force that has a say on state policies and corporation practices. They have more opportunities to monitor state and corporate practices, and question them when they threaten environmental sustainability and the interests of vulnerable communities. Although environmental activists still face enormous difficulties, compared to the New Order era, their situation has greatly improved; at the very least, they now enjoy freedom of speech and action without frequent threats to their lives.

Yet despite the democratization of the country after 1998, Indonesia remains a "flawed democracy" by Western standards. In that context, formal political channels do not provide an arena for average citizens to really influence the formulation of public policy in relation to the squandering of natural resources by capitalists and political elites. ENGOs have nevertheless become an important element of Indonesian civil society in advancing democracy. Their political engagement has become an example of how citizens banding together might navigate the circumscribed waters of Indonesian democracy and pressure the government to address their concerns.

NOTES

* The author would like to address special thanks to Paul Jobin and Rebecca Fite for their help and editing, as well as two anonymous reviewers for their suggestions.
1. www.globalforestwatch.org.
2. Three of Indonesia's environmental groups attempted to take part in the general election of April 2019, with the implicit backing of Walhi: the Green Union of Indonesia (*Sarekat Hijau Indonesia*, SHI), the Green Party of Indonesia (*Partai Hijau Indonesia*, PHI), and the Aceh Green Party (*Partai Atjeh Hijau*, PAH). Although none were able to meet the requirements to field candidates as an official registered party, some of the candidates they supported from other parties managed to be elected. Not long afterwards, in July 2019, Walhi announced its own bid to form the Indonesian Green Party in order to ensure that environmental issues are placed firmly on the political agenda.
3. Indonesians of Chinese descent who make up only about 4 per cent of the population control a vast range of business sectors. Since the Dutch colonial era, rampant anti-Chinese sentiment has provoked several out-

breaks of violence (the most dramatic occurring in 1740, 1946–49, 1965, and 1998).
4. See Government Regulation No. 2 of 2008 on Establishing Protected Forest Rental Tariffs for Forestry Activities Outside of the Forestry Sector.
5. This coalition consists of Walhi, AMAN, FWI, Semarang Legal Aid Institute, the Institute for Community Legal Resources Empowerment (LBBT), HuMa, Young Indonesian Foresters (*Rimbawan Muda Indonesia*, RMI), and Qbar.
6. Under the leadership of TuK, this coalition includes big ENGOs such as Walhi, the International NGO Forum on Indonesian Development (INFID), the Indonesian Consumers Protection Foundation (*Yayasan Lembaga Konsumen Indonesia*, YLKI), and new initiatives like the Welfare Initiative for Better Societies (*Perkumpulan Prakarsa*), Indonesian Corruption Watch (ICW), and Publish What You Pay.
7. This coalition included Walhi, Debt Watch Indonesia, HuMa, Greenpeace Indonesia, ICEL, AMAN, FWI, KpSHK, Wallacea Association (*Perkumpulan Wallacea*), and Transformation for Justice in Indonesia (*TuK Indonesia*).
8. KSTJ members include ICEL, the People's Coalition for Fisheries Justice (*Perkumpulan Koalisi Rakyat untuk Keadilan Perikanan*, Kiara), Walhi, LBH Jakarta, and the Indonesian Traditional Fishermen's Association (*Kesatuan Nelayan Tradisional Indonesia*, KNTI).

REFERENCES

Ahmed, Shamina and David M. Potter. 2006. *NGOs in International Politics*. Bloomfield: Kumarian Press.

Ambari, Muslim. 2016a. "Di Tengah Penolakan, 8 Perusahaan Pastikan Terlibat dalam Reklamasi Jakarta" [In the Middle of Rejection, 8 Corporations Involved in the Jakarta Reclamation]. *Mongabay*, 9 January 2016a. https://www.mongabay.co.id/2016/01/29/di-tengah-penolakan-8-perusahaan-pastikan-terlibat-dalam-reklamasi-jakarta/.

———. 2016b. "Memang benar reklamasi teluk Jakarta bisa dilanjutkan" [It is Indeed True that Reclamation of the Jakarta Bay May Continue]. *Mongabay*, 16 September 2016b. www.mongabay.co.id.

———. 2017. "Ada kejanggalan dalam prosedur pencabutan moratorium reklamasi teluk Jakarta, seperti apa?" [There are Procedural Irregularities in the Revocation of the Jakarta Bay Reclamation Moratorium. Like What?]. *Mongabay*, 11 October 2017. https://www.mongabay.co.id/2017/10/11/ada-kejanggalan-dalam-prosedur-pencabutan-moratorium-reklamasi-teluk-jakarta-seperti-apa/.

Arumingtyas, Lusia. 2016. "Penelitian temukan bank-bank ini berkontribusi pada kehancuran hutan" [Research Discovers That These Banks are Contributing to Deforestation]. *Mongabay*, 12 September 2016. https://www.mongabay.co.id/2016/09/12/penelitian-temukan-bank-bank-ini-berkontribusi-pada-kehancuran-hutan/.

———. "Kasus pulau G mahkamah agung tolak kasasi, warga langkah lanjutan" [The Supreme Court Rejects the G Island Appeal Case; Citizens Take Further Measures]. *Mongabay*, 15 August 2017. https://www.mongabay.co.id/2017/08/15/kasus-pulau-g-mahkamah-agung-tolak-kasasi-warga-langkah-lanjutan/.

Aspinall, Edward and Mada Sukmajati, eds. 2015. *Politik Uang di Indonesia: Patronase dan Klientelisme Pada Pemilu Legislatif 2014* [Money Politics in Indonesia: Patronage and Clientelism in the 2014 Legislative Elections]. Yogyakarta: PolGov UGM.

Astuti, Rini and Andrew McGregor. 2017. "Indigenous Land Claims or Green Grabs? Inclusions and Exclusions within Forest Carbon Politics in Indonesia". *The Journal of Peasant Studies* 44, no. 2: 445–66.

Bank, Nicola and David Hulme. 2012. "The Role of NGOs and Civil Society in Development and Poverty Reduction". *BWPI Working Paper* 171.

Bappenas. 2018. *Outlook Pembangunan 2018, Tantangan di Tahun Politik* [2018 Development Outlook: Challenges in the Political Year]. Jakarta: Bappenas.

Beetham, David. 1999. *Democracy and Human Rights*. Oxford: Polity Press.

Bharat, Shah S. 2018. "China's Belt and Road Initiative and Indonesia's Financial Security". *The Jakarta Post*, 1 October 2018. https://www.thejakartapost.com/academia/2018/10/01/chinas-belt-and-road-initiative-and-indonesias-financial-security.html.

Blanchard, Jean-Marc F. 2017. "China's Maritime Silk Road Initiative (MSRI) and Southeast Asia: A Chinese 'Pond' not 'Lake' in the Works". *Journal of Contemporary China* 27, no. 111: 329–43.

BPS (Biro Pusat Statistik, Central Bureau of Statistics). 2013. *Proyeksi Penduduk Indonesia 2010–2035* [2010–2035 Indonesia Population Projection]. Jakarta: BPS.

Burhani, Ruslan. 2009. "Pemerintah Agar Siapkan Dana Perubahan Iklim" [Government to Prepare Funds for Climate Change]. *Antaranews.com*, 28 October 2009.

Chandler, David. 2017. "Securing the Anthropocene? International Policy Experiments in Digital Hacktivism: A Case Study of Jakarta". *Security Dialogue* 48, no. 2: 113–30.

CSF. 2009. "Keadilan Iklim Tenggelam di Meja Negosiasi" [Climate Justice Sinks at the Negotiating Table]. *Down to Earth Indonesia*, 25 September 2009. https://www.downtoearth-indonesia.org/old-site/ICSF09.htm.

Damuri, Yose R., Vidhyandika Perkasa, Raymond Atje, and Fajar Hirawan. 2019. *Perceptions and Readiness of Indonesia towards the Belt and Road Initiative: Understanding Local Perspectives, Capacity, and Governance*. Jakarta: Center for Strategic and International Studies.

Darsono, Febryandi. 2011. "Koalisi Ornop Pasca Orde Baru: Studi tentang Jaringan Walhi dalam Kampanye Isu Hutan" [A Post-New Order Non-Government Organization Coalition: A Study on Walhi Networks in Forest Issue Campaigns]. *Masyarakat* 16, no 1: 27–48.

Diamond, Larry. 1999. *Developing Democracy: Toward Consolidation*. Baltimore: John Hopkins University Press.

Duile, Timo and Jonas Bens. 2017. "Indonesia and the 'Conflictual Consensus': A Discursive Perspective on Indonesian Democracy". *Critical Asian Studies* 49, no. 2: 139–62.

Eldridge, Philip J. 1995. *Non-Government Organizations and Democratic Participation in Indonesia*. Oxford: Oxford University Press.

Fairhead, James, Melissa Leach, and Ian Scoones. 2012. "Green Grabbing: A New Appropriation of Nature?" *Journal of Peasant Studies* 39, no. 2: 237–61.

Firmansyah. 2015. "Tarik Napas Panjang, Apakah Anda Mendengar Bumi Menangis" [Take a Deep Breath, Do You Hear the Earth Crying?]. *Kompas. com*, 7 December 2015.

ForBali. N.d. "Tentang ForBali" [About ForBali]. www.forbali.org/id/tentang-kami/ (accessed 30 January 2019).

Forest Watch Indonesia (FWI). 2014. *Potret Keadaan Hutan Indonesia Periode 2009–2013* [A Portrait of Indonesia's Forests in the 2009–2013 Period]. Bogor: FWI.

Friana, Hendra. 2017. "Anies akan bentuk tim khusus penghentian reklamasi teluk Jakarta" [Anies Will Form a Special Team to Stop the Reclamation of Jakarta Bay]. *Tirto.id*, 1 November 2017. https://tirto.id/anies-akan-bentuk-tim-khusus-penghentian-reklamasi-teluk-jakarta-czrG.

Ganie-Rochman, Muthia. 2002. *An Uphill Struggle: Advocacy NGOs under Soeharto's New Order*. Depok: Labsosio UI.

Gokkon, Basten. 2019. "No Environmental Permit for Bali Bay Reclamation Plan Amid Opposition". *Mongabay*, 25 June 2019. https://news.mongabay.com/2019/06/no-environmental-permit-for-bali-bay-reclamation-plan-amid-opposition/.

Greenpeace Indonesia. 2016. "Indonesia Meratifikasi Kesepakatan Paris: Kesenjangan antara Janji dan Kenyataan Lapangan" [Indonesia Ratifies the Paris Agreement: The Gap Between Promises and Actual Reality in the Field]. Jakarta: Greenpeace, 20 October 2016. www.greenpeace.org.

Hadiwinata, B. Sugeng. 2003. *The Politics of NGOs in Indonesia: Developing Democracy and Managing a Movement*. London: Routledge Curzon.

Hadiz, Vedi R. and Richard Robison. 2014. "The Political Economy of Oligarchy and the Reorganization of Power in Indonesia". In *Beyond Oligarchy: Wealth, Power and Contemporary Indonesian Politics*, edited by Michele Ford and Thomas P. Pepinsky. Ithaca: Cornell Southeast Asia Program Publications.

Haekal, Luthfian and Pungky Erfika Suci. 2018. "Kuasa dan Eksklusi REDD+ sebagai 'Climate Leviathan' dan Alih Fungsi Lahan di Indonesia" [Power and Exclusion: REDD+ as a 'Climate Leviathan' and Land Conversion in Indonesia]. *Balairung: Jurnal Multidisipliner Mahasiswa Indonesia* 1, no. 1: 110–25.

Hanif, Hasrul and Eric Hiariej. 2015. "Democratic Institutions from Good Governance to Vibrant CSOs". In *Reclaiming the State: Overcoming the Problems of Democracy in Post-Soeharto Indonesia*, edited by Amalinda Savirani and OlleTornquist. Yogyakarta: Polgov.

Hein, Jonas. 2013. "Reducing Emissions from Deforestation and Forest Degradation (REDD+), Transnational Conservation and Access to Land in Jambi, Indonesia". EFForTS Discussion Paper Series No. 2, University of Goettingen.

Heinrich, Volkhart F. 2005. "Studying Civil Society across the World: Exploring the Thorny Issues of Conceptualization and Measurement". *Journal of Civil Society* 1, no. 3: 211–28.

Hicks, Jacqueline. 2019. "Political Sensitivities Surround the BRI in Indonesia". *Asia Dialogue*, 30 January 2019. https://theasiadialogue.com/2019/01/30/political-sensitivities-surround-the-bri-in-indonesia/.

Hirsch, Philip and Carol Warren, eds. 1998. *The Politics of Environment in Southeast Asia: Resources and Resistance*. London: Routledge.

Ho, Ming-sho. 2019. *Challenging Beijing's Mandate of Heaven: The Sunflower Movement in Taiwan and the Umbrella Movement in Hong Kong*. Philadelphia, PA: Temple University Press.

Jakarta Post. "Anies Revokes Reclamation Project Permits". 26 September 2018. https://www.thejakartapost.com/news/2018/09/26/anies-revokes-reclamation-project-permits.html.

Jalal and Rahmawati R. Winarni. 2017. "Masukan Masyarakat Sipil atas rancangan peraturan otoritas jasa keuangan tentang penerapan keuangan berkelanjutan" [Civil Society Input on the Financial Service Authority Draft Regulation on Implementing Sustainable Finance]. Jakarta: TuK Indonesia, 11 June 2017. https://www.tuk.or.id/2017/06/masukan-masyarakat-sipil-atas-rancangan-peraturan-otoritas-jasa-keuangan-tentang-penerapan-keuangan-berkelanjutan/.

Jong, Hans Nicholas. 2019. "Customary Land Map, a First for Indonesia, Launches to Mixed Reception". *Mongabay*, 26 June 2019. https://news.mongabay.com/2019/06/customary-land-map-a-first-for-indonesia-launches-to-mixed-reception/.

Kalland, Arne and Gerard Persoon. 1998. *Environmental Movements in Asia*. Surrey: Curzon Press.

Katadata. 2018. "Inilah konsumsi listrik nasional" [This is the National Consumption of Electricity]. *Katadata*, 11 January 2018. https://

databoks.katadata.co.id/datapublish/2018/01/11/inilah-konsumsi-listrik-nasional.

Kenny, Paul D. 2018. *Populism in Southeast Asia*. New York: Cambridge University Press.

KPKK. 2007. *Mengapa Undang-Undang Kehutanan Perlu Direvisi? Argumentasi Kritis Terhadap Dampak Penerapan Undang-Undang Nomor 41 Tahun 1999 Tentang Kehutanan* [Why Does the Forestry Law Need to be Revised? A Critique on the Impact of Implementing Law Number 41 of 1999 on Forestry]. Jakarta: KPKK.

Lassa, Jonatan and Dominggus E. Li. 2015. "NGO Networks and the Future of NGO Sustainability in Indonesia". NSSC Publication – Research Series #4. https://www.ksi-indonesia.org/en/knowledge/detail/1016-nssc-publication-research-series-4-ngo-networks-and-the-future-of-ngo-sustainability-in-indonesia-by-jonatan-lassa-and-dominggus-elcid-li.

Lay, Cornelis. 2012. "Democratic Transition in Local Indonesia: An Overview of Ten Years Democracy". *Jurnal Ilmu Sosial Dan Ilmu Politik* 15, no. 3: 207–19.

Lee, Yok-shiu F. and Alvin Y. So. 1999. "Introduction". In *Asia's Environmental Movements: Comparative Perspectives*, edited by Yok-shiu F. Lee and Alvin Y. So. New York: M.E. Sharpe Inc.

Levitsky, Steven and Lucan A. Way. 2010. *Competitive Authoritarianism: Hybrid Regimes After the Cold War*. Cambridge: Cambridge University Press.

Mietzner, Marcus. 2012. "Indonesia's Democratic Stagnation: Anti-Reformist Elites and Resilient Civil Society". *Democratization* 19, no. 2: 209–29.

———. 2015. *Reinventing Asian Populism: Jokowi's Rise, Democracy, and Political Contestation in Indonesia*. Policy Studies 72. Honolulu: East-West Center.

Ministry of Environment of the Republic of Indonesia. 2012. *State of the Environment Report of Indonesia 2012*. Jakarta: Ministry of Environment.

Muhajir, Anton and Themmy Doaly. 2017. "Komnas HAM rekomendasikan rencana reklamasi teluk benoa dibatalkan" [The National Commission on Human Rights Recommends Abolishing the Benoa Bay Reclamation Plan]. *Mongabay*, 11 March 2017. https://www.mongabay.co.id/2017/03/11/komnas-ham-rekomendasikan-rencana-reklamasi-teluk-benoa-dibatalkan/.

Neilson, Jeffrey. 2017. "Indonesia: A Political-Economic History of Environment and Resources". In *The Routledge Handbook of the Environment in Southeast Asia*, edited by Philip Hirsch. New York: Routledge.

Nilan, Pam. 2017. "The Ecological Habitus of Indonesian Student Environmentalism". *Environmental Sociology* 3, no. 4: 370–80.

Nomura, Ko. 2007. "Democratisation and Environmental Non-governmental Organisations in Indonesia". *Journal of Contemporary Asia* 37, no. 4: 495–517.

Nugraha, Indra. 2015. "Responsi Bank dorong RUU Perbankan peka sosial dan lingkungan" [The Bank's Response Urges a Socially and Environmentally Sensitive Banking Bill]. *Mongabay*, 2 July 2015. www.mongabay.co.id.

———. 2016. "Tolak reklamasi teluk Benoa, 14 Bendesa Adat datangi Kantor Kepresidenan" [Reject the Reclamation of Bali Bay: 14 Village Heads go to the Presidential Office]. *Mongabay*, 18 February 2016. https://www. mongabay.co.id/2016/02/18/tolak-reklamasi-teluk-benoa-14-bendesa-adat-datangi-kantor-kepresidenan/.

Oxfam Indonesia. 2009. "Sarasehan Iklim untuk Petani dan Nelayan" [Climate Meeting for Farmers and Fishermen]. Jakarta: Oxfam, 29 October 2009. https://oxfamblogs.org/indonesia/digelar-sarasehan-iklim-untuk-petani-dan-nelayan/.

Raja, Muhammad Unies Ananda et al. 2018. "Antroposen". *Balairung: Jurnal Multidisipliner Mahasiswa Indonesia* [Multidisciplinary Journal of Indonesian Students] 1, no. 1: 6–143. https://jurnal.ugm.ac.id/balairung/issue/view/3380.

Resosudarmo, Budi P., Fitrian Ardiansyah, and Lucentezza Napitupulu. 2013. "The Dynamics of Climate Change Governance in Indonesia". In *Climate Governance in the Developing World*, edited by David Held, Charles Roger, and Eva-Maria Nag. Cambridge: Polity Press.

Rimayanti, R. 2013. "Forum Masyarakat Sipil Minta DNPI Lebih Efektif" [The Civil Society Forum Calls for the National Council on Climate Change to be More Effective]. *Ekuatorial*, 4 September 2013. https://www.ekuatorial. com/en/forum-masyarakat-sipil-minta-dnpi-lebih-efektif/.

Robison, Richard and Vedi R. Hadiz. 2004. *Reorganising Power in Indonesia: The Politics of Oligarchy in An Age of Markets*. London: Routledge Curzon.

Rosalina, M. Puteri. 2016. "Jalan Panjang Reklamasi di Teluk Jakarta dari era Soeharto sampai Ahok" [The Long Road to Reclamation of Jakarta Bay from the Soeharto Era through to Ahok]. *Kompas.com*, 4 April 2016.

Samadhi, Willy P. and Nico Warouw, eds. 2009. *Building Democracy on the Sand: Advances and Setbacks in Indonesia*. Yogyakarta: PCD Press & Demos.

Saturi, Sapariah. 2013. "Mahkamah Konstitusi putuskan hutan adat bukan hutan Negara" [The Constitutional Court Declares that Customary Forests are not State Forests]. *Mongabay*, 16 May 2013. https://www.mongabay. co.id/2013/05/16/mahkamah-konstitusi-putuskan-hutan-adat-bukan-hutan-negara/.

———. 2015. "Wah! 29 taipan kuasai 5 juta hekatr lebih lahan sawit" [Wow – 29 Tycoons Control More Than 5 Million Hectares of Oil Palm Plantations]. *Mongabay*, 13 February 2015. https://www.mongabay.co.id/2015/02/13/wah-29-taipan-kuasai-5-juta-hektar-lebih-lahan-sawit/.

Savirani, Amalinda and Olle Tornquist, eds. 2015. *Reclaiming the State: Overcoming the Problems of Democracy in Post Soeharto Indonesia*. Yogyakarta: Polgov.

Scanlon, Megan M. and Tuti Alawiyah. 2015. "The NGO Sector in Indonesia: Context, Concept, and an Updated Profile". Jakarta: KSI-Indonesia Brief,

16 December 2015. https://www.ksi-indonesia.org/assets/uploads/original/2020/02/ksi-1580493585.pdf.

Simangan, Dahlia. 2019. "Situating the Asia Pacific in the Age of the Anthropocene". *Australian Journal of International Affairs* 73, no. 6: 564–84.

Sinanu, Frieda. 2007. "Coming of Age: Indonesia's Environmental Network Faces Dilemmas as It Turns 25". *Inside Indonesia* 87, July–September 2007.

Stokke, Kristian. 2014. "Substantiating Urban Democracy: The Importance of Popular Representation and Transformative Democratic Politics". In *The Routledge Handbook on Cities of the Global South*, edited by Susan Parnell and Sophie Oldfield. New York: Routledge.

Suantika, Wayan. 2015. "Resistensi Masyarakat Lokal terhadap Kapitalisme Global: Studi Kasus Reklamasi Teluk Benoa Bali Tahun 2012–2013" [Resistence from Local Communities to Global Capitalism: A Case Study of the Reclamation of Benoa Bay in Bali in 2012–2013]. *Jurnal Hubungan Internasional* VIII, no. 1: 47–62.

Sugandi, Ahmad Thovan and Abdul Hakam Najjah. 2018. "Panggung Megah Itu akan Roboh: Di Ambang Batas Paradigma dan Harapan akan Revolusi" [The Magnificent Stage Will Crumble: On the Brink of Paradigm and Hope of the Revolution]. *Balairung: Jurnal Multidisipliner Mahasiswa Indonesia* 1, no. 1: 20–39.

Suharko. 2011. "The Limits of Indonesian CSOs in Promoting Democratic Governance". In *Limits of Good Governance in Developing Countries*, edited by Hirotsune Kimura, Suharko, Aser B. Javier, and Ake Tangsupvattana. Yogyakarta: Gadjah Mada University Press.

Suriyani, Luh De. 2016. "Desa adat sepakati pasubayan tolak reklamasi teluk Benoa seperti apa" [Indigenous Villages Agree to Reject the Reclamation of Benoa Bay. Like What?]. *Mongabay*, 24 March 2016. https://www.mongabay.co.id/2016/03/24/desa-adat-sepakati-pasubayan-tolak-reklamasi-teluk-benoa-seperti-apa/.

Syalaby, Achmad. 2016. "Lengkap kronologi reklamasi teluk Jakarta" [A Complete Chronology of the Jakarta Bay Reclamation]. *Republika.co.id*, 3 April 2016. https://nasional.republika.co.id/berita/o51dj4394/lengkap-kronologi-reklamasi-teluk-jakarta.

Tarrow, Sidney. 1994. *Power in Movement: Collective Action, Social Movements and Politics*. Cambridge: Cambridge University Press.

Törnquist, Olle. 2013. *Assessing Dynamics of Democratisation: Transformative Politics, New Institution, and the Case of Indonesia*. New York: Palgrave Macmillan.

TuK Indonesia. 2015. "Koalisi Masyarakat Sipil Luncurkan Platform Keadilan Iklim" [The Civil Society Coalition Launches a Climate Justice Platform]. Jakarta: TuK Indonesia, 12 December 2015. http://www.tuk.or.id.

————. 2020. "Serial Info Taipan HTI: Resiko Para Penyandang Dana Sektor Pulp and Paper di Indonesia" [HTI Tycoon Info Series: Risks of Funders in the Pulp and Paper Sector in Indonesia]. Jakarta: TuK Indonesia, 20 January 2020. http://www.tuk.or.id.

Uhlin, Unders. 1997. *Indonesia and the "Third Wave of Democratization": The Indonesian Pro-Democracy Movement in a Changing World*. London: Curzon Press.

Walhi. 2008. *Menjadi Environmentalis itu Gampang, Sebuah Panduan bagi Pemula* [Becoming an Environmentalist is Easy: A Guide for Beginners]. Jakarta: Walhi.

————. 2014. *Politik 2014: Utamakan Keadilan Ekologis, Tinjauan Lingkungan Hidup Walhi 2014* [2014 Politics: Prioritize Ecological Justice, Walhi 2014 Environmental Review]. Jakarta: Walhi.

————. 2015. *Menagih Janji Menuntut Perubahan, Tinjauan Lingkungan Hidup 2015* [Upholding Promises Demanding Change: 2015 Environmental Review]. Jakarta: Walhi.

————. 2016. *Keharusan Pembenahan Struktural untuk Perubahan Tata Kelola, Tinjauan Lingkungan Hidup 2016* [Structural Improvement is Needed for Changes in Governance: Environmental Review 2016]. Jakarta: Walhi.

Welker, Marina A. 2009. "Corporate Security Begins in the Community: Mining, the Corporate Social Responsibility Industry, and Environmental Advocacy in Indonesia". *Cultural Anthropology* 24, no. 1: 142–79.

Winarni, Rahmawati R. and Jalal. 2017. "Jalan panjang dan berliku keuangan berkelanjutan" [The Long and Winding Road to Sustainable Finance]. Jakarta: TuK Indonesia, 17 July 2017. https://www.tuk.or.id/2017/07/jalan-panjang-dan-berliku-keuangan-berkelanjutan/.

World Bank. 2014. "World Bank and Environment in Indonesia". *World Bank Brief*, 1 August 2014. https://www.worldbank.org/en/country/indonesia/brief/world-bank-and-environment-in-indonesia.

7

ENVIRONMENTAL ACTIVISM IN MALAYSIA: STRUGGLING FOR JUSTICE FROM INDIGENOUS LANDS TO PARLIAMENTARY SEATS

Fadzilah Majid Cooke and Adnan A. Hezri

Environmentalism can be seen as resulting from differences in material conditions and perspectives on how to live and develop sustainably. This chapter describes these differences and set them in the context of Malaysia's recent history. Following on from Guha and Martinez Alier (1997) and Martinez Alier (2002), we depart from the view that environmentalism is a luxury that emerges only when basic needs are fulfilled.[1] We rather consider that the positioning of environmental problems depends on the space available for doing so in the public sphere (Justus et al. 2009). Borrowing from the environmental justice approach, this chapter considers how environmental issues have become entangled with problems of land rights of Indigenous Peoples, particularly in East Malaysia.

Environmental justice is critical of the selective or complete exclusion of local communities for the sake of logging or mining interests, as well as deforestation for vast cash crops like rubber or palm oil (Sicotte and Brulle 2018). In early industrialized countries like the United States, environmental justice mobilizations started with conflicts over the unequal distribution of ecological burdens like waste disposal and air pollution. Although these sorts of conflicts have spread to developing countries, in the latter, social conflicts are still generally provoked by unfair access to natural resources or their destruction by mining, unsustainable logging, and the like (Aiken and Leigh 2015; Majid Cooke et al. 2018; Martinez Alier 2018). By extension, environmental justice is also critical of the cult of wilderness that, in the past, has equated conservation with preservation, for example, through the formation of national parks or the preservation of commons (Schlosberg 2013). Environmental justice has broadened conservation to consider landscapes and biospheres as places where people live, not museums to be preserved.

The discourse of "authentic native identity" aims at regaining the access of Indigenous Peoples to their customary lands. This narrative has won some support through the judicial system. The Orang Asli groups of West Malaysia and the myriad groups officially categorized as "natives" of East Malaysia (Sabah and Sarawak) have won a number of court cases through conservation claims as their livelihoods depend on the ecosystem of these places (Aiken and Leigh 2011). Although this strategy for recovering customary land rights has met with some success, in cases of conflicts over natural resources, the rhetoric of "authentic native identity" might exclude other "native" claims from individuals with equal rights (Murray Li 2001).

Actors from the oil palm and logging industries can also use the native framing to condemn shifting agriculture as unproductive or destructive under the "slash and burn" label (Cramb and McCarthy 2016). Together, the state, industry, and the market impose drastic changes in land use. Subsistence agricultural economies with minimal market involvement have been converted to cash crop production for export. The timber and oil palm industries both have a historical tendency to disregard ecological limits (Majid Cooke 1999), resulting in diminished forest coverage, and increasingly frequent and prolonged flooding (Teo et al. 2001; Merten et al. 2016), despite attempts to set ecological limits on them (Ivancic and Koh 2016). Included in the mix of industry and politics is a complex network of both non-native and *Bumiputra* "native" groups in East Malaysia and *Bumiputra* Malays in West

Malaysia.[2] Resistance against these entrenched forces of environmental degradation is not an easy task.

Despite governmental control and limitation of debate, elections can offer an opportunity for collective action separate from the legal system. The results of the 14th general election held in May 2018 (in Malay *Pilihan Raya ke14*/PRU-14) offer such a case study, as they surprised many analysts and even Malaysia's own citizens. These elections overthrew the government of Najib Razak, who had been Prime Minister since 2009 and, by the same token, put an end to the hegemony of the coalition Barisan Nasional (National Front). Surprisingly, the key actor of that political change was no other than Mahathir Mohamad, the very man who occupied Malaysia's socio-political and epistemological space from 1981 to 2003, leaving behind him the highly-controlled character of Malaysian democracy, or to say the least, its ambivalent nature.

We borrow from Gramsci the idea that, in a regimented democracy like Malaysia, the public sphere is not entirely independent from the state; it is, rather, an arena of contestation between state and counter-hegemonic forces (Ramasamy 2004). The control of Malaysia's social body by the state has been built up over several decades, and it is not limited to the most obvious forms of power, the power to control or repress.[3] However, the reaction of counter-hegemonic forces has been so strong that, in PRU-14, after sixty-one years in power, the political coalition Barisan Nasional, was finally defeated.

How was it possible for the opposition to organize in the face of the incumbent regime's power to exercise widespread and continued control? There are two ways of addressing this question. The first is to look at what went wrong with the regime; the second is to examine what have been the dynamics from below. We explore the second question by looking closely at the development of civil society, especially the environmental movement. Among these institutions we focus especially on Indigenous Peoples and conservation groups. For instance, many of the officials elected in PRU-14 have backgrounds in civil society organizations. However, in past elections, ecological concerns have not really been translated into votes at the ballot box when compared to other drivers of change, such as ethnicity or religion (Hezri 2016). By extension, civil society protests in the past failed to turn into a politically influential movement.

This chapter begins with this apparent contradiction within the dynamics of civil society by scrutinizing the environmental justice concerns that led to PRU-14. The sections that follow go back in history by contextualizing the evolution of environmentalism within the larger economic development of the country and the international influences that have had a bearing on local environmental problems. The last section analyses the protest movement resulting from the location in West Malaysia of a rare earth refinery by a subsidiary of Lynas, an Australian company. In addition to our extensive observation from living in East and West Malaysia, data for this chapter come from our involvement in research projects for more than fifteen years.

Our analysis of PRU-14 is confined to the processes that led to the election and to our observation a few months after the election; it is not meant to evaluate the performance of the Pakatan Harapan government.[4]

Environmental Activism and the 2018 Elections

In the evening of 9 May 2018, the day of the election, it was a shock for many to see that the coalition of the ruling party Barisan Nasional had only acquired seventy-nine seats in the national parliament, compared to 133 seats in 2013. The party also suffered a major defeat at the state level, with the Mahathir-led coalition, Pakatan Harapan, winning ten out of thirteen state governments. After sixty-one years of the Barisan's control over the Malaysian federation, these results therefore appeared to be a major change.

Interestingly, an array of the newly elected officials had background experience in non-governmental organizations (NGOs). Others had left the powerful and established ruling Barisan Nasional to join the opposition Pakatan Harapan, persuaded by the growing weight of public opinion regarding corruption, environmental damage, and the discourse on the "need to save Malaysia". This latter narrative moved some who had not previously been active in social movements or party politics. How could such a turnaround happen despite the continued strong restrictions on the civil sphere and the further introduction of new control mechanisms in the run-up to the election? Our analysis below will focus on the role of environmental issues. Table 7.1 shows the portfolios held by some ministers in the federal parliament and state legislative assemblies.

The table shows that there are strong civil society roots in the life experience of many newly elected members of Parliament. The range of backgrounds reflects well the standpoint that environmental justice in developing countries "is bridging ecological and social justice issues in that it puts the needs and rights of the poor, the excluded and the marginalised at the centre of its concerns" (Cock 2004, p. 2). The roots of environmental activism date back to long before the general election of 2018, and they have mainly been supported by two streams of thought. One stream reflects the position of Giddens (1994) that environmentalism has rarely been a self-contained matter but rather a vehicle for democratization, state accountability, or concerns about modernization in general. The second stream of thought pertains to Indigenous Peoples, how they have reacted to the experience of losing usufruct rights, access to customary land, and the bundle of rights and entitlements affecting their perceived attachment to place. To get an idea of how these two streams have contributed to the recent election of political representatives, let us take a closer look at three examples from Table 7.1.

Wong Tack (no. 7 in the table) once claimed to have initiated Malaysia's "green movement".[5] Back in the early to mid-2000s, in Sabah, he was involved in the successful struggle to prevent the construction of a coal-fired power plant in that region. Then, after having accumulated experience in environmental activism at the national and international level for more than twenty years, he returned to his home state of Pahang, where, in 2011, he launched an NGO named Himpunan Hijau ("Green Assembly"), which took the lead in the protest movement against the rare earth refinery of Lynas Corporation (Majid Cooke and Hezri 2017). People were anxious about the long-term consequences for public health of its radioactive waste. Protesters held demonstrations in many parts of West Malaysia and took the case to court against the government. The mobilization against Lynas became a vast campaign at a national level and included, for instance, the Indigenous Peoples Network of Malaysia (*Jaringan Orang Asal SeMalaysia*/JOAS) and the Coalition for Clean and Fair Elections or *Bersih* (meaning "clean" in Malay).[6]

Regarding the conjunction of clean environment and clean politics, the year 2012 clearly marked a turning point, with big rallies in Kuala Lumpur gathering twenty thousand people wearing green shirts for "clean politics and clean environment", while two hundred thousand

TABLE 7.1
Environmental Background of a Selection of Elected Representatives after Malaysia's 14th General Election (2018)

	Name	Current political position	Role in environmental issues	Outline of career
1	Baru Bian	Federal Minister of Works and Member of Parliament for the seat of Selangau, (Sarawak), under the Parti Keadilan Rakyat (PKR) or the People's Justice Party	A long-time activist and a lawyer for indigenous issues in Sarawak.	Lawyer → Indigenous activist → previously a state representative for the seat of Ba Kelalan and PKR representative in Sarawak → Member of the Federal Parliament (MP) Federal Minister under the Pakatan Harapan (PH) coalition government
2	Saifuddin Abdullah	Foreign Minister and MP representing the seat of Indera Mahkota, State of Pahang, under PKR	A long-time youth and education activist. In recent years, he has worked closely with the Malaysian coalition of social and solidarity economy and the Civil Society Alliance for Sustainable Development Goals. He has announced that apart from civil freedom, a significant focus of his Foreign Ministry is on environmental issues, especially those on sustainable development.	Student activist → Secretary General of Malaysian Youth Council → Author → MP and Deputy Minister under the former regime of Barisan Nasional → Secretary General of PKR → MP and Federal government Minister under the PH coalition

TABLE 7.1 (continued)

3	Dr Maszlee Malik	Federal Minister of Education and an MP for the seat of Simpang Renggam, under the Parti Pribumi Bersatu Malaysia (PPBM) or Malaysian United Indigenous Party	An academic-activist on a range of inequality issues covering education and health sectors.	Researcher and think-tank analyst → Education and health activist → MP and Federal Minister in the PH coalition government
4	Yeo Bee Yin	Federal Minister of Energy, Science, Technology, Climate Change and Environment; MP for the seat of Bakri, Johor (Democratic Action Party/ DAP)	Wrote one chapter each on energy, climate change and water governance in her 2018 book *Reimagining Malaysia*. She was vocal in seeking justice re: the Federal-Selangor State conundrum over water privatization issues and criticized the potential impact of the East Coast Railway Line (ECRL) project on the environment.	Petroleum engineer → DAP State Assembly Woman → Author → MP and Federal Minister in the PH government
5	Fuziah Salleh	Deputy Minister for Religious Affairs in the Prime Minister's Department; MP representing the seat of Kuantan, Pahang (under PKR)	Initiator of the many social groups related to the emergence of anti-Lynas environmental movement. Post-GE14, she was appointed by the Minister of Energy, Science, Technology, Climate Change and Environment to co-lead the review of the Lynas refinery plant under the Parliamentary Select Committee.	Corporate trainer and counsellor → Activist in Jamaah Islah Malaysia (JIM) → PKR Deputy Women Chief → MP and Federal Deputy Minister in the PH government

TABLE 7.1 *(continued)*

6	Sivarasa K. Rasiah	Deputy Minister of Rural Development; Member of Parliament for the seat of Sungei Buloh Selangor (under PKR)	A lawyer who was a human rights activist and inadvertently became involved in Indigenous Rights issues when he took up their cases for human rights for the NGO Suara Rakyat Malaysia (Citizens Voice Malaysia/SUARAM). He was elected to the state government of Selangor.	Human rights lawyer → formerly Member of the Selangor state legislature → now Deputy Minister for Rural Development for the PH government
7	Wong Tack	MP for the seat of Bentong, Pahang (DAP)	An environmental activist; after the elections of May 2018, he was appointed by the Minister of Energy, Science, Technology, Climate Change and Environment to co-lead the review of the Lynas refinery plant under the Parliamentary Select Committee.	Smallholder oil palm estate owner → Environmental activist → MP
8	Jannie Lasimbang	A member of Sabah state Legislative Assembly under DAP, and a Deputy Minister in the Sabah state/regional government headed by Parti Warisan Sabah, that came to power after PRU-14	An NGO activist with twenty years of national and international experience, as founder of the Indigenous rights NGO Pacos Trust in the 1980s, president of the Indigenous Peoples Network of Malaysia (JOAS), Commissioner of the Human Rights Commission of Malaysia (in Sabah) from 2009 to 2011. Abroad, she was the	Researcher → Indigenous Peoples' Activist → Human Rights Commissioner → Member of the state of Sabah Legislative Assembly for the seat of Kepayan in Sabah, and Deputy Minister for Law and Native Affairs in the Parti Warisan government of Sabah[7]

TABLE 7.1 (*continued*)

		Secretary General for Asian Indigenous Peoples' Pact in Chiang Mai, Thailand and an expert during several years at the United Nations Expert Mechanism for the Rights of Indigenous Peoples.	
9	Charles Anthony R. Santiago	MP representing Kelang, Selangor (PKR)	A long-time social activist working on water privatization issues and the distributional impact on Malaysian society.	Economist → Consultant → Water privatization activist → MP
10	Dr Azman Ismail	MP representing Kuala Kedah (PKR)	A champion for the issue of social and environmental justice for the paddy farmers in Kedah against the monopoly of rice production.	Medical doctor → Farmer activist → MP

Note: An arrow → denotes a progression in the public or professional lives of individual politicians yellow shirts contested the corruption of Prime Minister Najib Razak's government (Netto 2012). Police responded with tear gas and chemical-laced water, but in previous decades such protests would have met with a tougher response. In the 1980s, critical environmental voices were muted and labelled as being "against development" at best, or subversive at worst, followed by legal sanctions against them (Case 2001; Weiss and Hassan 2002; Doolittle 2007). In the next sections of this chapter, we will consider some emblematic cases that reflect this evolution.

Similarly, the environmental rights of Indigenous Peoples were well expressed by NGOs as early as the 1980s, for instance, through popular training on land rights (Majid Cooke 2004, 2013). Jannie Lasimbang (no. 8 in Table 7.1) is an activist from Sabah, who has a twenty-year history of advocacy work nationally and internationally. Her main message during the 2018 election was about correcting the mistakes made over decades by previous regimes and that it was time to have a different and more inclusive vision of development.[8] After the 2018 elections, she became Sabah Deputy Minister for Law and Native Affairs.

In Sarawak, the indigenous lawyer and activist Baru Bian (no. 1) has a twenty-five-year experience of dealing with customary land issues, from the early days of logging to more recent plantation development in oil palm. He has been involved in several dozen court claims for land use under Native Customary Rights.[9] In one case that was presented in Federal Court by Baru Bian in December 2016, the Chief Justice ruled against the claims of an indigenous group with the pronouncement that there was no law in Malaysia that allowed customary rights claims over virgin forests around their longhouses. Upon the defeat of the Barisan Nasional coalition in 2018, the then Chief Justice resigned from his post, as a result of public pressure over a conflict of interest in another matter (i.e., not a land issue). Baru Bian became a federal minister at the Ministry of Works in charge of public construction and infrastructure development in the Pakatan Harapan government.

In addition to the three examples above, several other members of the new government might not consider themselves environmentalists, although they have been involved with environmental issues at some stage of their career. Through their experience as health workers, lawyers or in other service industries, they have gained direct contact with

MAP 7.1

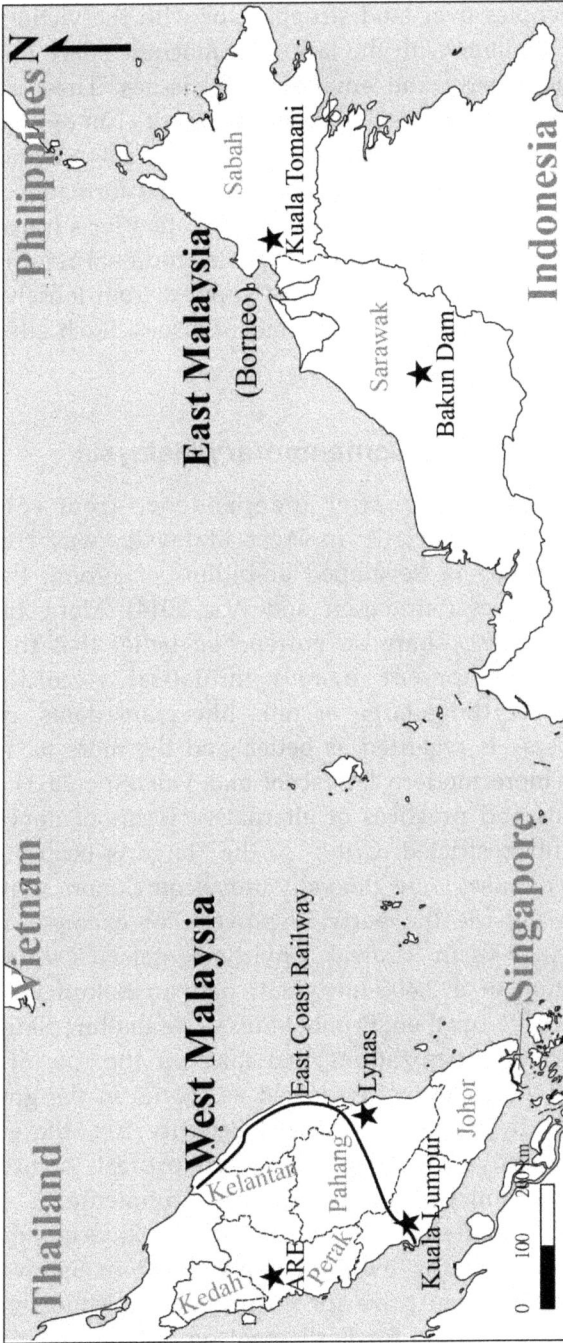

Selected sites of environmental disputes and Parliamentary seats in East and West Malaysia

Source: QGIS and Natural Earth.

Indigenous Peoples over land struggles, or with the victims of floods. They became familiar with the lack of democratic space to expose the links between poverty and environmental issues. These civil society organizers were elected largely because their criticism of the incumbent government emphasized state corruption, fiscal mismanagement, and the high cost of living; they presented the formation of a "new Malaysia" (*Malaysia Baharu*) as the logical solution for a transparent and ethical government, clean elections, and institutional reform to ensure fundamental freedoms. They received support from loosely organized civic groups concerned with a myriad of issues. Such support needs to be contextualized.

Environmentalism in Contemporary Malaysia

In the first thirty years after independence from colonial rule in 1957, poverty, especially in West Malaysia, was considerably reduced and Malaysia developed ambitions of joining the ranks of developed countries (Sundaram and Wee 2014). Many bureaucratic and political leaders share an entrenched belief that there is only one type of development, namely industrial. According to this perspective, everything large or tall—like giant dams, plantations, and skyscrapers—is regarded as better, and the more technologically complex, the more modern (Sovacool and Valentine 2011). The space for discussions and practices of alternative forms of development is therefore highly restricted. Critics of the "large is beautiful" type of development mindset were generally unwelcome, more so if they were coming from outside the party in power. For example, in the late 1980s to early 1990s in Sarawak, environmental NGOs that opposed the construction of a 2,400-megawatt dam in Bakun were labelled "crypto-socialists" by then Prime Minister Mahathir (Singh 2017, p. 43). Civil society organizations that take up the role of watchdog over government policy were viewed as thorns in the government's flesh. In 1987, by using the Internal Security Act, the government mounted a massive crackdown on civil protest, arresting social activists, opposition party politicians, environmentalists, and other concerned individuals (Weiss and Hassan 2002). Among them was Harrison Ngau, a young indigenous activist from Sarawak, who in 1990 won the Goldman prize for environmental leadership; he used the prize money to stand for Parliament on an anti-logging and anti-deforestation platform and won.[10] A few years later, after completing a law degree, he represented Indigenous Peoples in dozens of court cases involving claims to customary lands.[11]

Although the Internal Security Act has now been abolished, the political leadership's past discourse and practices have instilled a tendency to distrust NGOs or to regard them as enemies. Up to 2018, this culture has remained strong. In 2016, Maria Chin Abdullah, the leader of Bersih (Clean Politics Campaign), and several other civil rights and environmental activists were detained under Malaysia's Security Offences (Special Measures) Act, or SOSMA, a law introduced in 2012 to fight threats considered extremist and/or menacing to the country's security. Many of them were released soon after their arrests.[12] In 2017, Chin was arrested once again but released after several days in solitary confinement. These intimidation practices confirmed how NGOs have continued to move in an uncivil political environment since the 1980s. In March 2018, Chin left her responsibilities in Bersih to run as a parliamentary candidate under the Pakatan Harapan banner. Then, in PRU-14, she won the Petaling Jaya constituency against Barisan Nasional.

Despite tighter surveillance, the NGOs of the 1980s and 1990s have remained active until today, although progress has been incremental, and the root cause of environmental degradation—the developmentalist model—remains largely unaddressed (Hezri 2016; Majid Cooke and Hezri 2017). For example, activist and now-minister Baru Bian already mentioned above, has continued where Harrison Ngau left off in Sarawak. As we will see later in this chapter, the episodic protests against the Asian Rare Earth refinery in the 1980s became part of the larger social movement against Lynas.

Environmental Struggle and Indigenous Land Rights

Grassroots environmental struggles in East Malaysia often start with issues of land rights. Leaders and members of these organizations are largely Indigenous Peoples themselves, and, at the community level, the boundary between environmental NGOs and Indigenous Peoples' organizations becomes blurred. State agents encroach on their territories to impose development and modernization in a top-down manner, as if Indigenous Peoples (Orang Asli/Orang Asal) had no other alternative to avoid "being left behind". Faced with such an intrusion, local organizations try to defend their own epistemological space through the legal system (Majid Cooke 2012).

The courts have translated common law rights, which are derived from the colonial occupation of ancestral territories, into pre-existing customary laws (Aiken and Leigh 2011). Such rights, captured under native title rights, do not have their origins in legislative, executive, or judicial orders, and they have survived colonization under common law (Aiken and Leigh 2011). Consequently, one viable way of acquiring redress is to take grievances to court. In West Malaysia, some Indigenous Peoples' organizations won their cases against governments and developers who failed to compensate them properly for the lands taken away in land development schemes for infrastructure, housing or other projects such as airports.[13]

Defining indigenous territory is a major point of contention in such litigation. In Sabah, the establishment of the Kuala Tomani Forest Reserve included Murut land, which they claimed as part of their customary land. Local people considered that they were been trapped in a change of land use that was not conducive to their livelihood and culture (Majid Cooke 2013). NGOs organized paralegal training on customary rights and provided assistance in making claims. Customary rights are acknowledged in some sections of the Sabah Land Ordinance but are in fact often ignored by the administration.

As a means to convince the court, Indigenous Peoples' organizations use the technique of global positioning systems to translate mental maps of community territories into printed maps through Geographic Information Systems (Majid Cooke and Johari 2019). These counter-maps include features neglected in most maps of state forest reserves, such as burial grounds and evidence of occupation prior to the formation of the forest reserve, like the presence of fruit trees, village houses, or longhouses in Sarawak. Villagers have learned that while rubber trees are acceptable to the Sabah Forestry Department, oil palm is not considered a forest species.

However, in the Kuala Tomani Forest Reserve of Sabah, despite more than twenty years of wooing and pleading, the Murut communities failed to gain recognition of their land title by governmental issue. The villagers of Imahit took their case against the Sabah Forestry Department to court. At first instance, the Magistrate Court refused to recognize their land rights within the Forest Reserve; the High Court then ruled in their favour, but they finally lost a second time at the Court of Appeal in 2013 (Majid Cooke 2013).

The mobilizations of Murut communities in Sabah (and of other indigenous organizations in Sarawak and West Malaysia) are quite similar to the actions pursued by other natives around the world (e.g., the Awas Tingni in Nicaragua or the Nisga'a in Canada). In the 1990s and early 2000s, two groups, one led by Sagong Bin Tasi and the other by Adong bin Kuwau, took huge risks in bringing their cases to court and they ultimately won. In a lawsuit launched by the Iban community of Rumah Nor in Sarawak, the plaintiffs claimed that the Borneo Pulp and Paper plantation company had encroached on their longhouse territory. After a victory at the district level, they lost the case in the court of appeal. The case nevertheless set another precedent for customary rights (Aiken and Leigh 2011). Altogether, these three cases have tended to confirm that the common-law jurisdictions recognize the rights of Indigenous Peoples to their ancestral lands, thus providing sufficient stimuli for continued struggle. Between 2001 and 2010, in Sabah alone, there were 745 complaints about land, half of which were about defence of lands under customary claims (Suhakam 2013).

International discourse on environmental justice has paved an avenue for addressing land justice. But one needs to be careful how environmental justice is defined. For instance, Article Eight of the Convention on Biological Diversity (a multilateral treaty that entered into force in 1993) aims to protect traditional knowledge, lifestyles, and culture relevant to the conservation of biological diversity, and to guarantee the equitable allocation of benefits from conservation activities. This cult of the wilderness carries an unexpected effect for Indigenous Peoples: if they have constantly adjusted their livelihoods to cope with the demands of market forces and state interventions, then they may no longer correspond with the image of natives living in harmony with nature; in other words, they do not "fit the slot" required by the Convention (Murray Li 2001). But the Convention nevertheless also stipulates that before making any decision on development programmes on the lands of indigenous occupants, obtaining their free and prior informed consent should be a priority. So many NGOs and social enterprises emphasize this point, but promoting participation and protection of biological and cultural diversity has not been stellar (Majid Cooke et al. 2018).

Several organizations have played an instrumental role in these struggles, both in East and West Malaysia. The Indigenous Peoples

Network of Malaysia or *Jaringan Orang Asal SeMalaysia* (JOAS) has a membership of twenty-one community-based organizations that advocate at different levels for the rights of Indigenous Peoples. The Partners for Community Organizations Sabah (PACOS) focuses on the loss of customary lands and indigenous languages, whereas Friends of the Earth Malaysia (*Sahabat Alam Malaysia*) champions the livelihoods of many Indigenous Peoples in the regions of Baram and Tinjar in Sarawak.

In West Malaysia, a host of Orang Asli organizations engage in the fight against frequent displacement as a result of development implemented on their customary land (be it for plantation agriculture, an airport, or dam), while the first generation of NGOs, mostly urban, have been dealing with "brown issues" such as urban pollution, sanitation, waste removal, water supply, and electricity generation, as well as a new, additional set of problems from heavy industries, especially air pollution. Urban civil society organizations, which previously faced the effects of environmental degradation, are now confronting lifestyle issues such as high amounts of unnecessary wastage (uneaten food, throwaway plastic bags, etc.), gas-guzzling family cars and air conditioned bungalows (Hezri 2016, p. 151).

Additionally, diminishing forests and the threatened supply of clean water in West Malaysia has led to the formation of new NGOs such as the *Persatuan Aktivis Sahabat Alam* (KUASA or Association of the Friend of the Environment Activists) and *Pertubuhan Pelindung Khazanah Alam* (PEKA or Association of Nature Heritage Protectors). The latter's efforts against illegal logging in the forests of Gua Musang (state of Kelantan) and the construction of electric dams in the Sungai Jelai river basin (the state of Pahang), necessarily imply a fight against the injustice done to the place where the Indigenous Peoples of West Malaysia live.

The Mobilization Against Lynas

In November 2008, the Federal government granted a manufacturing licence and a twelve-year tax holiday for Lynas Malaysia Sdn Bhd[14] to produce rare earth oxides and carbonates. This wholly owned subsidiary of Lynas Corporation Limited from Australia was tasked with building and operating the Lynas Advanced Material Plant (LAMP) at the Gebeng Industrial Estate in Kuantan, on the east coast of West Malaysia. With a foreign investment of US$230 million, LAMP is by far the largest rare earth elements extraction and refinery plant outside of China. The plant imports its ore, which contains slightly radioactive thorium, from Mount Weld in Western Australia, and exports its refined products to hi-tech manufacturers in China, Taiwan, Japan, Korea, Europe, and North America. In contrast to the State of Pahang's willingness to locate the facility in the state, the neighbouring State of Terengganu (then under an opposition government) had rejected the investment opportunity in 2007 (Phua 2016).

The seeds of discontent were sown when local residents opposed LAMP because they had not been informed of it earlier. The local protest groups in Balok and Gebeng, Kuantan, which are located within a two-kilometre radius of LAMP, was led by a local opposition leader from the Islamic Party of Malaysia; the groups disbanded in 2010, when they were misled into believing that the project had been suspended (Yew 2016). However, the construction had quietly continued and remained unknown to the Malaysian public until March 2011, when the *New York Times* revealed that 90 per cent of the plant had been completed (Bradsher 2011a). What ensued was a series of larger and more organized protest actions with deep political consequences.

On 26 February 2012, about fifteen thousand people gathered in Kuantan to protest LAMP's location and commencement of operations. On 25 November that same year, over twenty thousand people joined a small group of protesters on their final leg of a fourteen-day, three-hundred-kilometre walk from Kuantan to Kuala Lumpur and picketing against LAMP. This march, also known as The Green Walk, was organized by the NGO Himpunan Hijau launched by activist Wong Tack (*supra* first section).

These gatherings were by far the largest protest actions Malaysia had ever seen. But far from giving in, the authorities doggedly defended Lynas and gave the plant a temporary operating licence until September 2014. Following this period, the Malaysian Atomic Energy Licensing Board granted LAMP a further two-year full operating licence. The Lynas imbroglio did, however, eventually weaken the political support for Barisan Nasional in Kuantan and other areas surrounding the state capital. In the general election of 2013 (PRU-13), Barisan lost four of five state constituency seats, a configuration retained in the 2018 voting.[15] Arguably, the anti-Lynas action represents Malaysia's most

FIGURES 7.1–7.2

A protest against Lynas supported by many civil society organizations, notably Himpunan Hijau, Bersih, and Indigenous groups at Gebeng, in the state of Pahang, 24 June 2012.

Source: Kelvin Chow.

far-reaching experience with environmental action, and it carries great importance for the political economy of the whole federation.

From the outset, there were multiple areas of concern associated with LAMP. The protest was a challenge to the ruling government, which was seen as putting profits before people by allowing Lynas to operate a risky facility without sufficient public consultation. The public was also riled by the competing claims in the media about the safety and health risks associated with the rare earth refinery (Ismail et al. 2016). The controversy divided the community of experts into pro- and anti-Lynas segments, each side marshalling its positions with scientific arguments and reports. The question of environmental justice emerged when the population of 700,000 inhabitants living within a thirty-kilometre radius of LAMP was allegedly at risk of suffering public health issues because of radiation and an unclear hazardous waste disposal plan. In addition, there are also other environmental and economic impacts once a plant with the capacity of 22,000 tonnes per annum begins operations. Public opinion about the danger of nuclear radioactivity was also shaped by the nuclear disaster of March 2011 in Fukushima, Japan.

The mobilization was also inspired by the collective memory of Mitsubishi Chemicals' Asian Rare-Earth (ARE) project, which started refining rare earth in Bukit Merah (north-central Malaysia) in 1982 but shut down ten years later when it became obvious that plant workers and nearby residents suffered from environmental radioactive contamination (Ichihara and Harding 1995; Singh 1992). In the ensuing years, ARE was also linked to a documented rash of birth defects, painful miscarriages, and leukaemia (CAP 1993). After many years with no leukaemia, a total of eight cases in a community of 11,000 happened within five years. As Mitsubishi Group was concerned that the scandal might damage its Southeast Asian operations, in 1992, the company decided to close the refinery and while denying any responsibility for illnesses, it avoided further scandal with an out-of-court settlement of $164,000 to the community's schools and an estimated $100 million to clean up the site (Bradsher 2011b). The clean-up operation is still ongoing after thirty years.

Lynas Corporation claims that, unlike the earlier scenario with the ARE plant, LAMP is not a threat to public health, because lanthanide (its raw material concentrate) emits very low levels of radiation. Yet compared to ARE, the extent of popular support for resisting Lynas has been much greater. As an activist from the Centre for Environment, Technology and Development, Malaysia (CETDEM) told us:

> Lynas has spread beyond Kuantan [state], but the Bukit Merah [the campaign against ARE] never spread beyond the Kinta Valley. Outside NGOs like ours went there in support, but the support remained limited at that time. I think because of the lack of Internet access, we relied on the mainstream media. *The Star* did some coverage and the Chinese papers were very supportive, but that was not enough.[16]

Arguably, the above quote confirms a degree of social learning from the past, which has energized the present movement. At Lynas, social media activism has played an important role in mobilizing support (Kaur 2015). Apart from postings on social media, the anti-Lynas groups also ran an unprecedented *"Bury Lynas with one million signatures"* online petition campaign, which was duly achieved. The anti-Lynas movement comprised not only local residents, but also various consumers, environmental and human rights groups, as well as individual technical experts from outside the state of Kuantan.

Along with local groups, some political actors took a leading role in the mobilization. In 2011, the groups of local residents linked to the Islamic Party (PAS) reorganized into a campaign named Anti Rare Earth Refinery or BADAR (for *Badan Bertindak*), under the leadership of Andansura Rabu, who two years later won the State Assembly seat of Beserah (Yew 2016). In September 2011, a coalition of twenty-two local groups launched the Stop Lynas Coalition (SLC), with the support of Kuantan's opposition member of parliament, Fuziah Salleh, then the Vice President of Parti Keadilan Rakyat (PKR) and, since May 2018, a deputy Federal Minister in the new cabinet.

Along with these opposition political parties, two groups played an instrumental role in the mobilization. One was Save Malaysia Stop Lynas (SMSL), which was launched by Tan Bun Teet, a former schoolteacher. Himpunan Hijau, another group founded by the charismatic Wong Tack, quickly grew into the umbrella group of the anti-Lynas movement, successfully organizing massive street rallies, online campaigns, and petitions. Although all these groups are guided by similar concerns over future socio-economic and ecological impacts in Kuantan, their working relations with the state differ, as explained by one informant:

SMSL and SCL basically have different and complementary approaches. Initially, SMSL members prefer working within the system to avoid too confrontational approaches. They try to utilize the existing networks of relations with decision-makers, to persuade them of what measures should be implemented. They try to be equidistant between opposing and ruling coalitions. [...] From early on, SLC decided that the only fruitful way was to organize a mass protest or street protests.[17]

Both SLC and SMSL have initiated a number of legal cases against Lynas Malaysia. The cases include filing for a judicial review on the issuance of a temporary operating licence for the refinery plant. The Lynas Corporation retaliated by filing a defamation suit against the key activists in the movement to stop them from publishing a joint statement against Lynas.[18]

SMSL poses a deeper challenge to the legitimacy of the state by also influencing NGOs and political leaders in Australia to take up action against the Lynas Corporation, be it from legal or market sanction mechanisms. The Australian Stop Lynas campaign has received strong support in Australia, ever since Australian activists visited the site in Malaysia in July 2011, at the invitation of SMSL. Furthermore, aiming for evidence-based advocacy, SMSL also invited an expert from the Öko Institut (Institute for Applied Ecology) in Germany, who later published a study confirming the radiological and environmental consequences of LAMP's operation and its waste (Schmidt 2013).

Within this movement, Malaysia's entrenched ethnicity-based social divisions have been blurring. According to one source:

> People are now trying to paint the Lynas controversy as a Chinese issue, but somehow it has not been so bad because the Malay group inside has been active from the beginning.[19]

In the 2013 general election, Himpunan Hijau's leader Wong Tack aimed to champion green issues through political representation in the Bentong Parliament as a candidate of the Democratic Action Party. Himpunan campaigned in support of opposition candidates fielded in what was dubbed the "Pahang Green Corridor", which covered a large area including Bentong, Cameron Highlands, Temerloh, and Kuantan. Wong Tack lost the 2013 election to the Barisan Nasional candidate by a slim majority, but he took his revenge five years later, in PRU-14, by winning a seat with a majority of 2,032 votes in a three-way contest. On 8 July 2018, the Minister of Energy, Green Technology,

Science, Climate Change and the Environment appointed Wong Tack and Fuziah Salleh to lead the review of Lynas' operation. Clearly, the energy from the anti-Lynas movement has successfully turned into a political force within Malaysian institutional politics.

As a final curtain to the Lynas story, in May 2019, Lynas announced plans to transfer its rare earth processing facility to Texas (the United States), partly because the Malaysian government requested that the company remove its accumulated waste.[20]

Conclusion

During the 2018 elections, criticism of the corruption, cronyism, and abuse of power of the entrenched elite was widespread. Ironically, it seems that Mahathir's entry in the election has swelled a movement of public opinion for inclusiveness, clean elections, and good governance. Such aspirations imbued even the newly elected who lacked an NGO background or were not particularly involved in the civil sphere prior to these elections. With the exception of a few (Singh 2017), members of environmental NGOs and other civil society organizations found it practical for their own survival to work alongside the state in a relationship of cautious optimism. However, in 2018, some environmental activists shared the perception of large sections of civil society that, since the first decade of the twenty-first century, Malaysia's political economy had deteriorated, and they had no other alternative but to participate in the elections "to save Malaysia". Some had already entertained the idea of being in government since the 2013 elections.

This trend can be traced to as early as the 1990s in Sarawak, when indigenous Kayan environmental activist Harrison Ngau became a member of the State Parliament, on an opposition ticket representing the indigenous Penan communities in their opposition to logging issues.[21] Baru Bian, an indigenous Lun Bawang, has continued the legacy of Harrison Ngau, as a lawyer and federal minister. Similarly, environmental activist Wong Tack has finally become a member of Parliament in the new government. In sum, although there is no "green party" as such, environmental activism has not shied away from state power, and the environmental movement has been gaining traction under the banner of social justice.

In addition, as the examples of Harrison Ngau and Baru Bian show, once initiated, grassroots organizing does not die in the face of state controls. The groups involved in the 1980s Asia Rare Earth protest in West Malaysia, later formed the backbone of the mobilization against Lynas. This environmental activism departs from the cult of wilderness and is best understood within the framework of environmental justice, linking issues of poverty and social inequality with democracy and indigenous rights.

The key factors contributing to a movement's failure or success have fuelled a lot of debates in social mobilization theory. The idea that social movements could be at times loosely organized, and ostensibly disappear, but then quickly regroup when necessary (Giugni 1998) seems apt in Malaysia. Within movements there are different definitions of success, so that taking over state power may not be regarded as a success story by some, as it is by others within the movement. Prior to 2018, considering the overarching control of state power over the social body, it was difficult to see the latent power within civil society, so that the regime change arrived as a surprise to many. But given the political economy that envelops Malaysian capitalism, it might be a long wait for the state to undo its own excesses on which its hegemony has thus far depended. How Malaysian environmental movements reshape and restrategize moving forward will certainly be the focus of further studies.[22]

NOTES

1. The intrinsic value of landscapes and ecosystems is assumed by a branch of environmentalism to be inherent in them and is independent of market-based assessment of instrumental value by valuers, such as humans (Justus et al. 2009).

2. *Bumiputra* meaning "sons of the soil" is a category introduced in the 1960s to refer to individuals viewed by the administrative apparatus as needing economic assistance via widespread affirmative action policy, which has lost aspects of its original intention because of bureaucratization (Majid Cooke and Johari 2019).

3. We need to look at various and subtler forms of power of control, which are exercised at "the point where power reaches into the very grain of individuals, touches their bodies and inserts itself into their actions and

attitudes, their discourses, learning processes and everyday lives" (Foucault 1978, p. 39).

4. The Pakatan Harapan government proved to be unstable, for it was a coalition of parties which included reformist leaders from civil society groups as well as political parties entrenched in the older style of patron-client leadership. The coalition lasted twenty-one months. For a state-centred analysis of the reasons for party implosion and future prospects for reform, see Moten (2020) and Ostwald (2020).

5. "Kinitalk: Wong Tack, the Person behind the Green Movement", *KiniTV*, 24 March 2013 (available on YouTube).

6. Netto (2012) and personal communication with the Centre for Orang Asli Concerns, 22 July 2018.

7. Under Malaysia's Federal System, the eastern states of Malaysia (Sabah and Sarawak) have their own political parties, some of which are unique to the state, and not replicated at the federal level. The Parti Warisan Sabah is an example of the Sabah ruling coalition that is not found at the federal level, but has "friendly relations" with Kuala Lumpur. There is a strong move now from Sabah and Sarawak to shift the status of these two states to regions, each of which to be regarded as equivalent in social, economic and political standing to the region of West Malaysia (containing eleven states), as per the Malaysia Agreement of 1963 in the formation of Malaysia.

8. "Impian rakyat Sabah: Membangun Kepayan Bersama Jannie Lasimbang" [The Dream of Sabah Citizens: Building Kepayan with Jannie Lasimbang], *Channel Rakyat*, 9 February 2018 (interview in Malay with Jannie Lasimbang, available on YouTube).

9. In legal documents, Indigenous Peoples in Sarawak and Sabah are referred as "natives" with rights to claim lands under specific sections of the land laws. Although it is limited to a few allowable methods, the modus operandi for making these claims under customary rights is enshrined in several sections of the Sarawak Land Code of 1958 and the Sabah Land Ordinance of 1930 (Majid Cooke 2003; Majid Cooke 2013). Despite being enshrined and confined to a few allowable options, the actual awarding of licences to native claimants is subject to intense bureaucratic hurdles, making the whole procedure serpentine.

10. "Harrison Ngau Laing, 1990 Goldman Prize Recipient", https://www.goldmanprize.org/recipient/harrison-ngau-laing/.

11. Our interview with Ngau in Miri, Sarawak, 4 July 2015.

12. "US 'Troubled' over Malaysia's Detention of Activist and Najib Critic", *The Guardian*, 24 November 2016.

13. Court cases in West Malaysia: *Sagong Bin Tasi v. the state government of Selangor* and *Adong bin Kuwau v. the Government of Johor* (Aiken and Leigh 2011).
14. Sdn Bhd stands for Sendirian Berhad, which designates a private limited company in Malaysia.
15. There are two Parliamentary seats for the Kuantan district, namely Kuantan and Indera Mahkota. Kuantan has three State legislative seats (Teruntum, Tanjung Lumpur, and Inderapura), while Indera Mahkota has two seats (Baserah and Semambu). In the 2008 election, Barisan Nasional won four seats except Baserah. In 2013, the opposition won four seats except Inderapura.
16. Interview in Kuala Lumpur, 10 March 2013.
17. Interview in Kuala Lumpur, 27 March 2013.
18. "Civil Society Organizations' Joint Statement on Lynas Issue: SMSL & Malaysian NGOs Statement against LYNAS", *Malaysia Today*, 11 April 2012.
19. Interview in Petaling Jaya, Selangor, 10 June 2013. The view that civil society is fragmented by ethnic groups (Malays, Chinese, Indians and Indigenous) is somewhat inaccurate in the environmental movement. In the Lynas campaign, Wong Tack and other leaders are supported by Malay politicians both established and aspiring (as in Fuziah Salleh mentioned in the text), and by Indigenous Peoples of West Malaysia (the Orang Asli). For other cases of environmental involvement, see also Singh (1992 and 2017). Indigenous Peoples' grievances are advocated in court by both Chinese and Indigenous lawyers (personal observations in Sabah and Sarawak, 2001, 2011, 2013).
20. "Lynas Plans New Plant in US after Facing Problems in Malaysia", *The Star*, 20 May 2019.
21. Penan and Kayan are among the group of Indigenous Peoples in Sarawak who are officially categorized as the Orang Ulu (upland people), although this category is imposed upon them by outsiders. The term Orang Ulu is specific to Indigenous Peoples living in the Sarawak hinterland (Majid Cooke 2002). While Orang Asli (Aboriginals) are indigenous to West Malaysia, Orang Asal (Original Peoples) refers to the umbrella term for all Indigenous Peoples of East and West Malaysia. The Malay group is also considered indigenous (*Bumiputera* or "sons of the soil") in policy terms, but not in the academic term because of its socially and politically dominant position.
22. The Perikatan government, formed in 2020 through elite political manoeuvring, has a strong coalition of Malay-oriented interests; because of legitimacy issues in a multicultural country (Ostwald 2020), it could be

prone to old-style top-down control measures. Under such conditions, social movements could reappear or regroup to take different forms under the impulse from a multitude of well-structured non-governmental think tanks. Another interesting development in the context of the Covid-19 pandemic is the movement initiated under the slogan of *kita jaga kita* ("we look after one another"), which includes a large range of issues, from student welfare and workers who have lost their jobs to assistance for flood victims and the indigenous Orang Asli communities.

REFERENCES

Aiken, S. Robert and Colin H. Leigh. 2011. "Seeking Redress in the Courts: Indigenous Land Rights and Judicial Decisions in Malaysia". *Modern Asian Studies* 45, no. 4: 825–27.

———. 2015. "Dams and Indigenous Peoples in Malaysia: Development, Displacement and Resettlement". *Geografiska Annaler: Series B, Human Geography* 97: 69–93.

Bradsher, Keith. 2011a. "Taking a Risk for Rare Earths". *New York Times*, 8 March 2011.

———. 2011b. "Mitsubishi Quietly Cleans Up Its Former Refinery". *New York Times*, 8 March 2011.

Case, William. 2001. "Malaysia's Resilient Pseudo-Democracy". *Journal of Democracy* 12, no. 1: 43–57.

Cock, Jacklyn. 2004. "Connecting the Red, Brown and Green: The Environmental Justice Movement in South Africa". *Globalisation, Marginalisation and New Social Movements in post-Apartheid South Africa*. Durban: School of Development Studies, University of KwaZulu Natal.

Consumers' Association Penang (CAP). 1993. *Wasted Lives: Radioactive Poisoning in Bukit Merah*. Penang, Malaysia: CAP.

Cramb, Robert and John McCarthy, eds. 2016. *The Oil Palm Complex: Smallholders, Agribusiness and the State in Indonesia and Malaysia*. Singapore: National University of Singapore Press.

Doolittle, Amity. 2007. "Native Land Tenure, Conservation and Development in a Pseudo-Democracy: Sabah, Malaysia". *Journal of Peasant Studies* 34, no. 3: 474–97.

Foucault, Michel. 1978. *Power/Knowledge: Selected Interviews and Other Writings*. New York: Pantheon Books.

Giddens, Anthony. 1994. *Beyond Left and Right: The Future of Radical Politics*. Cambridge: Polity.

Giugni, Margo. 1998. "Was It Worth the Effort? The Outcomes and Consequences of Social Movements". *Annual Review of Sociology* 24: 371–93.

Guha, Ramachandra and Joan Martinez Alier. 1997. *Varieties of Environmentalism: Essays North and South.* London: Earthscan.

Hezri, Adnan A. 2016. *The Sustainability Shift: Refashioning Malaysia's Future.* Penang: Areca Books.

Ichihara, Mika and Andrew Harding. 1995. "Human Rights, the Environment and Radioactive Waste: A Study of the Asian Rare Earth Case in Malaysia". *Review of European, Comparative & International Environmental Law* 4, no. 1: 1–14.

Ismail, T.H. Tengku, H. Juahir, A.Z. Aris, Sharifuddin M. Zain, and Armi Abu Samah. 2016. "Local Community Acceptance of the Rare Earth Industry: The Case of the Lynas Advanced Materials Plant (LAMP) in Malaysia". *Environment, Development and Sustainability* 18, no. 3: 739–62.

Ivancic, Helena and Lian Pin Koh. 2016. "Evolution of Sustainable Palm Oil Policy in Southeast Asia". *Cogent Environmental Science* 2, no. 1: 1195032.

Justus, James, Mark Colyvan, Helen Regan, and Lynn Maguire. 2009. "Buying into Conservation: Intrinsic Value versus Instrumental Value". *Trends in Ecology and Evolution* 24, no. 4: 187–91.

Kaur, Kiranjit. 2015. "Social Media Creating Digital Environmental Publics: Case of Lynas Malaysia". *Public Relations Review* 41: 311–14.

Majid Cooke, Fadzilah. 1999. *Forest Resource Policy in Malaysia 1970–1995.* Sydney: Allen & Unwin and University of Hawaii Press.

———. 2002. "NGOs in Sarawak". In *Social Movements in Malaysia: From Moral Communities to NGOs*, edited by Meredith Weiss and Saliha Hassan. London: Routledge.

———. 2003. "Maps and Counter-Maps: Globalised Imaginings and Local Realities of Sarawak's Plantation Agriculture". *Journal of Southeast Asian Studies* 34, no. 2: 265–84.

———. 2012. "In the Name of Poverty Alleviation: Experiments with Oil Palm Smallholders and Customary Land in Sabah". *Asia Pacific Viewpoint* 53, no. 3: 240–53.

———. 2013. "Constructing Rights: Indigenous Peoples at the Public Hearings of the National Inquiry into Customary Rights to Land in Sabah, Malaysia". *Sojourn: Journal of Social Issues in Southeast Asia* 28, no. 3: 512–37.

Majid Cooke, Fadzilah and Adnan A. Hezri. 2017. "Malaysia: Structure and Agency of the Environmental Movements". In *Handbook on the Environment in Southeast Asia*, edited by Philip Hirsch. London: Routledge.

Majid Cooke, Fadzilah, Adnan A. Hezri, Reza Azmi, Ryan Mukit, Paul Jensen, and Pauline Deutz. 2018. "Oil Palm Cultivation as Development Vehicle: Exploring the Trade-offs for Smallholders in East Malaysia". In *Handbook of Southeast Asian Development*, edited by Andrew McGregor, Lisa Law, and Fiona Miller. London: Routledge.

Majid Cooke, Fadzilah and Sofia Johari. 2019. "Positioning of Murut and Bajau Identities in State Forest Reserves and Marine Parks in Sabah, East Malaysia". *Journal of Southeast Asian Studies* 50, no. 1: 129–49.

Martinez Alier, Joan. 2002. *Environmentalism of the Poor*. Cheltenham: Edward Elgar.

———. 2018. "Ecological Distribution Conflicts and the Vocabulary of Environmental Justice". In *Ecology Economy and Society*, edited by Vickram Dayal, Anantha Duraiappa, and Naindan Nawn. Singapore: Springer.

Merten, Jennifer, Alexander Röll, Thomas Guillaume, Ana Meijide, Suria Tarigan, Herdhata Agusta, Claudia Dislich, Christoph Dittrich, Heiko Faust, Dodo Gunawan, Jonas Hein, Hendrayanto, Alexander Knohl, Yakov Kuzyakov, Kerstin Wiegand, and Dirk Hölscher. 2016. "Water Scarcity and Oil Palm Expansion: Social Views and Environmental Processes". *Ecology and Society* 21, no. 2: Art. 5.

Moten, Abdul Rashid Moten. 2020. "The Politics of Manipulation, Malaysia: 2018–2020". *Intellectual Discourses* 28, no. 2: 387–408.

Murray Li, Tania. 2001. "Masyarakat Adat, Difference, and the Limits of Recognition in Indonesia's Forest Zone". *Modern Asian Studies* 35, no. 3: 645–76.

Netto, Anil. 2012. "Malaysia's Green Movement Goes Political". *Inter Press Service*, 21 July 2012. http://www.ipsnews.net/2012/07/malaysias-green-movement-goes-political/.

Noh, Abdillah. 2014. "Malaysia 13th General Election: A Short Note on Malaysia's Continuing Battle with Ethnic Politics". *Electoral Studies* 34 (June): 266–69.

Ostwald, Kai. 2020. "The Impasse of Two-coalition Politics". *ISEAS Perspective*, no. 2020/25, 6 April 2020.

Phua, Kai Lit. 2016. "Rare Earth Plant in Malaysia: Governance, Green Politics, and Geopolitics". *Southeast Asian Studies* 5, no. 3: 443–62.

Ramasamy, Palanisamy. 2004. "Civil Society in Malaysia: An Arena for Contestation?" In *Civil Society in Southeast Asia*, edited by Lee Hock Guan. Copenhagen: Nordic Institute of Asian Studies Press and Singapore: Institute of Southeast Asian Studies, pp. 198–216.

Schlosberg, David. 2013. "Theorising Environmental Justice: The Expanding Sphere of a Discourse". *Environmental Politics* 22, no. 1: 37–55.

Schmidt, Gerhard. 2013. *Description and Critical Environmental Evaluation of the REE Refining Plant LAMP near Kuantan/Malaysia. Radiological and Non-Radiological Environmental Consequences of the Plant's Operation and its Wastes*. Darmstad: Öko-Institut e.V. (Institut für angewandte Ökologie). https://www.oeko.de/oekodoc/1628/2013-001-en.pdf.

Sicotte, Diane M. and Robert J. Brulle. 2018. "Social Movements for Environmental Justice through the Lens of Social Movement Theory". In

The Handbook of Social Movement Theory, edited by Ryan Holifield, Jayajit Chakraborty, and Gordon Wallace. London: Routledge, pp. 25–49.

Singh, Gurmit K.S. 1992. "Case Studies of Environmental Awareness in Malaysia". *Nature and Resources* 28: 30–37.

———. 2017. *Memoirs of a Malaysian Eco-Activist*. Penang: Areca Books.

Sovacool, Benjamin and Scott Valentine. 2011. "Bending Bamboo: Restructuring Rural Electrification in Sarawak, Malaysia". *Energy for Sustainable Development* 15, no. 3: 240–53.

Suhakam (Human Rights Commission of Malaysia). 2013. *Report of the National Inquiry into the Land Rights of Indigenous Peoples*. Kuala Lumpur: Human Rights Commission of Malaysia.

Sundaram, Jomo Kwame and Wee Chong Hui. 2014. *Malaysia@50: Economic Development, Distribution, Disparities*. Singapore: World Scientific Publishing.

Teo Cheong Hai, Andrew Ng, Cede Prudente, Caroline Pang, and Joseph Teck Choo Yee. 2001. "Balancing the Need for Sustainable Oil Palm Development and Conservation: The Lower Kinabatangan Floodplains Experience". Paper presented at the ISP national seminar on strategic direction for the sustainability of the oil palm industry, Kota Kinabalu (Sabah, Malaysia), 11–12 June 2001.

Weiss, Meredith and Saliha Hassan, eds. 2002. *Social Movements in Malaysia: From Moral Communities to NGOs*. London: Routledge.

Yew, Wei Lit. 2016. "Constraint Without Coercion: Indirect Repression of Environmental Protest in Malaysia". *Pacific Affairs* 89, no. 3: 543–65.

8

STATE, NGOS, AND VILLAGERS: HOW THE THAI ENVIRONMENTAL MOVEMENT FELL SILENT

Jakkrit Sangkhamanee[1]

Environmental problems do not occur solely as a result of natural phenomena, but are also a product of multi-faceted socio-political interactions. This is especially true in the Anthropocene era, in which the impact of human activities on the environment has been elevated to a geological scale. Such interactions likewise effect the mobilization that arises in response to environmental problems. This chapter highlights how, in Thailand, the political changes of the last twenty years— including mass mobilizations, military coups, constitutional reforms, and erratic government—have reoriented the country's environmental movement(s) away from the activism of earlier years, toward a more reactionary stance. In Thailand, as in other countries of the region, environmental politics largely focuses on the over-exploitation of natural resources, such as rainforests for logging and agribusiness, and rivers for the construction of hydroelectric dams. Resource politics is especially important if we consider the new forms of governance and institution required to cope with the challenges of the Anthropocene.

Environmental politics in Thailand goes far beyond formal political institutions with the government at the centre. In fact, it involves the dynamism of power relations and the wider processes of democratization, the politics of mass mobilization, knowledge production, emerging economic and social aspirations, as well as the rise and decline of relations between incumbent governments and civil organizations. These relations may be embodied in different ways— contestation, negotiation, cooperation, even impasse. The changing interactions among actors also create a new terrain in which various kinds of political manoeuvres can be achieved in the area of resource politics and in environmentalism more broadly.

In this chapter, I look at Thailand's environmental movement during the past two decades through the interaction between the state, non-governmental organizations (NGOs),[2] and the populations who are directly or indirectly affected by environmental issues. During the country's rapid economic growth in the 1990s, governments' development policies often caused all sorts of ecological problems, resulting in the dissatisfaction and mobilization of people demanding better management. During the 2000s, the political instability of the country added to the obstruction of sustainable development, especially the lack of meaningful participation of average citizens in the decision-making process. Such instabilities have created a new platform in which the former strategy of mass mobilization, namely, calling for the accountability of the incumbent government, has become ineffective. In addition, while the old relations between NGOs and rural people, articulated through street politics against the government, have become obsolete, a new kind of relations between elected governments and the agrarian masses has been formed through several natural resource and community development schemes.

Environmental Movements under Disparate Political Regimes

In considering Thailand's environmental politics, it is evident that "politics" cannot be solely limited to the actions of the government. In fact, environmental issues always involve a multiplicity of political actors. In this chapter, I argue that most of the environmental problems the country has experienced during the past decades—flooding, forest degradation, land rights and insecurity, chronic draught, river basin management, hydropower and coal-power production—often revolve around the triangulated relations between the government, NGOs, and citizens (see Figure 8.1).

As briefly mentioned above, many other actors have shaped the nature of resource politics in Thailand beyond the three principle ones. King Bhumibol and his irrigation projects in the highland territories, for example, have played a crucial role in legitimizing the role of the monarchy in natural resource discourse and practices (Blake 2015). In addition, the military and its security operations under the banner of rural development schemes acted as an "anti-politics" machine (Ferguson 1994) in bringing local villages into their political ideological construction (Sangkhamanee 2010).

Besides these domestic actors, external forces, like China and its investors in the Belt and Road Initiative projects (and similar pre-BRI undertakings) in Thailand, constitute major influences on environmental politics that go beyond the country's boundaries. A marked shift in geopolitical polarity from Western democratic ideals towards China's regional economic cooperation has also led to the transformation of the relations between civil society organizations and the state (Sangkhamanee 2014). Chinese investments in agriculture, trade, infrastructure, and the service industries in Thailand and the region have changed the nature of environmental impacts from domestically bounded to transnational. This poses a challenge for the NGOs in terms of their advocacy, which used to focus mainly on demanding accountability from their own national governments.

Recognizing that any account of environmental politics is necessarily a simplification of a far more complex reality, my analysis will concentrate on the relations between the state, civil society, and average citizens. Following on Rapin Quinn (1997)'s approach to Thai environmental politics between 1970 and 1990, I suggest that these three actors have continued to play a fundamental role over the last two decades.

Most of the recent studies on political relationships between the government, the general population, and NGOs in Thailand can be divided into two divergent approaches (Sangkhamanee 2013). The first entails the study of *parliamentary politics*, with a particular interest in the institutional approach to political relations which includes elections, the deposition of governments, and political reforms by urban and elitist networks (Callahan 2005; Callahan and McCargo 1996; McCargo 2005; Nishizaki 2001; Ockey 1996 and 2004; Phongpaichit and Baker 2009). In contrast, the second approach encompasses the *street politics* of social movements led by an alliance of NGOs and expressed through the mobilization of people residing mostly in rural areas and who suffer from policies destructive to their living environment (Phatharathananunth 2006; Missingham 2003). In this contribution, however, I will shed some light on an overlapping dimension beyond those two divergent approaches. I argue that, when examining environmental and resource politics, it can be observed that the triangulated relations between government, citizens, and networks of social movements bestride the dividing line between parliamentary and street politics. In addition, amidst the political unrest during the past two decades, such triangulated relations have continually been reshuffled. The unruly and unsettled relations among actors usually go beyond a fixed perception of antagonistic and cooperative relationships.

FIGURE 8.1

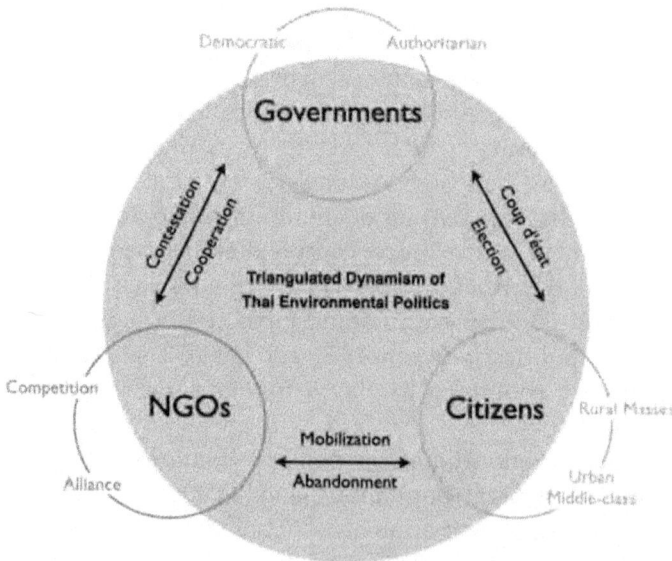

Triangulated dynamism between the government, NGOs, and citizens

Figure 8.1 portrays the triangulated, dynamic relations between different regimes of government (democratic and authoritarian-leaning), changing civil society relations (competition and alliance), and citizens of different backgrounds (rural and urban dwellers). It shows non-linear, co-evolutionary processes and relations occurring between the dominant politics of the day, and the ways in which environmental issues are framed and contested by Thailand's environmental movements during the past few decades. As will be discussed in detail later in this chapter, Thailand's environmental politics are very much shaped by how resources are framed and negotiated. Such a process does not occur in isolation; rather, it is embedded in the ways political contexts are formulated between different actors in their changing relations.

Let me provide a brief, concrete case to illustrate Figure 8.1. Each regime of government rose to power through their engagement with citizens and civil society organizations. It is necessary then to consider the triangulated relations in the context of frequent changes of political regimes from liberal democracy to authoritarianism, or in mixed regimes like Thaksin's populism. The rise to power of Thaksin Shinawatra between 2001 and 2006 as a result of electoral success, for example, certainly changed such triangulated relations and the way Thai environmental politics was understood during the authoritarian era. Even though many of his policies, such as the capitalization of assets, and mega-projects in resource development, as well as the use of various forms of populist policy, did not directly aim towards environmental management, such policies, however, had enormous effects on the environment and resource redistribution, particularly at the community level. This consequently led to heated criticism and stimulated wider political contestation among different groups in Thai society, led by conservative urban elites and communitarian-oriented NGOs.

As his electoral support was very much based in rural areas, Thaksin changed the relations between the government and villagers from an exploitative and antagonistic approach to a more collaborative and supportive one (Walker 2008 and 2012). Specifically, he enhanced economic opportunities based on local resource restructuring and management. Redefining environmental utilization and the establishment of collaborative relations between state and local communities weakened NGOs' role tremendously, particularly in their alliance with country folk who had protested against the unjust policies imposed by the government in the 1990s. In other words, through populist policy and elections, Thaksin moved environmental politics from street occupation to his electoral mobilization. He changed not only the way resources were allocated and distributed but also created a wider economic desire and political aspiration among the rural populace (Sangkhamanee 2013) that consequently led to the formation of new relations in environmental politics.

The 2006 coup d'état of the Thai military against Thaksin's government, achieved through accusations of corruption, tried to restore the original relationships wherein the government was the sole agent in determining the allocation of resources for its obedient citizens. This move was supported by the urban elites, who felt that Thaksin's populist patronage had raised unwarranted ambitions in the rural populace (Farrelly 2013; Glassman 2010; Walker 2012; Winichakul 2008; Chua 2018a).

During the 1990s, NGOs were able to be very active in supporting and protecting villagers with their environmental concerns. Between 2006 and early 2008, during the military government of General Surayud Chulanont, however, the role of NGOs in similar actions was almost unheard of. Then, between late 2008 and 2011, during the army-backed government of Abhisit Vejjajiva, while a few environmental NGOs were still active, their strategies and bargaining power had become much more limited compared to what they had been under previous civilian governments.

In Thailand, the urban elite and middle class have often overthrown governments that were elected by the rural population. According to Jim Glassman (2010), while urban movements are often associated with what are considered "progressive" political causes, divisions between Thailand's urban and rural populations have often superseded that tendency. For example, city dwellers often castigate their rural counterparts for what they deem short-term views, such as easily accepting vote-buying offers from local politicians (Sangkhamanee 2013). So, when the rural masses had an opportunity to elect the government they saw as better representing them—thanks to its promising policies toward rural development—the urban middle-class objected and chose rather to support the military to overthrow and silence the rural mandate.

This vicious cycle led to another major political crisis in early 2014. After a military coup, General Prayut Chan-o-cha took control of the country, replacing the democratically elected government of Yingluck Shinawatra. In the midst of the sluggish political reforms that have since followed, some prominent NGO representatives have been appointed as members of various commissions. However, local populations and environmental groups tend to encounter the deprivation of their rights in political expression and negotiation in the management of resources and environment (Thabchumpon et al. 2015).

In the following sections, I trace the dynamics of the triangulated relations of Thai environmental politics under the different political regimes of the last two decades. However, in order to examine the recent political instability, it is necessary to shed some light on the 1990s' legacy, a period that is often described as the pinnacle of Thailand's environmentalism and social movements.

Legacy of the 1990s Environmental Movements

In the mid-1990s, Thailand's economy had been substantially transformed, but its rapid development led to numerous negative consequences for the environment. To name some of the most spectacular or most problematic phenomena: the construction of dams to cope with the demand for electricity; the confiscation of villagers' lands for large eucalyptus plantations to supply the pulp and paper industry; the emergence of slum dwellings in Bangkok and other big cities due to labour migration and the lack of housing assistance; the decline of aquatic animals caused by the multiplication of commercial fisheries; the leakage of toxic substances from coal mining and industrial factories; and deforestation as a result of the expansion of agricultural areas, road construction, and military protection of the national borders (Bello et al. 1998; Delang 2002; Fahn 2003).

In response to these dramatic changes, in 1995, the Assembly of the Poor (AOP) was established on 10 December, International Human Rights Day. The AOP was formed as a nationwide network of locally active NGOs, particularly organizations working on issues of the environment and natural resources, as well as the alliance of villagers affected by various development projects. According to Bruce Missingham (2003, p. 3), the AOP "was the first national organization representing rural villagers' interests to emerge since the Peasant's Federation of Thailand in the mid-1970s". The environmental movements under the umbrella of the AOP had the ultimate goal of enhancing the political power of local inhabitants in negotiating with the government. Prior to the formation of the AOP, the different struggles of local NGOs and communities were dealt with individually. The nationwide alliance of environmental movements like the AOP allowed greater empowerment and more bargaining power.

In addition to the country's rapid economic development, environmental problems were also the result of inefficient bureaucracy combined with repressive governmental regimes (So and Lee 1999). The political upheaval of May 1992—also called Black May—emerged from the public demonstrations against the military-backed government of General Suchinda Kraprayoon. This uprising of citizens consequently led to a more open political space and facilitated competition between political parties. Furthermore, such changes in the political environment caused subsequent governments to become more interested in policies related to the livelihoods of their electoral constituency.

Institutionally, the political reform after Black May also led to the drafting of a new constitution. The 1997 Constitution emphasized the provision of the rights of citizens to monitor the government's exercise of power, as well as the restructuring of political institutions in a more transparent manner; civil society was thus enabled to gain more control of their own lives (Shigetomi 2002). The Constitution also granted citizens the right to manage natural resources and participate in the implementation of environmental policies. The emergence of street movements, especially the AOP nationwide protests fighting against the problems arising from development projects during the 1990s, was part of the process towards a more open political space.

Let me put forth one example of environmental movement that illustrates the intertwining relations of politics across the street and parliamentary arenas. During the late 1990s, one of the most important debates regarding environmental management centred on the issue of the highland agricultural practice popularly known as "shifting cultivation". In Thailand, "shifting cultivation" has often been pejoratively singled out as contributing to environmental problems, such as deforestation, soil erosion, and the destruction of natural water sources (Forsyth and Walker 2008). Such politicized environmental perceptions and discourses led to the expulsion of highland people from the forest and agricultural lands that they had relied on for generations.

Reacting to such environmental stigmatization, Towards Ecological Recovery and Regional Alliance (TERRA), a regionally-based, non-governmental organization, became actively engaged in contestation with specialists and decision-makers over forest management (Forsyth 1999; Laungaramsri 1999). In cooperation with scholars and local NGOs, they conducted field research on the upland agricultural areas of the Karen ethnic group in the northern region. The research aimed to provide an alternative view of upland agricultural practices and its environmental sustainability that would challenge technocratic expertise (Laungaramsri 2001; Santasombat 2003).

Culture and ethnic knowledge was viewed as the answer to environmental problems. Focusing on the practices of the Karen people, the research-action showed that highland agriculture should be redefined as a "rotational shifting cultivation" (*rai mun wian*) that does not encroach on forests, does not spoil water sources, and does not erode the soil. This type of agriculture based on local knowledge also plays a significant role in the conservation of biodiversity and develops the cultural capital of the Karen (Trakarnsuphakorn 2002). The way of life of these ethnic communities is mutually beneficial with the protection of the ecosystem (Ganjanapan 2000). The research subsequently led to a campaign for the Community Forest Bill in granting villagers the rights to utilize lands and forests in a sustainable manner.

While this cultural ecologist view towards upland agriculture empowered ethnic groups to gain better control over their environment, the proposition, however, became what Andrew Walker (2001) referred to as "the Karen consensus", in which the concerted environmentalist perspective towards the Karen people's agriculture tended to downplay the significance of market involvement in the livelihood of ethnic minorities. Instead of a unanimous political struggle over land tenure insecurity, Walker perceived that the campaign would carry a greater legitimacy if it acknowledged that the agricultural practices of ethnic groups are, in fact, connected with broader commercial networks that do not exclude developmental support from the neoliberal system (Walker 2004a, 2004b).

The campaign for the Community Forest Bill by TERRA and northern NGOs during the late 1990s and the 1997 AOP protest in front of the Government House brought environmental issues from demonstrations into a parliamentary discussion. In 1999, thanks to the new Constitution, which allowed fifty thousand eligible citizens to submit a petition to the parliament, the Community Forest Bill was successfully passed by the Legislative Assembly. Despite its final rejection by the Senate, this mobilization opened up the way for bringing ethnic rights and environmental issues into the parliament. The AOP, which demanded that the government resolve up to 125 issues, was eventually successful in settling an agreement that became a cabinet resolution during the period of General Chavalit Yongchaiyudh's government in 1997, but this agreement was later distorted by the following cabinet of Chuan Leekpai (1997–2001) and the poor response of his Democrat Party (Baker 2000). Though environmental movements were yet to be fully integrated into parliamentary politics, nevertheless, the 1990s ended with intense activity by NGOs that paved the way for a greater politicization of the environment.

A Shift from Street Politics to Knowledge Politics

At the beginning of 2001, Thaksin Shinawatra, a former telecommunications tycoon, won the general election by a landslide. When he assumed his position as Prime Minister in February, the AOP, which had been conducting a sit-in in front of the Government House, invited him for a "lunch meeting" to discuss the remaining problems he had promised to solve during his electoral campaign. Thereafter, Thaksin agreed to establish seventeen subcommittees to oversee the problems of villagers. After more than nine months of protest, the demonstrators ended their sit-in with a blessing ceremony for Thaksin to express their gratitude and a farewell (Missingham 2003).

During the early period of his administration, Thaksin succeeded in presenting himself as a leader attentive to country dwellers and their advocates' demands. In contrast with the previous government of Chuan Leekpai, he gained popularity and substantial support from civil society. For instance, when Thaksin faced a crisis of legitimacy due to a lack of transparency in concealing his assets, the villagers supported an initiative for amnesty if he were to be deemed guilty by the Constitutional Court. As a reward, the legal charges against two hundred villagers who had invaded the Government House during Chuan Leekpai's cabinet were withdrawn, and the lawsuit against the protest leaders was favourably settled during Thaksin's time (Missingham 2003).

Once Thaksin's political foothold became stronger, however, his relationship with environmental NGOs started to diverge. Thaksin was a politician who perceived the country as a big company and himself as the CEO (Phongpaichit and Baker 2009). To him, natural resources should be managed in a way that facilitated the economic development of the country. In 2002, Thaksin established the Ministry of Natural Resources and Environment (MNRE) by combining together the agencies administrating forests, wild animals, plant species, water resources (river basins, groundwater, and surface water), and mineral and coastal resources. It made sense, of course, to enhance the government's efficiency, but ultimately the bureaucratic centralization mostly allowed the government to utilize and regulate natural resources in a corporate-like manner.

Whereas the maturing of civil society during the late 1990s had mitigated state domination over environmental politics (Phongpaichit 1999), the enlarged and centralized ministry (MNRE) established by Thaksin was an attempt at a reversal. The power of the state was reinforced as the management of natural resources was identified as a platform for promoting state-initiated development projects. The centralization of power also proved helpful for the government in muffling the disruptive voice of mass mobilization and street demonstrations.

After the honeymoon period, the AOP and other environmental NGOs went back to the streets and often expressed their political discontent through protests and the occupation of public sites such as highways, trains, and provincial halls. This kind of political strategy was considered relatively efficacious when compared with the long-drawn-out process of voicing their concerns through local members of parliament. Nonetheless, Thaksin began to show intolerance towards such mobilized resistance that was contradicting his CEO-style management. He often adopted a paternalistic approach and perceived his relationship with the rural population as a constructive engagement through his new form of "social contract" (Hewison 2004). Thaksin's policies emphasized the development of rural areas within a broad picture. He thus perceived NGOs and the villagers who demonstrated against his development projects as a minority impeding the country's development. The disobedient villagers and troublemaking NGOs had no room for political manoeuvre in the face of Thaksin's rising political power (Phongpaichit and Baker 2009; McCargo and Pathmanand 2005).

During his administration, Thaksin initiated several mega-projects, such as the Thai-Malaysian gas pipeline, a gas separation plant and related industry project in Songkhla, a coal-fired power plant in Prachuap Khiri Khan, and rock-blasting of the Mekong river in Chiang Rai to improve navigation at the Thai-Laos border. These potentially contentious new projects were conducted and technically supported by state-sponsored consultant groups, private companies, and international experts. As Thaksin did not tolerate any more street protests, environmental NGOs sought an alternative way to formulate their grievances and political actions.

The first decade of the twenty-first century saw the environmental movement shifting from mass mobilization to epistemic contestation. This move employed local research to counterbalance the domination of experts' knowledge in justifying the social and environmental impacts of large projects. The Southeast Asia Rivers Network (SEARIN),

MAP 8.1

Selected sites of environmental disputes in Thailand

Source: QGIS and Natural Earth.

for example, was one of the organizations that drove this new approach, in collaboration with scholars from regional universities, local environmental groups, and the villagers who were affected by the construction of hydropower dams. Initially started with the Pak Mun dam, a controversial site at the frontier with Laos (SEARIN 2002), the Tai Baan ("the villager") research project borrowed from ethnomethodology and emphasized a localized relationship between ecology, cultural capital, and local wisdom. It pinpointed the limitations of standardized environmental impact assessments and instead highlighted the competency of local communities in comprehending the ecological system. The results of that research were further adapted to the study of the ecological effects of dam construction and water management in other river basins like Rasi Salai, Yom, Mekong, and Salween (SEARIN 2004, 2005, 2006).

Thaksinomics and the New Triangulated Relations

Although Tai Baan had changed the nature of environmental mobilizations from mass confrontation to a more subtle form of knowledge contestation, such a strategic move had limitations, however, as it relied on the context of the newly formed relationship between the government and the rural citizenry.

During his administration, Thaksin had successfully drawn villagers out from the NGOs' guardianship into an inclusive relationship with his government through so-called "Thaksinomics". This portmanteau word stands for a set of economic policies designed to increase domestic production and consumption, and implement welfare measures for the rural population (Phongpaichit and Baker 2008, 2009). Thaksin initiated or repackaged policies supposed to enhance both the livelihood of country dwellers and the management of natural resources (Phatharathananunth 2014; Walker 2012). The package included a four-year debt moratorium for farmers; financial support and capitalization of assets for local small and medium enterprises; an allocation of two million cattle to farmers; a better supply of water, Internet access, and solar energy; universal health care coverage; and a rice subsidy scheme. Political opponents to Thaksin viewed these measures as populist tricks (Hewison 2017; Kenny 2018).

In addition, Thaksin adopted a dual-track system that decreased domestic spending, but increased income and business opportunities by boosting the country's exports with an extensive use of natural resources (McCargo and Pathmanand 2005). Nonetheless, as Phongpaichit and Baker (2008, p. 62) argued, "his populism went beyond redistributive policies to include rhetorical rejection of Thailand's political elite, and denigration of liberal democracy in favour of personalised authoritarianism". The results of his populist policies consequently drew the rural population away from the environmental NGOs working in rural settings. Dissatisfied with this shift of power in the triangulated relations, in 2006, some leading environmental NGOs started a political movement against Thaksin.

Before that, the relationship between NGOs and rural inhabitants, to a certain extent, was paternalistic. NGOs portrayed the livelihood of villagers as inherently conservationist and bounded within the local ecology (Walker 2001). According to this culturalist and naïve view of ecology, the government and the capitalists were trying to infiltrate and eradicate the essence of rural communities. But Thaksin's populist policies did not only change the mode of production of agrarian citizens and their relation with their environment and natural resources. They also altered the relationship of villagers with the government, the market, and environmentalist NGOs.

Thaksin's landslide election victory in 2005 indicated that villagers had turned their back on the NGOs' outdated environmentalism. For Walker (2007, p. 5), "many rural voters seem to have embraced Thaksin's vision of market-oriented economic diversification". This "rural betrayal" resulted from "an increasing disconnect between academic and activist commentary and the rapidly changing livelihoods and aspirations of country dwellers. This disconnect is powerfully expressed in the NGO/academic rejection of Thaksin in contrast to his broad electoral popularity in many rural areas" (Walker 2007, p. 5; Sangkhamanee 2013).

Amidst the increasing popularity of Thaksin, it was undoubtedly challenging for the NGOs to restrain the paternalistic relationship as caregiver and protector of the rights of villagers. Assisting with the production of local knowledge, like the Tai Baan research programme, looked like one of the very few political tools left to NGOs for maintaining a relationship with the rural citizenry. While the majority of the latter had begun to establish a more rewarding relationship with Thaksin's government, it was now much more difficult for NGOs to fight against the intrusion of the government and capitalist forces into rural communities. The new wave of populist policies had won the match.

From the Patronage of Villagers to the Allegiance to Dictators

To a certain extent, the relationship between NGOs and country folk could be considered as a form of alliance-making, which helped to strengthen NGOs' power in the environmental struggle. Yet, there remains the question of whether such a relationship was fair and equal. It was also doubtful whether NGOs' conception of the environment and resource management truly reflected reality and the actual desires of the agrarian people (Chua 2018b; Elinoff 2014).

By and large, a substantial number of NGOs considered their attempts to protect the environment and the rights of villagers not merely as a political mission, but also as a moral pursuit. They saw themselves as the crucial supporters of an idealized community of villagers, especially protecting self-subsistent rural inhabitants from the intervention of an abusive government and depraved capitalism (Mukdawijitra 2005). As such, the relationship between NGOs and villagers therefore embraced the characteristics of political patronage, moral possession, and economic protection. Amidst the radical vigilance of the NGOs in crusading against the government's unjust projects, a significant number of NGOs even referred to the areas needing protection as "our communities" and "our villagers". With the patron-client relationship and the claiming of ownership over problematic issues, the Thai environmental NGOs did not only have to fight against the government, but they also had to compete among themselves in order to influence the masses and gain recognition, financial support, and hence the survival of their organization.

The antagonism among Thai environmental NGOs, and between NGOs and the governments of the late 1990s and the 2000s led to a nationwide environmental management impasse. There was almost no collaboration on development projects between the government and advocacy-based environmental NGOs. This stagnation incited the government to collaborate instead with the private sector on investments in neighbouring countries, particularly Laos and Myanmar. The example of the Xayaburi hydroelectric dam in Laos indicated that, since the case of the Pak Mun dam controversy during the 1990s and 2000s, the relationship between the government and NGOs was characterized by what I termed a "backwater", in which "the past contentions have fundamentally led to the deprecation of those who stand on opposing sides, creating significant obstacles to finding solutions together" (Sangkhamanee 2014, p. 97). For Thai NGOs, this situation brought a new kind of challenge, as they had lost their rural base and were now struggling to have any say in the government's agenda and decision-making process.

From the second half of the 2000s onwards, environmental NGOs thus began to ally themselves more with urban and middle class movements, and after the 2006 coup d'état, which toppled Thaksin, they became less reluctant to work with the junta governments. NGOs eventually shifted from allying with villagers to dealing with the authors of the "good" coup who rose to power by claiming an oligarchic political morality (Connors and Hewison 2008). There is no doubt that this change was in order to regain political capital. In fact, during the period of the junta and military-backed civilian governments (2006–11), the vital critical work of the environmental movement almost disappeared. In the 1990s, they were a driving force of the democratic movement (Phatharathananunth 2006; Phongpaichit 1999). But this political force now adopted a new ideology very much tied to the self-established legitimacy of oligarchic groups, the elite, and the military.

Overall, during the first decade after 2000, Thailand experienced a rapid economic transition, along with both the rise and fall of democracy. Despite this tumultuous situation, the relations between the state, environmental NGOs, and the rural population became much more entangled, but, as it turned out, far less concerned with environmental protection and participative democracy. To sum up, at least three factors caused NGOs to change their strategies, particularly during the period following the overthrow of Thaksin in 2006. The first factor was the "betrayal" of rural people (Walker 2007), who abandoned the crusade against the government and their alliance with environmental movements led by the NGOs. The agrarian populace welcomed the government's populist projects and their own incorporation into the market system. The second factor was the increased difficulty of NGOs in using the same protest tactics to influence the government, private sector, and cross-border development projects. The last factor was the tendency of NGOs to accentuate politics that rested on the morality of oligarchic and military-backed leaders. The government, run by a small group of conservative elites responsible for defining ideologies and patronizing the rural segment of society, subsequently caused the civil society movements to gradually transform into supporters of oligarchic forces (Kuhonta and Sinpeng 2014; Nethipo 2015; Pitidol 2016).

New Social Movements amidst Political and Environmental Turbulence

In the general election of July 2011, Yingluck Shinawatra, the sister of the ousted Prime Minister Thaksin, won a landslide victory. Her main political support came from the rural population, who benefitted from the development projects implemented by her brother. Unsurprisingly, Yingluck was not favoured by most of the conservationists, as she had a tendency to follow in her brother's footsteps in capitalizing on natural resources and the environment for economic development. She was also despised by the urban middle class, particularly in Bangkok, who saw her as a proxy of Thaksin, who had gained popularity from the politically illiterate country masses.

In addition to her lack of urban political support, Yingluck's legitimacy was further weakened by disastrous and expansive flooding that inundated Bangkok and the central provinces from mid-2011 to early 2012. Rather than politics shaping ecology, in this case, environmental disaster was a key factor in causing a tumultuous political storm against Yingluck's government (Maier-Knapp 2015). Handling such a great flood is not an easy task; it requires quick decisions and entails both environmental and political management (Marks 2015; Thabchumpon and Arunotai 2018). Yingluck did a poor job in coping with the crisis—from incompetent policy coordination among government offices and a lack of reliable technical data, to insufficient communication with the public and conflicts with the Bangkok Metropolitan Administration. The disgruntlement towards the government's approach to disaster management was overwhelming. The widespread use of social media by the urban population contributed to propagating harsh criticism of her administration.

Prior to this period, during the years 1990–2010, the mobilization of the environmentally affected generally comprised farmers from agrarian areas. The assembly of the rural masses was often negatively perceived by the urban dwellers. For them, farmers demonstrating and occupying *their* streets were nothing but troublemakers. However, the Bangkok inundation was a turning point. Although the flood prevented them from occupying the streets, the urban middle class expressed political discontent through social media, aggressively demanding efficiency in disaster management. As such, environmental politics was no longer limited to the circumscribed networks of NGOs, rural communities, and street politics. Through social networks, members of the urban middle class, who used to neglect environmental management, had suddenly turned into critical voices on the issue. The power of their movement derived from the ability to exploit both actual and virtual spaces to serve an agenda that bestrides the demarcation line between political and environmental advocacies.

Yingluck's undermined authority came from a combination of both environmental disaster and accumulated political discontent. In fact, it might be more accurate to say that, prior to the flood, there already existed ideological prejudice towards her role in political administration. The flood only precipitated an existing political discontent, bringing it to the surface. This partisan prejudice was confirmed in October 2017, under the administration of Prayut Chan-o-cha's military government, when floods once again struck Bangkok and the central region. Although this episode was not as severe as in 2011, this time, the urban middle class did not show anger or any specific urgency to solve the consequences of the flood. Such a discrepancy clearly reflected an ideological bias or partisan double standard in demanding a government response to the problem of recurrent flooding.

Yingluck's government was also marked by another important environmental movement in 2013. This was the campaign against the construction of the Mae Wong Dam, in the western forest area about fifty kilometres from the border with Myanmar. This mobilization, which became very popular, was led by Sasin Chalermlarp, the Secretary General of the Seub Nakhasathien Foundation, and a renowned environmental activist. The protest started in September 2013, as Sasin and his allies staged a campaign walk of 388 kilometres from Mae Wong National Park up to Bangkok. Thousands of people joined the march, particularly during its last days, and in the end, all the protestors assembled at the Bangkok Art and Culture Centre in the heart of the capital. The campaign crusaded against the approval of the Environmental Health Impact Assessment report on the construction of the dam, which, according to Sasin, failed to specify comprehensive details about the consequences for the environment and the local people (Fredrickson 2013). The dam was also criticized for encroaching on a vast area of forestland, and because, despite promises, it did not prevent further flooding. The campaign eventually compelled the government to suspend the project and look for an alternative approach to water management.

The changes of governmental regime crucially influenced the role of civil society over environmental policy. When the government was democratically elected, public scrutiny of mega projects was common and the lack of transparency in their implementation would generally lead to political movements. Nonetheless, after the 2014 coup d'état, Thai politics once again returned to a repressive regime of strict control and diminished civil liberties (Thabchumpon et al. 2015). Participation in any civil movement against state policy was perceived as a threat to national peace and security. Later, by the time that the construction of the Mae Wong Dam was resurrected under the military government, resistance from civil society had become almost impossible.

The Return of Autocratic Power in Environmental Politics

The lack of efficiency and transparency of Yingluck's government eventually provoked public demonstrations led by the urban elite and middle class, including some leaders from environmental NGOs. The street occupation from January to May 2014 led to a major ideological dispute, along with an economic and political deadlock. The dispute ended in May 2014 with the deposition of Yingluck's government in another coup d'état commanded by General Prayut Chan-o-cha and the National Council for Peace and Order (NCPO). One of their primary objectives was to eradicate the legacy of Thaksin and his sister. The NCPO also cancelled the democratic rule of the majority to install an oligarchic regime of self-proclaimed charismatic morality (Baker 2016). Right after its rise to power, the NCPO pushed forward political reform. The leaders of civil society who had supported the military to overthrow Yingluck's government were appointed to play a role in the decision-making process (Chua 2018a).

The military-style administration of the NCPO has substantially affected the environmental movements and the management of natural resources. One of the significant changes was the exercise of absolute power by virtue of the 2014 interim constitution, which allowed both private and public sectors to initiate big projects in parallel with the preparation of environmental impact assessments (*Prachatai* 2015, 2016a; *The Nation* 2016a). This change basically means that, whatever the result of these "assessments" might be, construction can go ahead with little or no opposition.

Under such a military regime, one might wonder what happened to the environmental movement: has it completely disappeared? For instance, the construction of the Mae Wong Dam was approved by a cabinet resolution during Yingluck's government in 2012, but was suspended during her administration as a result of the demonstration

FIGURE 8.2

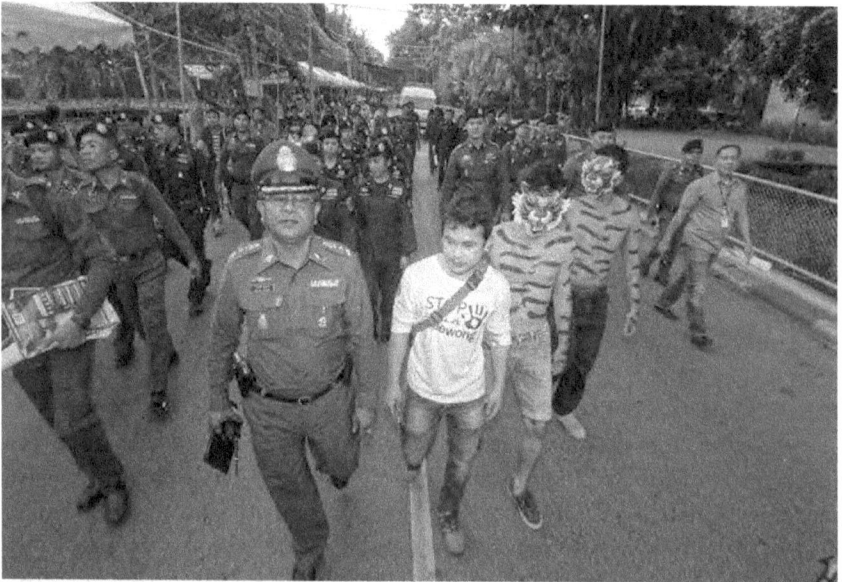

Thai police officers captured university students and activists during their protest against the construction of the Mae Wong Dam at Kasetsart University, Bangkok, 18 November 2014

Source: Abhisit Sapnaphapan and *Prachatai*.

led by Sasin and his conservationist allies. However, in February 2016, when military Prime Minister Prayut visited the area to announce the resumption of its construction (*Bangkok Post* 2016a, 2016b), previously critical actors kept silent.

With its authoritarian power, the government can also reinitiate and drive forward all the mega-projects that were previously a matter of conflict with local inhabitants and civil society organizations. These include the coal-fired power plant in Krabi, the dam on the Mae Wong river, ore mining in Loei, the Chao Phraya riverside promenade project in Bangkok, several Special Economic Zones, and other mega-infrastructure projects (Chambers 2018; *The Nation* 2016b, 2017). In 2016, the NCPO also passed a new Mineral Act, which enables private companies to start mining activities much faster and more easily, and with fewer restrictions regarding the negative effects for the local communities, the ecosystem of forestlands, and the water basins (*Prachatai* 2016b). The crusade against such projects has become more difficult since the dictatorial government can claim the maintenance of peace and stability of the nation as its primary mission; and the police or the army can now ban any assembly of more than five people (*Prachatai* 2016c).

Conclusion

Prominent Thai anthropologist and long-time observer of Thai environmental movements Pinkaew Laungaramsri raises the question of whether current social movements in Thailand have become an extension of the dictatorship (Laungaramsri 2017). According to her, during the past decades, social movements, and especially environmental NGOs, have often inclined towards being "tools of the state, political opportunists, and foes of democracy". As she further argues, while the electoral system has become an ineffective approach to promoting environmental protection, NGOs have become "a group of organizations that strengthened and allied with the government in exchange for their own survival without contemplating the future of the Thai society, while perceiving the quality of democracy no longer relevant to their mission" (Laungaramsri 2017, p. 56). As NGOs no longer serve as a watchdog over the government's management of the environment and natural resources—particularly under the current authoritarian administration—Laungaramsri (2017, p. 62) concludes that this spells "the end of environmental movements in Thailand".

This gloomy conclusion is relevant, though perhaps not entirely accurate. Since the beginning of the 2000s, Thai environmental movements have shifted from mass mobilization to knowledge contestation. This new strategy was achieved through various research endeavours conducted by NGOs and rural citizens in order to battle against technocratic authority in decision-making. These movements, however, have been suspended by political instability. Amidst the country's political polarization, civil society organizations tend to connect with the elitist and military oligarchy, bypassing the rural population's disapproval. Allying with undemocratic regimes, many Thai NGOs have lost their legitimacy to represent the struggles for the people's environmental and resource rights. In contrast with the brave actions of the late 1990s, NGOs now tend to look as if they were indistinct from other interest groups, lacking the courage to contest unrighteous power.

In this chapter, I have shed some light on the dynamism of environmental movements in Thailand, focusing on the shifting relations between keys actors as they seek to situate their political agenda within national environmental politics. I show that the 1997 Constitution opened up important processes of political decentralization and citizen participation, thus allowing the NGOs and environmental movements to flourish. It also became a bridge between country folk and the government for the allocation of natural resources. In the contentious readjustment of triangulated relations, the rather static and uncooperative NGOs lost momentum in responding to the changing desires and livelihoods of rural communities. NGOs used to be allied with villagers to fight against a government that they considered exploitative. But now they sit in a delicate position between a dictatorial government and rural masses whose political and ecological rights are at stake under the national political transformation.

The case of Thailand provides an insight into the important relationship between environmental social movements and political spaces that alternate between the confined and the dynamic. On the one hand, environmental movements can be considered as a driving force in the process of democratization at large, the idea popularized by new social movement scholars during the 1990s and 2000s (e.g., Missingham 2003; Peet and Watts 1996; Phatharathananunth 2006; Phongpaichit 1999; see also Mukdawijitra 2005). On the other hand, the context of political regimes in which environmental movements operate also shape the nature of their advocating agenda and actions. The dualistic relations between these two spheres of operation often fluctuate, influenced by the changing relations between diverse actors. As this chapter has illustrated, Thailand's environmental politics during the past few decades can be described as a triangulated relation, fundamentally shaped by the ever-changing state, civil society organizations, and citizens.

As is clear from Thailand's highly disputed national election in March 2019, political uncertainties still lie ahead. However, the power of the people is also getting stronger in demanding political transparency, good governance, the protection of rights, and the participation of the average citizen in decision-making. In the long run, the country's democratization process will be one of the key factors in determining the shape of environmental politics. But because of its legacy and contestation during the past few decades, we cannot deny that environmental politics has played an important role in creating, expanding, and multiplying political spaces in Thai society. This, in turn, has given way to a broader spectrum of actors involved in national politics.

NOTES

1. The research is funded by the Center of Excellence on Resource Politics for Social Development, Center for Social Development Studies (CSDS), Faculty of Political Science, Chulalongkorn University, Thailand.
2. In Thailand, despite the recent introduction of the term Civil Society Organizations or CSOs, the general term people often go by is still very much "NGOs". I use the term NGOs here to designate the environmental organizations formed and operated by civil groups with the aim of being a watchdog for government policies, protecting and empowering local communities' access to natural resources, and working to promote the issues of environmental problems to the wider public.

REFERENCES

Baker, Chris. 2000. "Thailand's Assembly of the Poor: Background, Drama, Reaction". *South East Asia Research* 8, no. 1: 5–29.
———. 2016. "The 2014 Thai Coup and Some Roots of Authoritarianism". *Journal of Contemporary Asia* 46, no. 3: 388–404.

Bangkok Post. 2016a. "Locals Urge Mae Wong Dam Build", 2 March 2016a.
———. 2016b. "No Need to Revisit Dam", 15 October 2016b.
Bello, Walden, Shea Cunningham, and Li Kheng Poh. 1998. *A Siamese Tragedy: Development and Disintegration in Modern Thailand.* London and New York: Zed Books.
Blake, David J.H. 2015. "King Bhumibol: The Symbolic 'Father of Water Resources Management' and Hydraulic Development Discourse in Thailand". *Asian Studies Review* 39, no. 4: 649–68.
Callahan, William A. 2005. "The Discourse of Vote Buying and Political Reform in Thailand". *Pacific Affairs* 78, no. 1: 95–103.
Callahan, William A. and Duncan McCargo. 1996. "Vote-Buying in Thailand's Northeast: The July 1995 General Election". *Asian Survey* 36, no. 4: 376–92.
Chambers, Paul. 2010. "Thailand on the Brink: Resurgent Military, Eroded Democracy". *Asian Survey* 50, no. 5: 835–58.
———. 2018. "In the Land of Democratic Rollback: Military Authoritarianism and Monarchical Primacy in Thailand". In *National Security, Statecentricity, and Governance in East Asia,* edited by Brendan Howe. Cham: Palgrave Macmillan.
Chua, Bencharat. 2018a. "When Democracy is Questioned: Competing Democratic Principles and Struggles for Democracy in Thailand". In *Political Participation in Asia: Defining and Deploying Political Space,* edited by Eva Hansson and Meredith L. Weiss. Oxon and New York: Routledge.
———. 2018b. "Thailand". In *Routledge Handbook of Civil Society in Asia,* edited by Akihiro Ogawa. Oxon and New York: Routledge.
Connors, Michael K. and Kevin Hewison. 2008. "Introduction: Thailand and the 'Good Coup'". *Journal of Contemporary Asia* 38, no. 1: 1–10.
Delang, Claudio O. 2002. "Deforestation in Northern Thailand: The Result of Hmong Farming Practices or Thai Development Strategies?" *Society & Natural Resources* 15, no. 6: 483–501.
Elinoff. Eli. 2014. "Unmaking Civil Society: Activist Schisms and Autonomous Politics in Thailand". *Contemporary Southeast Asia* 6, no. 3: 356–85.
Fahn, James D. 2003. *A Land on Fire: The Environmental Consequences of the Southeast Asia Boom.* Chiang Mai: Silkworm Books.
Farrelly, Nicholas. 2013. "Why Democracy Struggles: Thailand's Elite Coup Culture". *Australian Journal of International Affairs* 67, no. 3: 281–96.
Ferguson, James. 1994. *The Anti-Politics Machine: Development, Depoliticization, and Bureaucratic Power in Lesotho.* Minneapolis: University of Minnesota Press.
Forsyth, Tim. 1999. "Questioning the Impacts of Shifting Cultivation". *Watershed* 5, no. 1: 23–38.
Forsyth, Tim and Andrew Walker. 2008. *Forest Guardians, Forest Destroyers: The Politics of Environmental Knowledge in Northern Thailand.* Seattle and London: University of Washington Press.

Fredrickson, Terry. 2013. "Sasin Chalermlarp: 10 Lessons". *Bangkok Post*, 24 September 2013.

Ganjanapan, Anan. 2000. *Local Control of Land and Forest: Cultural Dimensions of Resource Management in Northern Thailand*. Chiang Mai: Regional Centre for Social Science and Sustainable Development, Chiang Mai University.

Glassman, Jim. 2010. "'The Provinces Elect Governments, Bangkok Overthrows Them': Urbanity, Class and Post-democracy in Thailand". *Urban Studies* 47, no. 6: 1301–23.

Hewison, Kevin. 2004. "Crafting Thailand's New Social Contract". *The Pacific Review* 17, no. 4: 503–22.

———. 2017. "Reluctant Populists: Learning Populism in Thailand". *International Political Science Review* 38, no. 4: 426–40.

Kenny, Paul D. 2018. *Populism in Southeast Asia*. New York: Cambridge University Press.

Kuhonta, Erik M. and Aim Sinpeng. 2014. "Democratic Regression in Thailand: The Ambivalent Role of Civil Society and Political Institutions". *Contemporary Southeast Asia: A Journal of International and Strategic Affairs* 36, no. 3: 333–55.

Laungaramsri, Pinkaew. 1999. "Rai, Rai Lu'an Loy, Rai Mun Wian and the Politics of 'Shifting Cultivation'". *Watershed* 5, no. 1: 39–46.

———. 2001. *Redefining Nature: Karen Ecological Knowledge and the Challenge to the Modern Conservation Paradigm*. Chennai: Earthworm Books.

———. 2017. "NGOs and Civil Society". In *A Molten Land: The Mandatory Transition*. Bangkok: Prachatai. (in Thai)

Maier-Knapp, Naila. 2015. "Betwixt Droughts and Floods: Flood Management Politics in Thailand". *Journal of Current Southeast Asian Affairs* 34, no. 1: 57–83.

Marks, Danny. 2015. "The Urban Political Ecology of the 2011 Floods in Bangkok: The Creation of Uneven Vulnerabilities". *Pacific Affairs* 88, no. 3: 623–51.

McCargo, Duncan. 2005. "Network Monarchy and Legitimacy Crises in Thailand". *The Pacific Review* 18, no. 4: 499–519.

McCargo, Duncan and Ukrist Pathmanand. 2005. *The Thaksinization of Thailand*. Copenhagen: NIAS Press.

Missingham, Bruce. 2003. *The Assembly of the Poor in Thailand: From Local Struggle to National Protest Movement*. Chiang Mai: Silkworm Books.

Mukdawijitra, Yukti. 2005. *Reading "Community Culture": Poetics and Politics of Watthanatham Chumchon Ethnography*. Bangkok: Same Sky Press. (in Thai)

Nethipo, Viengrat. 2015. "Thailand's Divided Civil Society at a Time of Crisis". In *Civil Society and Democracy in Southeast Asia and Turkey*, edited by N. Ganesan and Colin Dürkop. Ankara: Konrad-Adenauer-Stiftung.

Nishizaki, Yoshinori. 2011. *Political Authority and Provincial Identity in Thailand: The Making of Banharn-Buri*. Cornell: Cornell Southeast Asia Program Publications.

Ockey, James. 1996. "Thai Society and Patterns of Political Leadership". *Asian Survey* 36, no. 4: 345–60.

———. 2004. *Making Democracy: Leadership, Class, Gender, and Political Participation in Thailand*. Chiang Mai: Silkworm Books.

Peet, Richard and Michael Watts. 1996. *Liberation Ecologies: Environment, Development and Social Movements*. London and New York: Routledge.

Phatharathananunth, Somchai. 2006. *Civil Society and Democratisation: Social Movements in Northeast Thailand*. Copenhagen: Nordic Institute of Asian Studies.

———. 2014. "Civil Society Against Democracy". *Hot Spots, Cultural Anthropology*, September 2014. https://culanth.org/fieldsights/civil-society-against-democracy.

Phongpaichit, Pasuk. 1999. "Civilising the State: State, Civil Society and Politics in Thailand". *Watershed* 5, no. 2: 20–27.

Phongpaichit, Pasuk and Chris Baker. 2008. "Thaksin's Populism". *Journal of Contemporary Asia* 38, no. 1: 62–83.

———. 2009. *Thaksin*, Second Expanded Edition. Chiang Mai: Silkworm Books.

Pitidol, Thorn. 2016. "Redefining Democratic Discourse in Thailand's Civil Society". *Journal of Contemporary Asia* 46, no. 3: 520–37.

Prachatai. 2015. "Thai Government to Cut Short EIAs for Mega Projects", 4 November 2015. https://prachatai.com/english/node/5585.

———. 2016a. "Thai Junta Slashes EIA Procedures on State Projects", 9 March 2016a.

———. 2016b. "New Mining Bill Pleases Businesses But Harms Society: Civil Society Groups", 3 August 2016b.

———. 2016c. "Loei Villagers Barred from Meeting over Disputed Ore Mines", 16 February 2016c.

———. 2017. "Are Thai NGOs Tools of the Junta?", 2 August 2017.

Quinn, Rapin. 1997. "NGOs, Peasants and the State: Transformation and Intervention in Rural Thailand, 1970–1990". A thesis submitted for the degree of Doctor of Philosophy, The Australian National University, Canberra.

Sangkhamanee, Jakkrit. 2010. "Hydraulics of Power and Knowledge: Water Management in Northeastern Thailand and the Mekong Region". PhD thesis, The Australian National University, Canberra.

———. 2013. "Democracy of the Desired: Everyday Politics and Political Aspiration of Contemporary Thai Countryside". *Asian Democracy Review* 2: 5–37.

———. 2014. "From Pak Mun to Xayaburi: The Backwater and Spillover of Thailand's Hydropower Politics". In *Hydropower Development in the Mekong Region: Political, Socio-economic and Environmental Perspectives*, edited by Nathanial Matthews and Kim Geheb. New York: Routledge.

Santasombat, Yos. 2003. *Biodiversity, Local Knowledge and Sustainable Development*. Chiang Mai: Regional Centre for Social Science and Sustainable Development, Chiang Mai University.

———. 2004. "Karen Cultural Capital and the Political Economy of Symbolic Power". *Asian Ethnicity* 5, no. 1: 105–20.

Shigetomi, Shinichi. 2002. "Thailand: A Crossing of Critical Parallel Relationships". In *The State and NGOs: Perspective from Asia*, edited by Shinichi Shigetomi. Singapore: Institute of Southeast Asian Studies.

So, Alvin Y. and Yok-shiu F. Lee. 1999. "Environmental Movements in Thailand". In *Asia's Environmental Movements: Comparative Perspectives*, edited by Yok-shiu F. Lee and Alvin Y. So. Armonk, NY: M.E. Sharpe.

Southeast Asia Rivers Network (SEARIN). 2002. *Mun River: The Return of Fish Species after Opening the Dam's Gates*. Chiang Mai: Wanida Press. (in Thai)

———. 2004. *Mekong: River of Lives and Cultures*. Chiang Mai: Wanida Press. (in Thai)

———. 2005. *Rasi Salai: Knowledge, Rights, and Tham Forest Livelihood of Mun River Basin*. Chiang Mai: Wanida Press. (in Thai)

———. 2006. *Yom River: Golden Teak Forest and the Livelihood of Sa-Eab People*. Chiang Mai: Wanida Press. (in Thai)

Thabchumpon, Naruemon, Jakkrit Sangkhamanee, Carl Middleton, and Weera Wongsatjachock. 2014. "The Polarization of Thai Democracy: The Asian Democracy Index in Thailand". *Asian Democracy Review* 3: 65–87.

———. 2015. "Monopolization Strengthens: Thailand's Asian Democracy Index in 2015". *Asian Democracy Review* 4: 65–89.

Thabchumpon, Naruemon and Narumon Arunotai. 2018. "Living with and against Floods in Bangkok and Thailand's Central Plain". In *Living with Floods in a Mobile Southeast Asia: A Political Ecology of Vulnerability, Migration and Environmental Change*, edited by Carl Middleton, Rebecca Elmhirst, and Supang Chantavanich. Oxford: Routledge.

The Nation. 2016a. "PM: Support Transport Plans Facing EIAs", 5 November 2016a.

———. 2016b. "Mae Wong Dam Project a Test for Checks and Balances", 9 December 2016b.

———. 2017. "Chao Phraya River Project Approved Despite Criticism", 26 May 2017.

Trakarnsuphakorn, Prasert. 2002. "Local Wisdom in the Management of Biodiversity". *Watershed* 8, no. 2: 26–37.

Ungsuchaval, Theerapat. 2015. "NGOization and Civil Society in Thailand: A History and Development of Thai Nongovernmental Organizations". MA thesis, University of Kent.

Walker, Andrew. 2001. "The 'Karen Consensus', Ethnic Politics and Resource-Use Legitimacy in Northern Thailand". *Asian Ethnicity* 2, no. 2: 145–62.

———. 2004a. "Response". *Asian Ethnicity* 5, no. 2: 259–65.

———. 2004b. "Seeing Farmers for the Trees: Community Forestry and the Arborealization of Agriculture in Northern Thailand". *Asia Pacific Viewpoint* 45, no. 3: 311–24.

———. 2007. "Beyond the Rural Betrayal: Lessons from the Thaksin Era for the Mekong Region". Paper presented at the International Conference on Critical Transitions in the Mekong Region, Chiang Mai, 29–31 January 2007.

———. 2008. "The Rural Constitution and Everyday Politics of Elections in Northern Thailand". *Journal of Contemporary Southeast Asia* 38, no. 1: 84–105.

———. 2012. *Thailand's Political Peasant: Power in the Modern Rural Economy.* Wisconsin: The University of Wisconsin Press.

Winichakul, Thongchai. 2008. "Toppling Democracy". *Journal of Contemporary Asia* 38, no. 1: 11–37.

9

ENVIRONMENTAL MOVEMENTS IN VIETNAM UNDER ONE-PARTY RULE

Stephan Ortmann

Environmental activism is a recent phenomenon in Vietnam and, considering the authoritarian nature of the regime, it is still uncertain whether sustained environmental movements might yet emerge. A movement is here defined according to Tarrow (1994, p. 6) as "people with common purposes and solidarity in sustained interaction with elites, opponents and authorities", which distinguishes it from discrete instances of activism that do not challenge authority. This is the case in Vietnam, where campaigns are highly fragmented and generally do not last very long or have a deeper impact on the overall society. In order to thwart independent political association, the government has at first sought to engineer its own environmental movement with mass organizations and non-governmental organizations (NGOs) controlled by the government. This, however, has not been successful as the government and business interests are closely tied together. As such, the government has tolerated more independent activism in the form of NGOs, but they are not only required to register with the government but the institutional context forces them to remain small with insufficient financial resources. Moreover, rather than promoting grassroots environmental activism, they focus mostly on service delivery and policy advice. Even the formation of networks has not resolved this problem and may have instead reinforced it. Nevertheless, the government has encouraged environmental activism. There has been a rise in protests against serious pollution, which have generally been tolerated. The government-owned media has reported extensively about them. However, this changed in 2016 when the government heavily repressed nationwide protests in response to massive fish deaths caused by the Taiwanese-owned Formosa Ha Tinh Steel plant. The government's response to this protest movement reveals that, despite recent progress, a widespread environmental movement is unlikely to emerge.

This chapter will explore the progress and challenges of Vietnam's environmental activism. In the context of potential repression and deep fragmentation, traces of environmental movements can be found, but there are severe restrictions under the authoritarian one-party state. By examining the opportunities and obstacles of the various actors in this field, it is possible to map the changing situation in Vietnam and draw attention to both the opportunities and obstacles on the path toward a broad-based environmental movement. First, the chapter seeks to demonstrate that the Vietnamese government has effectively weakened the organizational basis of society for any sustained environmental movement to emerge. Following a discussion of the opportunities, I will focus on the organizational aspects of environmental activism. First, I will address the state's attempt to foster its own environmental movement within traditional structures as a substitute for bottom-up mobilization. Though it is far from sufficient, the government has granted journalists some space to report on environmental problems. However, their efforts are limited by the state's ability to censor the discussion of sensitive issues. Then the analysis will turn to grassroots efforts to develop a true environmental movement. It will be shown that NGOs have grown but remain very weak. While networks of associations have emerged, they have not been able to overcome this difficulty either. At the same time, and mostly separate from these formal organizations, there has been an increase in community activism, which has sometimes succeeded in challenging polluters. The government has often tolerated these initiatives. However, there are also limits because the government is deeply concerned about the ability of a broad-based movement to challenge the government and even lead to regime change, as has happened in other countries.

The Emergence of an Environmental Movement?

To determine the rise of an environmental movement, it is necessary to demonstrate sustained claim-making by activists. The key emphasis is on how we can determine whether a movement is sustained and has sufficient organizational capacity to effect change. McAdam's political process model provides a useful starting point to distil the various aspects necessary for a movement (McAdam 1999). A movement may emerge within a context of changing socioeconomic processes when political opportunities arise and there is sufficient organizational capacity. In addition, there must also be a growing awareness of the problem, which McAdam termed cognitive liberation. In order to maintain the movement, two more factors are of crucial relevance: the level of mobilization (or "insurgency" in McAdam's terms), which includes both the willingness to use protest and the ability to maintain pressure, and insufficient measures of government control.

The opportunity structure in Vietnam has been beneficial for the emergence of an environmental movement. In a climate of rapid economic development following economic reforms in 1986, known as *Doi Moi* ("renovation"), the natural environment has suffered significantly, creating the need for developing and improving environmental institutions. At the same time, international organizations have promoted a discourse of environmental sustainability and have created incentives for governments to shift toward sustainable development by tying environmental conditions to the provision of developmental aid. Reform-minded officials have continually improved the environmental law, set ambitious environmental targets, and strengthened the environmental ministry, including by establishing think tanks, an environmental police force, and many other institutional innovations. The latest version of the Vietnamese constitution even proclaims: "Everyone has the right to live in a clean environment and has the duty to protect the environment" (Article 43). Taken together, the government's concerted efforts have created the expectation of an effective solution to the problem.

The most important opportunity for environmental activism has been the result of the government's failure to implement its sophisticated legal framework. The primary reason for this situation is the problematic incentive structure of the Vietnamese state, which favours economic growth over other development objectives. The current Vietnamese Communist Party government is dominated by rent-seekers with only a small number of reformists and a faction of ideological hardliners (Kingsbury 2017). This rent-seeking is facilitated by the fact that local officials, who rely primarily on economic growth targets for promotion, are not under the direct control of the central government. Moreover, a good business environment is vital for local communities as companies provide jobs and tax revenue. Strict enforcement of regulations, however, would entail significant costs for business, which would need to update their equipment. The enforcement mechanisms of the government are in fact severely curtailed as fines are too low, monitoring companies' compliance is expensive and time-consuming, and the legal system is still underdeveloped. As the government falls short of its commitments, environmental activists both in NGOs and at the community level can capitalize on this failure. This is enhanced by the fact that reform-minded officials need to rely on these organizations to create pressure on local governments and on the media to shame errant local officials.

A third level of the opportunity structure has been several legal changes that have allowed individuals greater access to the political process. There have been efforts to strengthen democracy within communes, while a stronger emphasis on deliberations under the Grassroots Democracy Degree can provide the forum to legally voice grievances. The government has again broadened the space for societal activism in regard to the environment with the latest revision of the environmental law, enacted in 2015. In this latest version of the law, the government has dedicated a complete chapter (15) to societal organizations, which spells out a number of rights, including the right to obtain information, to be consulted, to investigate environmental problems, and to petition the government. These rights provide the legal justification for activists to rightfully resist environmental pollution, although they do not prevent government repression as it is impossible to claim these rights in the courts. The law does not make it clear how the provisions are legally enforceable. Nevertheless, there have been a growing number of environmental protests, which have mainly targeted highly polluting companies or the destruction of the limited nature present in the urban landscape.

Despite the increased amount of opportunities for environmental activism, the government has sought to contain the organizational capacity of the incipient movement both through legal means and repression. The government is greatly worried about the potential impact of more broad-based social movements, including those regarding the environment. Terms such as "civil society" (*xã hội dân sự*) and "non-governmental organizations" (*tổ chức phi chính phủ*) have been met with great concern from officials as these terms suggest a lack of government control and thus run counter to the idea of a unitary state. The government has failed to pass a new law to regulate private organizations despite going through eleven drafts (Vuving 2010). In particular, there was concern this could create "opposition organisations to sabotage the Party and State, which would violate political security, social order and safety" (cited in *VNS*, 25 September 2015). Instead, the newly arising bodies are labelled as "social organizations" or "people's organizations" (Wells-Dang 2012). A foreign concept such as "governance", which generally refers to partnerships between state and society, is often translated as "management" in Vietnamese, thus referring to the traditional top-down approach rather than indicating grassroots involvement.

In addition to containing autonomous environmental activism, the government has also resorted to repression whenever it has felt threatened. In at least two instances, repression was used against environmental grassroots activists who had sought to build alliances with other organizations. In the anti-Bauxite campaign of 2009 and the protest movement against the "Formosa incident" of 2016, activists cooperated with other groups, including those within the growing democracy movement, human rights activists, and members of the Catholic Church. The increasingly broad-based movement indicated a potential threat to the one-party regime. As environmental activists had played a prominent role in the democratization process of a number of Eastern European countries as well as in Taiwan (Tang and Tang 1997; Jancar Webster 1998; Ho 2011 and Chapter 2 in this book), it was probably not a surprise that the government sought to suppress the budding movement with media censorship and the arrest of activists.

The Attempt to Engineer an Environmental Movement

The social movement literature generally considers environmental movements to be driven by social actors and in conflict with existing forces from the state to the private sector. However, the Vietnamese case shows that states may also have an interest in fostering their own environmental movements, partly in response to growing international pressure. In order to avoid any challenge to existing power structures, the "movements" should remain within the institutional framework of the Communist Party regime, which has no clear separation between state and society and regards mass organizations as the primary driver of societal change. The most notable among them are the Women's Union, the trade unions, the Ho Chi Minh Communist Youth Federation, the Farmers' Union, and the Association of Veterans. Due to their vast membership bases, they have significant power to influence behaviour. In regard to the environment, they can be useful for quickly mobilizing larger numbers of people for mass campaigns. For instance, the Women's Union with its approximately fourteen million members has been rallied for efforts in climate change adaptation, rural sanitation, and waste clean-up. In a period of nine months from 2011 to 2012, volunteers successfully collected more than eighteen trillion tonnes of garbage, which had been discarded along 1,600 kilometres of road (Minh 2012). Mass organizations can also provide a channel for members to raise issues with the government. The Farmers' Union, for example, has been used by farmers to raise concerns about the worsening water pollution that affects their livelihoods.

The mass organizations, however, cannot provide the proper basis for an effective environmental movement. First of all, they are too closely tied to the state and hierarchically organized. Consequently, they lack the flexibility and innovativeness necessary to deal with many newly arising problems. None of the traditional organizations can adequately deal with a complex issue such as environmental protection. Mass campaigns are single events that do not last very long and thus rarely achieve any long-term effects. Moreover, not all environmental issues can be tackled with mass actions and instead need to take into account the different interests of the pluralizing society. For while some profit from the environmental degradation, others suffer. Last but not least, there is no real mass organization that is specifically targeted toward this issue and, as I will show below, creating an environmental group modelled on mass organizations is difficult due to the close link between the government and economic interests.

Determined to resolve the issue within the current institutional framework, the government has established the Vietnam Union of Science and Technology Associations (VUSTA) directly under the Fatherland Front, which makes it similar to other mass organizations. However, instead of having a mass membership, it is an elite governmental organization for scientists. VUSTA primarily serves as the registrar for many of the small, technical and scientific NGOs, which must be registered with a government organization. As such, it functions primarily to control fledgling environmental activism, which will be discussed below.

VUSTA has played a direct role in promoting environmental issues but has been hampered by its close links with business interests. This can be illustrated by a case in 2010, when it awarded an environmental prize to a known polluter. Although the media had reported widely about excessive air and water pollution by the Luks Group, a cement producer based in Hong Kong, which had also drawn local protests, VUSTA nevertheless awarded the company the "Sustainable Green Brand" award. This triggered massive outrage in the Vietnamese media and VUSTA was subsequently forced to strip the company of the award. In its defence, VUSTA claimed that it had not properly consulted local officials about the company (Thu 2011). Whether this occurred as a failure of the internal vetting process—which would raise serious concerns about its management—or whether there was another reason, it was clear that VUSTA's primary incentives were driven by economic and not environmental concerns.

In 1988, VUSTA decided to establish a structure specifically dedicated to the environment in the form of the Vietnam Association for Conservation of Nature and Environment (VACNE), which has since evolved into a government-organized non-governmental organization (GONGO). Although formally separate from the government, VACNE's head is a retired government official, Dr Nguyen Ngoc Sinh, who still maintains close relations with other officials. Despite these links, the organization claims to have achieved a certain degree of autonomy because its primary funding does not come from the government but from other sources, including membership fees and international donors. Nevertheless, in the tradition of mass organizations, VACNE also acts as an umbrella organization for a variety of member associations that include other non-governmental organizations, research centres, media outlets, and businesses. In addition to these organizations, there are also ten thousand individual members who profit from the ability to participate in conferences, are allowed to take part in elections, and have access to information, facilities, projects, and training programmes. Despite its apparently large size, the organization has only two small offices, in Hanoi and Ho Chi Minh City, and employs fewer than twenty people.

As was the case for VUSTA, VACNE has also struggled with its close linkage to business interests. In fact, 65 of its 175 member organizations come from the business sector, making it the largest segment of the overall organization. In 2011, VACNE suddenly changed its position in regard to the construction of two controversial dams along the Dong Nai river near Ho Chi Minh City, which according to environmental activists would have caused serious harm to society, the fish population, and the surrounding environment. Many people would have to be resettled as well as large forests cleared. Associate Professor Dr Nguyen Dinh Hoe, who heads the Social Review Committee, had publicly spoken out against the project at the beginning of the consultation period but, merely half a year later, reversed his position and indicated his support. Although it is not known what led to this about-face, other environmental organizations that were involved in the project naturally questioned the organization's objectivity (Tran 2011). Meanwhile, as VACNE had changed its mind, the government also reversed its position and abandoned the dam project following the release of the environmental impact assessment report. Nevertheless, VACNE had suffered a serious blow to its reputation.

The Media as a Link Between State and Society

Realizing the shortcomings of creating top-down environmental activism, reform-minded government officials have sought to promote relatively independent environmental journalism. While the central government has little direct control over local governments, journalists facilitate the monitoring of local officials by highlighting serious problems at the community level. Despite this instrumental nature, many environmental journalists consider themselves to be the voice of the public. For instance, reporters believe they can speak for the people who suffer from environmental pollution. In addition, the media has begun to play a special role for budding environmental movements because it provides the necessary cognitive liberation for environmental activists. Reports about environmental issues, problems, and protests are now common in the press (Bass et al. 2010). Media coverage can not only create awareness but also influence government policy-making and implementation.

The unique role of the media in Vietnam as both a tool of the government and a tool of activists can only be understood in its particular context. All of the media in Vietnam is owned by the government, and yet since the introduction of economic reforms, the news media has become more diverse and thus more willing to report on controversial topics. After a period as the mouthpiece of the government, the media has enjoyed increased freedom and investigative reporting has become possible under certain circumstances, even on corruption (Kerkvliet 2001) and environmental problems. Indeed, the government actively promotes environmental journalism directly through its official propaganda. Many of the stories that appear on government websites have in fact first appeared in the media. To assist environmental journalists, the Vietnam Forum of Environmental Journalists (VFEJ) was founded in 1998 and currently has over one hundred members. It formally comes under VACNE, although according to interviews, the two are not only organizationally separate but also disagree on many issues. The VFEJ was established to foster more professional environmental journalism and facilitate the cooperation between journalists across borders. In addition, the separate organization allows environmental journalists greater autonomy than other journalists, who are represented by the Vietnam Journalists' Association. This may well be reflected in their reporting, which often touches on controversial topics such as environmental protests.

Despite the advances, however, it is important to recognize that the state's influence over the press limits the media's ability to maintain accountability (Bass et al. 2010; Abusza 2001). Reporting on environmental problems is only possible when it does not threaten the legitimacy of the Communist Party (Cain 2014). In recent years, there have been cases in which the government has opted for censorship over objective reporting. For example, when in 2016, the Taiwanese-owned Formosa steel plant heavily polluted the ocean and caused massive fish deaths, the media had to follow tight guidelines set by the government. There was hardly any coverage of the ensuing protests, which spread nationwide. Instead, protest leaders were criticized and blamed for illegal mobilizations and being in cahoots with "foreign forces", demonstrating the limits of reporting. Virtually any news article may become sensitive and journalists can end up on the wrong side of the law, which induces a degree of self-censorship. Once the government has made a formal declaration about how a topic has to be covered, the traditional press must report according to these official mandates; the role the media can play in any sustained environmental movement is therefore clearly circumscribed.

The Rise of Non-Governmental Organizations

While the attempt to foster an environmental movement from above has not succeeded, there has been bottom-up activism, signifying the beginning of a genuine environmental movement. In fact, there has been an increase in the number of autonomous environmental NGOs, which theoretically could provide the organizational network necessary for sustained mobilization. While many of them are small, elitist technical or scientific organizations, there is growing interest in voluntarism, indicating embryonic social activism. In 1992, the government enacted Decree 35/HDBT, which allowed the formation of non-profit science and technology associations. As mentioned above, these scientific associations had to be registered under VUSTA and were thus only partially autonomous from the state. Despite many limitations on the operation of organizations, their numbers have increased over the years. As of 2017, VUSTA had 928 members listed on its homepage. Of these, 611 were linked directly to the central office, 107 were national science and technology associations, and 210 were provincial science and technology associations. According to research in 2008, more than 70 per cent of the organizations were established after 1998 and were thus relatively young (Le and Khuat 2008). With respect to the environment, O'Rourke (2004) identified about 150 officially registered environmental research centres, institutes, and organizations in 2004.

As of 2017, there were about 180 organizations with an environmental focus registered with VUSTA, with the majority (160) linked to the central office (based on a conservative count of organizations whose name indicates environmental issues as their mission).

The international community has sought to foster the development of NGOs. One condition for aid was the involvement of non-state actors, which are believed to be more effective and less prone to corruption. How international organizations have sought to foster local organizational development can be illustrated by the case of the local branch of Live & Learn International, a network of localized NGOs registered under VUSTA; active in eleven countries, it focuses on the promotion of an environmentally-friendly lifestyle among young people. In Vietnam, the organization has supported youth activism on university campuses in twenty provinces. According to the organization's own assessment, the students' willingness to participate in environmental issues has grown. In Hanoi, a group of youngsters mapped the public transport system and sought to motivate the government to enhance its user-friendliness. Despite its primarily educational nature, the network potentially spawns wider social activism that could lead to a more participatory society. For instance, in 2015, hundreds of people in the city protested against the cutting down of 25 per cent of the trees in the downtown area. Almost 60,000 people liked a webpage that had asked for 6,700 people to protect 6,700 trees. The action proved to be successful as the government suspended the clearance after cutting five hundred trees (Thompson 2015; Vu 2017).

Overall, Vietnamese NGOs have also been able to increase their political space even within the narrow confines of the state. This was already visible in the 1990s (Sidel 1995) and was the consequence of the inconsistency between government policy-making and implementation. The failure to enact many of the ambitious government policies provided significant opportunities for these organizations to step in to assist the government in strengthening its enforcement mechanisms (Wells-Dang 2010). In the process, NGOs have been able to conduct their projects autonomously as the government provides them with little funding. Fewer than 15 per cent of these organizations rely on government support (Wischermann 2003). According to many observers, there is a sense that compared to the past the political environment has become more open (London 2009; Wells-Dang 2010), which has created some optimism about the future as organizations seek to expand (Taylor et al. 2012).

Although there have been some improvements over the years, Vietnamese NGOs still face many difficulties. Overall, relatively autonomous organizations remain too small in terms of funding and employees to contribute to the development of a sizeable environmental movement. They are dependent on foreign donor money for most of their operations since they receive hardly any money from Vietnamese individuals or the government (Taylor et al. 2012; Aschhoff 2008), so naturally their main agenda has shifted toward meeting the demands of foreign organizations and away from local priorities. To make matters worse, the authoritarian system and the promotion of materialism have resulted in an overwhelmingly apathetic population that shows very little interest in participating in any form of activism (Hostovsky et al. 2010).

In addition, the relationship with the authoritarian government can also prove to be difficult to say the least (Bui 2005). The government has created onerous rules for setting up membership organizations that can draw funds from the general public and thus be more independent from both the government and international donors (Nguyen 2008). Moreover, setting up an association takes sixty days, while a company only requires three days (VUSTA, 4 September 2015). This demonstrates that the legal framework is designed to curtail these organizations (Wischermann 2013). The government can also easily deregister any errant organization, which has created a climate of caution within civil society. For instance, in 2017, the Research Institute for Agricultural Mechanization in the Southeast (Viện Nghiên cứu cơ giới hóa nông nghiệp Đông Nam Bộ) was dissolved after less than a year in operation because it was "insufficiently financed and lacked resources for sustainable development" (VUSTA 2017). The government's main objective is to avert the emergence of any large-scale organizations that could rally support against it, which reveals an overwhelming social control response.

Not only is it difficult to register new organizations, but also there are many rules that complicate the NGO's daily operation as well as their ability to expand (Bui 2013), thereby inhibiting any sustained activism. As a consequence, many of the small organizations go to great lengths to demonstrate that they can be trusted by the government, for instance by refraining from criticizing the authorities. Some even publicly declare their support for the government:

> Since its founding, the [Environmental and Social Science] Institute has been actively participating in the research and development of various topics, projects and communication activities, thereby successfully implementing the guidelines and policies of the Party and the State and contributing positively to the cause of socio-economic development of the country (ESSI 2016).

As such, they position themselves more in the emerging notion of top-down governance in which NGOs act as service providers for the government and help in the implementation of policies. As O'Rourke (2004) noted, these NGOs tend to be closer to consultation firms rather than advocacy organizations that seek to shape environmental politics.

The many challenges facing NGOs can be illustrated by one of the more successful of them, People and Nature Reconciliation (PanNature), a small non-profit organization focusing on nature conservation, established in 2004 and formally registered in 2006 under VUSTA. Its history shows how difficult it is to establish a registered organization in Vietnam. At the beginning, PanNature was fully reliant on volunteers, which is not easy in a developing country. Moreover, it had to share an office with a company, which provided free office space for the four founders and a volunteer. In order to obtain funding and be able to hire any staff, it needed to become registered. The registration process for social organizations such as PanNature, however, is very onerous and takes much patience and perseverance (Nguyen 2008). Prior to its official registration, the organization needed to discuss and get approval for its by-laws, organizational strategy and mission, as well as an acceptable name. While PanNature managed to register, survival remains an ongoing challenge and constantly depends on the ability to gain external funding. As of 2017, the organization had twenty-nine staff members. Its budget must fund five policy experts; only about 2 per cent of it is used for research meant to influence government policy. While it was involved in the recent revision of the environmental law, enacted in 2015, PanNature's efforts remain extremely limited due to its very small size. In particular, it has no ability to monitor the actual implementation of environmental laws, which is arguably the most serious problem right now.

The Formation of Societal Networks

In order to enhance the organizational strength of the small environmental organizations, various networks have been formed to enhance collaboration and mutual assistance. Through frequent meetings, non-governmental organizations can learn from each other and strengthen their ability to deal with various other actors, from the government to international organizations. Better access to these players ensures the ability of small NGOs to be considered as reliable partners. The meetings are also a way to share knowledge and find common ground to cooperate on projects. Of course, the most important function is greater access to external funding, which helps sustain these organizations. While membership in networks is generally viewed as an advantage for small groups, it also increases competition over limited resources and may cause other conflicts. As a consequence, some organizations, such as PanNature, see little use in joining a network.

Networks of NGOs exist both for domestic and international organizations active in the country. The two, however, are somewhat separate from each other due to different challenges but also some disagreements. International NGOs often have significant financial resources, which dwarf the wherewithal of local organizations and make them not only more effective actors in service delivery but also more attractive to potential employees. In consequence, it is very difficult for local groups to compete. It is thus perhaps not surprising that around 90 per cent of the organizations in the urban areas of Hanoi and Ho Chi Minh City claimed that they were members of networks. Nevertheless, not everyone is an active contributor. Wells-Dang (2012) found that approximately 25 per cent of all organizations are inactive because they do not want to waste time and effort and they are thus viewed negatively by others in the network. In addition, NGOs complain about discrimination against newer members (Taylor et al. 2012). Overall, a network's effectiveness is not measured by its size, but rather by the extent to which the links between members are strengthened by the community (Wells-Dang 2012).

For Vietnam's fledgling environmental NGOs, the most important network has been the so-called Vietnamese Non-Governmental Organizations and Climate Change (VNGO&CC) which was formed in 2008. It can trace its roots to the Vietnamese NGO Network for

Community Development (VNGO), which was established in 2001 with the support of international organizations; its primary goal was to deal with poverty in rural communities while fostering sustainable development and enabling people to participate in grassroots democracy, something the government also sought to promote (Zink 2013). By 2008, the topic of climate change had become dominant within international organizations. International NGOs had established the Climate Change Working Group, and the Vietnamese version was a direct response to it. For instance, Nguyen Huu Ninh, a climate scientist, argued that Vietnamese organizations would be better equipped to deal with climate change in the country because they were familiar with the country's traditions and lifestyle (Clark 2008). The network was established by the Centre for Sustainable Rural Development (SRD), the Centre for Marinelife Conservation and Community Development (MCD), the Centre for Environment Research, Education and Development (CERED), and the Institute for Social Studies (ISS). Its official goal has been to provide advocacy as well as feedback on the implementation of climate change efforts at both the grassroots and government levels, which it seeks to achieve through capacity-building, strengthening communications and providing training for local communities. Despite the organizational separation, both the local and international NGO networks signed a common memorandum of understanding (MoU) in 2011 with the Department of Meteorology, Hydrology and Climate Change of the Ministry of Natural Resources and Environment.

Another formal NGO alliance, called the Vietnam Rivers Network, was formed by Vietnamese NGOs in 2005; according to its own assessment, this alliance enhanced the "awareness on environmental protection [...] evidenced by the close cooperation among network members, the state agencies and the media" (VRN 2015). The network deals with the country's rivers, streams, and lakes, which are not only threatened from growing pollution but also face the challenge of dam development inside the country and beyond. The Mekong River, one of the crucial lifelines for Vietnam and neighbouring countries, is subject to the development of many new dams that threaten the ecosystem of the river and reduce the number of fish, which may no longer freely migrate along the river. Although the builders of dams include mitigation measures for fish, it is as yet unclear how effective those can be. As a consequence of slowing down the river, less water ultimately arrives at the coast, deeply impacting the people in the delta, which produces approximately 50 per cent of the country's main food supply and 90 per cent of its rice exports (Fawthrop 2016). In addition to these problems, the construction of dams also results in the displacement of people, which can cause serious social problems in the densely populated country.

The Vietnam Rivers Network, which boasts around three hundred members across the country, is basically an open forum facilitating the discussion of important topics as well as the exchange of information between various organizations including NGOs, researchers, government officials, and anyone else who is interested. It has engaged in a wide variety of activities, which has been useful to its members. Particularly beneficial is the training of member organizations to enhance group capacity. As a collective, the network has facilitated contact between NGOs and the government in the form of enabling input to impact assessments, the provision of scientific studies to the government, and the collection of public feedback to the lawmaking process. It thus seeks to gain support from within the government coalition that can overcome the overemphasis on short-term economic benefits, which often has detrimental consequences for the sustainability of rivers (Nga Dao 2011). Finally, the network also seeks to gain media attention by organizing field trips, workshops, conferences, and seminars for journalists, as well as writing and distributing articles about its activities and scientific research. This proved to be a very effective strategy in the campaign against two dams along the Dong Nai River, intended to produce clean electric power. After the environmental impact assessment report was released in 2013, the government recognized the serious consequences and decided to terminate the two projects (Ha 2014).

The network's formation has enhanced the organizational structure among non-governmental organizations, but its efforts have been limited due to the same constraints as those that apply to NGOs in general. Not only are the networks primarily geared toward better service delivery and resource concentration, they also rely on international organizations for their support. For instance, the Vietnam Rivers Network receives its funding from the Interchurch Organization for Development Cooperation (ICCO) of the Netherlands and the McKnight Foundation, an American organization. Aside from foreign funding, the networks also depend greatly on government support for most environmental projects. As such, the networks must avoid becoming too confrontational. Not surprisingly, they are unlikely to align themselves with other societal actors, such as local communities, that are willing to challenge the government more openly.

Environmental Protest Movements at the Grassroots Level

Separate from the world of environmental projects and NGO networks, there has been growing grassroots discontent about the deterioration of the environment as it has affected the life of ordinary Vietnamese. Much of the direct activism has been targeted at air and water pollution because they have had the most immediate and visible impact on the population. Dark smoke billowing out of factory smokestacks, pungent smells, discoloured liquids that change streams and rivers, and most importantly, the massive impact on livelihoods—from fish deaths to the destruction of farmland—are directly felt by local residents. Desperate about the situation and aware that the government should help them, many have been willing to protest against such activities by going into the streets, blocking the entrance of offending factories or the roads that lead to them, and even committing forceful entry, the clogging of exit pipes, or other forms of violence.

Protests usually erupt when a serious situation has festered for a significant period of time while attempts are made to solve the problem through official channels. In most cases, community members are seriously worried about their own health while the quality of their daily life suffers from the impact of the pollution. Attempts to talk with government officials and company representatives, along with petitions to local and even central government officials, are often made initially before residents decide to take action against a polluter. This, however, happens quite frequently, as reports in the Vietnamese press attest. There are many news reports detailing the desperate reaction of local communities to polluting factories or landfills in their neighbourhoods.

While many of the protests are small, some have drawn hundreds or even thousands of people. In general, protests start off as peaceful actions outside a company or at the local government office. Protesters surround the company and make their demands known. When there is no response, they will try to block staff from entering or leaving the company. The reports about environmental protests, however, also show that in some cases protesters take more extreme measures and enter the companies to confront workers or managers, which can result in physical confrontations and even the destruction of company property. Some protesters have tried to block exhaust pipes so that they could no longer pollute.

One reason that protests have become more common is the fact that they may potentially achieve some of their goals. Success, however, is not assured and according to O'Rourke (2004) depends primarily on the degree of community cohesion, the community's linkage to outside actors including the government, and the type of strategies used. In addition, Ortmann (2017) argues that success has also hinged on the salience and magnitude of each case of pollution. In particular, instances that draw heavy media attention can raise the chances of a positive outcome. While the rise in the number of protests suggests that a growing number of people see protest as an effective method to deal with serious pollution, defining the meaning of success has become very difficult. First of all, any action to reduce the problem can be regarded as a "success", but a serious situation may only be mitigated rather than resolved. Furthermore, compensation payments may be insufficient or unfairly distributed. As a consequence, protests may continue even after a company has been fined and agreed to pay compensation, as was the case in 2016 with Formosa, which will be discussed later. It is clear, however, that protests have not solved the underlying institutional weaknesses and the enforcement of environmental regulations remains highly selective.

In most cases, environmental protests have remained isolated community actions that draw on Vietnam's traditionally strong community organization. As the protests do not seek to achieve broader policy change and instead focus on particular cases of pollution, they can be described as not-in-my-backyard activism, or NIMBYism. These are generally tolerated by the authorities. Protesters refer to their right to a clean environment and the right to participate in local affairs, which has been formalized in Vietnamese law. In China, this form of activism has been called "rightful resistance" and has received a very similar response from the government (O'Brien 1996; O'Brien and Li 2006). Scholars focusing on community activism in China have even argued that the central government is supportive of such protests because they are useful for detecting problems at the local level (Chen 2012; Heurlin 2016). Authoritarian regimes generally lack sufficient information about social problems and the protests allow officials to determine local discontent.

Although protests have generally remained localized affairs, they have demonstrated the ability of residents to cooperate with each other without formal organization. These local movements are often sustained over many years because a single major protest may not resolve the crisis. Companies may continue to pollute even if there is massive media attention and government officials speak out against the company. Because dealing with the problem is often very expensive, due to the high costs of compensating affected residents as well as the need to adopt costly pollution prevention and mitigation measures, companies can be reluctant to respond positively.

In urban contexts, Wells-Dang (2012) and Vu (2017) have shown that the opposition to urban redevelopment projects has involved informal networks, which have emerged in recent years as demands for a green environment and heritage protection have grown. The primary organizational basis is social media, which has become particularly prominent among intellectuals and the urban middle class (Mol 2009). Many discussions can be found online that do not exist in the print media (Wells-Dang 2010). In particular, Facebook and WhatsApp are used to maintain contact, mobilize new members, communicate goals and strategies, and organize events.

Not surprisingly, the government has become increasingly concerned about the democratizing effect of online media. It has passed a number of laws that were designed to limit its impact. For instance, in 2013, the government enacted Decree 72, which declared that blogs should only be used "to provide and exchange personal information". This suggested that the sharing of news articles or even government information on personal websites and social media would no longer be allowed (Palatino 2013). In addition, the law also required foreign Internet content providers to maintain local servers in the country (*BBC* 2013). From time to time, the government has also blocked websites such as Facebook. Nevertheless, the Vietnamese government has been far less successful than China, which is known for its "Great Firewall", because not only does it lack the technological capabilities to develop a sophisticated censorship system, it also relies heavily on the free exchange of information for economic development. The pressure to lift the ban on Facebook usually comes from businesses, as they rely on the social media platform for advertising. In 2011, when Facebook was blocked, Hanoi's airport continued to use its Facebook page as

its homepage, leading unsuspecting foreign travellers to land on an
error page. This demonstrated not only that most Vietnamese are savvy

MAP 9.1

Selected sites of environmental disputes in Vietnam

Source: QGIS and Natural Earth.

enough to circumvent the block, but also that Facebook has become an important part of the emerging economy.

Although social media plays a growing role in Vietnam, it is unclear whether these informal networks can translate into more effective and sustainable organizations that might develop into a social movement. So far, the network of social activists has failed to create any formal organizations. And while NGOs and grassroots activists collaborated for the first time in the campaign to save Hanoi's trees, the movement remained focused on only this particular issue within the narrow limits of the city of Hanoi (Vu 2017). In order to assess whether localized protests could evolve into a broader environmental movement, it is helpful to discuss two cases in which the movement expanded to the national level: the anti-Bauxite campaign of 2009 and the protest movement following the Formosa incident in 2016–17.

The Rise and Fall of the Anti-Bauxite Movement

While environmental protests have often remained confined to a particular locality and environmental activism constrained to government-controlled organizations, there has been a growing trend toward less formal networks and loose cooperation over social media, which have evolved from support for localized protests to foster incipient national movements. This was particularly visible in 2009 in the campaign against planned Bauxite mining. Unlike in other protests, the government eventually decided to use repression against the activists and silenced the movement.

The opposition to a Bauxite mining project in 2009 emerged from deep concerns over the potentially hazardous impact of unearthing the mineral because the surface-strip mining would not only completely alter the landscape, any potential runoff from the mines could destroy the neighbouring environment. Although tight protections can prevent any spills, activists were worried that the government would be unable to enforce strict management on the mining corporations. This was coupled with the fact that the mining companies were Chinese, which are considered to have a poor environmental record. Due to this, many locals were deeply worried about the potential harm to their country. At the same time, it also raised nationalist concerns about Vietnam selling out its natural resources to China. One year earlier, the Vietnamese and Chinese leaders had come together to announce the project in a joint statement, and the Vietnamese government granted the Chinese state-owned mining company Chinalco the right to operate the mine and even bring in its own workers (Womack 2009). There was concern, moreover, that the Chinese were interested in the project because it was close to the border with Laos and would allow Chinese soldiers masquerading as workers into the country (Hoa and Turner 2010). According to Morris-Jung (2013), the whole programme would include more than twenty mines in the Central Highlands, at the frontier with Laos and Cambodia, most of which lies in the provinces of Dak Nong, at the frontier with Cambodia (thirteen mines), and Lam Dong province (five mines).

While there was a growing informal coalition of opponents, the movement lacked a strong organizational basis as well as strong leadership that could have effectively coordinated the opposition (Hoang 2009). One could find voices against the project not only among local residents, scientists, and the state media, but even from soldiers. One hundred and thirty-five prominent scholars and scientists signed a petition against the project, and a Pastoral Letter by the archbishop of Ho Chi Minh City indicated the Catholic Church's opposition to it. Perhaps the most prominent opponent was General Vo Nguyen Giap, who was the only remaining founding member of the country and thus wielded significant symbolic legitimacy (Vuving 2010). For observers of Vietnamese politics, the growing opposition was significant. Morris-Jung (2011), for instance, claimed that it was "one of the most significant expressions of public dissent against the single-party state since the end of the Vietnam War (1959–1975)". However, the criticism was too fragmented to evolve into a sustained movement.

The mere threat of an emerging coalition contributed to the decision to use repression against the movement. Pro-democracy activists and leading members of the movement were arrested. For instance, the scientist Dr Cu Huy Ha Vu, who had attempted to sue the prime minister, was arrested for "propaganda against the state" and "plotting to overthrow the communist government of Vietnam". The government also enacted Decision No. 97, which makes it harder to criticize the government because comments must now be made directly in person and privately (Vuving 2010). For reporting on the China-Vietnam issue, the Vietnamese news magazine *Du Lich* (*Tourism*) was taken out of circulation for three months (*The Economist*, 23 April 2009). To this day, Chinese investments and the Belt and Road Initiative, which is officially supported by the Vietnamese government, are considered sensitive topics; they may draw little media attention but still hold the potential for serious political discontent, as reflected in a number of nationalist protests. A website set up for reporting on Bauxite mining was attacked by hackers and then the web master decided to block Vietnamese visitors to prevent further hacking attacks.[1] As the topic became politicized, the anti-Bauxite website was recast as a forum for political change and no longer targets the original issue. It continues to be banned within Vietnam.

The movement did lead to some compromises. In order to assuage the nationalist concerns, the government conducted a review of the project and fined six Chinese companies because they had not obtained the necessary permit for employing Chinese miners. Otherwise, however, the project proceeded as planned. The economic benefits from the mining project clearly outweighed any potential risks. In particular, the prime minister at the time, Nguyen Tan Dung, was convinced that the project was of strategic importance to the country, calling it "a major policy of the party and the state" (quoted in Hoang 2009). Clearly, the government did not want to forgo the estimated US$15 billion in investments in this field by 2025, or the jobs, related businesses, and other benefits that come with it.

The "Formosa Incident" and Another Growing Environmental Coalition

Environmental protests have, as mentioned above, occurred frequently across Vietnam, and they still happen on and off. However, in most instances, the anger remains localized and protesters, company representatives, and the government can find a mutually agreeable resolution. While leaders are sometimes arrested, the protests are generally tolerated and appear as objective news stories in the Vietnamese press. The case of the protest movement against the steel producer Formosa, owned mainly by two Taiwanese companies, Formosa Plastics and China Steel (with the minor capital participation of Japanese steel maker JFE), in the southern part of Ha Tinh province was very different. I will argue that the reasons for this trajectory are very similar to the anti-Bauxite movement. First of all, the movement became more than just localized opposition when it attracted support from across the country. Secondly, it gained the support of the overseas

Vietnamese community, which is viewed as a threat to the regime. Thirdly, the protests involved criticism of Chinese involvement and thus raised nationalist concerns. Last but not least, the protests raised questions about the legitimacy of the Vietnamese Communist Party.

The whole affair began when dead fish appeared in fish farms and were washed ashore starting on 6 April 2016, in a stretch of about two hundred kilometres of coastline, affecting the four provinces of Ha Tinh, Quang Binh, Quang Tri, and Thua Thien-Hue, in Central Vietnam. At the time, fishermen were clueless as to the reason for this dire situation that would deeply affect their livelihoods. A company called Formosa Ha Tinh Steel had used three hundred tonnes of toxic cleaning material for its exhaust pipes, which was then released untreated into the ocean. At first, the government investigation was unable to link the fish deaths to the actions of the company. The Deputy Minister of Natural Resources and Environment, Võ Tuấn Nhân, suggested on 27 April that there could be other reasons for the disaster, such as a red tide or pollution from individual households. However, people were not convinced by this explanation and were angered by the company's Hanoi office head, Chou Chun Fan, who asserted: "You have to decide whether to catch fish and shrimp, or to build a modern steel industry" (Bui 2016). On the official Labour Day, 1 May, protests were organized across the country, including in Hanoi and Ho Chi Minh City, rallying against Formosa and the failure to respond to the crisis. Many shouted "I choose fish" in response to Chou's statement.

The quickly spreading movement, which was mainly driven by social media, suggested an increasingly effective mobilizational capacity, even if the organization remained highly fragmented. Aside from environmental activists, many of the protesters were supporters of democracy and human rights, as well as members of the Catholic Church. This raised concerns within the government about the potentially subversive nature of the movement, which could threaten the regime. On the website dedicated to the current president, Tran Dai Quang, an article on 1 May 2016, denounced the involvement of so-called "reactionary forces" and asserted that they only used "the case of the dead fish and the marine pollution as an excuse for these forces to incite violence and to overthrow the government" (Vinh An 2016). The article names a number of dissidents, including human rights activist Bui Tuan Lam of the Vietnam Path Movement (Phong Trào Con đường Việt Nam), which is derided as a reactionary organization. This claim is probably based on the group's re-evaluation of the country's history without a Communist Party bias. The article is also interesting for the fact that it describes the dissidents as "collaborators of overseas media companies", probably as a result of giving interviews to international media outlets. Although the protests remained peaceful, the government asserted that these individuals and organizations were intent on creating riots.

Despite the growing protest movement, it took until 30 June 2016 for the government to finally announce that Formosa was responsible for the pollution, which the company accepted. As a consequence, Formosa was made to pay US$500 million in compensation to those affected by the pollution. In 2017, the government also disciplined four senior local government officials for neglect, including Nguyen

FIGURE 9.1

A protest near the entrance of Formosa Ha Tinh Steel, Ký Anh, 4 October 2016

Source: Paulus Lê Sơn.

FIGURE 9.2

Fishermen on the beach near Formosa Ha Tinh Steel, Ký Anh, 4 February 2018

Source: Paul Jobin.

Minh Quang, the former environmental minister of Ha Tinh province, Bui Cach Tuyen and Nguyen Thai Lai, his two deputies, and Vo Kim Cu, the former party chief secretary of the province. According to the media, they were punished because of "irresponsible and loose management and supervision in regard to environmental safety, which led to serious damage to the environment and local people" (*Reuters/ Tuoi Tre News* 2017). Vo Kim Cu was also later forced to resign from his position in the National Assembly.

Although the protests could thus be seen as partially successful, the process of identifying victims and distributing the compensation—which many consider insufficient—has been a fraught process with many problems that are difficult to manage for Vietnam's administrative state. As a consequence, accusations of corruption and abuse surfaced, leading to discontent among those affected, especially due to the slow and uneven distribution of the money. Protests erupted again in early

2017 as anger at local officials grew. Most of the protests occurred in early April in Nghe An, Ha Tinh, and Quang Binh provinces when an estimated five hundred people were arrested (Hutt 2017). Directly affected Catholic communities played a particularly prominent role and many of the most prominent activists were church members.

The government has repeatedly responded with repression against these activists. On 14 February, a march of a few dozen people from Nghe Anh Province, which had been excluded from the compensation payments, managed to walk only twenty kilometres of a planned two-hundred-kilometre march to the People's Court in Ky Anh, where the Formosa plant is located, when it was interrupted by the police (Reuters Staff 2017; Nguyen 2017). The government accused the protesters of "opposing the government" and using violence against the police. As Catholic priests played a key role in the protest and were effective in mobilizing large crowds, the government sought to counter this trend. Following an "offending" sermon by one of the activist priests, in which he had argued for a re-evaluation of Vietnamese history, thousands of people were mobilized to protest against the supposedly traitorous priest. As the Communist Party draws legitimacy from its victory in the war against the United States, the war for national liberation, any re-evaluation of that event is regarded as a betrayal of the nation. For the first time, there was a pro-government protest against activists who were deeply concerned about the impact of the massive pollution on the livelihoods of the people. The government has also cracked down on a number of individual activists and bloggers, including Nguyễn Ngọc Như Quỳnh, known as Mother Mushroom (Mẹ Nấm), for fear the growing environmental movement could eventually evolve into an anti-government movement.

Conclusion

This chapter has demonstrated, based on the political process model, that despite periods of increasing environmental activism, a sustained environmental movement is unlikely to emerge in Vietnam. The reason for that is primarily that the government maintains tight control over all formal organizations in the country, stifling the organizational structure necessary for movements to emerge. Instead, the Communist Party state prefers mass organizations that are hierarchically organized and under full control of the government. They can be quickly mobilized for their vast membership bases but lack the voluntary spirit. As such, they have been used as a tool in environmental campaigns like waste collection and tree planting, but such events have necessarily been episodic.

In terms of creating awareness about the worsening natural environment, environmental journalists have enjoyed greater freedom than other reporters and, since many see themselves as advocates of the people, they have frequently pressed for environmental concerns. As the media is under the control of the government, they are, however, bound to the state and are prone to censorship in regard to sensitive issues. This places a great limit on the media's role.

Vietnam has also seen growth in the number of non-governmental organizations, but they, too, are tightly regulated and limited in their capabilities due to a severe lack of funding. This has been slightly mitigated through the formation of networks, but Vietnamese NGOs still remain largely service providers for donors or the government.

In contrast, the mostly informal community organizations tend to be the least restricted. Across the country, an increasing number of people have protested against egregious pollution. In some cases, protests have been able to achieve some success, for example, compensation, the installation of pollution-control systems, and even relocation. However, the government has dealt harshly with attempts to create a broader and sustained nationwide environmental movement involving other activists and individuals. This largely corresponds with the nationalist protests identified by Kerkvliet (2019, p. 142), in which the government cracked down on activism that "became lengthy, happened several weekends in a row, threatened to grow nationwide, or occurred in defiance of orders explicitly prohibiting them".

In conclusion, Vietnam's authoritarian regime does not allow the emergence of an organizational basis for a sustained environmental movement, which could threaten the dominance of the Communist Party. Although Vietnamese society has become more plural in recent years, the institutional framework does not allow broad-based independent activism that is beyond the control of the ruling elite. A sustainable environmental movement can only emerge in the context of political liberalization, which, however, appears remote at this point.

NOTE

1. http://www.boxitvn.net/BauxiteViệtNam.

REFERENCES

Abuza, Zachary. 2001. *Renovating Politics in Contemporary Vietnam*. Boulder: Lynne Rienner.

Aschhoff, Niklas. 2008. *What Role Can NGOs Play to Support Grassroots Democracy? The Example of the Vietnamese NGO CRP*. Sankt Augustin: Konrad-Adenauer-Stiftung.

Bass, Steve, David Annandale, Phan Van Binh, Tran Phuong Dong, Hoang Anh Nam, Le Thi Kien Oanh, Mike Parsons, Nguyen Van Phuc, and Vu Van Trieu. 2010. "Integrating Environment and Development in Viet Nam: Achievements, Challenges and Next Steps". Paper resulting from the Viet Nam Environmental Mainstreaming "Lessons Learned Review" of March 2009 organized by IIED in association with the Viet Nam/UNDP Poverty Environment Programme.

BBC. 2013. "Vietnam Internet Restrictions Come into Effect", 1 September 2013. https://www.bbc.com/news/world-asia-23920541.

Bui, Duyen. 2016. "Amid Protests, Vietnamese Look to Obama's Visit". *The Diplomat*, 18 May 2016.

Bui The Cuong. 2005. "Issue-Oriented Organizations in Hanoi: Some Findings from an Empirical Survey". In *Towards Good Society: Civil Society Actors, the State, and the Business Class in Southeast Asia—Facilitators of or Impediments to a Strong, Democratic, and Fair Society?*, edited by Heinrich Böll Foundation. Berlin: Heinrich-Böll-Stiftung.

Bui, Thiem H. 2013. "The Development of Civil Society and Dynamics of Governance in Vietnam's One Party Rule". *Global Change, Peace & Security* 25, no. 1: 77–93.

Cain, Jeffrey. 2014. "Kill One to Warn One Hundred: The Politics of Press Censorship in Vietnam". *The International Journal of Press/Politics* 19, no. 1: 85–107.

Chen, Xi. 2012. *Social Protest and Contentious Authoritarianism in China*. Cambridge: Cambridge University Press.

Clark, Helen. 2008. "Vietnam: Heeding Climate Change Warnings". *Inter Press Service*, 28 September 2008. http://www.ipsnews.net/2008/09/vietnam-heeding-climate-change-warnings/.

Environmental and Social Science Institute (ESSI, Viện Khoa học Môi trường và Xã hội). 2016. "Lời nói đầu (Preface)", 25 August 2016. http://essi.org.vn.

Fawthrop, Tom. 2016. "Killing the Mekong, Dam by Dam". *The Diplomat*, 28 November 2016.

Ha Thi Quynh Nga. 2014. "Climate Change and Energy in Vietnam: Is the Door Open for Civil Society?" Bonn: Friedrich Ebert Stiftung Sustainability, 8 April 2014.

Heurlin, Christopher. 2016. *Responsive Authoritarianism in China*. Cambridge: Cambridge University Press.

Ho, Ming-sho. 2011. "Environmental Movement in Democratizing Taiwan (1980–2004): A Political Opportunity Structure Perspective". In *East Asian Social Movements*, edited by Jeffrey Broadbent and Vicky Brockman. New York: Springer, pp. 283–314.

Hoa, Nguyen Kim and Bryan S. Turner. 2010. "The Fourth Indo-China War". *Society* 47, no. 3: 246–53.

Hoang, Duy. 2009. "Vietnam Bauxite Plan Opens Pit of Concern". *Asia Times*, 17 March 2009.

Hostovsky, Charles, Virginia MacLaren and Geoffrey McGrath. 2010. "The Role of Public Involvement in Environmental Impact Assessment in Vietnam: Towards a More Culturally Sensitive Approach". *Journal of Environmental Planning and Management* 53, no. 3: 405–25.

Hutt, David. 2017. "Formosa Factory Restart Favors Foreign over Local Interests". *Asia Times*, 10 April 2017.

Jancar Webster, Barbara. 1998. "Environmental Movement and Social Change in the Transition Countries". *Environmental Politics* 7, no. 1: 69–90.

Kerkvliet, Benedict J. Tria. 2001. "An Approach for Analysing State-Society Relations in Vietnam". *Sojourn: Journal of Social Issues in Southeast Asia* 16, no. 2: 238–78.

———. 2019. *Speaking Out in Vietnam: Public Political Criticism in a Communist Party-Ruled Nation*. Ithaca and London: Cornell University Press.

Kingsbury, Damien. 2017. *Politics in Contemporary Southeast Asia: Authority, Democracy and Political Change*. London and New York: Routledge.

Le Bach Duong and Khuat Thu Hong. 2008. "Third Sector Governance in Vietnam". In *Comparative Third Sector Governance in Asia: Structure, Process, and Political Economy*, edited by Samiul Hasan and Jenny Onyx. New York: Springer, pp. 309–23.

London, Jonathan. 2009. "Viet Nam and the Making of Market Leninism". *The Pacific Review* 22, no. 3: 373–97.

McAdam, Doug. 1999. *Political Process and the Development of Black Insurgency, 1930–1970*. Chicago and London: University of Chicago Press.

Minh Yen. 2012. "Thanh Hóa: Xây dựng, bảo vệ môi trường xanh – sạch – đẹp" [Than Hoa: Constructions, Environmental Protection – Green, Clean, Beautiful]. *Vietnam Women's Union website*, 11 October 2012.

Mol, Arthur P.J. 2009. "Environmental Governance through Information: China and Vietnam". *Singapore Journal of Tropical Geography* 30: 114–29.

Morris-Jung, Jason. 2011. "Prospects and Challenges for Environmental Politics: The Vietnamese Bauxite Controversy". Paper presented at the 2011 Vietnam Update: The Environment: Change, Challenge and Contestations, Australian National University, 17–18 November 2011.

———. 2013. "The Vietnamese Bauxite Mining Controversy: The Emergence of a New Oppositional Politics". PhD dissertation, Department of Environmental Sciences, Policy and Management, University of California, Berkeley.

Nga Dao. 2011. "Damming Rivers in Vietnam: A Lesson Learned in the Tây Bắc Region". *Journal of Vietnamese Studies* 6, no. 2: 106–40.

Nguyen, Hai Hong. 2016a. *Political Dynamics of Grassroots Democracy in Vietnam*. London: Palgrave Macmillan.

———. 2016b. "Resilience of the Communist Party of Vietnam's Authoritarian Regime since Doi Moi". *Journal of Current Southeast Asian Affairs* 35, no. 2: 31–55.

Nguyen, Hai Hong and Minh Quang Pham. 2016. "Democratization in Vietnam's Post-Đổi Mới One-Party Rule: Change from Within, Change from the Bottom to the Top, and Possibilities". In *Globalization and Democracy in Southeast Asia*, edited by Chantana Banpasirichote Wungaeo, Boike Rehbein, and Surichai Wun'gaeo. London: Palgrave Macmillan, pp. 131–55.

Nguyen, Joseph. 2017. "VietNam: Police Violently Attacked Priest and Faithful during Formosa Protest". *VietCatholic News*, 18 February 2017.

Nguyen, Manh Cuong. 2008. *A Theoretical Framework and Principles for the Establishment and Management of Civil Society Organizations in Vietnam*. Hanoi: Institute for Social Studies.

O'Brien, Kevin J. 1996. "Rightful Resistance". *World Politics* 49, no. 1: 31–55.

O'Brien, Kevin J. and Lianjiang Li. 2006. *Rightful Resistance in Rural China*. Cambridge: Cambridge University Press.

O'Rourke, Dara. 2004. *Community-Driven Regulation: Balancing Development and the Environment in Vietnam*. Cambridge, M.A. and London: MIT Press.

Ortmann, Stephan. 2017. *Environmental Governance in Vietnam: Institutional Reforms and Failures*. Cham: Palgrave Macmillan.

Palatino, Mong. 2013. "Decree 72: Vietnam's Confusing Internet Law". *The Diplomat*, 8 August 2013.

Reuters/Tuoi Tre News. 2017. "Vietnam Punishes Officials over Formosa Incident". *Tuoi Tre News*, 22 April 2017.

Reuters Staff. 2017. "Vietnam Police Stop Fishermen Marching to Make Claims at Steel Firm". *Reuters*, 14 February 2017.

Sidel, Mark. 1995. "The Emergence of a Nonprofit Sector and Philanthropy in the Socialist Republic of Vietnam". In *Emerging Civil Society in the Asia Pacific Community: Nongovernmental Underpinnings of the Emerging Asia Pacific Regional Community*, edited by Tadashi Yamamoto. Singapore and Tokyo: Institute of Southeast Asian Studies and Japan Center for International Exchange.

Tang, Shui-Yan and Ching-Ping Tang. 1997. "Democratization and Environmental Politics in Taiwan". *Asian Survey* 37, no. 3: 281–94.

Tarrow, Sidney. 1994. *Power in Movement: Social Movements, Collective Action and Mass Politics*. Cambridge and New York: Cambridge University Press.

Taylor, William, Nguyen Thu Hang, Pham Quang Tu, and Huynh Thi Ngoc Tuyet. 2012. *Civil Society in Vietnam: A Comparative Study of Civil Society Organizations in Hanoi and Ho Chi Minh City*. Hanoi: The Asia Foundation, 2012.

Thayer, Carlyle A. 2009a. "Political Legitimacy of Vietnam's One Party-State: Challenges and Responses". *Journal of Current Southeast Asian Affairs* 28, no. 4: 47–70.

———. 2009b. "Vietnam and the Challenge of Political Civil Society". *Contemporary Southeast Asia* 31, no. 1: 1–27.

The Economist. 2009. "Bauxite Bashers: The Government Chooses Economic Growth over Xenophobia and Greenery", 23 April 2009.

Thompson, Ashley. 2015. "Hundreds in Hanoi Protest Tree Cutting". *Voice of America*, 23 March 2015.

Thu Hang. 2011. "Gây ô nhiễm vẫn được giải thưởng hiệu xanh" [Polluter Still Awarded Green Brand]. *Thanh Nien*, 12 May 2011. https://thanhnien.vn/thoi-su/gay-o-nhiem-van-duoc-giai-thuong-hieu-xanh-430573.html.

Tran Minh Quan. 2011. "Today's mistake to harm the future". *VietnamNet Bridge*, 18 October 2011.

Viet Nam News (VNS). 2015. "NA debates new law on civil associations", 25 September 2015.

Vietnam Rivers Network (VRN). 2015. "Vietnam Rivers Network's 2015 Annual Meeting". *VRN website*, 31 December 2015.

Vietnam Union of Science and Technology Associations (VUSTA). 2015. "VUSTA Discusses Draft Law on Association". *VUSTA homepage*, 4 September 2015. http://www.vusta.vn/en/news/Our-Partners/VUSTA-discusses-draft-law-on-association-55662.html# (accessed 18 March 2016).

Vinh An. 2016. "Biểu tình ngày 1/5: Cá chết và ô nhiễm biển chỉ là vỏ bọc để thực hiện các âm mưu đen tối" [May 1 Protests: The Dead Fish and Marine Pollution are Just a Cover for Carrying out a Dark Plot]. *Trần Đại Quang*. http://trandaiquang.org/.

Vu, Ngoc Anh. 2017. "Grassroots Environmental Activism in an Authoritarian Context: The Trees Movement in Vietnam". *VOLUNTAS: International Journal of Voluntary and Nonprofit Organizations* 28, no. 3: 1180–1208.

VUSTA. 2017. "Thông báo về việc giải thể Viện Nghiên cứu cơ giới hóa nông nghiệp Đông Nam Bộ" [Announcement on the Dissolution of the Institute for Agricultural Mechanization in the Southeast]. *VUSTA Homepage*, 24 July 2017. http://vusta.vn/chitiet/cac_to_chuc_khac/Thong-bao-ve-viec-giai-the-Vien-Nghien-cuu-co-gioi-hoa-nong-nghiep-Dong-Nam-Bo-1008.

Vuving, Alexander L. 2010. "Vietnam: A Tale of Four Players". *Southeast Asian Affairs*: 366–91.

Wells-Dang, Andrew. 2010. "Political Space in Vietnam: A View from the 'Rice-Roots'". *The Pacific Review* 23, no. 1: 93–112.

——. 2012. *Civil Society Networks in China and Vietnam: Informal Pathbreakers in Health and the Environment*. Houndmills and New York: Palgrave Macmillan.

Wischermann, Jörg. 2003. "Vietnam in the Era of *Doi Moi*: Issue-Oriented Organizations and their Relationship to the Government". *Asian Survey* 43, no. 6: 867–89.

——. 2010. "Civil Society Action and Governance in Vietnam: Selected Findings from an Empirical Survey". *Journal of Current Southeast Asian Affairs* 29, no. 2: 3–40.

——. 2013. "Civic Organizations in Vietnam's One-Party State: Supporters of Authoritarian Rule?" *GIGA Working Papers*, No. 228. Hamburg: German Institute of Global and Area Studies. https://www.giga-hamburg.de/en/publication/civic-organizations-in-vietnams-one-party-state-supporters-of-authoritarian-rule.

Womack, Brantly. 2009. "Vietnam and China in an Era of Economic Uncertainty". *The Asia-Pacific Journal* 36, no. 2 (7 September 2009). http://japanfocus.org/-Brantly-Womack/3214.

Zink, Eren. 2013. *Hot Science, High Water: Assembling Nature, Society and Environmental Policy in Contemporary Vietnam*. Copenhagen: Nias Press.

10

THE CAMBODIAN NEOPATRIMONIAL STATE, CHINESE INVESTMENTS, AND ANTI-DAM MOVEMENTS

*James W.Y. Wang**

Since it toppled the Khmer Rouge in 1979 with the help of Vietnam, the Cambodian People's Party (CPP) has been Cambodia's ruling party, under the strong leadership of Hun Sen who, since 1985, has doubled as the Prime Minister. Hun Sen and the CPP have thus ruled the country for over three decades. The CPP's legitimacy as a hegemonic party is based internally on its capacity to maintain political order and develop the economy, and externally on its ability to work with international aid donors, with different geopolitical agendas (China and the United States, in particular). Since the early 1990s, and thanks to the regional stability provided by the country's adhesion to the Association of Southeast Asian Nations (ASEAN) in 1997,[1] Cambodia has experienced a rapid economic transformation built with the support of considerable financial aid from international donors, as well as the ruthless exploitation of the country's natural resources. The institutional basis for this political economy is a patronage network controlled by the CPP and its local allies, who reap financial windfalls from lucrative land deals (MacInnes 2015). This commercialization of the land encourages illegal logging and land grabs, which have already caused massive biodiversity loss and declining fish stocks (Connell and Grimsditch 2017). The forced dislocation of local populations has provoked indignation from international donors and reduced the CPP's popular approval. Nevertheless, state patronage based on land concessions and a brutal exploitation of natural resources remains the regime's strongest political asset.

Max Weber (1978, pp. 231–32) defined patrimonialism as a form of traditional domination: as long as the ruler abided the tradition, he could treat the administration and the military as his personal instruments. As in feudalism, under traditional patrimonialism, the subordinates accept submission to the ruler's personal power in return for various advantages (Weber 1978, p. 1026). In his study of sub-Saharan Africa, Eisenstadt (1973) drew on Weber to underline that the lack of political modernization exacerbates practices of patronage and clientelism, a mechanism which he described as a modern form of patrimonialism or "neopatrimonialism". Some recent studies have applied the notion of neopatrimonialism to the Cambodian context, to spotlight how the state apparatus has been captured by particular patronage interests (Cock 2011), and the consequences of that functional threat for nature-society relations (Milne et al. 2015).

Generally speaking, a political system based on patronage, asymmetrical power relations, and subjugation of the people to the state is inimical to a healthy civil society (Springer 2015). However, since the 1991 Paris Peace Accords and the subsequent UN intervention in Cambodia, socio-political dynamics and associations have been evolving. Cambodian NGOs have blossomed into lucrative businesses that generate considerable revenue and perform many functions. International donors and investors are the major funding sources for most NGOs in Cambodia. NGOs' connections to international donors have enabled campaigners to enjoy political opportunities in a large range of issues including healthcare, agricultural development, and humanitarian aid (Coventry 2017).

Foreign NGOs working locally in Cambodia and committed to advocacy, human rights, and environmental issues are generally more willing to expose the Cambodian government's failings and shortcomings and to demand accountability and transparency (Henke 2011). However, conservation campaigns at the subnational and local levels are risky and potentially fatal. Numerous committed environmental activists have lost their lives while campaigning at work sites. These tragedies have inspired more international NGO campaigners to cooperate with local activists to enhance the effectiveness of conservation campaigns (Lambrick 2012).

In addition to the exploitation of rainforests, the provision of stable and cheap sources of electricity has been a priority of economic development (Middleton et al. 2015; Middleton and Lamb 2019; Bong 2019). In this context, China's aid and investment have been warmly welcomed, in particular for the construction of hydroelectric dams (Moore 2018; Middleton and Allouche 2016). This welcome by the Cambodian government contrasts with the tensions that Chinese dam projects have generally provoked in other countries of the Southeast Asian mainland (Keskinen et al. 2008). However, the decision to contract with China's state-owned dam builders has lacked both transparency and accountability (Schmeier 2009; Li et al. 2011). With the Chinese dam builders uninterested in environmental and social safeguards and the Cambodian government focused on short-term interests, these dam-building projects have therefore incited strong protests and vehement criticism.

Through a review of the scholarly literature and the press, this chapter investigates the tensions between civil society and state patronage over environmental issues, paying special attention to geopolitical perspectives and political implications. We will see in particular how a coalition of local activists and inhabitants in Cheay Areng, supported by foreign NGOs, has halted one of these dam-building projects. But the anti-dam movement also provides a good picture of the fragilities of the Cambodian environmental movement, which is contingent on an uncertain political opportunity structure and risks facing human rights violations.

State Patronage and the Predation of Resources

Cambodia's neopatrimonial regime has deep historical roots and matured through several stages. After one of the deadliest civil wars of the twentieth century, the combatants agreed to sign the

Paris Peace Accords in October 1991. Cambodia was to establish a multiparty democracy starting with a national election in 1993 under the authority of the United Nations (Akashi 2012). National reconciliation was achieved through diplomatic engagement with the former King Sihanouk. During this period of transition, Prime Minister Hun Sen, who had served in that role since 1985, replaced socialism with economic liberalization. Another strong man was Chea Sim, who acted as the CPP's President from 1991 to 2015, and as President of the National Assembly from 1981 to 1998, and then President of the Senate from 1999 to 2015. Over the years, through the CPP's network and chain of command, Hun Sen, Chea Sim, and the rest of their clique were gradually mobilizing state resources.

As required by the United Nations and foreign donors, democratic elections were organized in 1993. Hun Sen and his allies ran against the popular royalist party, FUNCINPEC, led by former King Sihanouk's son Norodom Ranariddh. Despite intimidating and threatening voters, Hun Sen lost by seven points but refused to step down and proposed a political arrangement: he would share power with Ranariddh as the "First Prime Minister", while he himself would humbly serve as the "Second Prime Minister". However, in 1997, Hun Sen ousted Ranariddh in a military coup. According to Milne et al. (2015), following the coup, Hun Sen secured his rule by developing a personal patronage network, which paralleled the formal government, like a shadow state. Milne and Mahanty (2015, pp. 31–33) further argue that the neopatrimonial regime that emerged from this strategy has developed fundamentally into a mechanism to exploit natural resources and distribute the resulting revenue in exchange for political allegiance.

Since their introduction in 1993, elections have continually been marked by intimidation and the bribing of voters. For a time, moderate elements of the CPP attempted to cooperate with the Cambodian National Rescue Party (CNRP) in efforts to liberalize the regime. But Hun Sen, seeking to prevent this from happening, in 2015 finally forced the opposition leader, the CNRP's Sam Rainsy, into exile. Then, in the lead-up to the 2018 national election, the CNRP's president Kem Sokha was arrested on the charge of treason for plotting a coup supposedly backed by the United States. Two months later, the Supreme Court ruled to forcibly dissolve the CNRP. As Hun Sen's electoral victory was considered both flawed and illegitimate, the United States threatened to impose sanctions and the European Union warned of similar economic measures.[2] Inversely, at the same time, China's diplomatic and economic support grew stronger than ever.

For Cock (2011, p. 28), bureaucratic politics in Cambodia bear characteristics of a "patrimonial administrative state", in which the ruling elite governs the state without obligation for accountability over its administrative responsibilities, blurring the boundary between the public and private spheres. The result is a state apparatus captured by individual patronage interests. And for Cock, Hun Sen, with this neopatrimonial administration, does not need to exercise coercive capacity to dominate the CPP. For he can simply tap into existing patronage arrangements to cultivate his personal reputation and ruling legitimacy, which then can further cement patrimonial relationships. This patronage encourages extra-bureaucratic forces to overwhelm the bureaucracy and diminish state control over this "economy". The contradiction is apparent only, as business entities take advantage of the state's political influence to advance their own interests.

Moreover, despite abundant international aid and resources, Hun Sen's patronage network has stockpiled resources as a hedge against international pressure (Un 2011). Hun Sen has continued to persuade international donors that political change was imminent, without ever actually delivering on the promise. Ear (2013) posits that Western efforts to promote democratic norms through financial aid were doomed to fail. Southeast Asian regional integration—which has achieved substantial progress (Kim and Schattle 2012; Schmiegelow and Schmiegelow 2007) and was confirmed, in 2016, by the establishment of the ASEAN Economic Community—has encouraged Cambodia to pursue foreign direct investment and technology transfers. But the main source of revenue for the regime has primarily come from enclosures and land grabs at the expense of agrarian peasants, who have tried to oppose them with "resistance from below" (Hall et al. 2015).

The remainder of this section presents three patterns of patronage that engage with different levels of state power: the central elite, the provincial elite, and the village heads. These different scales of the neopatrimonial state have prompted resistance from affected inhabitants, mainly rural populations of either Khmer or other indigenous peoples.

The first pattern consists in state-sponsored land-grabbing that aims to maintain the CPP's legitimacy. As the ruling group, the Phnom Penh-based CPP and the government have claimed forest resources through the introduction of Economic Land Concessions (ELCs), appropriating vast areas of state land to transform them into for-profit operations as patronage for the connected elite. Through these legal concessions issued by the state, privileged CPP officials, local strongmen, and tycoons have expedited the predation of natural resources and thereby earned themselves a windfall of personal profits.

The government has also crafted legislation to exert its control over the country's land and resources. For instance, through the 2001 Forest Estate and Protected Areas Law, the Cambodian state monopolized control of luxury timber extraction and the issuance of concessions. Some progress appears to have been made on the legal framework for preventing illicit activities concerning natural resources. Under pressure from foreign donors, the 2002 Forest Law put a ban on illegal logging, and the 2008 Protected Areas Law institutionalized the protection of national parks and wildlife sanctuaries from illegal activities. The Cambodian government alleges that 60 per cent of the country's territory is under protection and overseen by the Forestry Administration. But in practice, the ruling elite uses the state machinery to turn natural resources into monetary gains that have little to do with natural protection, as "protected" land is not immune from forest conversion under ELCs. And while ostensibly granted for specific development purposes—generally in agriculture or mining—the ELCs are also responsible for the indiscriminate clearing of evergreen forests (Neef et al. 2013).

Furthermore, the lack of transparency surrounding ELCs, together with feeble enforcement of environmental protections, has enabled illegal logging to flourish. For example, the post-2009 boom in China's furniture market led to a high demand for rosewood, which encouraged illegal logging in the Cardamom Mountains. Most illegally logged luxury timber has been transported to the Chinese market. According to an anecdotal estimation, at least half a billion US dollars of revenue was generated from this timber logging and shared between the tycoon Try Pheap and relatives of Hun Sen (Milne 2015). In 2019, the corruption intrinsic to this illegal logging resulted in sanctions from the United States on Try Pheap and his companies, which blocked all assets within or transiting U.S. jurisdictions and banned American citizens and companies from any business with Pheap.[3]

Large-scale development projects in general provide great cover for illegal logging and mining operations. After 2007, China became the primary donor of aid and investment in large-scale infrastructure projects, largely because of its geostrategic objective to acquire energy and natural resources. China's state-owned dam builders, such as Sinohydro Corporation, China International Water & Electric Corp., and China Gezhouba Group Company Ltd., are the main dam construction contractors hired by the governments of Cambodia, Myanmar, Laos, the Philippines, and Vietnam (Urban et al. 2018, p. 8). The process for selecting a contractor for these dam-building projects generally lacks transparency and accountability. Forest clearing and illegal timber logging always ensue, causing severe environmental and social harm that leads to protests and conservation campaigns.

The second pattern of patronage concerns development projects supported by provincial elites. Cambodia's subnational bureaucracy has experienced various phases of transformation since the 1980s, transitioning from state-building to regular governance. All along this transition, business entities at the subnational level have nurtured a regional oligarchy composed of provincial bureaucrats. The Cambodian regional oligarchy derives substantial benefit from opportunistic alliances with the state apparatus. The 1990s in Cambodia were marked by a rapid increase in the demand for timber, which may be understood as a postwar conversion of forest resources into cash and political capital. Thanks to the economic spurt that followed, the regional elite's influence over provincial officials has continued to grow (Hughes and Un 2011). Cock's review of land dispute cases at the subnational level demonstrates how justice is perverted by the symbiotic relationship between provincial officials and large oligarchic, elite-owned business entities (Cock 2011, pp. 31–47).

Any provincial official with a close connection to a high-ranking official can easily use the subnational state apparatus to his advantage. For example, Keat Kolney, sister of the Minister of Economy and Finance and wife of a Secretary of State in the Ministry of Land Management, sought to purchase 450 hectares of land from villagers of the Jarai ethnicity in Ratanakiri's O'Yadaw district and planned to convert the land into a rubber plantation. The Jarai villagers, represented by the Community Legal Education Centre and Legal Aid of Cambodia, filed a complaint in the Ratanakiri Provincial Court, alleging that Keat Kolney obtained the land through threats. The villagers claimed to have been deceived by local officials who used fake documents to mislead them into believing that Prime Minister Hun Sen would expropriate their land and distribute it to disabled soldiers (MacInnes 2015, p. 108). The judge who received the complaint slow-walked the legal process. Keat Kolney herself insisted on the legal integrity of the land deal. She also filed a complaint with the Cambodian Bar Association against the lawyers of the Community Legal Education Centre and Legal Aid of Cambodia, alleging that they had manipulated Jarai villagers (Cock 2011, p. 34). To tip the scale in Kolney's favour, local officials selected villagers to provide testimony and evidence to support Kolney's counterclaim.

The third pattern of patronage is the exploitation of natural resources at the commune level. Communes are responsible for everyday administration, the registration of births, deaths, and marriages, and for maintaining electoral rolls. Through these frequent encounters with the population, the village heads develop patrimonial links. According to So (2011), community chiefs' roles can be categorized as local government officials, spiritual leaders, or influential businessmen—or any combination thereof. Commune and village chiefs generally remain influential for a long time. Some local leaders may have opportunities to move up in the bureaucratic hierarchy. Non-state community leaders may also assume leadership roles in communes on behalf of formal organizations, but they may also lead social movements in case of dispute with provincial or central elites. Foreign NGOs are active in communities and villages and often successfully cultivate mutual trust with inhabitants (Sedara and Öjenda 2011). In some cases, NGOs, campaigners, communes, and villages are motivated to resist land privatization and enclosure when local livelihoods stand to be negatively affected (So 2011).

In their study of various communes, Hughes et al. (2011) described in particular how one commune in the Northeast faced threats of deforestation and expulsion. Traditional social ties suffered, and villagers deprived of land had to turn to a commercial microcredit agency for financial support. In 2007, a Sam Rainsy Party (SRP) candidate managed to win the election for commune chief after he exposed the corruption and internal conflict of the CPP camp. In addition, the inhabitants' livelihoods had been negatively affected by land concessions. Yet, to assist the commune's inhabitants, the SRP community chief had to overcome exclusion by the CPP commune chiefs and a boycott by the provincial authorities (Diepart and Schoenberger 2017).

In the case of a commune adjacent to Tonle Sap Lake, the village demonstrated solidarity with its grassroots organizing and helped to advance the cause of the poor. The villagers who entered a land dispute against the local authorities were also critical of the use of the lake's water. The CPP invited a farmer trusted by the other villagers to become the community councillor. But after he accepted the position, he was viewed as politically co-opted and lost his influence among the villagers in other land-grab incidents (Hughes et al. 2011, p. 262). In the system of patronage operated by the CPP in community life, the distribution of profits and handouts is an everyday practice. Protecting the poor from the negative effects of economic transformation and creating alternative opportunities for earning a living are especially important at the commune level. Solidarity between NGOs, campaigners, and local inhabitants is key to communal resistance against environmental injustice. The third level of local neopatrimonialism is therefore ambiguous, as it can act both as support of and opposition to the state and the CPP.

These observations on the relations between the state and population over land issues at the national, subnational, and local levels indicate that, since the end of the civil war, Cambodia's political economy has involved a complicated set of dynamic interactions between the state, the CPP-connected elite, and affected inhabitants, as well as national and international NGOs. The CPP aims at sustaining its rule through a balance of patronage distribution and the extraction of environmental resources.

The architecture of the Cambodian neopatrimonial regime resembles a web extending from the centre of Phnom Penh to the subnational and local levels. To consolidate the CPP's rule, Hun Sen and the Phnom Penh-based ruling elite have established patronage networks, which engaged in lucrative activities such as cross-border trade, goods smuggling, and the exploitation of natural resources, especially luxury timber and fish (Hughes 2003). Superficially, the Cambodian government declared its intention to reform, but the patronage-based alliances and natural resource extraction of the shadow state have continued unabated.

At the national level, the power and patronage surrounding Prime Minister Hun Sen has strengthened and centralized over time. Key governmental positions have largely been filled by his cronies—in the Council of Ministers; the central Ministries of Economy and Finance and the Interior; and the directly involved Ministries of Agriculture, Forestry, and Fisheries; Land Management, Urban Planning, and Construction; and Mines and Energy. At the subnational level, the capital and 24 provinces, 165 districts and 26 municipalities, and 1,646 communes constitute the nodes of the patronage network. The national and subnational levels of the state apparatus informally channel personal patronage, political funds, and economic benefits in exchange for political allegiance so as to consolidate the CPP's rule and ensure electoral victories. Over the years, the government has implemented several reform packages to decentralize and shift administrative power to the provinces, which has contributed to the rise of a regional oligarchic elite.

According to Milne et al. (2015) and Cock (2011), subnational administrators, such as community councils, are not delegated specific functions apart from basic infrastructure development and promoting people's welfare and environmental protection. But with no jurisdiction over forestry or land management and no basis on which to formally collect community-based revenue, these councils are very limited in what they can do. And although provincial governments have increasingly been delegated more power to collect minor taxes and revenues, their operations continue to depend on fiscal allocations from the central government. The true rationale for decentralization reform is the CPP's desire to uphold the legitimacy of local rule while still controlling the valuable resources of land, forests, mines, and fisheries.

Because subnational institutions remain financially starved, provincial governments are forced to seek revenue from surrounding natural resources. The CPP established the Party Working Group for Helping the Local Level (PWG) to deliver mass patronage (Hughes et al. 2011). The PWG is headed by key party officials and is responsible for mobilizing resources to build local infrastructure that will be used for election-related purposes. The PWG has branches in each province, district, and commune. Party officials, businessmen, tycoons, and even NGOs must all contribute to the PWG. Milne et al. (2015) argue that the PWG is considered a successful model for establishing subnational support, and it has contributed to the CPP's electoral triumphs since 1998. The PWG model has thus been replicated in other CPP-sponsored organizations such as the Cambodian Red Cross and Party Youth Group.

Last but not least, Cambodian tycoons and some foreign investors play a part in this patronage system, as they provide major donations to the PWG in exchange for government non-interference with their commercial operations. Land deals and concessions for logging and dam construction are the main sources of their lucrative business. Political contributions to the PWG are critical to obtaining licences to operate. Economic liberalization in the past decade has multiplied the opportunities of state officials and the CPP-connected elite to engage in natural resource management. Natural resource exploitation and related entrepreneurial activities are an especially valuable channel of extra income for local authorities and military personnel in the countryside. The CPP has indulged local party cadres with generous concessions in exchange for political allegiance, and the exploitation of timber and land is thus fundamental to state patronage.

The China Factor in Cambodian Politics

China's geostrategic interest in Cambodia dates back five decades, but China's relations with post-war Cambodia resumed relatively late. In Beijing's 1955 "Principles of Peaceful Coexistence", China appealed to Southeast Asia to respect the sovereignty and territorial integrity of all states, to not engage in acts of aggression against other states, to adopt a "no strings attached" policy toward the internal affairs of other states, to promote equality, mutual benefits, and peaceful coexistence. During the Cold War period, China's relationships with Vietnam, Laos, and Cambodia underwent ups and downs. Wars, territorial disputes, and ideological rows with Russia disturbed bilateral relationships (Baviera 2016). Cambodia gained independence from France in 1953, and established formal relations with China in 1958. In 1970, Cambodia's monarchy was abolished, and from 1972 to 1978, China supported the genocidal Pol Pot's Communist Party of Kampuchea. In 1978, Vietnam invaded Cambodia and later fought against China. During the 1990s, after Vietnamese soldiers withdrew, Cambodia established a multiparty democracy. When his coup d'état in 1997 met with international condemnation, Hun Sen re-established ties with China to escape his country's diplomatic isolation, having already visited Beijing in July 1996 and accepted the shutting down of the Taiwanese trade liaison office in Phnom Penh. The bilateral relationship that subsequently developed between the two countries can be understood from three perspectives: geopolitical, economic, and political (i.e., its effect on Cambodia's national politics).

Let us first consider the geopolitics of the Sino-Cambodian rapprochement. By the end of the 1990s and the turn of the century, China aimed to extend its influence in mainland Southeast Asia through a "charm offensive", so Cambodia's diplomatic isolation and China's geopolitical strategy appeared to be a perfect match (Beech 2018). Through this new ally, China has acquired a spokesperson inside ASEAN, and military access to mainland Southeast Asia. Between 2005 and 2007, China donated nine patrol boats and five warships to Cambodia. China claimed the boats were purely to strengthen Cambodia's marine capacity to fight pirates and drug smugglers. The Port of Sihanoukville was renovated to host facilities for commercial shipping and a greater naval presence. This came with the construction of roads, highways, and bridges connecting Phnom Penh to the port. China's increasing presence thus transformed Cambodia into a strong ally. But the two countries' security cooperation stirred suspicion from Cambodia's neighbours, with Thailand, Vietnam, and Malaysia becoming concerned that the improved coastal military infrastructure could be used for military purposes in the Gulf of Thailand (Jeldres 2012; Cáceres and Ear 2013).

Second, from an economic perspective, another goal for China has been to ensure access to Cambodia's natural resources, and for Cambodia, China's aid and investment promised energy sufficiency. The rapid expansion of China's economy created enormous demand for energy and natural resources, and Cambodia's abundance of resources, notably its forests and rivers, could satisfy part of that demand (Cáceres and Ear 2013). The special relationship with China has thus boosted Cambodia's economy through both primary and secondary infrastructure projects. The Chinese market's growing demand for energy and resources drove state-owned electricity generators and dam builders to seek cooperative partners in mainland Southeast Asia. Hydropower schemes have provoked protests, but as a country desperate for a sufficient supply of electricity, the Cambodian state is prone to ignoring environmental and social safeguards in its quest for hydropower development.

Third, the scale of China's aid packages and direct investment has been unprecedented (Sullivan 2011); this flow of money has had a considerable influence on Cambodian national politics. After 1997, as the bilateral relationship stabilized, China's aid and investment in Cambodia increased, as did the power of Sino-Khmer lawmakers and pro-China officials who began to assume key positions. China actively supported the rebuilding of the Chinese community in Phnom Penh, opening Chinese language schools and promoting business links with Sino-Khmers. In 2007, for the first time, China joined Cambodia's foreign donors in pledging an aid package at the regularly held government-donor forum. From that point on, China escalated the scale of its presence in Cambodia to become the main donor, investor, and political ally of Hun Sen's regime. In principle, China proclaims to apply the principle of "non-interference" in internal politics, and that is true as far as the nature of the regime (i.e., electoral democracy or another system) is concerned. But in practice, China's aid and investment packages for large-scale infrastructure projects constitute a major sponsor of Hun Sen's neopatrimonial system, which itself forms the core of Cambodia's political regime. Consequently, the symbiotic relationship between China and the Cambodian elite has further undermined democratic progress, something that has not, moreover, been strongly demanded by international donors (Un 2011).

China's enormous influence on the Cambodian political economy poses a threat to the country's autonomy. The majority of infrastructure projects in Cambodia are entirely financed by Chinese banks in concert with Chinese government. After China's state-owned enterprises invested billions of dollars in dams, oilfields, highways, textile factories, and mines, the Cambodian economy took off, but efforts from the Cambodian government to diversify economic development were hardly effective (Ear 2013). As argued by Sullivan (2011, p. 64), natural resource extraction by Chinese companies and the importation of cheap Chinese goods may be stunting the growth of Cambodia's fledgling industrial sector and entrenching the core-periphery relationship. Consequently, the Cambodian market is disproportionally dominated by Chinese corporations and this financial reliance on China substantially undermines Cambodia's bargaining power. In the long term, such dependence is likely to harm Cambodia's autonomy, both economically and in other spheres.

China's investment decisions and aid to Cambodia generally follow the "no strings attached" approach, that is to say, unconditional funding for infrastructural projects. As argued by Sullivan (2011, p. 67), most western donors attach conditions to grants of aid packages that the Cambodian government refrain from human rights violations and the oppression of dissidents or other misuse of power. China, however, requires neither good governance nor human rights. What China cares for is that the Cambodian governement serves as a strong ally to its geostrategic interests. The government and local politicians must sometimes not only shut their eyes to labour abuses committed by Chinese investors, but also provide vast land concessions for dam building or other industrial projects. Obviously, the rise of the Chinese-Cambodian aid relationship bodes ill for Cambodia's governance practice; instead it erodes the already opaque decision-making on the extraction of environmental resources (Ear 2013, p. 51).

Chinese investments are not only engaged in controversial infrastructure projects, they have exacerbated Cambodia's poor record on human rights. The two countries have proved quite willing to shrug off this range of issues for the sake of not interfering with each other's internal politics. For instance, in December 2009, twenty members of the Uighur minority were forcibly repatriated from Cambodia to China, prior to the signing of a bilateral $1.2 billion aid and soft-loan accord (Mydans 2009). This sort of "cooperation" has grown substantially since China launched its Belt and Road Initiative in 2013.

The Cambodian government established a legal framework for land deals in 2000. The 2001 Land Law and 2005 Sub-Decree of ELCs legalized foreign investment in land deals. Once China became the main investor in agribusiness after 2007, deforestation, land-grabbing, and forced displacement all increased considerably. Although the new wave of land grabs generated a terrific amount of wealth, it was shared exclusively by the coalition consisting of Chinese business concerns and Cambodian dignitaries. Chinese investors also leveraged this mutually beneficial partnership to keep government officials onside and circumvent the 10,000-hectare limit of land ownership stipulated by the Land Law. In response, there occurred during these years numerous cases in which affected communities took action to fight or protest against the activities of these concessionaires, as violations of human rights and the destruction of livelihoods have provoked widespread dissatisfaction. But affected inhabitants and villagers were denied justice by the authorities, and their protests were met with lethal threats (Connell and Grimsditch 2017). China's investment thus makes the affected inhabitants and displaced villagers even more vulnerable to the conduct of the concessionaires (Coventry 2017; Henke 2011). The following section examines the specific case of Chinese dam projects.

China's Hydro-politics in Cambodia

China's state-owned hydropower dam builders are now notorious for being the object of criticism and protests from inhabitants and villagers affected by controversial hydropower projects (Bosshard 2009; McDonald et al. 2009; Hensengerth 2015; International Rivers 2012; Del Bene et al. 2018; Siciliano et al. 2019). For example, in Sudan in the mid-2000s, Sinohydro Corporation and its international partners on the Merowe dam project failed to respect the United Nations' request to properly compensate villagers for relocation and, as a result, local villagers were flooded out (Siciliano et al. 2019). Another emblematic case is China Power Investment's Myitsone dam in Myanmar (on the Salween River), which was suspended in 2016 after vehement opposition by regional and national civil society organizations (Middleton and Lamb 2019).

Given the geographic proximity, China's geostrategic priorities, and the high potential of rivers such as the Mekong, Chinese hydropower investments have shown a predilection for mainland Southeast Asia (Li et al. 2011; Middleton and Allouche 2016; Moore 2018). An important literature has already been devoted to the various problems spawned by these projects, in particular with regard to the Cambodian case (Hensengerth 2013, 2015, 2017; Sullivan 2015; Urban et al. 2015; Siciliano et al. 2015, 2016; Pheakdey 2017; Kirchherr et al. 2017). This section highlights the main problems at issue in relation to the Cambodian neopatrimonial state and conflicts with the local population. I show that, in the face of the Cambodian state and Chinese state-owned firms, Cambodian environmental movements have little margin left for agency; nonetheless, thanks to emerging civil society networks across the Mekong region, the situation is not yet totally desperate. For more than a decade, protests against large hydropower dams built by Chinese state-owned enterprises along the Mekong and the Salween rivers (Middleton and Lamb 2019) have prompted NGOs and the neighbouring communities to build networks of resistance.

With its "Go Out" policy launched in 2006, the Chinese government has encouraged its state-owned enterprises to explore business opportunities in emerging markets. Through aggressive bids with very competitive prices or tempting offers of build-operate-transfer (BOT) arrangements—under which the host country is exempt from all costs and responsibilities for the project—Chinese firms have been aggressively seeking out dam-building opportunities in the global market, with special attention paid to countries with weak social and environmental safeguards and pliable governments. Cambodia meets these conditions.

Soon after the inception of China's "Go Out" policy, Prime Minister Hun Sen started to frame hydropower as a priority of his "Power Development Plan" for energy policy: a network of seventeen dams that would generate sufficient electricity to meet domestic demand and export surplus energy abroad, with an ultimate aim to transform Cambodia into an electricity provider for the whole of mainland Southeast Asia. As of June 2020, Cambodia has a total of six hydroelectric dams under construction. All of these sites are BOT projects under the supervision of Chinese firms, including one joint venture between Cambodia and China, and another one between China, Cambodia, and Vietnam. China also plans to build hydroelectric dams along the Mekong River in Laos and Cambodia (see Table 10.1).

The first of these projects was inaugurated in 2011 on the Kamchay River, in Kampot Province, in the southwest of the country, about 100 km east of the Gulf of Thailand and 150 km west of Phnom Penh (see Map 10.1). This case has been particularly well studied.[4] It was built by the Sinohydro Corporation, the world's largest hydropower construction company, with 50 per cent of the global market share; in addition to Southeast Asia, the firm is currently engaged in dam-building projects in South Asia, Africa, Latin America, and Eastern Europe. Sinohydro had planned to build another dam, the Cheay Areng dam in Koh Kong Province (also in the southwest of the country, see Map 10.1). In 2014, China's Hydrolancang launched a project to build the Lower Sesan 2 Dam in northeastern Cambodia. Dam projects in Kamchay, Cheay Areng, and Se San have all met with protests from the local populations. But while the mobilization failed in the case of Kamchay, it proved relatively fruitful in the case of Lower Sesan 2 and in Cheay Areng successfully brought construction to a halt.

TABLE 10.1
Chinese Involvement in Cambodian Hydropower Development

Project	Capacity (MW)	Chinese Project Company/lead Sponsor	Year Completed	Type of Agreement
Kiriom 1	12	CETIC International Hydropower Development Co.	2002	BOT
Kamchay	193.2	Sinohydro Corp.	2011	BOT
Kiriom 3	18	CETIC International Hydropower Development Co.	2012	BOT
Stung Tatay	246	China Gezhouba Group Corp.	2014	BOT
Stung Atay	120	China Datang Corp.	2014	BOT
Russei Chrum Krom	338	China Huadian Corp.	2015	BOT
Lower Sesan 2	400	China Hydrolancang International Energy Co.	2018	BOT
Sambor	2600	China Southern Power Grid Co.*	After 2030	BOT

Note: * China Southern Power Grid Co. signed a memorandum of understanding with the Ministry of Industry, Mines, and Energy of the Cambodian Government in 2006, but in 2011, after a feasibility study including a geological assessment were conducted, the firm withdrew from the project.

Sources: Middleton et al. (2015), pp. 132–33; websites of international think tanks, international news agencies, international NGOs, the Chinese press, and official websites of Chinese dam-builders

MAP 10.1

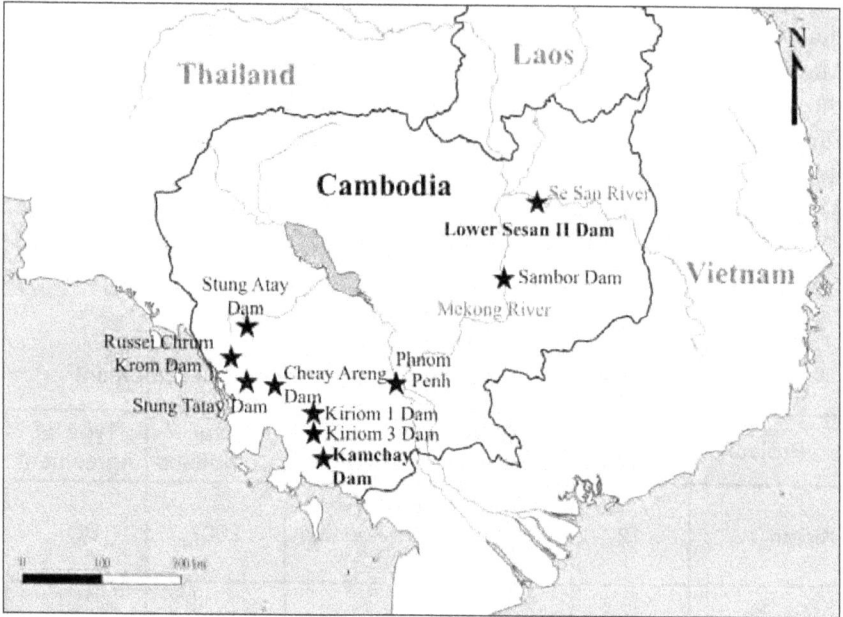

Dam projects with Chinese participation in Cambodia

Source: QGIS and Natural Earth.

All these projects have been marked by an opaque decision-making process. In the case of the Kamchay dam, for instance, after Hun Sen approved the project, the Ministry of Industry, Mines, and Energy signed a contract with Sinohydro for its realization and the Export-Import Bank of China for its funding, but the deal was kept completely confidential; local authorities and the affected inhabitants were never consulted (Sullivan 2011). Generally, once a project is revealed, the blatant lack of public consultation in the decision-making generally provokes public mistrust, and it may prompt protests, as in the cases of Kamchay, Se San, and Cheay Areng.

An important reason to keep the deal secret is that China's state-owned enterprises are notorious for their reluctance to conform to international standards of environmental and social protection. Another reason, ecologists argue, is that dam-building projects are also great cover for illicit activities, chiefly the lucrative businesses of illegal logging and mining. These projects may then be the target of strong disapproval. International and local NGOs, environmental campaigners, affected inhabitants, and opposition political parties can all challenge the legitimacy of dam-building projects, as was the case for the Kamchay dam, as well as the Stung Atay dam, built by the China Datang Corporation and inaugurated in 2013.

Around 2010, as the construction of dams was progressing, local NGOs and village representative groups formed a united front, before seeking support from foreign NGOs. In 2009, the California-based NGO International Rivers held a policy dialogue with Sinohydro concerning environmental policy and social safeguards in the global market (International Rivers 2012; Pye 2014). Sinohydro later delivered a broad but vague commitment to sustainable development and the pursual of sound health, safety, and ethical policies. Although the firm's announcement did not have a significant effect on other Chinese companies, this concession indicated that international NGOs and conservation campaigners, alongside inhabitants and villagers at the local level, could together exert some sort of pressure.

In the Stung Tatay project, located in the southern Cardamom Mountains, the dam builder China National Heavy Machinery Corporation was also heavily criticized by International River, which highlighted the inconsistencies and insufficient consultation over environmental concerns.

The Lower Sesan 2 dam was proposed by the Asian Development Bank in 1992 as a part of a vast power grid development in the Greater Mekong Subregion (GMS). The Chinese government has provided substantial funds for that programme, and with even greater enthusiasm after the launch of the Belt and Road Initiative in 2013. Along with the Asian Development Bank and the Cambodian government, Chinese hydropower companies have designed a waterscape that has simply ignored the ethnic minorities located in the areas upstream and downstream of the project. At no stage of the preparations were they consulted. It was therefore not surprising that, when they finally were notified, they refused to move to the designated resettlement sites. With the support of Cambodian and foreign NGOs, these communities protested against the dam and petitioned the government. This case sent a warning that unless the needs of affected communities were taken into consideration, a dam project could face serious resistance (Hensengerth 2017).

The UK-based organization Global Witness has been especially committed to monitoring Cambodian forests (e.g., Global Witness 2003, 2007); in fact, its very first campaign, in 1993, exposed Khmer Rouge involvement in the illegal logging trade. While initially tolerated by the regime, Global Witness's reporting on military and government complicity in the illegal timber trade—which notably involved much of Hun Sen's family—led to the 2005 closure of its local office, a visa ban on foreign investigators, and the harassment of its allies within Cambodia. Despite this, the NGO has continued to probe environmental malfeasance in the country. International Rivers and Global Witness have been particularly critical of the Cheay Areng project and the Lower Sesan 2 dam on the Se San River (or Tonlé San River, a major tributary of the Mekong), in Stung Treng Province, not far from the Laos border (see Map 10.1), built by a joint venture between the Royal Group of Cambodia, China's Hydrolancang International Energy (a subsidiary of China Huaneng Group), and the Vietnamese company EVN, with respective participation shares of 39, 51, and 10 per cent (Parameswaran 2015; Middleton et al. 2015). These two dam projects have not only posed enormous ecological threats to endangered species, they have also displaced thousands of inhabitants (Hensengerth 2017).

However, to hedge their bets, other foreign organizations like Conservation International, Flora and Fauna International, and the Wildlife Alliance have built close relationships with the Cambodian government (Sullivan 2015). Both Conservation International and the Wildlife Alliance are working in areas close to the Chinese-contracted hydropower projects in the Cardamom Mountains. International organizations must carefully choose their positions and consider how to achieve viable solutions to targeted problems. Conservation International's close work with Forestry Administration officials and the military to prevent illegal logging has received criticism for ineffectively engaging with partners in the government. As ground operations in Cambodia become more constrained, international organizations and donors must leverage more resources to achieve effective actions.

With the help of environmental NGOs that are not afraid to be critical of the government and Chinese firms, affected inhabitants and opposition political parties can nevertheless challenge the legitimacy of these construction projects. The last section takes a closer look at the Cheay Areng case, which the solidarity between NGOs, activists, and villagers succeeded in stopping.

The Mobilization Against the Cheay Areng Dam

In 2006, the Cambodian government decided to build a mega hydropower dam in the Areng Valley. The Areng Valley is located in the 400,000-hectare Central Cardamom Protected Forest, which is one of Cambodia's last pristine natural forests in Koh Kong Province. The Chong people, one of Cambodia's oldest ethnic groups, have resided in this area for centuries. The Areng Valley is also home to a number of rare and endangered animals, including the Asian arowana, Asian elephants, and Siamese crocodiles. The Siamese crocodile is classified as critically endangered on the Red List of Threatened Species of the International Union for Conservation of Nature. This project would flood at least 26,000 acres and displace over 1,500 people in an area recognized as one of the last few natural and cultural treasures in Cambodia.

Prime Minister Hun Sen has been considering constructing at least eleven dams in the Cardamoms. An initial proposal for the Cheay Areng dam involved a memorandum of understanding between the state-owned enterprise China Southern Power Grid and the Cambodian Ministry of Industry, Mines, and Energy to conduct a feasibility study (Yeophantong 2014). China Southern Power Grid's study was delivered in 2008. The proposed scheme received strong criticism from conservation groups, such as the U.K.-based Fauna and Flora International, with regard to its adverse ecological impact. Facing increased scrutiny, China Southern Power Grid pulled out of the project, but China Guodian, another major Chinese power generation corporation, stepped in. Once again, the company signed a memorandum of understanding with the government to conduct a feasibility study, which reached the same conclusion: at an estimated cost of $400 million for a generating capacity of only 108 MW, the dam-building scheme was not economically viable (Sullivan 2015). With two Chinese dam builders having now pulled out of the project, it thus appeared that the dam-building project in the Areng Valley had been dropped.

But the project was revived after China and Cambodia strengthened their bilateral relationship with the 2011 conclusion of the "Cambodia–China Comprehensive Strategic Partnership of Cooperation", which was celebrated with the inauguration of the Kamchay dam. Two years later, in June 2013, Chinese and Cambodian dignitaries gathered in Phnom Penh to celebrate the fifty-fifth anniversary of diplomatic relations, and soon after, the Cambodian government announced that Sinohydro Resources Ltd., a holding company of Sinohydro Group, would replace Guodian to resume the Areng dam-building project in 2014, but without undertaking another feasibility study. To cap off the contract, the CPP senator and tycoon Lao Meng Khin and his wife became board members of Sinohydro (Sullivan 2015). Conservation campaigners alleged that the true reason for this alliance was not so much to generate hydroelectricity, but because the reservoir-clearing process could be used as a cover for the logging of luxury timber and illegal mining. Sinohydro's decision to take on the dam project might have had more to do with cultivating political connections and satisfying the short-term personal gains of Cambodian politicians, than with the long-term sustainability of the dam itself. This sort of deal is representative of the symbiotic relationship that unifies Cambodian neopatrimonialism with Chinese investors. Debunking and defeating such an alliance is not an easy task.

To complicate matters, Cambodia has a long history of cracking down on environmental activists. In 2012, the journalist Taing Try was shot dead while investigating illegal logging in the southern Kratie Province. That same year, Chut Wutty, the prominent environmental activist and director of the Natural Resources Protection Group, was killed by a security guard while investigating large-scale illegal logging in an area adjacent to hydropower projects. It was later discovered that the security guard who shot Chut Wutty to death was a military policeman working for Timbergreen, a Cambodian logging company. The murder drew worldwide media attention and was the inspiration for the ongoing Global Witness campaign documenting the killings of environmentalists throughout the world.[5] Activist Leng Ouch won the Goldman Environmental Prize and Asia Game Changer Award for exposing illegal logging and corruption in 2016 and, a year later, lost his left leg during his investigation of an illegal-logging incident. In March 2020, Ouch was detained with three other forest monitors (one of whom was beaten) by guards of the Think Biotech company—whose plundering of the "protected" Prey Lang Forest the four were investigating—and then turned over to Cambodian police; though released after three days, the four remain under investigation. Ouch's strategy has been to clandestinely gather evidence of illegal logging activities and later release the photos and video footage to expose criminal collusion between timber companies and government officials (RFA 2017). With environmentalists increasingly barred from forest areas by a combination of Ministry of Environment rangers and private company guards, Ouch and his colleagues have to rely more and more on satellite technology to monitor deforestation. The government, unsurprisingly, is threatening to ban such activity (Global Witness 2020).

Despite the risks, the Spanish- and Khmer-speaking environmental activist Alejandro Gonzalez-Davidson has engaged in leading a campaign against dam-building activities in the Areng Valley. In 2013, when he learned the Cambodian government was determined to revive the dam project, he founded the environmental organization Mother Nature (Gonzalez Davidson 2015). Together with local activists, he started to inform people living in the Areng Valley about the truth concerning the project and produced advocacy videos that were distributed through Facebook. His efforts successfully aroused public attention, as many local inhabitants and NGOs learned about the situation and offered their support for the campaign.

By that time, the political opportunity for fledgling environmental movements was minimal. But the Areng Valley campaign boosted the anti-dam movement and contributed to the poor performance of the CPP in the 2013 national election and 2017 local communal elections.[6] Declining support has forced the CPP to respond more cautiously to local communities resisting resettlement. Inversely, the Cambodian National Rescue Party has supported the campaign against the Cheay Areng dam, attracting national attention. The CPP was facing a serious challenge as its system of delivering personal patronage in exchange for political loyalty was fading away. The CPP had concerns that mishandling the anti-dam campaign could cost more seats in the election. In addition, after the initial assessment of the environmental impact, Sinohydro considered the dam project economically unfeasible.

The Cambodian government and Sinohydro, however, did not easily give in to anti-dam sentiment. In September 2014, the mega dam projects were revived once more. When Gonzalez-Davidson and local activists staged a protest to stall the project, the government and Sinohydro dispatched provincial officials and experts to conduct studies at the project sites. Fearing that the hydroelectric dam projects would wipe out the ancestral home of the Chong and destroy the biodiversity in the Areng Valley, roughly 250 locals and activists established a roadblock to prevent provincial governor Phon Lyvirak and the Sinohydro experts from accessing the site (RFA 2014; Harbinson and Mongabay 2016). A few engineers disguised as tourists managed to sneak in before they were identified and forced to leave by the locals. To heighten public awareness, Areng villagers and monks also engaged in a hunger strike in front of the Chinese embassy (Seangly and Pye 2014). Mother Nature's Facebook profile page amassed hundreds of thousands of fans, spreading messages to gain support from like-minded young people, middle-class Khmers, and opposition party members. As people from across the country visited the Areng Valley, awareness of the issue rose among the public. Monks organized ceremonies to wrap one hundred ancient trees—some fourteen metres in diameter—with eighty-meter saffron cloths; according to Cambodian Buddhist beliefs, cutting down any of these trees would be tantamount to killing a monk. The visual aesthetic and strong symbol of the scene attracted widespread media attention.

In 2015, to save face, the government and Sinohydro declared that more studies were needed before any construction could begin on the proposed dam, and in an act of retaliation, Gonzalez-Davidson was deported after his visa renewal was refused. The anti-dam movement had nevertheless won a battle against the CPP in this case. Since then, the project has been on hold. But the war is not over. Commenting on the case, Sarah Milne (2017) warned that the CPP was still able to trigger local divisiveness between the southern side of the Areng Valley, which is strongly united against dam building, and the northern side, which is reluctant to express opposition as the village leadership has been co-opted by the CPP. Moreover, after Gonzalez-Davidson was deported, the main local indigenous leader was arrested, and an activist monk went into hiding. So, while the dam-building project may be stopped for now, environmental justice hinges on political opportunity

FIGURE 10.1

The venerable But Buntenh leads a group of monks from the Independent Monk Network for Social Justice as they travel from the capital city of Phnom Penh to support the people of Areng Valley in their protest against the construction of a hydroelectric dam in Southwestern Cambodia

Source: Fight for Areng Valley.

FIGURE 10.2

But Buntenh and his fellow monks from the Network for Social Justice perform a tree ordination ceremony as part of the effort to prevent the construction of the Areng Valley hydroelectric dam in Southwestern Cambodia

Source: Fight for Areng Valley.

structure. The absence of vigilant and vocal activist-leaders could loom as an environmental and social threat. The Cambodian government has claimed that the Cheay Areng dam project was suspended because domestic demand for stable electricity had been met; if accurate, that would mean that the construction of hydropower generators would soon cease, which is not at all the case. The reason lies in the nature of China's aid to and investment in Cambodia: its continuing geopolitical considerations, and the maintenance of a strong political and economic connection with the CPP ruling elite in Phnom Penh.

Conclusion

In this chapter, I have described Cambodia's neopatrimonial state as a system in which patronage is delivered in exchange for political loyalty at multiple levels. Exploitation of natural resources, collusion of political and economic elites with Chinese officials regarding aid and investment, and suppression of the voices of local inhabitants are the central dynamics of a malign system resulting from client-state patronage. The cases of China-sponsored dam-building projects demonstrate well how the CPP consolidates its rule though development and piecemeal reforms. But the China factor in Cambodia's neopatrimonialism should first be understood from a geopolitical perspective: although the CPP is currently unchallenged, the future of Cambodian neopatrimonialism is deeply influenced by China's strategic intervention in mainland Southeast Asia.

From the perspective of environmental movements, although environmental activists have been intimidated, threatened, and imprisoned, the seeds of a nationwide environmental movement have been planted in Cambodia. Nonetheless, international NGOs and environmental campaigners continue to express grave concerns about the near-total prioritization of economic gain over environmental and social safeguards, particularly with respect to these controversial hydropower projects and the likely irreversible consequences of such construction. The threats posed to inhabitants' livelihoods and the biodiversity of a large swathe of Cambodia's last pristine forested areas are potentially catastrophic. Most dam-building projects are linked with mining, agriculture, and concomitant illegal logging and land-grabbing. National laws and regulations governing project design are always subject to compromise under political pressure. The apparent disregard for environmental and social safeguards by the Chinese state-owned dam builders carries enormous environmental and social risks. The livelihoods of traditional and rural communities are being privatized, commodified, and exploited, in tandem with the biodiversity loss and declining fish stocks caused by such concessions.

As I have shown, these environmental grievances are embedded in a complicated nexus of state and non-state actors at the local, national, and international levels. The CPP's corruption and mishandling of natural resources has contributed to the increase in electoral share of the opposition Cambodian National Rescue Party. But since the CNRP was made illegal by decision of the Supreme Court in 2018, Cambodian environmental defenders have lost a precious ally. Moreover, with Chinese investments like those in hydropower constantly on the rise, the voices of Western critical NGOs has become less influential.

NOTES

* The author would like to address special thanks to Paul Jobin and Rebecca Fite for their help and editing, as well as two anonymous reviewers for their suggestions.

1. Though internal political upheaval prevented Cambodia from taking up membership in ASEAN until 1999.
2. The US House of Representatives threatened to cut business ties and froze Hun Sen's assets, and the European Union, which counted for 45 per cent of Cambodia's exports, began to review Cambodia's "Everything But Arms initiative", the tax-free access to developing countries. Most of the 118 opposition figures who were banned from politics for five years refused to trade their political allegiance for the reinstatement of political rights. Sam Rainsy, who could not return home, promised to lead a revolt against Hun Sun for Cambodia's Independence Day on 9 November 2019, but despite widespread national and international attention, it did not happen (Onishi 2019).
3. The sanctions are administered and enforced by the Office of Foreign Assets Control, a division of the US Treasury Department. See https:// www.federalregister.gov/d/2019-28231/p-29.
4. Urban et al. (2015), Middleton et al. (2015), Hensengerth (2015), Siciliano et al. (2015, 2016), Sullivan (2015), Pheakdey (2017); and for a good summary of the case, see the Global Atlas of Environmental Justice (EJAtlas), https:// ejatlas.org.

5. From the 26 April 2012 article "Death of a Comrade" at www.globalwitness. org.
6. Cambodia's local communal elections held in June 2017 saw nearly 90 per cent turnout of registered voters, an increase from previous years. The opposition Cambodia National Rescue Party won more than 400 seats out of 1,646, up from only 40 in the 2012 elections (VOA 2017).

REFERENCES

Akashi, Yasushi. 2012. "An Assessment of the United Nations Transitional Authority in Cambodia (UNTAC)". In *Cambodia*, edited by Pou Sothirak, Geoff Wade, and Mark Hong. Singapore: Institute of Southeast Asian Studies, pp. 153–65.

Associated Press (AP). 2015. "Cambodia Leader says Work on Mega-dam Will Not Start Until At Least 2018: Hun Sen Attempts to Stop Opposition to Dam in Areng Valley, a Day after Cambodia Deported Spanish Activist Alex Gonzalez-Davidson". *The Guardian*, 24 February 2015.

Baviera, Aileen S.P. 2016. "China's Strategic Foreign Initiatives under Xi Jinping". *China Quarterly of International Strategic Studies* 2, no. 1: 57–79.

Beech, Hannah. 2018. "Embracing China, Facebook and Himself, Cambodia's Ruler Digs In". *New York Times*, 17 March 2018.

Bong, Chansambath. 2019. "Cambodia's Disastrous Dependence on China: A History Lesson". *The Diplomat*, 4 December 2019.

Bosshard, Peter. 2009. "China Dams the World". *World Policy Journal* 26, no. 4: 43–51.

Cáceres, Sigfrido Burgos and Sophal Ear. 2013. *The Hungry Dragon: How China's Resource Quest is Reshaping the World*. London: Routledge.

Cock, Andrew Robert. 2011. "The Rise of Provincial Business in Cambodia". In *Cambodia's Economic Transition*, edited by Caroline Hughes and Kheang Un. Copenhagen: NIAS Press, pp. 27–49.

Connell, Jessie and Mark Grimsditch. 2017. "Forced Relocation in Cambodia". In *The Handbook of Contemporary Cambodia*, edited by Katherine Brickell and Simon Springer. London: Routledge, pp. 223–32.

Coventry, Louise. 2017. "Civil Society in Cambodia: Challenges and Contestations". In *The Handbook of Contemporary Cambodia*, edited by Katherine Brickell and Simon Springer. London: Routledge, pp. 53–63.

Del Bene, Daniela, Arnim Scheidel, and Leah Temper. 2018. "More Dams, More Violence? A Global Analysis on Resistances and Repression Around Conflictive Dams through Co-produced Knowledge". *Sustainability Science* 13, no. 3: 617–33.

Denyer, Simon. 2015. "China's Back Yard Cambodia: The Push and Pull of China's Orbit". *The Washington Post*, 5 September 2015.

Diepart, Jean-Christophe and Laura Schoenberger. 2017. "Concessions in Cambodia: Governing Profits, Extending State Power and Enclosing Resources from the Colonial Era to the Present". In *The Handbook of Contemporary Cambodia*, edited by Katherine Brickell and Simon Springer. London: Routledge, pp. 157–68.

Ear, Sophal. 2013. *Aid Dependence in Cambodia: How Foreign Assistance Undermines Democracy*. New York: Columbia University Press.

Eisenstadt, Shmuel Noah. 1973. *Traditional Patrimonialism and Modern Neopatrimonialism*. London: Sage Publications.

Global Witness. 2003. "Taking a Cut: Institutionalised Corruption and Illegal Logging in Cambodia's Aural Wildlife Sanctuary". https://cdn2.globalwitness.org/archive/files/import/takingacuthighres.pdf.

———. 2007. "Cambodia's Family Trees: Illegal Logging and the Stripping of Public Assets by Cambodia's Elite". https://cdn2.globalwitness.org/archive/files/import/cambodias_family_trees_low_res.pdf.

———. 2020. "Threats Against Cambodian Forest Defenders Escalate Amid Covid-19". https://www.globalwitness.org/en/blog/threats-against-cambodian-forest-defenders-escalate-amid-covid-19/.

Gonzalez Davidson, Alejandro. 2015. "Cambodia: Peaceful Direct Action Has Saved One of Our Most Beautiful Forests". *The Guardian*, 27 October 2015.

Hall, Ruth, Marc Edelman, Saturnino M. Borras Jr., Ian Scoones, and Ben White. 2015. "Resistance, Acquiescence or Incorporation? An Introduction to Land Grabbing and Political Reactions 'From Below'". *The Journal of Peasant Studies* 42, no. 3–4: 467–88.

Harbinson, Rod and Mongabay. 2016. "Cambodia: Indigenous Eco-defender Released After Five Months Jail on False Charges". *Ecologist*, 22 March 2016.

Henke, Roger. 2011. "Ngos, People's Movements and Natural Resource Management". In *Cambodia's Economic Transition*, edited by Caroline Hughes and Kheang Un. Copenhagen: NIAS Press, pp. 288–309.

Hensengerth, Oliver. 2013. "Chinese Hydropower Companies and Environmental Normsin Countries of the Global South: The Involvement of Sinohydro in Ghana's Bui Dams". *Environment, Development and Sustainability* 15, no. 2: 285–300.

———. 2015. "Global Norms in Domestic Politics: Environmental Norm Contestation in Cambodia's Hydropower Sector". *The Pacific Review* 28, no. 4: 505–28.

———. 2017. "Regionalism, Identity, and Hydropower Dams: The Chinese-Build Lower Sesan 2 Dam in Cambodia". *Journal of Current Chinese Affairs* 46, no. 3: 85–118.

Hughes, Caroline. 2003. *The Political Economy of Cambodia's Transition, 1991–2001*. London: Routledge.

Hughes, Caroline, Eng Netra, Thon Vimealea, Ou Sivhuoch, and Ly Tem. 2011. "Local Leaders and Big Business in Three Communes". In *Cambodia's Economic Transition*, edited by Caroline Hughes and Kheang Un. Copenhagen: NIAS Press, pp. 245–65.

Hughes, Caroline and Kheang Un. 2011. "Cambodia's Economic Transformation: Historical and Theoretical Frameworks". In *Cambodia's Economic Transition*, edited by Caroline Hughes and Kheang Un. Copenhagen: NIAS Press, pp. 1–26.

International Rivers. 2012. "The New Great Walls: A Guide to China's Overseas Dam Industry". https://archive.internationalrivers.org/resources/the-new-great-walls-a-guide-to-china's-overseas-dam-industry-3962.

Jeldres, Julio A. 2012. "Cambodia's Relations with China: A Steadfast Friendship". In *Cambodia*, edited by Pou Sothirak, Geoff Wade, and Mark Hong. Singapore: Institute of Southeast Asian Studies, pp. 81–95.

Keskinen, Mark, Katri Mehtonen, and Varis Olli. 2008. "Transboundary Cooperation vs. Internal Ambitions: The Role of China and Cambodia in the Mekong Region". In *International Water Security: Domestic Threats and Opportunities*, edited by Nevelina I. Pachova, Mikiyasu Nakayama, and Libor Jansky. Tokyo: United Nations University Press, pp. 79–109.

Kim, Sunhyuk and Hans Schattle. 2012. "Solidarity as a Unifying Idea in Building an East Asia Community: Toward an Ethos of Collective Responsibility". *The Pacific Review* 25, no. 4: 473–94.

Kirchherr, Julian, Nathanial Matthews, Katrina J. Charles, and Mathew J. Walton. 2017. "Learning It the Hard Way: Social Safeguards Norms in Chinese-led Dam Projects in Myanmar, Laos and Cambodia". *Energy Policy* 102: 529–39.

Lambrick, Fran. 2012. "Who is Responsible for the Death of Cambodia's Foremost Forest Activist?" *The Guardian*, 1 May 2012.

Li, Zhiguo, Daming He, and Yan Feng. 2011. "Regional Hydropolitics of the Transboundary Impacts of the Lancang Cascade Dams". *Water International* 36, no. 3: 328–39.

MacInnes, Megan. 2015. "Land is Life: An Analysis of the Role 'Grand Corruption' Plays in Enabling Elite Grabbing of Land in Cambodia". In *Conservation and Development in Cambodia: Exploring Frontiers of Change in Nature, State and Society*, edited by Sarah Milne and Sango Mahanty. London: Routledge, pp. 95–119.

McDonald, Kristen, Peter Bosshard, and Nicole Brewer. 2009. "Exporting Dams: China's Hydropower Industry Goes Global". *Journal of Environmental Management* 90: 294–302.

Middleton, Carl and Jeremy Allouche. 2016. "Watershed or Powershed? Critical Hydropolitics, China and the 'Lancang-Mekong Cooperation Framework'". *The International Spectator* 5, no. 3: 100–17.

Middleton, Carl, Nathaniel Matthews, and Naho Mirumachi. 2015. "Whose Risky Business? Public–Private Partnerships (PPP), Build-Operate-Transfer (BOT) and Large Hydropower Dams in the Mekong Region". In *Hydropower Development in the Mekong Region: Political, Socio-economic and Environmental Perspectives*, edited by Nathanial Matthews and Kim Geheb. London: Earthscan, pp. 224–37.

Middleton, Carl and Vanessa Lamb, eds. 2019. *Knowing the Salween River: Resource Politics of a Contested Transboundary River*. New York: Springer.

Milne, Sarah. 2015. "Cambodia's Unofficial Regime of Extraction: Illicit Logging in the Shadow of Transnational Governance and Investment". *Critical Asian Studies* 47, no. 2: 200–28.

———. 2017. "On the Perils of Resistance: Local Politics and Environmental Struggle in Cambodia". *The Newsletter* 78 (Autumn).

Milne, Sarah, Pak Kimchoeun, and Michael Sullivan. 2015. "Shackled to Nature? The Post-Conflict State and Its Symbiotic Relationship with Natural Resources". In *Conservation and Development in Cambodia: Exploring Frontiers of Change in Nature, State and Society*, edited by Sarah Milne and Sango Mahanty. London: Routledge, pp. 28–50.

Milne, Sarah and Sango Mahanty. 2015. "The Political Ecology of Cambodia's Transformation". In *Conservation and Development in Cambodia: Exploring Frontiers of Change in Nature, State and Society*, edited by Sarah Milne and Sango Mahanty. London: Routledge, pp. 1–27.

Moore, Scott. 2018. "China's Domestic Hydropolitics: An Assessment and Implications for International Transboundary Dynamics". *International Journal of Water Resources Development* 34, no. 5: 732–46.

Mydans, Seth. 2009. "After Expelling Uighurs, Cambodia Approves Chinese Investments". *New York Times*, 21 December 2009.

Neef, Andreas, Siphat Touch, and Jamaree Chiengthong. 2013. "The Politics and Ethics of Land Concessions in Rural Cambodia". *Journal of Agricultural and Environmental Ethics* 26, no. 6: 1085–103.

Onishi, Tomoya. 2019. "Cambodian Leader Releases Activists to Save EU Trade Perks: Hun Sen Eases Grip on Opposition after Blocking Sam Rainsy's Homecoming". *Nikkei Asian Review*, 16 November 2019.

Parameswaran, Prashanth. 2015. "Cambodia Suspends China Dam Project to Silence Opposition". *The Diplomat*, 25 February 2015.

Pheakdey, Heng. 2017. "Hydropower and Local Community: A Case Study of the Kamchay Dam, a China-Funded Hydropower Project in Cambodia". *Community Development* 48, no. 3: 385–402.

Pye, Daniel. 2014. "Areng Valley Mining May Unseat Dam". *The Phnom Penh Post*, 25 March 2014.

Radio Free Asia (RFA). 2014. "Cambodian Police Detain Activists Against China Dam Project", 15 September 2014.

———. 2017. "Interview: 'I Have to Take Risks to Make Change'", 3 November 2017.

Reaksmey, Hul. 2014. "Environment Minister Asks for Patience on Areng Valley Dam". *The Cambodia Daily*, 25 November 2014.

Sam Rainsy. 2020. "Sam Rainsy: Cambodia's Ruling Party is More Divided than the Public Knows". *The Diplomat*, 6 February 2020.

Schmeier, Susanne. 2009. "Regional Cooperation Efforts in the Mekong River Basin: Mitigating River-Related Security Threats and Promoting Regional Development". *Austrian Journal of South-East Asian Studies* 2, no. 2: 28–52.

Schmiegelow, Michele and Henrik Schmiegelow. 2007. "The Road to an Asian Community". *Internationale Politik Global Edition* 8, no. 4: 10–17.

Seangly, Phak and Daniel Pye. 2014. "Standoff in Areng Valley Continues". *The Phnom Penh Post*, 18 March 2014.

Sedara, Kim and Joakim Öjenda. 2011. "Accountability and Local Politics in Natural Resource Management". In *Cambodia's Economic Transition*, edited by Caroline Hughes and Kheang Un. Copenhagen: NIAS Press, pp. 266–87.

Siciliano, Giuseppina, Daniela Del Bene, Arnim Scheidel, Juan Liu, and Frauke Urban. 2019. "Environmental Justice and Chinese Dam-building in the Global South". *Current Opinion in Environmental Sustainability* 37: 20–27.

Siciliano, Giuseppina, Frauke Urban, May Tan-Mullins, Lonn Pichdara, and Sour Kim. 2016. "The Political Ecology of Chinese Large Dams in Cambodia: Implications, Challenges and Lessons Learnt from the Kamchay Dam". *Water* 8, no. 9 (online).

Siciliano, Giuseppina, Frauke Urban, Sour Kim, and Pich Dara Lonn. 2015. "Hydropower, Social Priorities and the Rural-Urban Development Divide: The Case of Large Dams in Cambodia". *Energy Policy* 86: 273–85.

So, Sokbunthoeun. 2011. "The Politics and Practice of Land Registration at the Grassroots". In *Cambodia's Economic Transition*, edited by Caroline Hughes and Kheang Un. Copenhagen: NIAS Press, pp. 136–60.

Springer, Simon. 2015. *Violent Neoliberalism: Development, Discourse and Dispossession in Cambodia*. New York: Palgrave Macmillan.

Sullivan, Michael. 2011. "China's Aid to Cambodia". In *Cambodia's Economic Transition*, edited by Caroline Hughes and Kheang Un. Copenhagen: NIAS Press, pp. 50–69.

———. 2015. "Contested Development and Environment: Chinese-Backed Hydropower and Infrastructure Projects in Cambodia". In *Conservation and Development in Cambodia: Exploring Frontiers of Change in Nature, State and*

Society, edited by Sarah Milne and Sango Mahanty. London: Routledge, pp. 120–38.

Un, Kheang. 2011. "Cambodia: Moving Away from Democracy?" *International Political Science Review* 32, no. 5: 546–62.

Urban, Frauke, Giuseppina Siciliano, and Johan Nordensvard. 2018. "China's Dam-Builders: Their Role in Transboundary River Management in South-East Asia". *International Journal of Water Resources Development* 34, no. 5: 747–70.

Urban, Frauke, Johan Nordensvard, Giuseppina Siciliano, and Bingqin Li. 2015. "Chinese Overseas Hydropower Dams and Social Sustainability: The Bui Dam in Ghana and the Kamchay Dam in Cambodia". *Asia and Pacific Policy Studies* 2, no. 3: 573–89.

Voice of Cambodia (VOA). 2017. "Hun Sen 'Willing to Do Anything to Cling to Power'", 16 June 2017.

Weber, Max. 1978 [1922]. *Economy and Society*. Berkeley: University of California Press.

White, Christine Pelzer. 1986. "Everyday Resistance, Socialist Revolution and Rural Development: The Vietnamese Case". *The Journal of Peasant Studies* 13, no. 2: 49–63.

Yeophantong, Pichamon. 2014. "Cambodia's Environment: Good News in Areng Valley?" *The Diplomat*, 3 November 2014.

11

CONCLUSION: ENVIRONMENTAL MOVEMENTS AND POLITICAL REGIMES, OR WHY DEMOCRACY STILL MATTERS IN THE ANTHROPOCENE

Paul Jobin

In the introduction, we adopted the notion of the Anthropocene as a symbol of the planetary scale of the environmental crisis, and a time marker for the last two decades (see Chapter 1). Given Southeast Asia's rich biodiversity and its pivotal role in global capitalism—with hubs like Taiwan, Hong Kong, and Singapore—the countries we chose to focus on in this book bear an important responsibility in the Anthropocene in general, and its Asian version in particular. But they are interesting for other reasons, which lie in the dialectics between civil society and political regimes, and the contribution of their environmental movements in a geopolitical context marked by China's growing hegemony.

In the previous chapters, we have seen a great variety in the repertoire of collective action, with different levels of engagement and risk. For example, in the case of the Philippines (Chapter 5), while online petitions on climate change policy may present no risk for those who click to sign, court litigation and protest marches against coal plants require greater commitment and do not exclude perils such as police brutality, and disruptive actions against illegal logging and agribusiness thugs entail considerable danger such as "extra-judicial killings". Cambodian environmental activists are likewise exposed to the risk of murder. Such dramatic endings are thus far unheard of in Taiwan, Singapore, or Vietnam, although in Vietnam activists might be condemned to long prison sentences on false pretexts. These examples suggest that opportunity structures for environmental activism vary greatly depending on patterns of political regime. One goal of our book has been to examine the evolution of this interaction between environmental movements and political regimes in our selection of East and Southeast Asian countries over the first two decades of the twenty-first century.

In the collective opus published twenty years ago—and which inspired the present book—Lee et al. (1999, chapter 9) evaluated the impact of democratization on environmental movements in East Asia. In the cases of South Korea, Taiwan, and the Philippines, the authors found that environmental movements played a significant role in the process of political liberalization, democratization, and democratic consolidation. They called these environmental movements *partners* or *guardians* of the democracy movement (i.e., partners in the democratization process while it was still in the making, and guardians once significant steps towards democratization had been achieved). But they discovered that environmental groups could also be dissociated from or gradually lose connections with the democracy movement to become *bystanders* of democratization, as occurred in Hong Kong in the 1990s, when the territory was preparing its transition back to China. Let us see to what extent this typology remains operational in the new context of the Anthropocene and China's hegemony in the region.

During the last two decades, the push for democracy from Hong Kong has grown in intensity despite Beijing's authoritarian response. As James K. Wong and Alvin Y. So show in Chapter 3, while managerial environmentalism has remained a bystander of the movement for democracy, a new radical branch has emerged as a full partner in Hong Kong's struggle against Beijing's rule. The radicalization of some environmental activists has significantly contributed to the democracy movement. Under the new security law imposed on the territory by Beijing in July 2020, the movement is likely to enter a period of repression and silence. However, the initial meaning of *movement* should remind us to look at these interactions as constant potential agents of change.

In Chapter 2 on Taiwan, I concur with the now largely accepted view that, despite economic and military pressure from China, Taiwan has consolidated its democracy, and environmental groups have confirmed their role as a vital part of its civil society. Taiwan's environmental movements have clearly worked as active partners of democratization. I further highlight that eco-nationalism—i.e., the conjunction of a concern for ecology and national identity sentiment—is an essential component of that virtuous evolution, thus marks a departure from the generally negative views of nationalism in the literature.

The chapters on Indonesia and Malaysia also tend to show that environmental movements have been, at different times, either the partners or the guardian of democratization. In Indonesia, Suharko (Chapter 6) finds that since Suharto's authoritarian "New Order" was finally defeated in 1998, environmental non-governmental organizations (ENGOs) have greatly benefitted from the democratization of the country's institutions, and they have themselves contributed to the development of its civil society. Despite persistent constraints from the state and agribusiness, Indonesian ENGOs have been committed to saving the rainforests through legal initiatives. Their active cooperation with international organizations such as Greenpeace and the United Nations (in programmes such as REDD+) further attest to the democratization of the country (although one might argue that Greenpeace also manages to work with China's authoritarian regime).

Fadzilah Majid Cooke and Adnan A. Hezri, in their observation of Malaysian environmental activists (Chapter 7), highlight the benefits of their involvement in areas ranging from social movements to political careers and state responsibilities. In the 2018 elections, the Barisan Nasional coalition was defeated after a sixty-year rule. The authors' analysis shows what this landmark result owes to the long-term efforts of environmental activists. Because they focus on the internal dynamics, the authors set aside the China factor of this election. But we should keep in mind that Mahathir Mohamad's electoral campaign against Najib Razak resorted abundantly to anti-China rhetoric, accusing his rival of selling the country for the sake of Chinese-backed infrastructure projects, including a long railway line that has raised environmental concerns. In the year that followed the election, however, Mahathir gave up his rhetoric against China to renegotiate with Beijing in order to reduce the cost of the infrastructure projects.[1] Yet, at least so far, Chinese investments do not seem to be perverting the democratic game.

In Singapore, after the transfer of power from Lee Kuan Yew to his son Lee Hsien Loong (in 2004), the regime underwent gradual liberalization. Nevertheless, compared to their Indonesian and Malaysian counterparts, environmental groups remain cautious in challenging the state and corporations. As Harvey Neo describes their depoliticized style of activism, these organizations have thus far focused on the protection of wild animals, keeping their distance from more sensitive issues that would challenge the responsibility of the Capitalocene's "garden city". Consequently, if we consider the difference between democratization and liberalization, which I will discuss further below, the Singaporean environmental movement can be defined as a *bystander of liberalization*, an additional category of the typology established by Lee et al. (1999).

The case of the Philippines is quite difficult to classify. After the country rid itself of Ferdinand Marcos' dictatorship in the mid-1980s, grassroots environmentalism flourished, inspired in particular by left-wing liberation theology, thirty years ahead of Pope Francis' encyclical on ecology *Laudato Si'*. In that sense, Filipinos were the Asian pioneers of a radical movement for environmental justice. Today, while the influence of the Catholic Church remains strong in Philippine society, neither the Church nor environmental activism seems to exert a significant role in the political life of the country. If President Rodrigo Duterte does not openly adhere to the climate-scepticism of Western right-wing populism (Lockwood 2018), as Francisco Magno highlights in Chapter 5, climate change is obviously not a salient priority of what Kenny (2018, p. 49) defines as Duterte's "penal populism". Furthermore, despite relatively smooth general elections in May 2019, the country is at risk of falling back into an authoritarian regime. We might therefore consider the Philippine environmental movement as oscillating between attempts to remain a *guardian of democracy* and becoming a *bystander of autocratic populism*.

In Thailand, the situation is currently quite gloomy. Jakkrit Sangkhamanee (Chapter 8) reminds us that in the 1990s the country enjoyed a promising movement for environmental justice with all sorts of interesting initiatives for eco-friendly rural development, thanks in part to cooperation with educated activists from urban areas. There were good reasons to hope that such a social movement would contribute to the democratization of the country. However, as Sangkhamanee observes, not only has Thailand not gotten rid of its "addiction" to coups d'état, but the fracture between urban elites and the rural masses has worsened, and ENGOs and other civil society organizations have become instruments of the military junta. Apart from a few statements, environmental groups have remained mostly absent from the large students protests of 2020, which have received popular support in the polls despite their unprecedented demands for reform of the Thai monarchy (Sangkhamanee 2021). From this analysis, we shall therefore state that the Thai environmental movement has been limited to the role of bystander, whether of populism or autocracy.

Despite Vietnam's very different political regime, Stephan Ortmann makes a similar observation in Chapter 9. While the few environmental "government-organized NGOs" that are eager to push for radical change in environmental policies attest to the dynamism of Vietnamese civil society, calling these organizations "partners of democratization" would be a gross exaggeration, and "bystanders of autocracy" would be similarly inappropriate. As Ortmann demonstrates, given the strong hold of the Communist Party, environmental organizations have little room for manoeuvre. The scale of the movement is a decisive factor: as long as it remains local, the party does not fear for its authority. If contention reaches the national level, repression is ineluctable. Besides, it happens that the largest protest movements were against bauxite mines sponsored by China, and against a large steel mill, which the Vietnamese perceive as Chinese-owned investment even though it is a Taiwanese firm. These two mobilizations were thus fuelled by an anti-Chinese historical trope railing against its giant neighbour's domination. This anti-Chinese sentiment has recently been revived by China's intrusions in the Vietnamese waters of the South China Sea—known in Vietnam as the East Sea—for fishing, oil exploration, and the installation of military bases. But the popular resentment against China is also camouflage for expressing dissatisfaction toward Vietnam's one-party regime.

In the last chapter on Cambodia, James Wang shows that despite massive Chinese investment in dams and logging, which have already turned the country into a client state and a biased democracy, anti-Chinese sentiment is not the main driver of environmental mobilization. Rather, environmental criticism addresses the nepotism of the Cambodian regime itself. Despite the important presence of Western NGOs, activists are exposed to a high risk of brutal repression similar to that of the Philippines. Confronted with the predation of resources under a system of state patronage, the Cambodian environmental movement alternates between positions as a brave guardian of democracy and a protester against autocracy. But this situation remains as fragile as the resistance of the political opposition.

From this country by country review, we see that compared to the situation twenty years ago, the interaction between Asian environmental movements and political regimes has become more complex. Among the new factors at issue are the ambiguity of populist regimes toward democratic forces (in the case of Thailand and the Philippines, but also Indonesia), and the growing presence of Chinese investments throughout the region (even in Taiwan, during the period of 2008–16). How can we further unravel this complexity? To what extent do regional geopolitics interfere with each country's environmental politics? And what about the influence of China, the new Asian juggernaut? In twenty years, China has shifted from a developing country into a world power: if not yet the world leader, at least the biggest challenger to the US domination. While the fault lines in European and American democracy become more and more apparent, Southeast Asian countries have closely witnessed China's growing importance over the last thirty years, and its ability to uphold stability and increase its power internationally has reinforced the possibility of decoupling political from economic freedoms (Boisseau du Rocher and Dubois de Prisque 2019, pp. 231–42). But given China's legitimate appetite for energy and other primary resources, environmental issues have increasingly become drivers of geopolitical conflicts, in addition to their influence on regional and national policies (Tan-Mullins 2017). These are the questions that I would like to address in the remainder of this concluding essay, in hopes of providing a basic analytical framework for further studies.

China, Singapore, and the Temptation of Environmental Authoritarianism

In the 1970s, the "tragedy of the commons" (Hardin 1968) and the "limits to growth" (Meadows et al. 1972) inspired economist Robert Heilbroner (1974) and ecologist William Ophuls (1977) to propose a blueprint for an ecologically-motivated authoritarianism. A fair distribution of risk and responsibilities—as was later formulated by the environmental justice movement—was the least of their concerns. The main concern was to prevent a global environmental disaster. Toward that end, a strong political regime of "ecological mandarins"[2] was envisioned as a necessary evil, or, as stated by Hardin (1968, p. 1247): "Injustice is preferable to total ruin."

As observed by Shahar (2015), though this literature vanished with the decline of the USSR's socialist model in the late 1980s, it later reappeared with China as its new poster child, and with "hybrid regimes" (somewhere between authoritarianism and liberal democracy), like Singapore and other Southeast Asian countries, as alternative pathways. This renaissance of environmental authoritarianism started around the mid-2000s with some scholars of Chinese politics and economics, such as Daniel A. Bell—a professor at Princeton who also teaches in China—and Peter Hugh Nolan—a chair professor at Cambridge—who have seen in the Chinese Communist Party and its thousands of devoted eco-technocrats a model of enlightened leadership to solve the world's ecological crisis.[3] Using Singapore as a model of environmental authoritarianism, Shearman and Wayne (2007) further declared the complete failure of liberal democracy to tackle climate change, while Schneider-Mayerson (2017), taking a critical look at this literature, has noticed that Singapore has indeed been competing with China to become the champion of eco-authoritarianism.

Mark Beeson (2010), a frequent reference on this topic, has further enlarged the Chinese model to East and Southeast Asia. Given the state-led capitalism the region has been through, Beeson argues, environmental authoritarianism is a logical outcome for confronting the depletion of natural resources and the resource-intensive economic development: "In much of Southeast Asia and China the forces supporting environmental protection are comparatively weak and unable to overcome powerful vested interests intent on the continuing exploitation of natural resources" (Beeson 2010, p. 282).

For Beeson, who endorses the thesis that cultural determinism of East and Southeast Asia tolerates authoritarian regimes, China's unambiguously assumed authoritarian regime is likely to reinforce an illiberal approach in Southeast Asia. To be fair to Beeson, he is right to notice that, despite a rhetorical preoccupation with the promotion of democracy, when American hegemony was at its zenith in Southeast Asia, the United States tolerated and even encouraged authoritarian regimes in the region. Another concession to Beeson is the case of Japan: since the 1980s, Japanese multinationals have been at the centre of a ruthless exploitation of Southeast Asian natural resources (Lim and Valencia 1990; Dauvergne 1997; Hirsch and Warren 1998). If we go further back in history, we could add the predatory colonialism of the Dutch in Indonesia, the Spanish in the Philippines, the French in Indochina (today's Cambodia, Vietnam, and Laos), and the British in Burma and Malaysia. And if we consider the marine pollution caused by two Taiwanese firms in Vietnam, we might also say that Taiwan is not really doing any better in that range of issues.

But it is one thing to concede the contradictions of liberal democracies, their double standards, and past (neo)colonial crimes; it is quite another to avoid discussion of the neocolonial practices of the new Chinese "empire" or to encourage the arrival of environmental authoritarianism as a desirable prospect. Or as Beeson (2016, p. 529) put it more recently: "It may prove to be wishful thinking, but it is important to recognize how astounding and unprecedented China's experience has already been."

Such wishful thinking has turned out to be right on at least one point: the authoritarianism of China continues unabated. In the 1990s, there was a strong liberal expectation that China would follow the track of Taiwan and South Korea and liberalize along with the development of a market economy. But now that the Chinese Communist Party seems stronger than ever, under the quasi-absolutist leadership of Xi Jinping, the transition of China to democracy is no longer a matter for debate. Many scholars are tempted to see in China's current authoritarianism the sole possible horizon for political economy and, given its growing influence around the world, a likely outcome for other countries.

The new Silk Road of the Belt and Road Initiative (BRI) is likely to increase China's political influence all over the world, starting with Southeast Asia, which China considers its "backyard" (Morris-Jung 2018). As China challenges the US hegemony and aims at reshaping the world order in line with its own standards, its roadmap necessarily includes a diplomatic and political agenda, which has become even more obvious since the Covid-19 pandemic. Even before the pandemic, Hamilton (2018) had, for example, illustrated the surprisingly deep influence of China on Australian politics.

However, as with the neo-colonial practices of the American "empire", there is no simple causality, and popular reactions against a possible or effective loss of sovereignty are not to be neglected. Yet China's political influence needs to be carefully examined country by country (Morris-Jung 2018; Diokno et al. 2019). For instance, in Myanmar, the country has turned to democracy after decades of authoritarianism despite China's considerable investments in infrastructure projects like dams (Tang-Lee 2018; Chen 2019). In Malaysia, the incumbent Prime Minister Najib Razak lost the 2018 general elections after a financial scandal revealed the billions of dollars missing from state funds, along with the risk that China's massive investments entailed for the federation (Boisseau du Rocher and Dubois de Prisque 2019, pp. 237–40, see also Ngeow 2019).

Beeson's prophecy has nevertheless nourished an abundant literature on China's environmental authoritarianism, which alternates between a critical evaluation of the efficiency (or lack thereof) of the authoritarian system as a whole (Gilley 2012; Eaton and Kostka 2014, 2018; Moore 2014; Kostka and Zhang 2018; Shin 2018), and an emphasis on the environmental initiatives that manage to elude Beijing's rigid control (Huang and Li 2019; Zeng et al. 2019). In a critique of the system's efficiency, Kostka and Zhang (2018, p. 778) posit that "China's nascent green transformation shows that authoritarian states can, under certain circumstances, be responsive to public demands for improved environmental governance." The authors' main concern is "about the utility and viability of environmental authoritarianism with Chinese characteristics in the longer run" (p. 771). Kyoung Shin further questions the alleged efficacy of environmental authoritarianism, while admitting that "Xi Jinping's drive toward environmental authoritarianism is an ongoing process, and it may be premature to conclude how effective it will ultimately be" (Shin 2018, p. 846).

As for those focusing on the latitude for action through the cracks of Beijing's "fragmented authoritarianism" (Lieberthal and Oksenberg 1988), Huang and Li (2019), for instance, aim to show that despite the "authoritarian governance system in China, different transition actors demonstrate significant agency in shaping urban energy transitions". For Zeng et al. (2019), environmental NGOs in China can achieve some policy changes if they align with the central state, but they have little chance of getting any result if they adopt a critical tone. Interestingly, they chose the case of Greenpeace's campaign to mitigate deforestation in Indonesia with the cooperation of China's regional government (Yunnan) as an example of a wise adaptation to the rhetoric of Beijing's central state. Many specialists of environmental sociopolitics in China thus tend to accept that authoritarianism is now strongly established and the best thing to do is to just cope with it somehow.

Xi Jinping's current tight grip on China's "environmental governance" follows on Hu Jintao's concept of "ecological civilization", which he introduced at the 17th National Congress of the Chinese Communist Party in 2007, the very year China became the greatest global emitter of CO_2 (Heurtebise 2017). A culturalist interpretation of Chinese classics, "ecological civilization" has been invoked to rescue an industrial growth threatened with asphyxia from horrific levels of air and river pollution. For Kostka and Zhang (2018), environmental protection has become a matter of regime legitimacy for the Party. Indeed, China's influence in international organizations dealing with global warming and other environmental policies has continued to grow, especially since Donald Trump chose to abnegate US responsibility. China's "ecological civilization" is of course just one aspect of China's soft-power rhetoric against the Western climate-change deniers (whose "denial countermovement" has both a long history and an impressive network, see Dunlap and McCright 2015). Moreover, China possesses its own share of climate scepticism, which flirts with a nationalist tone of conspiracy theories against Western hegemony (Liu 2015).

Although we should refrain from Cold War rhetoric, we must seriously consider that the menace may not only be ecological. The ecological politics of a rising China is intimately mingled with geopolitics and traditional security threats, so that more countries are coerced into "dancing to China's tune" (Tan-Mullins 2017). For instance, the already endangered fish and corals of the South China Sea are being further depleted by the construction of military bases and by the vessels of government-controlled fishermen that China is using to expand its control of the region. Another example is the multiplication of dam projects in mainland Southeast Asia that are planned by or linked to Chinese firms (e.g., along the Mekong River). What Carl Middleton and Jeremy Allouche (2016) call "China's hydrodiplomacy" is gradually influencing the whole region, from Myanmar to Thailand, Laos, Cambodia, and Vietnam, dangerously threatening aquatic ecosystems and encouraging land-grabbing and illegal logging.

This new form of neo-colonialism is therefore the target of various environmental mobilizations. As James W.Y. Wang shows in Chapter 10, despite China's tremendous influence on Cambodian politics, a coalition of environmental groups was successful in halting the dam project led by China's Sinohydro Corporation, the world's largest hydropower construction company. But this success story looks rather like an isolated case and, given the now almost perfect symbiosis between China and the Cambodian state's patronage system, it is likely that in the future, the Cambodian environmental movements will have much more difficulty seeking help from Western NGOs. Other emblematic examples of how environmental issues entangle with the China factor of geopolitics are the anti-Bauxite and the anti-Formosa campaigns in Vietnam, analysed by Ortmann (Chapter 9) and evoked by Jobin (Chapter 2).

Horn and Bergthaller (2020) conclude their excellent book on the Anthropocene by confessing a certain admiration for China's green authoritarianism as a welcome challenge to the West's confidence in democracy as a vehicle for the challenges of the Anthropocene.[4] However, we hope to have shown in this book that the longing for democracy is not only a Western fantasy—or a "contamination" by the West of Asian values and ontologies—but that democracy is clearly compatible with concern for the environment. Furthermore, we concur with Shahar (2015) that eco-authoritarianism is at best only capable of more or less matching the performance of market liberalism, but it comes at the clear cost of renouncing individual and political rights with no clear benefit. So why throw the baby out with the bath water? The next section considers to what extent the resistance of Hong Kong and Taiwan against Chinese authoritarianism reflect this intuition.

Hong Kong, Taiwan, and the Challenge of Green Democracy

Against the temptation of China's authoritarian model, what are the possibilities for achieving environmental goals without throwing away aspirations to democracy? Faced with the pressure of environmental authoritarianism, recent years have seen a recrudescence of theoretical efforts to reassess the importance of environmental democracy—also called ecological democracy, or green democracy (Coles 2015; Disch 2016; Wong 2016; Baber and Bartlett 2018; Eckersley 2019; Schlosberg et al. 2019). Some of these studies address the specific challenges that the Anthropocene poses for democracy (Karlsson 2013; Eckersley

2017; Dryzek and Pickering 2019). Other authors look at concrete applications, such as energy policies or climate mobilizations (Szulecki 2018; Delina 2018).

As James Wong (2016) sees it, the opposition between environmental authoritarianism and ecological democracy can be synthesized into an opposition between environmental ends and democratic means: for Robert Goodin (1992), environmental ends justify any means, be they democratic or not, but the early and unwavering proponents of green democracy, like John Dryzek or Robyn Eckersley, have upheld that democratic means are at least as important as environmental ends. Wong identifies a further conundrum for green democrats. There is no decision-making process that can at once provide (1) robustness to pluralism—accepting any logically possible combination of individual opinions; (2) consensus preservation—adopting a solution chosen by all citizens; and (3) green outcomes—ensuring that the decision process always generates a green outcome. Wong concludes that to achieve green outcomes democratically, either pluralism or consensus needs to be relaxed, and compromises must be found through a pragmatic or probabilistic approach.

In their contribution to this book, James K. Wong and Alvin Y. So (Chapter 3) depict how Hong Kong's environmental movements alternate between a non-confrontational approach and a more radical form of mobilization. While the former is a narrow example of green pragmatism, exemplified by organizations like Greenpeace and the World Wide Fund for Nature that focus on less politically sensitive topics, the latter leads to brand new directions, such as the Umbrella Movement of 2014, which urged Beijing to keep its word to implement universal suffrage in the territory. The protesters failed to obtain what they were asking for and the leaders of the movement were sentenced to prison. From June 2019 until early 2020 (when the coronavirus lockdown curtailed the protests), people once again took to the streets en masse to fight a proposed law that would allow those charged in Hong Kong to be extradited to China. Although such resistance against China's authoritarianism has not been primarily motivated by environmental issues but rather concerns for political freedom, Wong and So show that mobilizations over issues of land justice and the protection of cultural landscapes have played a significant role in the radicalization of civic action in Hong Kong.

Faced with the security law voted by the National People's Congress and imposed on Hong Kong on 1 July 2020 (the highly symbolic date when control of the territory passed from the UK to China in 1997), it remains uncertain as to where the democratic movement will be heading. In the future, many people might be forced into exile or long prison sentences, and politically sensitive actions such as labour strikes and electoral activities are likely to be scrutinized by the police. Such a critical context might see the return of low-profile initiatives for environmental protection as well as the preservation of urban heritage and rural landscapes.

In his analysis of the first twenty years of Taiwan's environmental movement, Ming-sho Ho (2006) used the notion of green democracy as a metaphor to depict different phases of interaction between democratization and environmentalism, a process that he called "environmental democratization" (*huanjing minzhuhua*). During the first phase starting in the mid-1980s, the mobilization of intellectuals and grassroots citizens, for example against nuclear and petrochemical plants, provided a significant contribution to the liberalization of the country toward partisan pluralism, ultimately putting an end to martial law and decades of dictatorship. Thereafter, as the country resolutely shifted to democracy with increasingly transparent elections and universal suffrage, environmental movements did not obtain the green outcomes they had expected (e.g., on the nuclear issue), but they nevertheless became an essential part of Taiwanese civil society. In Chapter 2, Jobin further analyses this process as an expression of eco-nationalism and the development of a national identity distinct from China. While China's regime is becoming more and more authoritarian, Taiwan in contrast is now labelled as a beacon of liberal democracy and civic activism. For instance, in May 2019, the island nation made the headlines worldwide when it became the first Asian country to legalize same-sex marriage. Taiwan's environmental mobilizations are an essential part of this process of social transformation at large.

Together, Taiwan and Hong Kong represent a thorn in the side of Beijing's "mandate of heaven" (Ho 2019). Despite the apparent failure of Hong Kong's movement for democracy (as of July 2020) and the growing menace to Taiwan's de facto independence, these two polities are, to say the least, an obvious indication that China's authoritarianism is not necessarily an attractive model to all Chinese speakers. The next section identifies the scenarios of interaction between different political regimes and various sorts of environmental achievements, with a focus on East and Southeast Asia.

Ecology and Political Regimes: An Analytical Framework

In 2015, the World Resources Institute launched the Environmental Democracy Index, based on the 2010 United Nations Environment Programme's Bali Guidelines, to measure the scope and coherence of environmental laws and rights in a selection of seventy countries, as well as their effective practice. For instance, is the public allowed free access to timely information and can environmental injustices be challenged before an independent legal authority? The index was supposed to be updated every two years, but unfortunately, this interesting initiative has not been repeated and the list of seventy countries selected does not provide enough clues about the countries at issue in this book. Thus, if we are to sketch a theoretical framework for understanding the potential interactions between environmental mobilizations and different political regimes, we are compelled to cross indexes of two different sorts: the first category deals with the evaluation of political regimes; the second aims to address environmental performance. Fortunately, there is a good deal of exhaustive and reliable metrics in both fields.

Following on the efforts of the Washington-based Freedom House (founded in 1941) with its annual Freedom in the World survey, the past two decades have seen a multiplication of systematic surveys based on large datasets regarding the levels of freedom and democracy around the world. Despite their inherent limitations, these indexes provide useful information. Table 11.1 presents a selection of countries in the Asia-Pacific region, based on the most recent reports showing indicators of the evolution over the last two decades, from Freedom House, The Economist Intelligence Unit (London), and the V-Dem Institute (University of Gothenburg, Sweden). The countries appear in the order of their aggregate score in the Freedom House ranking.

In the long run, democracy has expanded and autocracies diminished, particularly if we look at the global evolution over the twentieth century (Lührmann et al. 2018). However, after a long wave of democratization that started in the mid-1970s and peaked in 2008, there has been an overall erosion of democracy during the last ten years. Still, it continues to prevail in a majority of countries worldwide, and Asia has shown

Table 11.1
Democracy Rankings
(for the countries covered in this volume)

	Freedom House: Regime type and aggregate freedom score out of 100		The Economist Democracy Index: Regime type, overall score out of 10, (Rank among 165 countries)		V-Dem Democracy Report: Regime type, score out of 1.00 (Rank among 179 countries*)	
	2003	2019	2006	2018	2000	2018
Taiwan	Free 86	Free 93	Flawed Democracy 7.82 (32)	Flawed Democracy 7.73 (5)	Liberal Democracy 0.67	Liberal Democracy 0.7 (37)
Indonesia	Partly free 58	Partly free 62	Flawed Democracy 6.41 (65)	Flawed Democracy 6.39 (65)	Electoral Democracy 0.52	Electoral Democracy 0.5 (63)
Philippines	Free 73	Partly free 61	Flawed Democracy 6.48 (63)	Flawed Democracy 6.71 (53)	Electoral Democracy** 0.49	Electoral Democracy** 0.32 (101)
Hong Kong	Partly free 60	Partly free 59	Flawed Democracy 6.03 (78)	Flawed Democracy 6.15 (73)	Closed Autocracy 0.33	Closed Autocracy 0.3 (107)
Singapore	Partly free 43	Partly free 51	Flawed Democracy 5.89 (84)	Flawed Democracy 6.38 (66)	Electoral Autocracy 0.32	Electoral Autocracy 0.33 (100)
Malaysia	Partly free 42	Partly free 52	Flawed Democracy 5.98 (81)	Flawed Democracy 6.88 (52)	Electoral Autocracy 0.18	Electoral Autocracy 0.29 (109)
Thailand	Free 72	Not free 30	Hybrid regime 5.67 (90)	Hybrid regime 4.63 (106)	Electoral Democracy 0.39	Closed Autocracy 0.1 (156)
Cambodia	Not free 31	Not free 26	Authoritarian 4.77 (105)	Authoritarian 3.59 (125)	Electoral Democracy 0.14	Closed Autocracy 0.08 (164)
Vietnam	Not free 13	Not free 20	Authoritarian 2.75 (145)	Authoritarian 3.08 (139)	Closed Autocracy 0.1	Closed Autocracy+** 0.16 (138)

Notes: * For 2018 only.
** The minus and plus signs attached to a category indicate that taking uncertainty into account, the country could also belong to the lower or higher category.

an overall positive trend, with South Korea and Taiwan frequently mentioned as models of the path to democratization.

Based on a list of 171 questions on political rights and civil liberties, Freedom House distributes its results in three categories: "free", "partly free", and "not free" countries. A country that has met certain minimum standards for political rights and civil liberties is designated an "electoral democracy"; most "free countries" might be considered liberal democracies (implying a greater observance of democratic ideals and civil liberties), while some "partly free" countries might qualify as electoral democracies. According to these definitions, apart from a bottom pack of "non-free" regimes, a majority of the countries in Table 11.1 meet the criteria of an electoral democracy.

The Economist and V-Dem offer additional, "thicker" definitions of political regimes. In the Economist index, New Zealand and Australia are the only exemplars of "full democracy" for the Asia-Pacific region. They are followed by South Korea, Japan, and Taiwan atop nine "flawed democracies", which include Singapore and Hong Kong (as of 2019). Thailand is the sole case of a "hybrid regime". A bottom echelon of authoritarian regimes is headed by China and, unsurprisingly, North Korea closes the ranks.

The V-Dem index is generally congruent with The Economist's, but it uses a different vocabulary: the category of "liberal democracy" is a rough equivalent of "full democracy"; "electoral democracy" corresponds more or less to "flawed democracy"; and "electoral autocracy" dovetails with "hybrid regime"; while "closed autocracy" stands for an authoritarian regime. But these categories do not always match, and in some cases, V-Dem's definitions present counterintuitive situations: Japan and Taiwan are ranked as "liberal democracies", despite having lower scores than South Korea, which remains an "electoral democracy" (with a plus sign to indicate that it could be ranked higher); Hong Kong drops to the infamous group of "closed autocracies", whereas Vietnam and Laos are promoted to "electoral autocracies", despite their very low scores.[5] Using probabilities with a dataset of 400 variables, V-Dem's latest edition (Lührmann et al. 2018) forecasts that the Philippines presents a 75 per cent risk of adverse regime transition within a two-year window; in other words, the Philippines could turn into an electoral autocracy.

In addition to a multiparty system and a diversity of free media, peaceful transfers of power after free and fair elections, an independent judiciary, freedom of association, the possibility of peaceful demonstrations, and the absence of brutal means of repression like torture are all essential variables in these rankings. In countries such as Cambodia and the Philippines, where environmental activists are frequent targets of extreme violence, these factors are also of crucial importance for environmental mobilizations.

Table 11.2 presents a selection of three environmental performance rankings. Our selection of countries is listed in order of their ranking

TABLE 11.2
Environmental Rankings
(for the countries covered in this volume*)

	Yale Environmental Performance Index Score/100 (Rank/180 countries)		Global Footprint Network				Germanwatch Climate Change Performance Index Score/100 (Rank/60 countries)	
			Ecological biocapacity reserve (+) or deficit (−) in global hectares (gha)			Earth overshoot day		
	2012**	2018	1961	2000	2016	2018	2009	2018
Taiwan***	62.23 (29)	72.84 (23)		−			51.5 (32)	28.8 (56)
Singapore	56.36 (52)	64.23 (49)	−	−7.9	−5.8	12 April		−
Malaysia	62.51 (25)	59.22 (75)	+4.7	−0.8	−1.6	1 June	44.3 (52)	38.08 (51)
Philippines	57.4 (42)	57.65 (82)	+0.1	−0.7	−0.7	−		−
Thailand	57.4 (34)	49.88 (121)	+1.7	−0.8	−1.3	28 Aug	50.2 (35)	48.71 (37)
Vietnam	59.98 (79)	46.96 (132)	+0.6	−0.1	−1.1	8 Oct		−
Indonesia	52.29 (91)	46.92 (133)	+1.3	0.0	−0.4	18 Dec	53.8 (27)	48.68 (38)
Cambodia	55.29 (59)	43.23 (150)	+0.1	0.0	−0.3	−		−

Notes: * Except Hong Kong, which is not mentioned by any of these environmental indexes.
** Due to methodology change in 2012, comparisons with earlier reports are not possible.
*** Referred to as "Chinese Taipei" in the Germanwatch index

by the Environmental Performance Index (EPI) conducted by Yale University since 2002. The latest edition of its annual report (Wendling et al. 2018) covers a large range of topics, from air quality and water management to biodiversity, forests and fisheries, climate and energy, etc. For Southeast Asia, the report emphasizes the tree cover loss over the past decade in Indonesia (at an equal rate with Brazil) and the Mekong region from Myanmar to Thailand, Laos, Cambodia, and Vietnam. In Laos, illegal logging accounts for the massive increase in timber exports, around two-thirds of which go to China. In Indonesia, palm oil producers use "slash-and-burn" practices, not only destroying forests but also sending large quantities of smoke across the archipelago. Despite these criticisms, the general tone of the Yale EPI report is rather positive, highlighting examples of "good governance", such as Singapore's water management system or Taiwan's air pollution policy. The EPI could therefore be criticized for adopting a consensual tone that lacks the sense of urgency required to deal with the challenges of the Anthropocene.

Since 1961, the Global Footprint Network has measured the "ecological footprint" of approximately two hundred countries. Counted in the number of global hectares of land that are required to fulfil current levels of consumption, the ecological footprint is used to measure the surplus or deficit of ecological biocapacities. There is a deficit when the footprint of a population exceeds the biocapacity of the natural resources available to it, meaning that the country is exhausting its ecological assets, or else borrowing biocapacity from other countries through trades or the emission of wastes into the global commons (the atmosphere, oceans, etc.). In other words, countries in deficit are consuming more than what the earth can renew. Compared to 1961, world biocapacities have plummeted. In 2016, only fifty-one countries maintained a surplus. With an ecological footprint exceeding its biocapacity by 9,950 per cent in proportion of its population, Singapore ranks first among the countries in deficit, far beyond even Korea's 797 per cent or China's 278 per cent. The "Garden City" and other rich countries have amassed a huge ecological debt. Since this index is based exclusively on data released by UN organizations, Taiwan does not appear, but it is reasonable to expect that its ecological footprint is also far above its capacity.

The "earth overshoot day" is another—and perhaps more striking— way to represent the exhaustion of biocapacities: the earlier in the year, the worse it is. For example, by 12 April 2018, Singapore had already exhausted its biocapacities. In other words, for the rest of the year, Singapore was relying on—or borrowing from—other countries such as Indonesia, which is the last country in the world to exhaust its biocapacities. Yet that does not mean that Indonesia is doing enough; despite its huge reserves, after 18 December, Indonesia also found itself in the red.

The Climate Change Performance Index released by the Germanwatch Institute since 2005 compares the energy policies of fifty-six countries and the European Union (EU), which together are responsible for more than 90 per cent of global greenhouse gas emissions. The scope of this index is thus much more limited, but it provides contrasting results worth considering. For instance, according to Yale's 2018 EPI report, Taiwan ranks as a world leader (global rank: 4) in climate change and energy policies. However, for Germanwatch, Taiwan—labelled "Chinese Taipei"—falls to the bottom of the list, along with Japan, South Korea, Australia, and the United States.

We will not go into a detailed comparison of these different indexes. What we need for sketching a theoretical framework for future research is to cross Tables 11.1 and 11.2, as summed up in Table 11.3. Countries that have already achieved a certain level of democratization (full and flawed democracies, or liberal and electoral democracies) and a relatively good environmental performance can be considered on the path to becoming green democracies (category 1). A good environmental performance without sufficient democratization or showing clear signs of autocratization (hybrid and authoritarian regimes, or electoral and closed autocracies) implies a trend toward a green autocracy (or green authoritarianism, category 2). On the flip side, countries with a poor environmental performance are also distributed between democracies (3) and autocracies (4); in reference to the purple colour used to map high levels of air pollution (see Chapter 2 on Taiwan), we call these regimes *purple democracies* and *purple autocracies*. The countries move horizontally in the chart depending on their political regime, and vertically depending on their environmental performance.

In contrast with the homogeneous results of the democracy indexes, environmental indexes are more disparate. If we take Yale's EPI as a reference, for instance, with a demarcation score above or below 50, several countries get the laurels of a green democracy, including Taiwan, Malaysia, and the Philippines. However, if we refer to the Footprint

Network, only New Zealand, Australia, and Mongolia would meet the selection criteria; Japan, Korea, Malaysia, Philippines, and probably Taiwan would fall into category 3 and purple democracy; China and Singapore would be retrograded down to purple autocracies (4), whereas Myanmar and Laos would just pass the test for green autocracies (2). If we use the standards of the Germanwatch ranking, no Asia-Pacific country could be classified as a green democracy, and indeed only a dozen countries in the world—mostly in Western Europe—would do

TABLE 11.3
Environmental Performance and Political Regime
(A classification with exemplars focused on Asia-Pacific;
the country cases in this book appear in boldface.)

	Democratization	Autocratization
Good Environmental Performance	1) Green Democracy	2) Green Autocracy
Yale's EPI: Overall score over 50	*New Zealand, Australia, Japan, **Taiwan**, South Korea, **Malaysia**, **Philippines**, Mongolia*	***Singapore**, China, Brunei*
Global Footprint: Positive biocapacity	*New Zealand, Australia, Mongolia*	*Myanmar, Laos*
Germanwatch: High overall score (over 60)	*India, European Union (average)*	*Morocco, Ukraine*
Poor Environmental Performance	3) Purple Democracy	4) Purple Autocracy
Yale's EPI: Overall score below 50	***Indonesia***	***Thailand, Vietnam, Cambodia**, Laos, Myanmar*
Global Footprint: Negative biocapacity	*Indonesia, Japan, Korea, **Malaysia, Philippines, Taiwan?***	***Singapore**, China*
Germanwatch: Low overall score (below 60)	*New Zealand, Australia, Japan, Korea, **Taiwan**, **Indonesia, Malaysia***	*China, **Thailand***

so.[6] These results contradict those of the Global Footprint Network, suggesting either different methodologies and criteria of evaluation, or a lack of robustness of these environmental indexes compared to democracy benchmarks. In either case, we shall keep this problem in mind in the following typology.[7]

So, if we accept the basic hypothesis that a relatively good environmental performance can, in theory, be achieved under either democracy or autocracy or, in other words, that the level of liberalization of a political regime is immaterial to its environmental performance, the next important question for environmental politics and sociology will be: to what extent do environmental mobilizations contribute to reinforce democracy and achieve a better environmental performance?

As evoked above, despite important institutional constraints, Chinese ENGOs can still mobilize with the state in a common effort to engage in the "war against pollution" or fight against the depletion of Indonesian forests. Seen like this, however, environmental NGOs are completely detached from a broader understanding of civil society organizations, especially in their "check and balance" role of holding the authorities to account. While they may be not totally controlled by the state, some environmental groups must compromise to such an extent that they might be called *hybrid* organizations, hence the oxymoron of "government-organized NGOs" used in the literature about China and Vietnam.

In liberal democracies, many environmental NGOs are also dependent on state subsidies. But as analysed by Jakkrit Sangkhamanee regarding Thailand (Chapter 7), and Stephan Ortmann in the case of Vietnam (Chapter 8), the hybrid character of environmental NGOs brings forth fundamental questions for the very meaning of *environmental movements*.

Another issue that would be worth further study is the role of nationalism in environmental movements. In Chapter 2, Jobin emphasizes the mutually reinforcing role of Taiwan's environmentalism, the spirit of democracy, and national identity. The recent events in Hong Kong also suggest that a local identity distinct from the rest of China has been a fundamental ingredient of the movement for democracy, and so far, the tougher the repression from Beijing, the stronger that identity. Similar observations could apply to other countries; for instance, the aggressive behaviour of Chinese fishermen in the South China Sea often provoke anger in the Philippines and Vietnam. To what extent might popular expressions of national anger turn into larger and better organized environmental movements? Such a consideration must not lose sight of the impact of environmental movements on the scale and scope of the environmental emergency itself.

The Anthropocene is already affecting territorial sovereignties; think for instance of a city like Jakarta and other large areas of land threatened by rising sea-levels. But it does not mean that nations do not have their say in the response to the Anthropocene. To borrow from Craig Calhoun (2007), we might argue that in the Anthropocene nations still matter, perhaps more than ever, in fact. During the last four decades, the wishful thinking of neoliberalism has spread the illusion that authoritarianism, civil wars, and global issues such as environmental problems were soluble in the globalization of trade; consequently, nations were thought to no longer be so important, as multilateralism was gradually imposing an international rational order.

Actually, the concept of the Anthropocene, which serves as the temporal context of this book, appears to have been relatively poorly assimilated into the rhetorical motivations of each nation's environmental movements. As we discussed in the introduction, the Anthropocene is not an obligatory theoretical framework for addressing the current environmental crisis; drawing on Lidskog and Waterton (2016), we gave it ourselves a "cautious welcome". More problematic actually is the lack of a serious societal debate about the climate emergency and the massive depletion of biodiversity. In Western nations and some other countries of South Asia, Africa, and Latin America, the existential threat posed by the climate emergency has been widely assimilated into environmental movements such as Extinction Rebellion (which started in London in 2018), and the Global Climate Strike stamped by the iconic leadership of Greta Thunberg and other young urban middle class Western teenagers. However, thus far, these movements have found little echo in East and Southeast Asia.

For instance, in addition to four Western languages and Japanese, the Global Climate Strike's website offers pages in Bahasa Indonesia, which reflects the commitment of Indonesian NGOs since the climate conference held in Bali (see Chapter 6); but there is no sign of Chinese or other Asian languages. Although Malaysia shares with Indonesia a mutually intelligible idiom (Bahasa) and a part of its territory (Borneo), the Malaysian movements for the protection of rainforests and indigenous lands show no sign of cooperation with their Indonesian counterparts to scale up their grievances and link them to the climate emergency.

   In the Philippines, participation in the coalition of developing countries most exposed to the consequences of global heating (the Climate Vulnerable Forum) and in litigation against the carbon majors are significant movements, but they seem to remain isolated from initiatives in Western countries, and in Asia, they have not received any visible support from wealthy countries like Taiwan, Singapore, Japan, and South Korea. These countries host an important number of Philippine migrant workers who could relay this type of concern for their homeland; but generally their labour and living conditions do not allow them sufficient time and peace of mind required for such civic engagement.

   Instead, in most Asian countries, rather than a societal awareness that the region is on the front line of both the anthropogenic climate change crisis and a focal point of the Sixth Mass Extinction, the main concerns within the environmental movements remain relatively parochial issues.[8] In countries like Taiwan and Vietnam, domestically oriented environmental mobilizations partly reflect nationalist concerns in the face of China's aggressive moves. Yet confronted with a common global threat, these different expressions of eco-nationalism might also nurture a sense of emergency and international solidarity. The dialectic of nationalisms and the climate emergency stirs a set of questions that will be worth further exploration in the years ahead.

NOTES

1. Keith Schneider, "Despite Fiery Campaign Rhetoric, Chinese-backed Projects in Malaysia Steam Ahead", *Mongabay*, 28 June 2019.
2. Ophuls (1977, p. 163), quoted by Shahar (2015).
3. See for instance Bell (2006), and his most recent books, Bell (2015), and Bell and Pei (2020). For a brief but pertinent criticism of his narrative from the standpoint of Taiwan, see Chuang (2015, pp. 72–73).
4. Although I disagree with it, to be fair, their argument is worth a long citation. It shows how China's model can be tempting for Western liberal minds:

   More than any other country in the world, China has sought to replace gross domestic product (GDP) as a measure of economic well-being with a so-called "green GDP"—a form of accounting which would factor in ecological costs. [...] For many people in the West, such a development would come as a shock, because it would put into question the conviction, widely shared in the West, that only a democratic, emancipatory politics will be able to meet the challenges of the Anthropocene [...]. By contrast, the path that China seems to have chosen might best be described as a radical and authoritarian form of ecomodernism, and it is not unlikely that many Asian countries will follow its lead. [...] In combination with a social credit system, such as the Chinese government has been experimenting with over the past few years, this could give rise to a comprehensive system of biopolitical control which completely dissolves the boundary between the private and the public sphere. Whether such a system would actually be able to get the ecological problems of the Anthropocene under control is an open question. From a Western standpoint, it certainly represents a terrifying vision—but that is something we also like to say about climate change, even as we comfort ourselves that we are helping to save the Earth by lugging our groceries home in a cotton tote bag. Given the glaring inability of liberal democracies to limit consumption [...], the West would be well-advised to tone down the moral outrage. If humanity is to have a desirable future, we must not only change our habits of consumption, but our economic, political and legal systems, our infrastructure, our pedagogy, our art, and our everyday lives (Horn and Bergthaller 2020, pp. 174–75).

5. V-Dem's classification of electoral or liberal democracy and electoral or closed autocracy is based on a decision tree with eight levels (Lührmann et al. 2019). In a nutshell, if the executive and legislature are not selected through multiparty elections, the country is classified as a closed autocracy (as is the case of Hong Kong). The distinction between electoral and liberal democracies rests mainly on the scores of three variables: access to justice for both men and women, transparent law enforcement, and a general liberal component. The reason that South Korea remains classified as an electoral democracy is due to its rating of slightly below 3 regarding transparent law enforcement. (Thanks to Yi-Ming Wang for this explanation).

6. Remember, however, that the Germanwatch list is restricted to a group of fifty-six countries which are responsible for 90 per cent of global greenhouse gas emissions; all other countries are left off the radar.

7. There is good reason to be cautious with regard to the index study, which can be terribly simplifying since it attempts to put different things on the same scale. This is particularly problematic as the Anthropocene in fact requires renewed attention to problems of scale, both for time and space (Horn and Bergthaller 2020, chapters 10 and 11). And when comparing environmental policy-making, the time factor might be more decisive than the level of democracy (Haddad 2015). Cross-country comparisons are notoriously tricky, given the vast differences in natural endowment and geographical factors (in the case of the environment), and the unique mix of historical, geopolitical, economic, and demographic influences that shape each individual nation. Pigeonholing these diverse entities into a single schema necessarily robs them of some of their complexity and may distort the perception of them to fit into a study's world-view. For example, is Taiwan a green democracy

or a purple democracy? The judgment can be very different depending on whose narrative we emphasize. Many environmentalists will think that Taiwan performs poorly and could do much better, but "objectively", as Yale's EPI suggests, Taiwan is ahead of many Southeast Asian countries in terms of public awareness, legal framework, and air quality. Therefore, although we present these comparisons here—for they do provide a useful basis for reflecting on the general state of the region's performance and the divergences within it—we believe that a diachronic comparison of each country's past and present might be more meaningful, as indeed we have aimed to provide with the chapters in this book.
8. I thank an anonymous reviewer for this remark.

REFERENCES

Baber, Walter F. and Robert V. Bartlett. 2018. "A Rights Foundation for Ecological Democracy". *Journal of Environmental Policy and Planning*. https://doi.org/10.1080/1523908X.2019.1566059.

Beeson, Mark. 2010. "The Coming of Environmental Authoritarianism". *Environmental Politics* 19, no. 2: 276–94.

———. 2016. "Environmental Authoritarianism in China". In *The Oxford Handbook of Environmental Political Theory*, edited by Teena Gabrielson, Cheryl Hall, John H. Meyer, and David Schlosberg. Oxford: Oxford University Press, pp. 520–32.

Bell, Daniel A. 2006. *Beyond Liberal Democracy: Political Thinking for an East Asian Context*. Princeton: Princeton University Press.

———. 2015. *The China Model: Political Meritocracy and the Limits of Democracy*. Princeton: Princeton University Press.

Bell, Daniel A. and Wang Pei. 2020. *Just Hierarchy: Why Social Hierarchies Matter in China and the Rest of the World*. Princeton: Princeton University Press.

Boisseau du Rocher, Sophie and Emmanuel Dubois de Prisque. 2019. *La Chine e(s)t le monde. Essai sur la sino-mondialisation*. Paris: Odile Jacob.

Calhoun, Craig. 2007. *Nations Matter: Culture, History and the Cosmopolitan Dream*. London: Routledge.

Chen, Ian Tsung-yen. 2019. "China's Economic Offensive and Its Discontent in Southeast Asia: Diminishing Footprints in Myanmar". In *China's Footprint in Southeast Asia*, edited by Maria Serena I. Diokno, Hsin-Huang Michael Hsiao, and Alan H. Yang. Singapore: National University of Singapore Press, pp. 63–89.

Chuang, Ya-Chung. 2018. "Democracy under Siege: *Xiangming* Politics in Sunflower Taiwan". *Boundary* 2 45, no. 3: 61–77.

Coles, Romand. 2015. *Visionary Pragmatism: Radical and Ecological Democracy in Neo-Liberal Times*. Durham: Duke University Press.

Dauvergne, Peter. 1997. *Shadows in the Forest: Japan and the Politics of Timber in Southeast Asia*. Cambridge, MA: MIT Press.

Delina, Laurence. 2018. "Climate Mobilizations and Democracy: The Promise of Scaling Community Energy Transitions in a Deliberative System". *Journal of Environmental Policy and Planning*: 1–13.

Diokno, Maria Serena I., Hsin-Huang Michael Hsiao, and Alan H. Yang. 2019. *China's Footprints in Southeast Asia*. Singapore: National University of Singapore Press.

Disch, Lisa. 2016. "Ecological Democracy and the Co-Participation of Things". In *The Oxford Handbook of Environmental Political Theory*, edited by Teena Gabrielson, Cheryl Hall, John M. Meyer, and David Schlosberg. Oxford: Oxford University Press, pp. 624–39.

Dryzek, John S. and Jonathan Pickering. 2019. *The Politics of the Anthropocene*. Oxford: Oxford University Press.

Dunlap, Riley E. and Aaron M. McCright. 2015. "Challenging Climate Change: The Denial Countermovement". In *Climate Change and Society: Sociological Perspectives*, edited by Riley E. Dunlap and Robert J. Brulle. New York: Oxford University Press, pp. 300–32.

Eaton, Sarah and Genia Kostka. 2014. "Authoritarian Environmentalism Undermined? Local Leaders' Time Horizons and Environmental Policy Implementation in China". *The China Quarterly* 218: 359–80.

———. 2018. "What Makes for Good and Bad Neighbours? An Emerging Research Agenda in the Study of Chinese Environmental Politics". *Environmental Politics* 27, no. 5: 782–803.

Eckersley, Robyn. 2017. "Geopolitan Democracy in the Anthropocene". *Political Studies* 65, no. 4: 983–99.

———. 2019. "Ecological Democracy and the Rise and Decline of Liberal Democracy: Looking Back, Looking Forward". *Environmental Politics*: 1–21.

Gilley, Bruce. 2012. "Authoritarian Environmentalism and China's Response to Climate Change". *Environmental Politics* 21, no. 2: 287–307.

Goodin, Robert E. 1992. *Green Political Theory*. Cambridge, UK: Polity Press.

Haddad, Mary Alice. 2015. "Paradoxes of Democratization: Environmental Politics in East Asia". In *Routledge Handbook of Environment and Society in Asia*, edited by Paul G. Harris and Graeme Lang. London: Routledge, pp. 86–104.

Hamilton, Clive. 2018. *Silent Invasion: China's Influence in Australia*. Melbourne: Hardie Grant Books.

Hardin, Garrett. 1968. "The Tragedy of the Commons". *Science* 162: 1243–48.

Heilbroner, Robert. 1974. *An Inquiry into the Human Prospect*. London: Calder & Boyars.

Heurtebise, Jean-Yves. 2017. "Sustainability and Ecological Civilization in the Age of Anthropocene: An Epistemological Analysis of the Psychosocial and

'Culturalist' Interpretations of Global Environmental Risks". *Sustainability* 9, no. 8. https://doi.org/10.3390/su9081331.

Hewison, Kevin. 2017. "Reluctant Populists: Learning Populism in Thailand". *International Political Science Review* 38, no. 4: 426–40.

Hirsch, Philip and Carol Warren, eds. 1998. *The Politics of Environment in Southeast Asia: Resources and Resistance*. London: Routledge.

Ho, Ming-sho. 2006. *Luse minzhu: Taiwan huanjing yundong de yanjiu* [Green Democracy: A Study on Taiwan's Environmental Movement]. Taipei: Socio Publishing.

———. 2019. *Challenging Beijing's Mandate of Heaven: The Sunflower Movement in Taiwan and the Umbrella Movement in Hong Kong*. Philadelphia, PA: Temple University Press.

Horn, Eva and Hannes Bergthaller. 2020. *The Anthropocene: Key Issues for the Humanities*. London: Routledge.

Hsiao, Hsin-Huang Michael. 1999. "Environmental Movements in Taiwan". In *Asia's Environmental Movements: Comparative Perspectives*, edited by Yok-shiu F. Lee and Alvin Y. So. Armonk, New York: M.E. Sharpe, pp. 31–54.

———. 2019. "Observations on Rising Populism in Taiwan Politics". *Global Taiwan Institute Brief* 4, no. 15, 31 July 2019. http://globaltaiwan.org/wp-content/uploads/2020/02/4.15-PDF-GTB.pdf.

Hsiao, Hsin-Huang Michael, On-Kwok Lai, Hwa-Jen Liu, Francisco Magno, Laura Edles, and Alvin Y. So. 1999. "Cultures and Asian Styles of Environmental Movements". In *Asia's Environmental Movements: Comparative Perspectives*, edited by Yok-shiu F. Lee and Alvin Y. So. Armonk, New York: M.E. Sharpe, pp. 210–29.

Huang, Ping and Ping Li. 2019. "Politics of Urban Energy Transitions: New Energy Vehicle (NEV) Development in Shenzhen, China". *Environmental Politics* 29, no. 3: 1–22. https://doi.org/10.1080/09644016.2019.1589935.

Hughes, Alice. 2019. "Understanding and Minimizing Environmental Impacts of the Belt and Road Initiative". *Conservation Biology* 33, no. 4: 883–94.

Karlsson, Rasmus. 2013. "Ambivalence, Irony, and Democracy in the Anthropocene". *Futures* 46: 1–9.

Kenny, Paul. 2017. *Populism and Patronage: Why Populists Win Elections in India, Asia, and Beyond*. Oxford, UK: Oxford University Press.

———. 2018. *Populism in Southeast Asia*. Cambridge, UK: Cambridge University Press.

———. 2019. "'The Enemy of the People': Populists and Press Freedom". *Political Research Quarterly* 73, no. 2: 261–75. https://doi.org/10.1177/1065912918824038.

Kostka, Genia and Chunman Zhang. 2018. "Tightening the Grip: Environmental Governance under Xi Jinping". *Environmental Politics* 27, no. 5: 769–81.

Lai, On-Kwok, Hsin-Huang Michael Hsiao, Hwa-Jen Liu, Somrudee Nicro, and Yok-shiu F. Lee. 1999. "The Contradictions and Synergy of Environmental Business Interests". In *Asia's Environmental Movements: Comparative Perspectives*, edited by Yok-shiu F. Lee and Alvin Y. So. Armonk, New York: M.E. Sharpe, pp. 269–86.

Lee, Su-Hoon, Hsin-Huang Michael Hsiao, Hwa-Jen Liu, On-Kwok Lai, Francisco A. Magno, and Alvin Y. So. 1999. "The Impact of Democratization on Environmental Movements". In *Asia's Environmental Movements: Comparative Perspectives*, edited by Yok-shiu F. Lee and Alvin Y. So. Armonk, New York: M.E. Sharpe, pp. 230–51.

Lee, Yok-shiu F. and Alvin Y. So, eds. 1999. *Asia's Environmental Movements: Comparative Perspectives*. New York: M.E. Sharpe.

Lidskog, Rolf and Claire Waterton. 2016. "Anthropocene: A Cautious Welcome From Environmental Sociology?" *Environmental Sociology* 2, no. 4: 395–406.

Lieberthal, Kenneth and Michel Oksenberg. 1988. *Policy Making in China: Leaders, Structures, and Processes*. Princeton, NJ: Princeton University Press.

Lim, Teck Ghee and Mark J. Valencia, eds. 1990. *Conflict over Natural Resources in Southeast Asia and the Pacific*. Tokyo: United Nations University Press.

Liu, John Chung-En. 2015. "Low Carbon Plot: Climate Change Skepticism with Chinese Characteristics". *Environmental Sociology* 1, no. 4: 280–92.

Lockwood, Matthew. 2018. "Right-Wing Populism and the Climate Change Agenda: Exploring the Linkages". *Environmental Politics* 27, no. 4: 712–32.

Lührmann, Anna et al. 2019. *V-Dem Annual Democracy Report 2019*. Gothenburg: V-Dem Institute.

Lührmann, Anna, Marcus Tannenberg, and Staffan I. Lindberg. 2018. "Regimes of the World (RoW): Opening New Avenues for the Comparative Study of Political Regimes". *Politics and Governance* 6, no. 1: 60–77.

Maréchal, Jean-Paul. 2018. "La Chine: nouvel *hegemon* du régime climatique mondial?" *Monde chinois nouvelle Asie* 56: 9–27.

Meadows, Donella H., Dennis Meadows, Jergen Randers, and William W. Behrens, III. 1972. *The Limits to Growth: A Report for the Club of Rome's Project on the Predicament of Mankind*. New York: New American Library.

Middleton, Carl and Jeremy Allouche. 2016. "Watershed or Powershed? Critical Hydropolitics, China and the 'Lancang-Mekong Cooperation Framework'". *The International Spectator* 51, no. 3: 100–17.

Moore, Scott. 2014. "Modernisation, Authoritarianism, and the Environment: The Politics of China's South–North Water Transfer Project". *Environmental Politics* 23, no. 6: 947–64.

Morris-Jung, Jason, ed. 2018. *In China's Backyard: Policies and Politics of Chinese Resource Investments in Southeast Asia*. Singapore: ISEAS – Yusof Ishak Institute.

Müller, Jan-Werner. 2016. *What is Populism*. Philadelphia: University of Pennsylvania Press.

Ngeow, Chow Bing. 2019. "The Political Economy of China's Economic Presence in Malaysia". In *China's Footprint in Southeast Asia*, edited by Maria Serena I. Diokno, Hsin-Huang Michael Hsiao, and Alan H. Yang. Singapore: National University of Singapore Press, pp. 90–116.

Ophuls, William. 1977. *Ecology and the Politics of Scarcity: Prologue to a Political Theory of the Steady State*. San Francisco: W.H. Freeman and Co.

Sangkhamanee, Jakkrit, 2021. "'Wither the Environment? The Recent Student-led Protests and (absent) Environmental Politics in Thailand'". *Kyoto Review of Southeast Asia* 30 (Environmental Politics in and after Military Authoritarianism in Thailand), March 2021. https://kyotoreview.org.

Schlosberg, David, Karin Bäckstrand, and Jonathan Pickering. 2019. "Reconciling Ecological and Democratic Values: Recent Perspectives on Ecological Democracy". *Environmental Values* 28, no. 1: 1–8.

Schneider-Mayerson, Matthew. 2017. "Some Islands Will Rise: Singapore in the Anthropocene". *Resilience* 4, no. 2–3: 166–84.

Shahar, Dan Coby. 2015. "Rejecting Eco-Authoritarianism, Again". *Environmental Values* 24, no. 3: 345–66.

Shearman, David and Joseph Wayne. 2007. *The Climate Change Challenge and the Failure of Democracy*. Westport, Connecticut: Praeger.

Shin, Kyoung. 2018. "Environmental Policy Innovations in China: A Critical Analysis from a Low-Carbon City". *Environmental Politics* 27, no. 5: 830–51.

Szasz, Andrew. 1994. *Ecopopulism: Toxic Waste and the Movement for Environmental Justice*. Minneapolis: University of Minnesota Press.

Szulecki, Kacper. 2018. "Conceptualizing Energy Democracy". *Environmental Politics* 27, no. 1: 21–41.

Tan-Mullins, May. 2017. "Dancing to China's Tune: Understanding the Impacts of a Rising China through the Political-Ecology Framework". *Journal of Current Chinese Affairs* 46, no. 3: 3–32.

Tang-Lee, Diane. 2018. "Complex Contestation of Chinese Energy and Resource Investments in Myanmar". In *In China's Backyard: Policies and Politics of Chinese Resource Investments in Southeast Asia*, edited by Jason Morris-Jung. Singapore: ISEAS – Yusof Ishak Institute, pp. 204–28.

Wendling, Z.A., J.W. Emerson, D.C. Esty, M.A. Levy, A. de Sherbinin et al. 2018. *Environmental Performance Index*. New Haven, CT: Yale Center for Environmental Law & Policy. https://epi.yale.edu/.

Wong, James. 2016. "A Dilemma of Green Democracy". *Political Studies* 64, no. 1S: 136–55.

Zeng, Fanxu, Jia Dai, and Jeffrey Javed. 2019. "Frame Alignment and Environmental Advocacy: The Influence of NGO Strategies on Policy Outcomes in China". *Environmental Politics* 28, no. 4: 747–70.

INDEX

Note: Page numbers followed by "n" refer to endnotes.

www.ingramcontent.com/pod-product-compliance
Lightning Source LLC
Chambersburg PA
CBHW072044020426
42334CB00017B/1387